MULTIREGIONAL ECONOMIC MODELING:
PRACTICE AND PROSPECT

Studies in
Regional Science
and Urban Economics

Series Editors

ÅKE E. ANDERSSON
WALTER ISARD

Volume 9

NORTH-HOLLAND PUBLISHING COMPANY – AMSTERDAM • NEW YORK • OXFORD

Multiregional Economic Modeling: Practice and Prospect

Editors

BORIS ISSAEV
PETER NIJKAMP
PIET RIETVELD
FOLKE SNICKARS

1982

NORTH-HOLLAND PUBLISHING COMPANY – AMSTERDAM • NEW YORK • OXFORD

ISBN: 0 444 86485 7

Publishers:
NORTH-HOLLAND PUBLISHING COMPANY
AMSTERDAM • NEW YORK • OXFORD

Sole distributors for the U.S.A. and Canada:
ELSEVIER SCIENCE PUBLISHING COMPANY, INC.
52 VANDERBILT AVENUE
NEW YORK, N.Y. 10017

HT
391
. M82
1982

PRINTED IN THE NETHERLANDS

INTRODUCTION TO THE SERIES

Regional Science and Urban Economics are two interrelated fields of research that have developed very rapidly in the last three decades. The main theoretical foundation of these fields comes from economics but in recent years the interdisciplinary character has become more pronounced. The editors desire to have the interdisciplinary character of regional sciences as well as the development of spatial aspects of theoretical economics fully reflected in this book series. Material presented in this book series will fall in three different groups:

- interdisciplinary textbooks at the advanced level,
- monographs reflecting theoretical or applied work in spatial analysis,
- proceedings reflecting advancement of the frontiers of regional science and urban economics.

In order to ensure homogeneity in this interdisciplinary field, books published in this series will:

- be theoretically oriented, i.e. analyse problems with a large degree of generality,
- employ formal methods from mathematics, econometrics, operations research and related fields, and
- focus on immediate or potential uses for regional and urban forecasting, planning and policy.

Åke E. Andersson
Walter Isard

This book is the result of a research collaboration between the Regional Development Group, International Institute for Applied Systems Analysis (IIASA), Laxenburg, Austria, and the Department of Regional Economics, Free University, Amsterdam. The work stems from the conviction that the field of multiregional economic (ME) modeling has reached such a stage of maturity that it is worthwhile to provide a worldwide survey of the current practice of that class of economic model building, and to review the major development trends. The project has been an effort to bring together the expertise in the area, using IIASA as a clearing-house for theories, models and applications stemming from different countries, different planning systems, and different modeling traditions. This book may be used both as a source of reference and guide to current applied ME models, and as a volume of structured analyses of the field.

Three delimitations form the fundamental basis for giving the survey a distinct focus. They all relate to the concept of an applied ME model. The first prerequisite for a model to qualify for this classification is that it should contain a description of a more or less complete economic system. This means that models treating only one sector of the production system have been excluded, together with models including the economic system in a peripheral way. The second prerequisite is that this description should be given for at least two regions, each one of them of such a geographical scale that commuting is not a major mechanism for labor market equilibrium. The third prerequisite is that this model should be operational, implying either that it has been applied to a policy or other issue or that such an application is feasible. This rules out theoretical model constructs not yet at the stage of application and not intended for applied use.

With these delimitations this volume contains a comprehensive set of reviews and analyses of the current practice of ME modeling in North America, Western Europe, Eastern Europe, and the Pacific Area. The term "current" is interpreted as indicating that models included should exist in a physical sense at the time of the survey, either in the form of computer systems or technical descriptions. The volume also embraces some examples of prospective empirical models currently under construction or model approaches planned or pleaded for.

In the study 50 models have been reviewed and classified. This review is based on a questionnaire circulated to almost 100 researchers or research institutions. An advisory group has been used to convey information on the potential contributors to the study.

The material contained in this volume has been reviewed carefully, both by direct contacts with the survey respondents and through a conference at IIASA in November 1981. The introductory and concluding chapters of the book are based on material provided by a large group of researchers at the conference. We acknowledge especially the contributions of David Batten, David Boyce, Takao Fukuchi, Norman Glickman, Curtis Harris, C.S. Holling, Leen Hordijk, John Kim, Lars Lundqvist, and Karen Polenske. A second group of researchers have contributed directly via independent chapters written specifically for this volume. These persons, and all other contributors to the survey and the conference, are thanked for their participation and help in bringing the study to a successful conclusion. Penelope Beck, Olivia Carydias, Judy Pakes, and Ineke Vos are thanked for efficient co-editorial, organizational and secretarial assistance. Steven Flitton, Valerie Jones, and Derek Delves

helped in editing the book, and Linda Foith and Rosemary Flory typed the final version. Paul Makin negotiated, planned and coordinated the editing and production.
We thank all of them for their efforts in producing the book so quickly and efficiently.

A survey study of the type presented in this volume should not be repeated too
often. On the other hand, measures should be taken to maintain the network of contacts and accumulation of knowledge represented herein. Such an activity can take
different forms, ranging from networking to clearing-house conferences. With this
volume, we have set the stage for recurrent activity in this field, where an international institution such as IIASA has an important role to play.

Although a worldwide coverage has been attempted in the survey, we are aware
that the material is still incomplete in several respects. Models developed within
academic institutions may be over-represented. We may have overlooked modeling
efforts directed toward the developing world. Language barriers may have delimited
the scope of the study by excluding models not intended for international audiences.

Furthermore, we may not have succeeded in achieving a proper balance between
ME modeling in market and planned economies. Western experiences and approaches
have perhaps been given greater coverage than Eastern. This is an additional strong
reason for the continuation of East-West scientific exchange in this area, and for
a second study at some time in the future.

Boris Issaev
Peter Nijkamp
Piet Rietveld
Folke Snickars

CONTENTS

CHAPTER 1

MULTIREGIONAL ECONOMIC MODELS: AN INTRODUCTION TO THE SURVEY

Peter Nijkamp
Piet Rietveld
Folke Snickars

1 Background

1.1 The evolution of regional economic modeling

The construction of models has a long tradition in economics. Since the pioneering work of Tinbergen (1956) considerable effort has been made in an attempt to
get more insight into the complexities of the economic world by means of statistical, econometric, and modeling techniques. The main aim of these methods has been
to describe the interwoven economic mechanisms in quantitative terms so as to arrive
at reliable predictions or adequate policy decisions. Nowadays, various economic
models are widely used in many countries as a means for integrated economic policy
analysis (Adams and Glickman 1980).

Regional economics is a discipline developed more recently. Ever since its
emergence in the 1950s it has also had a strong quantitative orientation. During
the 1970s especially many regional, multiregional, and interregional models were
developed. The first *regional economic models* were essentially spatial input-output
models, but very soon more elaborate models were developed, including labor market
components, consumer and investment behavior modules, and public policy elements.
Such regional economic models are being currently employed in planning practice in
many countries.

The *first* generation of regional economic models, developed in the sixties,
might be characterized as a search for systematic and quantitative representations
of spatial economic systems. Much emphasis was placed on the definition and specification of the *components* and *interactions* in these systems. At the end of the
1960s and the beginning of the 1970s, the regional models were increasingly used as
tools for planning and policy making in space and time; examples are urban land-use
models and transportation models. In this period many crude *programming* models
were designed to compute the most desirable state of a system according to welfare
criteria given *a priori*. This development of models based on optimality concepts
was paralleled by a strong trend towards *econometrically specified* regional economic models. Those econometric models (see Glickman 1982) were most often built
on structural frameworks other than the input-output one. Rather, direct causal
relationships were sought between output and factor input, infrastructure policy,
and location variables. The latter subset of models, developed in the last stage
of the first generation, were in general based on assumptions of infinite resources,
so limitations emerging from environmental constraints, energy availability, land
use, quality of life, and equity considerations were not taken into account.

During the 1970s the awareness of limited resources has led to a new trend in
regional model building in which the impacts of *constraints* and *limits* have played
an especially major role. Examples are regional environmental and energy models.
This motivates the assertion of a *second* generation of models emerging in the
regional economic field.

From the middle of the 1970s onward, efforts have been made to design *integrated* (and sometimes comprehensive) spatial economic models that are suitable for
an evaluation of actual regional trends by means of a whole spectrum of (sometimes
conflicting) regional objectives and/or side-conditions. Some of these models
are multidisciplinary or even interdisciplinary in nature, incorporating also

1

demographic, environmental, energy, and social variables. They also focus the
attention on a *multiregional* rather than on a *single-region* system. In this *third*
generation, the regional economic models have a clearer multiregional orientation
than before.

1.2 Introducing the multiregional framework--considerations of theory and
     application

It has been argued that the general practice during the period of building
single-region models was unsatisfactory for two principal reasons (see Bolton 1980,
Glickman 1982). From a *theoretical* point of view, the design of single-region
models has been questioned since the models altogether ignored links between the
regions studied and other regions. The ensuing neglect of feedback could give rise
to misleading results. This is a reason for demanding the introduction of direct
links between subregions, which might be extended to a demand for consistency between the outcomes of the single-region models and a national model. A class of
multiregional economic models subject to the structure and outcomes of national
economic models would emerge from these considerations. From a *policy* viewpoint,
multiregional economic (ME) models appeared to be able to respond to the needs of
the decision makers better than the single-region ones. The measurement of the
effect of a regional policy, even at the national level, might be more precise if
a multiregional framework is adopted. Economic decline might call for a framework
in which leading and lagging regions can be analyzed simultaneously. Large-scale
indivisible infrastructure projects might have interregional spillover effects both
directly and indirectly. Several countries adopting decentralized regional development strategies need tools to appraise the overall consequences of such policies.
We are thus saying that a multiregional framework has been increasingly employed by regional economic model builders both as part of the introduction of
more fully fledged regional economic theory and as a response to emerging policy
issues. It is evident that interactions among regions should be properly represented in applied ME models. This goes without saying for models of national-
regional planning and policy levels. It is less obvious, but still warranted, for
cases where one region is in the focus of the analysis and the others serve as
composite system exteriors.
Without a consideration of interregional and national-regional links, there
is no consistency guarantee for a spatial system as a whole. Only if the focus of
the analysis is oriented to a single region that forms a more or less closed system, and if the macroeconomic (national and international) development pattern is
given, may a single-region approach at the level of states or local units be regarded as reasonable.
Usually, however, there are various kinds of direct and indirect cross-regional
linkages caused by spatiotemporal feedback and contiguity effects, so that regional
developments may have nationwide effects. In addition, national or even international developments may significantly affect a spatial system; this is especially
important because such developments may affect the competitive situation of regions
in a spatial system. For instance, a nationwide innovation policy may favor especially the areas with bigger agglomerations. Thus, the diversity in an open spatial-
economic system requires coordination of policy handles on the national and regional
level, leading to the necessity of using ME models in attempts to include regional
welfare variables in national-regional development planning. Some countries (e.g.
France, the Netherlands) have even mandated the use of integrated ME models for
setting up regional and industrial plans. Unfortunately, there is too little information available on the *ex ante* policy impacts and on the *ex post* performance of
ME models. The evaluation of the use of ME models in the policy arena no doubt
deserves more attention.
In this respect, the community of regional model builders and of regional
planners and decision makers have to cooperate closely, as only an interface between model builders and users will lead to a full exploitation of the potential
of ME models.

1.3 Why a survey of multiregional economic models?

We have stated above that currently the development of ME models is being given priority in several countries, although many models are still in the phase of amendment and extension.

Some comparative studies have been made (Bolton 1980, Hordijk and Nijkamp 1980, Glickman 1982, Courbis 1982), but these have been limited to subsets of models: Bolton and Glickman consider American models, while Hordijk and Nijkamp, and Courbis restrict themselves mainly to certain Western European models. It is natural to extend their work towards a more internationally oriented comparative study.

Another reason why an international comparison of the practice of multiregional modeling may be meaningful stems from observations that our capacity to develop theoretical models has outrun our capacity to implement them (Miernyk 1976). It is important, therefore, to try to decide which elements of theoretical models have proved to be applicable and to discover those directions where further research is most promising.

The increasing use of ME models, especially in the industrialized nations, is to some extent due to the growing (and urgent) need for precise assessment of the spatial dimension of economic development. Regional development issues tend to form an increasingly large part of economic and physical planning efforts. The economic recession during the last few years has especially evoked the need for more attention to the friction inherent in economic distribution policies. In various countries ME models are being used as tools for investigating the consequences of regional economic policies, facility planning, and resource use. In this way, alternative policy instruments, future policy scenarios, and conflicting policy options can be judged.

Nijkamp and Paelinck (1976) have argued that quantitative regional economic models may lead to an operational approach to analyzing regional problems. Models provide a precise and consistent definition and use of concepts, hypotheses, variables, and structural relationships and a systematic assessment and formal description of interdependencies, parameter shifts, structural change, and policy impacts on the regional economy. The possibilities of formal consistency checks on model predictions by means of statistical and econometric tools provide for more appropriate tests of the validity of policy measures by means of inferences drawn from model experiments and simulations (provided that the·database is satisfactory).

It should be noted, however, that ME modeling also has limitations and pitfalls. A model builder and/or user should carefully examine the assumptions, theory, and data while applying a model to a specific problem. A comparison of ME models currently in use also demonstrates differences in structure and scope of these models. Ideal models do not exist; each model is limited by its purpose (descriptive versus predictive), its required database (survey versus nonsurvey), and the prevailing institutional structure (regional autonomy versus centralization).

It is important to note that in related fields, modeling efforts have been heavily attacked. For example, Lee (1973) states with respect to urban modeling that

(1) the models were designed to replicate too complex a system in a single shot; and
(2) they were expected to serve too many purposes at the same time.

A related critique has been produced by Sayer (1976). He argues that standard urban modeling is based on very poor theory; identification errors occur in urban modeling and disequilibria are inadequately dealt with. Urban models legitimize the status quo and obscure the possibilities for radical change of the system structure. Similar criticisms can be found in Brewer (1973).

It is evident, that--after a decade of experiences with ME models--a careful investigation of the features and performances of these models is desirable. Research should not exclusively be directed to the formulation of sophisticated conceptual models, but also to the experiences with models that have been operational for some time. The idea of a survey would then be to review the currently existing operational ME models, attempting to achieve a worldwide coverage, and to scrutinize these models from a systematic perspective. We believe that such an approach, of careful analysis, is more fruitful than merely a listing of aspects. It should produce a grid of reference for current model builders to relate their work to. It should respond to the set of expectations that a current or future model user might have. It should provide a source of inspiration for prospective model builders in the field. Finally, it should convey information to the general scientific audience on the current state of the art in ME modeling.

2 Methodological Framework

2.1 The range of multiregional economic models

Models can be devised for different purposes. A standard classification inherited from operations analysis is to subdivide a model class into descriptive, predictive, and planning segments. This classification is not unique for ME models but could refer to any field of application. One of the aims of the survey is to obtain insight into the emphasis on each of these purposes in ME modeling. Is the scope and range of this type of model work different from that in other branches of economics? What is the balance between models used in a policy generation and policy evaluation context?

The range of ME models can also be delimited in a narrower sense as a statement about the coverage of the current study. In this introduction, we will not go into such practical matters. Instead, this structuring work will be presented in the introduction to Part A. It may suffice here to say that a reasonably strict scheme has been adopted, cutting out models that do not have a distinct multiregional context, a reasonably well integrated model of an economic system, and a clear direction towards application.

To stress the importance of the policy direction to the study, we again refer to the standard formulation of Tinbergen (1956) concerning the use of models to develop policies. According to Klaassen *et al.* (1979), this paradigm presupposes that there is a relatively simple system of equations adequately describing the main features of the economic development. There should be a predetermined set of goal variables and the public is free to use existing policy instruments or choose new ones. There is also a certain assumption of controllability, i.e., a statement that the goals can be attained by proper use of instruments.

The characteristic features of regional policy making are such as to demand complex models simply because of the spatial contiguity effects. The field of regional planning is also multidimensional, simply because of its direction towards many policy fields. Additionally, the scope of the diverse policies in regional planning is generally small, given the fact that the national policies have a constraining effect as well. Furthermore, the local nature of the planning leaves room for pressure from interest groups.

It is clear that many models have been designed to serve more than one of the modeling purposes mentioned above and therefore it may make little sense to classify a model as exclusively prediction or policy oriented (Sharpe and Karlqvist 1980). The importance of the distinction is that it points to the institutional context of modeling efforts. This context is relatively simple when analytical purposes dominate. When forecasting, and certainly when policy purposes prevail, the contextual issue is much more intricate, however, and consequently deserves considerable attention when developing a framework for a comparison of models.

2.2 Alternative methods of model classification

Several possibilities exist for developing a framework of classifying ME models: (a) construction of a list of attributes characterizing aspects of the models; (b) specification of a set of criteria serving as a general evaluation framework; (c) construction of an "ideal" model as a frame of reference for judging all other models; and (d) cross comparison of models on the basis of general structure characteristics of these models. Clearly, these possibilities are not mutually exclusive, but they reflect different viewpoints for arriving at a systematic

classification of multiregional models. The four dimensions mentioned may be interpreted hierarchically where (a) would be at the first level, and (b) at the second.
With the help of these two schemes an ideal (case (c)) or a set of nondominated
models may be discerned (see Figure 1).

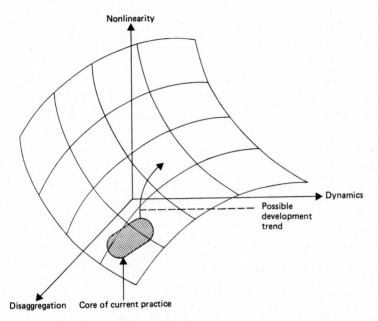

Figure 1. The efficiency frontier in a three-dimensional ME modeling space

     The survey should indicate the shape of the efficiency curve by providing
sample points on it. It should also locate the strong point of current practice
on the surface and the main direction of change. The anticipation of that focus
is that at present disaggregation is favored in relation to nonlinearity and
dynamics.
     Alternative (d) represents another way of approaching the classification. It
does not take a stand on the issue of efficiency but adopts an analytical framework
for cross comparisons of the models in the sample.

     (a) Attributes of models. The choice of a set of attributes constitutes a
descriptive approach to characterizing ME models without providing an explicit
judgement framework. Hordijk and Nijkamp (1980) have listed some such features:

     static, comparative static, or dynamic structure;
     cross section or time series estimation;
     goodness-of-fit of estimations;
     accuracy of predictions;
     degree of connectivity with national models;
     size and number of regions;
     size and number of sectors;
     size and number of groups and/or spatial actors;
     kind of estimation method used; and
     computer time for running the model.

     A typological approach is necessary for obtaining a general insight into the
components of ME models. As will be indicated later, this approach has also been
utilized in the present study.

(b) General evaluation criteria. The specification of a set of general evaluation criteria is based on the aim of seeking for more generality in judging and
building multiregional models. Hordijk and Nijkamp (1980) made an attempt to construct such a list of criteria. Two sets of criteria have been distinguished in
their analysis: *methodological/theoretical* criteria and *practical/empirical* ones
(see Table 1).

Table 1. A set of methodological and practical evaluation criteria for ME models

Methodological	Practical
Isolation of groups of actors	Transferability
Integration and comprehensiveness	Decision support orientation
Testability of behavioral relationships	Data demands
Correspondence between spatial units and problems	Predictive properties
Consistent introduction of policy levers	Adaptability

Such a list of evaluation criteria is, however, not always entirely satisfactory. It can only be applied if the purposes of all models under consideration are
known, if information is available on the database for estimating these models, and
if the institutional policy structure for the spatial system at hand is known. In
general, however, such information for a collection of ME models is not available;
the documentation of most models does not facilitate generalizations. Therefore,
the above mentioned normative approach is not viable when there is a large number
of ME models to be judged. However, several aspects of the list of criteria can
be used to make a cross comparison of such models. This will be further discussed
under point (d).

(c) "Ideal" models. An "ideal" model is supposed to provide the best available
structure of an ME model under theoretically optimum circumstances. Practical bottlenecks in building such a model are normally neglected. There are two reasons
that prevent "ideal" model concepts being used as a general judgement framework:

(i) the properties of any particular model depends very much on its theoretical
     foundations, on its role in a planning and management system and on the level
     of resources put into the building of it;
(ii) each ME model is built for a specific regional economic system, for specific
     policy issues, for specific information systems and for specific future ques-
     tions, so that comparability is an illusion.

Clearly, it may be possible to use notions from such "ideal" models in order
to arrive at a better understanding of models actually used. However, we will not
employ the "ideal" as a reference point in this study, other than in qualitative
terms.

(d) Cross comparison of model structures. Besides the elements of ME models,
their structure also deserves a closer examination. By analyzing and comparing the
structure of models, a deeper insight can be obtained into spatial economic mechanisms, impacts of public policy measures, interregional and intersectoral linkages,
causality patterns, top-down and bottom-up patterns, and so forth. This structure
analysis also makes up a substantial part of the cross comparison of ME models
presented later in this study.

The approaches proposed in (a) and (d) are especially viable ways of studying,
characterizing, and comparing in a systematic way an extensive set of ME models.
They will be used in particular in Chapters 2-6 of this book.

The number of dimensions in an aspect-based comparison may be discussed at length. We have given the matter considerable attention and derived the frame outlined below.

3 Outline of the Book

3.1 General remarks

This book is aimed at giving a comprehensive picture of the current practice in the building and application of ME models. The review is based on an extensive survey made with the help of a formal questionnaire and a large set of background papers. We will not employ the results of this exercise to draw inferences in statistical terms from the sample of 50 models in the survey. Neither will we adhere strictly to the structure of the questions put to the model builders. Rather, we will use the response pattern to attempt to make meaningful cross comparisons. The meaningfulness of a comparison along a certain dimension depends of course on the frequency of treatment of that aspect. Thus, if no models treat the wage formation process endogenously there is nothing to compare.

To complement these questionnaire-based cross comparisons we have asked a number of scientists to contribute to the volume with their view of the practice of ME modeling in different countries with different regional economic problems and different planning and management systems. Special consideration is given to the prospects of ME modeling both in relation to existing and new economic theories, and to emerging problem areas. In this book these aspects are treated in the first three parts. An Appendix containing a summary of information on the 50 models included in the survey constitutes an important part of the documentation. This concludes the book.

3.2 Choice of comparative dimensions

We have chosen to separate five dimensions for the descriptions of the general results of the survey in Part A of the volume. They are:

    model purpose;
    model size;
    model structure;
    model estimation and validation;
    model use.

Apart from these attempts to review the existing body of models (see Chapter 2), by isolating clusters of similar models and modeling techniques, we have chosen to perform cross comparisons in another four dimensions. These dimensions have been chosen after a consideration of the traits of the models in the survey. These are some of the dimensions in which the current modeling practice is varied and important enough to warrant a deeper analysis.

Causality structures. The earlier surveys in the field (Glickman 1982, Courbis 1982) attempted to distinguish top-down and bottom-up approaches to national-regional interactions. Many models fall between these two categories and we will also attempt to structure this area somewhat further. It is shown in Chapter 3 that this cannot be done without analyzing the substitution between a detailed treatment of the intraregional production systems, and an emphasis on national-regional links.

Interregional linkages. This topic is at the core of ME modeling. As shown in Chapter 4, the treatment of trade with products and factors is still incomplete although there have been some interesting steps forward in the last few years.

Effectiveness of regional policies. The majority of ME models are aimed at some type of policy impact analysis. Chapter 5 indicates the necessity of considering policy impact analysis in a more comprehensive framework than normally done when taking recourse to simple types of sensitivity analyses.

Planning and management systems. A special emphasis will be given in the
current study to worldwide comparisons. The role of ME models is different in
market, mixed, and planned economies (see Albegov *et al.* 1982). These issues are
dealt with in Chapter 6 where a description is given of the use of models in the
regional planning system of the USSR, with comparisons with the French planning
experience. Considerable attention is also given to the role of ME models in the
planning systems in the countries of Eastern Europe in Chapters 9, 10, and 11.
In several cases there is a striking similarity in the outlook on model design of
East and West.

The practice of ME modeling is heterogeneous in different countries. There is
even a whole range of operational models, from partial labor demand constructs to
comprehensive dynamic simulation models, even for a single country. We have chosen
to give the discussion of trends in modeling by country or country group.
The trends in Western Europe are clearly towards models that redefine the concept of region, to deal with either different types of functional regions or regions
crossing national boundaries. The labor market aspect is important as shown in
Chapters 7 and 8.
The development of large-scale ME models has been pushed forward substantially
in North America in the last few years. This shift in emphasis from urban to interregional modeling is clear from both the review paper (Chapter 12) and the prospects
one (Chapter 13). In fact, Chapter 14 indicates a strong push towards more comprehensive regional development models in Japan as well.
This trend towards comprehensiveness and complexity through disaggregation is
questioned in Chapter 15 where it is argued that new theories should be brought to
bear in ME modeling. The claim for an integrated location-transportation analysis
is coupled with a demand for a considerably more ambitious treatment of dynamic
technological change and capital mobility.
In the concluding summary section of the book the arguments are developed in
terms of constraints that separate the current *ex post* practice of ME modeling
from the prior objectives. The scope of the models is deficient from a policy
analysis viewpoint since the economic subsystems are treated in an uneven way. The
environmental, population, social, and other subsystems attached to the economic
sphere are not given in enough detail to attain credibility. Such views on disaggregation and integration are confronted with the development of the paradigms
in other scientific disciplines.
Among the aspects warranting more attention in future ME modeling efforts, we
include flexible and systematic information systems, adoption of modern convergent
rather than heuristic solution techniques, a more differentiated view of the appropriate scale of models and their submodules, the treatment of dynamics of change,
and an increased policy relevance.
It is asserted that the development should be conducted along different complementary dimensions. Comprehensiveness must not supersede a sharp problem focus.
Theoretical sophistication must not be given priority before computational flexi-
bility and user credibility. The current volume should encourage prospective model
builders in the 1980s to choose carefully among theories, tools, and information
systems before engaging in large-scale ME modeling without a precise focal point.

References

Adams, F.G., and N.J. Glickman (eds.) (1980), *Modeling the Multiregional Economic
    System* (Heath, Lexington, MA).
Albegov, M., A.E. Andersson, and F. Snickars (eds.) (1982), *Regional Development
    Modeling: Theory and Practice* (North-Holland, Amsterdam).
Bolton, R. (1980), Multiregional Models: Introduction to a Symposium, *Journal of
    Regional Science*, 20, 131–142.
Brewer, G.D. (1973), *Politicians, Bureaucrats, and the Consultants* (New York Basic
    Books, NY).
Courbis, R. (1982), Multiregional Modeling: A General Appraisal, in M. Albegov
    et al. (eds.), *Regional Development Modeling: Theory and Practice* (North-
    Holland, Amsterdam).

Glickman, N.J. (1982), Using Empirical Models for Regional Policy Analysis, in M. Albegov *et al.* (eds.), *Regional Development Modeling: Theory and Practice* (North-Holland, Amsterdam).

Hordijk, L., and P. Nijkamp (1980), Integrated Approaches to Regional Development Models, *Research Memorandum 1980-4* (Free University, Department of Economics, Amsterdam).

Klaassen, L.H., J.H.P. Paelinck, and S. Wagenaar (1979), *Spatial Systems* (Saxon House, Westmead, U.K.).

Lee, D.B. (1973), Requiem for Large-Scale Models, *Journal of the American Institute of Planners*, 39, 163-178.

Miernyk, W.H. (1976), Comments on Recent Developments in Regional Input-Output Analysis, *International Regional Science Review*, 1, 47-55.

Nijkamp, P., and J.H.P. Paelinck (1976), *Operational Theory and Method in Regional Economics* (Saxon House, Farnborough, U.K.).

Sayer, R.A. (1976), A Critique of Urban Modelling, *Progress in Planning*, 6(3), 187-254.

Sharpe, R., and A. Karlqvist (1980), Towards a Unifying Theory of Modelling Urban Systems, *Regional Science and Urban Economics*, 10, 241-257.

Tinbergen, J. (1956), *Economic Policy: Principles and Design* (North-Holland, Amsterdam).

PART A

A REVIEW OF MULTIREGIONAL ECONOMIC MODELING

Part A of this volume is devoted to a review of the current practice in multiregional economic (ME) modeling. In this introduction we will first give a precise indication of the types of model included in and excluded from the review, and will then consider the way in which the basic material for this overview has been collected (see Appendix). Finally, we will give a short introduction to the contents of the chapters which make up this review.

The subject of the review can be described as *operational multiregional economic modeling*. For a clarification of this description, which is at the same time a delimitation of the scope of this book, we will first give a precise definition of each of the elements included in this expression.

Operational. Operationality refers to the stage of development of a model. We have excluded models that have only been developed in conceptual form, without empirical content. Only models that have already been used for empirical studies or that are intended to be used in the very near future are included. Further, we have excluded models that have been used in the past, but are not intended for future use. The effect of the last inclusion is that apart from one or two exceptions, only models that have become operational since 1970 are taken into account.

The choice for operational as opposed to conceptual models had consequences for the design of the review and the whole book; most attention is paid to the structure and application of the models and the theoretical background receives less attention. This does not mean to say, however, that the theoretical background is completely ignored. For example, Chapter 15 is devoted to it.

*Multi*regional. Models dealing with only one region have been excluded, as have models of the satellite type in which the main variables referring to a single region are driven by a national model. We have interpreted "multiregional models" as meaning models containing an integrated description of more than one region. Interregional models, containing direct relationships between regions, are obvious members of the set of multiregional models but they do not exhaust this set: models with indirect relationships between regions (via national variables) also belong there.

Multi*regional*. We have restricted our attention to regions that are so large that the labor commuting between regions is relatively insignificant, so that the regional labor markets are closed to a large extent. This delimitation has the important implication that urban models are not taken into account. Of course, we are aware that multiregional economic and urban models share many features, so a fruitful cross fertilization might be achieved by a combined study. We have decided, however, to focus explicitly on multiregional economic modeling. Another field of multiregional modeling not taken into account is the linkage of existing national models by means of international trade relationships. Here again interesting possibilities for a combined study exist but we have opted for depth rather than breadth in the current analysis.

Economic. We have restricted our attention to models with a more or less complete description of the economic system. This means that we have excluded models focusing on only one particular sector (e.g., agriculture) or that treat the economic system in a peripheral way (as is the case in certain demographic models). Obviously, this does not mean to say that we have excluded models that, in addition to an economic system also contain other systems such as demographic, environmental,

11

and water resource systems. Several such integrated models are present in the
survey.

Modeling. We define a model as a set of formal relationships between variables
that are formulated in such a way that it is possible to find the impacts of each
variable on the others. This definition means that we have not taken into account
informal or qualitative procedures to arrive at impact statements or predictions.
It also means that we have paid no attention to data systems of an exclusively
descriptive nature such as input-output tables. Only if these data systems are
used in the context of a model as defined above are they taken into account. We
use the term modeling rather than models; this means that we have restricted our
attention not only to the formal structure of models, but activities such as estimation, validation and builder-user communication have also been taken into account.

We will now give some information about the course of the survey study, which
is important for a good understanding of the survey results published in this book.
In the summer of 1980 the Regional Development Group of IIASA, Laxenburg, Austria,
and the Department of Regional Economics, The Free University, Amsterdam, The
Netherlands, agreed to start a collaborative study of multiregional economic modeling. An advisory group of eight model builders from various countries was formed
to provide information on the items to be dealt with in the survey and on names of
researchers active in the field to be covered. In November 1980, a background
paper was written (Nijkamp and Rietveld 1980) and a questionnaire was designed.
From December 1980 to December 1981 approximately 100 questionnaires were sent out.
In 63 cases model builders returned a completed form. Thirteen of the models did
not satisfy the delimitations formulated above. Thus, we arrived at a set of
exactly 50 multiregional economic models. Some readers might infer that we have
aimed at this outcome, but it really was a coincidence!

For an assessment of the completeness of the survey, it is important to pay
attention to the 37 model builders who did not return a completed form. In approximately ten cases, the addressee informed us that he or she had nothing to report
on multiregional economic modeling activities. From the rest we did not receive
any response at all. Obviously, two types on nonresponse may be distinguished:
those where there is a model to report and those where there is not. It is our
impression that the latter group is larger than the former one. Only in a few
cases are we certain of the existence of a multiregional economic model not covered
by the survey.

By the summer of 1981 most of the responses to the questionnaire had been received, and these formed the main inputs for a preliminary version of the model
descriptions contained in the Appendix and for the chapters included in Part A of
this book. In November 1981, a conference was held at IIASA with approximately
50 participants on the theme "Practice and Prospects of Multiregional Economic
Modeling", during which the provisional results of the survey were presented. We
encouraged the participants to inform us about modeling efforts not included in the
papers at that time; according to the participants the coverage of the field was
fairly complete.

The main source of information for the chapters in Part A is the set of 50
model descriptions in the Appendix. These descriptions have been authorized by
the respective model builders. All references to this set of models will be made
by means of the acronyms of the models, which can be found at the beginning of the
Appendix. For models without an existing acronym we have designed one ourselves
to facilitate the referencing process. Explicit references to publications relating to a particular model are only given if information not contained in the main
publication mentioned in the Appendix is at stake.

The subjects covered in Part A are as follows. Chapter 2 is devoted to a
general overview of multiregional economic models. In this chapter the majority
of the entries in the Appendix are reviewed. These entries pertain, among other
things, to model purposes, elements, structure, use, and documentation.

Since the study is explicitly model-oriented, formal features of multiregional
modeling are in the foreground to some detriment for considering problems of reality in international and regional-national relations in different countries, as
well as for substantial analysis of mechanisms reflected by the models.

The other chapters contain more specific treatments of some model aspects that are of particular importance for multiregional economic models. The interrelationships between nations and regions, and interregional relationships receive attention in Chapters 3 and 4, respectively. In Chapter 3 attention is also paid to the question of to what extent model outcomes are determined by demand variables, supply variables, or both.

The focus in Chapters 5 and 6 is on the use of multiregional economic models for policy or planning purposes. Chapter 5 is devoted to the use of these models for policy analysis. In Chapter 6 the implications of the type of planning system for the features of multiregional economic models are discussed.

Reference

Nijkamp, P., and P. Rietveld (1980), Towards a Comparative Study of Multiregional Models, *IIASA Working Paper* WP-80-172 (International Institute for Applied Systems Analysis, Laxenburg, Austria).

CHAPTER 2

A GENERAL OVERVIEW OF MULTIREGIONAL ECONOMIC MODELS

Piet Rietveld

1 Introduction

In this chapter, a general overview is given of the state-of-the-art in multi-regional economic modeling. The overview is mainly based on the summary descriptions of 50 multiregional economic models from 20 countries in the Appendix.

As explained in the introduction to Part A, use has been made of a questionnaire to obtain the information for the summary descriptions. Due to space limitations, not all the information contained in the responses to the questionnaire could be included in these descriptions. Some of the information excluded from the descriptions has been used directly in the present chapter, however. Examples are: information on the impacts of model outcomes and on the communication between model builder and model user. For information on the way in which the set of models has been delimited and on the course of the survey study, we refer the reader to the introduction to Part A.

Not all the relevant features of multiregional economic modeling are covered in the present chapter. In Chapters 3-6 a more elaborate discussion will be given of specific model aspects such as interregional linkages, and the use of models for policy purposes.

An important question to be considered is whether the set of models described in the Appendix is (approximately) exhaustive. The answer is not entirely positive: in some cases it appeared to be impossible to get in touch with model builders; in other cases we had to accept the problem of nonresponse. Given this result, one may wonder whether the models included in the survey form a representative subset of the complete set of models. Table 1 presents the distribution of the models among the 20 countries. It is clear from this table that the developing countries are underrepresented. This may also hold true for the USSR.

Table 1. Models included in the survey

Country	Number of models	Country	Number of models
FRG	4	Yugoslavia	1
The Netherlands	4	Czechoslovakia	1
Belgium	5	Poland	1
France	1	USSR	2
Italy	2	Canada	2
UK	2	USA	9
EEC	1	Japan	4
Austria	1	Australia	2
Sweden	5	Korea	1
Norway	1	Kenya	1

Given these gaps one should be careful in making general statements about the present state of multiregional economic modeling. This does not alter the fact that, according to our impression, the survey provides a reasonable coverage of the complete set of multiregional economic models and that it contains the large majority of the models at the frontiers of the multiregional economic modeling field. The survey is undoubtedly the most complete one in the history of multiregional economic modeling.

It should be emphasized that all the models included are operational or close to being operational. Theoretical model proposals have been left out of consideration in the survey.

The following sections mainly consist of frequency tables, contingency tables and Venn diagrams with brief comments. If the number of models in the tables or diagrams is not equal to the sample size (50) the reason is missing information, unless otherwise stated. In general, the number of models with missing information is small.

The following subjects will be discussed in this chapter. In Section 2, attention will be given to model purposes. Section 3 will be devoted to the elements of multiregional economic models: size aspects, the types of region, the time dimension and the scope of the models. In Section 4, we will deal with various aspects of model structure such as production structures and the role of prices, investments, and the labor market in the models. In Section 5 we will focus on the estimation and validation of multiregional economic models. Section 6 will be devoted to model use: types of users, builder-user communication, etc. Finally, in Section 7, attention will be given to model documentation.

2 Model Purposes

When one wants to do justice to a model, it is important to know the purposes for which it has been built. For example, when a model is exclusively built for forecasting purposes, one should not be surprised when it contains only a small number of policy handles. Table 2 presents the frequencies of the two most important purposes per model. It is clear from the table that the models have mainly been developed for policy (*ex ante*) forecasting and analytical studies. The lack of interest in *ex post* policy studies is remarkable, especially when one knows that the majority of the models have been built at public academic institutions (see Section 2.6). If there is a place where conditions for an impartial analysis of regional policies of the past are favorable, it is at these institutions. The relatively minor attention paid to *ex post* policy studies will be further discussed in Chapter 5.

Table 2. Frequency of model purposes in multiregional
         economic models

Purpose	Number of models
Policy studies (*ex ante*)	35
Forecasting studies	29
Analytical studies	24
Policy studies (*ex post*)	7
Educational purposes	5

One of the conclusions that can be drawn on the basis of the survey is that most of the models can be used for most of the purposes mentioned in Table 2. This means for example, that it may be misleading to call a model a "forecasting" model. A better terminology--which will be used in this study--is to speak in such a case of a model designed or used for forecasting purposes.

Obviously, model purposes have more dimensions than the one described in Table 2. The purpose of a model may, for example, also refer to the time span or the scope of a model. These elements will be discussed in the following section. Also, in the final chapter, an integrative analysis of model purposes in the process of multiregional economic modeling will be given.

3 Elements of Multiregional Economic Models

3.1 Size aspects

In this section, various size aspects of multiregional economic models will be discussed: the number of regions, number of sectors, and number of endogenous variables.

The number of regions distinguished in the models is represented in Table 3. Clearly, the variation is large. The largest share of the models describe only a relatively small number of regions. The median number of regions is nine. There are some models with very large numbers of regions, however: MULTIREGION deals with 173 regions, while MRMI even contains a spatial disaggregation of up to 3103 counties. In some models, one has the possibility of selecting the appropriate level of spatial detail. The above mentioned MRMI model, for example, can be run for 3103, 435, or 51 regions.

Table 3. Frequency distribution of the number of
         regions in multiregional economic models

Number of regions	Number of models
2 - 8	21
9 - 20	13
21 - 100	13
> 100	2

In Table 4, the frequency distribution of the number of sectors in the model is displayed. It appears that some models have no sectoral disaggregation at all (e.g., MACEDOINE, IRUD). The median number of sectors is 20. Models with a large number of sectors are: MRMI (108 sectors) and SCIIOM (200 sectors). In Chapter 5 special attention will be paid to a separate treatment of the public sector. This subject will also be addressed in the concluding chapter.

Table 4. Frequency distribution of the number of
         sectors in multiregional economic models

Number of sectors	Number of models
1 - 10	17
11 - 20	9
21 - 40	11
41 - 100	10
> 100	2

It is clear that the sectoral detail in the models is on average larger than the spatial detail. Table 4(a) presents the joint distribution of the number of

Table 4(a). Contingency table of numbers of regions and sectors in multiregional
            economic models

		Number of sectors		Σ
		1 - 20	≥ 21	
Number of regions	≥ 10	7	16	23
	2 - 9	19	7	26
Σ		26	23	49

regions and sectors. The distribution of the models among the classes in the table
is certainly not uniform. There is a clear tendency for models with a large number
of regions to describe a large number of sectors as well. The number of models in
the north-east and south-west corner is relatively small. This means that model
builders have a tendency to build models in which the sectoral and regional detail
are in equilibrium. The number of models in which the sectoral detail is clearly
above average and the regional detail is clearly below average (and vice versa), is
relatively small.
      We will next consider model size as measured by the number of endogenous vari-
ables (see Table 5). The median number of endogenous variables is roughly 800.
Model size is clearly above average in North America and somewhat below average in
Western Europe. The largest models have been listed in Table 6.

Table 5. The number of endogenous variables in multiregional economic models

	Number of endogenous variables		Σ
	< 800	≥ 800	
Western Europe	13	7	20
Scandinavia	3	3	6
Eastern Europe	3	2	5
North America	1	10	11
Pacific	4	2	6
Developing countries	1	1	2
Σ	25	25	50

Table 6. Models with a large number of endogenous variables

Model	Country	Number of variables
REGINA	France	8 000
MULTIREGION	USA	14 000
NRIES	USA	14 000
MREEED	USA	≥ 40 000
MRMI	USA	≥ 50 000
SMOPP	USSR	≥ 100 000

In most cases the large models have relatively large numbers of regions and sectors, but there are exceptions (e.g., REGINA). The exceptions indicate that model size is not only a function of the number of regions and sectors, but also of model scope and model completeness (see also Section 3.4).

3.2 Types of regions

It is important to note the type of region used in the models: are the basic spatial units functional or administrative regions? In almost all cases, model builders use regional data collected by statistical offices for general purposes. In the large majority, these offices employ administrative regions as spatial units, although there are exceptions such as the Bureau of Economic Analysis in the USA which generates data for functional economic areas (these data are inputs of the MULTIREGION model).

This choice of administrative regions as the basic spatial units is not in agreement with the way in which the models are usually specified: most multi-regional economic models are based on the implicit assumption that the spatial units are functional economic regions. For example, most models assume that the regions are relatively independent of each other, so that interregional relationships are only specified for a limited number of phenomena (see Chapter 4). Obviously, this discrepancy gives rise to specification errors and hence to unreliable results. On the other hand, an advantage of models based on administrative regions is that they can be used for policy purposes.

In some models, regions are classified according to the degree of urbanization (e.g., urban versus rural). These models are: REGINA, REMO, and IRUD. The regions obtained in this way are more or less homogeneous according to the human settlement patterns. Models based on these classes of regions are especially suitable for studying migration, commuting, suburbanization, physical planning problems, housing markets, etc. It is not a coincidence that the distinction between urban and rural areas is at the core of many models for developing countries (see Sanderson 1980).

An especially interesting treatment of urban versus rural regions is contained in REGINA. In this model, the urban-rural breakdown is embedded in a three-level hierarchical framework: (1) nations; (2) regions; (3) urban and rural areas. A similar introduction of a regional hierarchy can be found in the NRWF model. Some models have been especially devised to study a particular region in a larger system of regions. In these models, some regions receive a more detailed treatment than others. Some of these models only deal with two regions: region x versus the rest of the country--MEEI and VERDI (see NORD-SUD). Other models contain a spatial breakdown of the region of interest (NRWF and HESSEN).

3.3 The time dimension

In this section we will first look at the time dimension *of* multiregional economic models (year of construction, most recent data available) and then at the time dimension *in* these models (short-term versus long-term dynamics).

In the survey, we have restricted our attention to operational models. This means that we have excluded models that have only been developed in conceptual form. Only models that have been used for empirical studies or that are intended to be used in the near future have been included. Models that have been used in the past but that are not intended for future use have been left out. Table 7 shows that the last delimitation implies that almost all models became operational after 1970.

The table seems to suggest a certain growth of the number of new models in the course of time. One should be careful with the interpretation of the table, however. We know several models that were built in the early 1970s but are not operational now (e.g., CANDIDE-R, developed by d'Amours *et al.* 1975). Therefore it is not clear whether there has really been an increase in regional modeling efforts during the 1970s.

In the survey we describe the models as they are at the beginning of 1982. This means that they are at different stages: some are not yet fully operational, others are in a process of updating, refinement or extension, others have not been used for some time and may be near to a silent death. We know much more about the

Table 7. The age of multiregional economic models

Period in which the model became operational	Number of models
Before 1970	2
1970-73	9
1974-77	12
1978-81	19
Not quite operational	8

first stages of models than about the final ones. This is a pity, since information on the origins of the collapse of models may improve future model building. Model builders seldom or never report in professional journals why they decided to stop the maintenance and use of their models.

The availability of data is an important determinant of the scope and quality of a model. Table 8 presents the most recent regional data used in the models. The median delay is six years. This means that 50% of the models are exclusively based on data from the period before 1975. This period is characterized by a rather stable growth pattern as opposed to the period since 1975. This inadequacy of the database leads to a decrease in the relevance of the models for the problems of the 1980s. It is by no means sure that models that have been validated for periods of stable development are useful for turbulent periods. We note, for example, that stable development gives rise to little variability in the data, which hampers the estimation of statistically significant coefficients.

Table 8. Availability of regional data

Most recent regional data used	Number of models
1963-69	5
1970-74	16
1975-77	16
1978-81	9

We will next discuss the time dimension *in* multiregional economic models. The time scope of the models as intended by the model builders can be found in Figure 1. The figure indicates that four models are exclusively meant for short-term purposes (BREIN, KIM, MAG, and OTSIS), 17 models are exclusively meant for the medium-term, and one model is exclusively meant for long-term purposes (MFM). There is a clear tendency towards the medium-term: all but five models have been intended for this time class (among others).

A model suitable for short-term analyses should satisfy the following requirements. It should take note of business cycles and inventory formation, and it should preferably also contain quarterly data and seasonal variations. Figure 1 indicates that 14 models have been intended for this time class (among others). The requirements are, however, seldom met by these models. There is, for example, only one model with quarters as the time unit: MEPA.

A model suitable for long-run analyses should, among other things, satisfy the requirements that it is an integrated (nonpartial) model and that attention is paid to the development of resources such as population, capital, and energy. Further, such a model should not be based on the constancy of certain coefficients that may be expected to change in the future. Figure 1 indicates that 17 models have been intended for long-run analyses. However, most of these models do not satisfy these

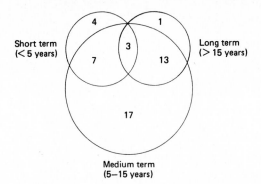

Short term
(< 5 years)

Long term
(> 15 years)

Medium term
(5—15 years)

Figure 1. The intended time scope of models

requirements. Of the 17 models only four contain a complete economic system (see
Section 2.6): BACHUE, MFM, MREEED, MEPA. Of these four models, BACHUE is the only
one that treats demography in a sufficiently sophisticated way to make it suitable
for long-run analyses. We may conclude that although some model builders may have
other intentions, the large majority of the models is not particularly useful for
short- and long-term problems. The time span that remains is the medium-term.

Finally, we will consider the role of dynamics in multiregional economic
models. A model is called dynamic when it allows one to follow the effects of a
jump in an exogenous variable during period t on the endogenous variables in
periods t, $t + 1$, $t + 2$, etc. One of the reasons why it is important to know
whether the model is dynamic is that policy questions often include a time element
(e.g., short-run versus long-run consequences of certain policies). Another reason for it being important to pay attention to dynamics in a model is that certain
important phenomena, such as capital formation and technological change, cannot be
dealt with in a static model in an adequate way. It appears that of the 50 models,
33 are dynamic, while 17 are static. This reveals the limited scope of some of the
multiregional economic (ME) models. For a further discussion of the role of dynamics in ME models, we refer the reader to Chapters 5 and 15.

3.4 The scope of multiregional economic models

One of the conditions imposed on the models included in the survey is that
they should contain a more or less complete description of an economic system. Not
surprisingly, the models differ significantly in the amount of detail used and in
the extent to which other systems are also taken into account (e.g., environment,
energy, demography). Figure 2 gives an indication of the scope of the models by
means of Venn diagrams.

Figure 2(a) indicates that in 24 models both employment and production are
endogenous. In nine cases, only production is endogenous, while employment is not
included or is exogenous. These models appear to be ordinary input-output models
such as BREIN and MRIO. In another nine cases, only employment is endogenous, while
production is not included or absent. Examples of these multiregional labor market
models are REGAM and MULTIREGION. We may conclude that a considerable part of the
models is clearly partial. Obviously partial models are by definition useful for
a smaller set of purposes than more comprehensive models. In Section 2.6 it will
be shown, however, that partial models are very well represented in the set of
models with the broadest range of users. Thus, there is no reason to look upon
these partial models as less relevant than more comprehensive models.

In Figure 2(b) attention is given to demographic elements in the models. It
appears that in 25 cases the population size is endogenous. In most cases, the
treatment of population is rather crude: no detailed study of various age-sex

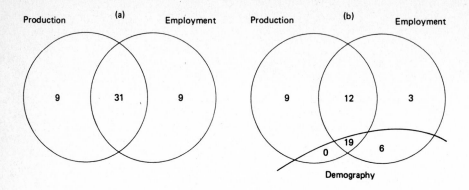

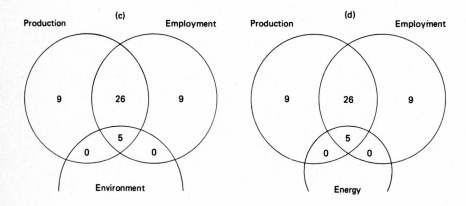

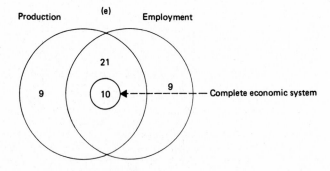

Figure 2.   The scope of multiregional economic models

classes. Notable exceptions are NRWF, BACHUE, MULTIREGION, and ECESIS. Obviously, when demography is crudely treated or even missing in a model, such a model is less suitable for long-run analyses. Here we find a clear indication that most models in the survey are only useful for the short- and medium-run.

Figure 2(c) shows that in five cases environmental variables are endogenous. These models are: HESSEN, MEEEI, TLM, MREEED, and RDM. Five models contain a detailed treatment of the energy sector (see Figure 2(d)): MEEEI, TLM, MORSE, MAG, and MREEED. One may conclude that in only a small part of the models has the economic system been linked with the energy or the environmental system.

Diagram (e) indicates that ten of the models contain a "complete" economic system. We call an economic system complete when production, employment investments, and prices/wages are endogenous. These models are: REM, RENA, SERENA, REGINA, BACHUE, MFM, MREEED, MEPA, ECESIS, and NRPEM. We note that this number is relatively low, and that the distribution among the various countries seems to be rather regular.

4 The Structure of Multiregional Economic Models

4.1 Production structures

In this section, attention will be given to interindustrial relations and production functions in multiregional economic models. A common classification in the field of (multi) regional economic modeling is the one between input-output and econometric models (Glickman 1977, Polenske 1980). From the survey we may conclude, however, that this distinction is not accurate. Table 9 shows that in 29 models input-output relationships have been specified. In no less than 11 cases, it appears, however, that these input-output relationships are embedded in a model estimated by means of econometric techniques (e.g., HESSEN, TLM, REGINA, MEPA, RDM). This result indicates that there have been considerable efforts to integrate detailed information on interindustry and behavioral relationships estimated by means of econometric methods.

Table 9. Input-output, and econometric models

	Input-output	Noninput-output	Σ
Noneconometric	18	2	20
Econometric	11	19	30
Σ	29	21	50

We now turn to the specification of production functions. The production factors distinguished are represented in Figure 3. The figure shows that labor is the production factor that occurs most frequently in the models (40 times). In ten models, no attention is paid to any production factor at all. In the figure no distinction is made between public and private capital. It appears that in five models public capital is taken into account explicitly: REGAL, BALAMO, NRPEM, EPAM, and OTSIS. More attention is paid to the treatment of public capital in Chapter 5.

Production functions of various types have been used (see Table 10) in a direct or indirect way (for example, as a basis for factor demand functions). In a large majority of the models, no production function at all or a traditional production function is used. Models with distinguishing features are SERENA, in which a vintage approach is used, and MEEEI and MREEED, which make use of so-called translog functions.

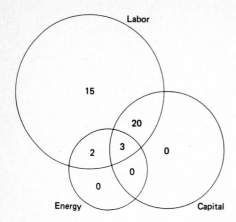

Figure 3. Frequency of occurrence of production factors

Table 10. Frequency distribution of various types of production functions

Types of production function	Number of models
Cobb-Douglas	11
Constant elasticity of substitution	2
Putty-clay vintage	1
Other forms	6
Fixed technical coefficients	11
No production function	19

4.2 The modeling of private investments

    It is a well known fact that the modeling of private investments is one of the more difficult steps in the construction of economic models. It is therefore worth-while to consider how private investments are modeled in ME models. The survey reveals that various approaches have been used by model builders:

(1) In 20 models, investments have been completely taken out of consideration;
(2) In seven models, investments play a role as exogenous variables. In some cases investments are exclusively treated as a component of final demand (e.g., MRIO). In other cases attention is only paid to the effect of investments on production capacity (e.g., MACEDOINE);
(3) In six models, investments are instrument variables in a programming model (e.g., MORSE, SMOTR);
(4) In 12 models, investments are endogenous. In some cases regional investments are determined by applying fixed proportions to national investments (e.g., REGION). In most models, however, the specification of regional investments is based on location theory. This means that the distribution of investments among regions depends on variables such as rental cost of capital and labor market tightness, both relative to the national level. Examples of this approach are REM and RDM.

    It is well known that regional data on investments and capital are in general weak. This is reflected by the fact that these variables are rather often left out of consideration in ME models. It is clear, however, that if these models are to be used for medium- to long-term studies, they should include the capital formation process. An attractive property of investment equations based on location theory, as mentioned earlier, is that they provide an important policy handle: investment subsidies. Hence these models can be used to study the effectiveness of investment subsidies on regional investments (see also Chapter 5).

4.3   The modeling of the labor market

Regional labor market problems have been one of the reasons for the construction of ME models. It is therefore interesting to investigate the ways in which regional labor markets have been treated in ME models. In Chapter 7 such an investigation has been carried out for the models developed in Western Europe. In this section, we will focus on the modeling of one particular aspect of the labor market: unemployment. It appears that regional unemployment is endogenous in 21 models included in the survey. Given the fact that employment plays a role in 40 models, we may conclude that a considerable part of the models does not give a very complete description of the labor market.

Two different approaches to the modeling of unemployment can be distinguished. In the majority of the cases, regional unemployment is determined in the models as the difference between regional labor demand and regional labor supply. An example of such a regional labor market model is represented in Figure 4(a). In this figure are also included the discouraged labor effect (impact of employment on labor supply) and a Phillips curve relationship (impact of unemployment on wages). Examples of this approach are: IMPE, REM, REGAM, RENA, and REMO.

In the majority of cases labor supply is determined as the result of labor demand and unemployment (see Figure 4(b)). Examples are LPFM, NRIES, MAG, and MACEDOINE. Although there does not seem to be a clear theoretical justification of this approach, Ledent (1981) has shown that the latter approach in general gives rise to more satisfactory prediction errors than the former one. This is clearly a result that deserves further attention in (multi)regional labor market modeling.

(a)

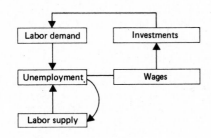

(b)

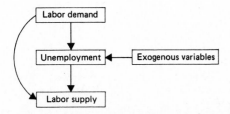

Figure 4.   Two versions of regional labor market models

All models in the survey share the property that vacancies are absent on the labor market which means that excess supply and excess demand are treated in an asymmetric way. This may give rise to an inadequate specification of adjustment processes on the labor market. The obvious reason for the neglect of vacancies is the lack of reliable regional data.

Another crudeness in modeling regional labor markets is discovered when one considers the treatment of occupational mobility. When demand and supply are confronted with each other in the models, usually an aggregation is applied over all sectors or occupational categories. There are few models in which the implicit assumption of perfect occupational mobility is absent: REMO and MEPA. The REMO model contains an explicit treatment of the educational system as a means of achieving upward occupational mobility. In MEPA, the introduction is proposed of a "trained labor force" variable for each industry. This variable indicates the number of people with job experience per industry (Treyz 1980).

4.4 Modeling of prices and wages

The way in which prices and wages are modeled forms an important aspect of the structure of ME models. For example, prices and wages have impacts on:

income formation, which has effects on intra- and interregional income differentials;
interregional migration and location of investments;
substitution of production factors;
supply-demand adjustments on various markets.

In a substantial number of models (19), prices and wages have been left out completely. This is obviously a handicap for an adequate analysis of the above mentioned phenomena.

In four cases, prices and wages play a role as exogenous variables (e.g., RDM). In such cases wages and prices may indeed give rise to adjustment processes as described above, but there is no feedback from the development of the real variables on the prices.

In 11 programming models, prices may play a role of importance via the objective function. For example, in transportation models (exogenous), transport costs have an impact on interregional trade patterns. Besides, the dual variables found in programming models often have a clear meaning as shadow prices of certain resources. MRMI is an example of a model in which dual variables are used intensively.

In the remaining 16 models, wages and/or prices are endogenous. In these cases they perform one or more of the functions mentioned above. There is a tendency in the models for prices to be determined at the national level, so that interregional price differentials are assumed to be absent. On the other hand, in all these models, wages are determined at the regional level. Examples involving this asymmetric treatment of wages and prices are RENA and NRIES. This approach clearly reflects that the labor market functions for most occupational categories at the regional level, while for many goods the national market prevails.

An interesting treatment of wages is provided by REGINA in which wages in provincial regions are influenced by wages in the Parisian region. Due to these interregional wage dynamics, an increase in the Parisian wages may have a substantial impact on the national price level. This is an example of an inflation theory based on interregional wage dynamics.

4.5 Functional forms and solution methods

The functional forms specified in models have repercussions on the way in which the models can be solved and on the estimation techniques to be used. Table 11 shows that approximately 50% of the models are completely linear while in the other 50% linearity still plays an important role.

The methods used for solving the models have been displayed in Table 12. In this table a distinction has been made between programming models and simulation models. Nine of the 15 programming models have been solved by means of well known

Table 11. Functional forms of relationships

Functional form	Number of models
Linear	26
Linear and log-linear	8
Linear and information term	2
Linear and quadratic	2
Various forms	11

Table 12. Solution methods for multiregional economic models

Solution method	Number of models
Programming models	
Linear programming	8
Quadratic programming	1
Nonlinear programming	5
Multiobjective programming	1
Simulation models	
Recursive structure	9
Standard linear structure	12
Gauss–Seidel	4
Numerical method not specified	9
Eigenvalue method	1

methods such as linear and quadratic programming. In the other six cases more advanced methods have been applied such as nonlinear programming and multiobjective programming; these are REGAL, IRUD, FRET, INTEREG, DREAM, and MACEDOINE.

In 21 of 36 cases, the solution of the simulation model is straightforward: either the model is recursive, or it allows the application of standard methods for solving systems of linear equations. In 14 cases more complex solution methods have to be used. In ho case did the model builder report on problems with these more complex methods. This is, to a certain extent, a surprise since in many of these methods iterative procedures are involved that do not necessarily converge towards a unique solution.

Finally, it is interesting to note that in the two largest models of the survey (SMOPP and MRMI) use is made of linear programming. This clearly indicates the power of linear programming algorithms to deal with large-scale models.

4.6 Programming versus simulation models

In the preceding section we introduced the distinction between programming and simulation models. One usually assigns to programming models the property that they are normative, while simulation models are usually assumed to serve descriptive purposes. A careful analysis of the models in the survey reveals that the above assignment of properties is completely incorrect, as will be clarified by the following two statements.

(1) *Not all programming models serve normative purposes.* We note that some programming models are exclusively used for descriptive purposes: IMPE, MRMI, FRET, and INTEREG. For example, in MRMI interregional trade is determined by a linear programming model. The dual variables are interpreted as location

rents and used as explanatory variables of interregional location. Thus, programming can simply be looked upon as a solution method for a system of equations and inequalities. There are also some programming models in the survey that are used for both descriptive and normative purposes: MORSE, REGAL, and IRUD. For example, REGAL has been used to determine the most desirable distribution of investments among regions, and also to determine the most probable one. For the last purpose, use has been made of an information term to find the interregional distribution nearest to the existing distribution while it obeys the restrictions imposed by economic structure, physical planning, etc.

(2) *Almost all simulation models can in principle be used for normative purposes.* A common classification of exogenous variables is the one between instruments (exogenous variables that can be controlled) and autonomous variables (variables that cannot be controlled). Consequently, as soon as certain instruments can be identified in a model, the model can in principle be used to find the values the instrument variables have to assume in order to arrive at desired outcomes for endogenous variables. For an elaboration of this approach we refer to Chapter 5, where we find that a considerable number of models have been used for this purpose.

There is another pair of concepts that yields insight when confronted with the pair programming versus simulation models, namely econometric versus noneconometric models. The coefficients of programming models are usually not obtained by means of econometric methods; see Table 13. Econometric methods appear to play an important role in the estimation of the coefficients of only four programming models: IMPE, HESSEN, TLM, and MACEDOINE. There is no intrinsic reason for econometric methods being more suitable for simulation than for programming models, however. One might question the usefulness of econometric methods for programming models by saying that these models may give rise to outcomes far outside the range within which the models have been estimated. This is not a convincing argument, however, since it may also be raised against the use of econometrics in simulation models. In our opinion this problem can in principle be avoided by an appropriate model specification. We conclude therefore, that there is scope for an increased use of econometric methods in programming models. This aspect will be taken up in Chapter 16.

Table 13. The coincidence of programming and econometric models

	Programming	Simulation	Σ
Econometric	4	26	30
Noneconometric	11	9	20
Σ	15	35	50

5 Estimation and Validation

In Sections 4.1 and 4.5 we considered the extent to which econometric methods are used for the estimation of models. It appears that for 20 models, econometric methods have not been used at all. Input-output models are strongly represented among these 20. In these models, coefficients are usually obtained by elementary operations applied to observations from one year. In some cases the coefficients are based on informed guesses. Various methods for updating input-output coefficients are used. We mention especially information theoretic approaches, used in MORSE, GISSIR, and OTSIS.

The econometric methods used to estimate the remaining models are represented in Table 14. For some models, use has been made of more than one technique. The table shows that in the large majority of cases the model equations have been

Table 14. Estimation methods for multiregional economic models

Econometric method	Number of models
Ordinary least-squares	29
Two-stage least-squares	5
Maximum likelihood	2
Nonlinear regression	3

estimated separately. It appears that the possibility of spatial autocorrelation is completely neglected in the models, indicating that the econometric methods usually employed in multiregional economic models are not very advanced.

Once a model has been estimated, the question of validity arises: does the model yield meaningful results given the purposes for which it has been built. This formulation indicates that the appropriate validation strategy for a model depends on the purposes of the model. Chaubey (1979) has formulated a validation plan for a multiregional economic model in which the forecasting purpose takes a central place. He proposes to carry out tests concerning: (1) the ability of a model to generate reliable forecasts; (2) the stability of a model.

The first test has the following features. Let t_1 and t_2 represent the time bounds within which a model has been estimated. Then the model can be used for the following activities:

(a) *ex post simulation:* the model is used to generate endogenous variables for the period from t_1 to t_2, given the actual values of exogenous variables during this period;

(b) *ex post forecast:* the model is used to generate endogenous variables for the period after t_2, given the actual values of exogenous variables;

(c) *ex ante forecast:* the model is used to generate endogenous variables for the period after t_2, given predicted values of exogenous variables.

Various concepts have been developed to measure the extent to which values generated by the model are in accordance with the model: MAPE, MSE, etc. The second test (only applicable to dynamic systems) can be carried out by examining the characteristic roots of the system.

In Table 15 we have given the frequency of occurrence of the validation activities. For only 19 models did we find that numerical results of validation tests had been published. *Ex post* simulation, which is the least radical way of validity testing, has been applied most frequently (14 times). Characteristic roots have been computed for MACEDOINE and GISSIR.

If we use the above validity tests as a frame of reference for ME models, we arrive at the conclusion that the (scientific) community is insufficiently informed about the validity of the majority of these models. For only approximately 50% of the fully operational models, have results of validation tests been published. This does not mean, of course, that for the other 50% validation has been completely neglected, but less strict validation procedures may have been carried out. For

Table 15. Frequency of occurrence of validation activities

Validation activity	Number of models
Ex post simulation	14
Ex post forecast	7
Ex ante forecast	3
Computation of characteristic roots	2

example, some of these models have been employed by a wide range of users for several years, which indicates that these models yield results that are considered meaningful by those users. Although such support is not worthless, it should be supplemented with information about stricter tests to allow definite statements to be made about the validity of a model. We conclude, therefore, that validity tests deserve more explicit attention in ME modeling.

6 Model Use

Information on model use is often one of the weaker points of models. Therefore, we pay special attention to it in this section. We start with a description of the linkages between model users and model builders. The extent to which models are used appears to depend considerably on the type of institution where the model has been developed. We distinguish four types of institutions:

A : academic institutions (universities, academies of science);
C : consultancy agencies;
G_N: national governmental agencies;
G_R: regional governmental agencies.

In Table 16 the numbers of models developed in these institutions are given, and we have confined our attention to models that have been operational for a long enough time to allow them to be applied. The majority of the models have been built in academic institutions. The number of models built by consultancy agencies and governmental agencies is considerably smaller.

Table 16. Builders and users of models

Model builders	Number of models	Mean number of users per model
Academic institutions	25	1.2
Consultants	4	2.2
National governmental agencies	9	1.6
Regional governmental agencies	–	–

In the questionnaire the model builders were asked in which of the types of institutions mentioned above have results of their models been used. Thus, the maximum possible number of users per model is four. The mean number of users per model appears to be 1.4. The distribution among the types of model builders has been given in the last column of Table 16. The (not very surprising) conclusion is that the number of users is on average largest for consultancy agencies, and smallest for academic institutions. Generally, model builders can also be considered as users of their own models; this kind of use has been excluded in Table 16. The extent of model use appears to vary considerably from country to country; for example, the mean number of users in North America (2.7) is clearly above average.

We will next give closer inspection to the models with the widest range of users, as defined above. One can conjecture, for example, that the more comprehensive a model is, the larger the range of potential users will be. In Table 17 are listed the models that have been used in three or four different types of institutions. The above conjecture is not confirmed by this list: most of the models included are clearly partial. For example, the first three models exclusively deal with labor markets. Models 4-6 are models in which the focus is predominantly or exclusively on input-output relationships. The only exception is MRMI, which gives a rather complete description of the economic system and related systems.

Table 17. Models with a wide range of users

Model	Country
(1) WREM	UK
(2) LPFM	Sweden
(3) MULTIREGION	USA
(4) SCIIOM	Canada
(5) MRIO	USA
(6) IDIOM	USA
(7) MRMI	USA

Another feature of the listed models is that they provide considerable regional and sectoral detail. The median numbers of regions and sectors in these models are 51 and 79, respectively. The median values for the whole set of models have been reported in Section 2: they are nine and 20, respectively. This is quite a substantial difference.

One of the problems in modeling is that the communication between users and builders does not usually proceed smoothly. The complaints about model builders who produce irrelevant results or about users who do not recognize the importance of results or who misuse results are common. Part of these problems can be explained by the large distance between model users and model builders. In Table 18 three ways of communication between model builder and user are distinguished. In seven cases there is a short distance between model (builder) and model user: the user directly takes care of the runs of the model. In 21 cases the model builder has access to users by means of oral presentation of model results. In 17 cases model results are only presented in written form; there is no room for a discussion between the two parties.

We now turn to the question of whether outcomes in multiregional economic models have had impacts on (regional) policy making. It is not easy to answer this question since model outcomes may influence policies in several direct and indirect ways. For example, they may give governmental agencies a better understanding of the problems they face, but they may also provide pressure groups with arguments against certain proposed policies. Table 19 contains a summary of the answers of the model builders to the above question. It appears that in approximately a third of the operational models, a clearly positive answer is given. The table also shows that model builders in national governmental agencies are clearly more confident that their models had an impact than the model builders.

Obviously, there are several reasons why the results of Table 19 have to be interpreted carefully. One may expect a tendency for model builders to be overoptimistic about the impacts of their models. In some cases models may be built

Table 18. Modes of communication in multiregional economic models

Mode of communication between model builder and model user	Frequency of use of communication modes	
(A) Model builder runs model, presents results in written form	Only A	17
(B) Model builder runs model, presents results in a briefing to model user	Both A and B, not C	14
(C) User agency directly runs model and analyzes results	Both A, B and C	7

Table 19. Impacts of model outcomes on regional policy making

Impact of model outcomes on regional policy making	Academic institutions	Consultants	National governmental agencies	Σ
(1) Direct impact (e.g., model forecasts served as a basis for five-year plan)	9	–	6	15
(2) Indirect impact (e.g., model outcomes led to improved understanding of problems)	5	4	1	10
(3) No impact or too early to say	11	–	2	13
Σ	25	4	9	38

and used to enable politicians to postpone difficult decisions. Sometimes models seem to be used exclusively as a justification for certain policies. It is not impossible, therefore, that less positive outcomes would have been obtained had the question been asked of the model users (see also Fromm *et al.* 1975).

7 Documentation

An often neglected aspect in the development and maintenance of models is the provision of appropriate documentation. Various types of documentation can be distinguished, each suitable for certain purposes:

(1) documentation aiming at enabling potential users to understand the structure and limitations of the model;
(2) documentation enabling potential users to run the model (e.g., user manual, testing data);
(3) documentation enabling other model builders to replicate the model.

In the questionnaire we asked the model builders to indicate the extent to which this documentation is available for the models. The responses for the models that have already been used for some time are represented in Table 20. Here again, there may be a tendency for model builders to be overoptimistic about the quality and quantity of their model documentation.

If one wants to make a model accessible to the scientific community so that it is possible to arrive at a well founded opinion of it, the availability of documentation of type (1) is essential. It appears that approximately 20% of the models do not fully satisfy this condition. Obtaining documentation of types (2) and (3) is even more problematic. Table 20 shows that the transferability of models from the model builder to model users and to other model builders is clearly impossible for the majority of the models. This means that it is impossible for outsiders to come to know what is really going on in these models.

We conclude that in many cases a model is actually the property of one person or of a very small group of persons. Essential information for the understanding, maintenance, use, and development of models is often only present in the memory of one person (or of a small group). This is a regrettable state of affairs since it makes the models concerned vulnerable; e.g., if one or more persons move to another job, special measures have to be taken to prevent the collapse of such a model. Besides, it hampers progress in the modeling field since other people are not sufficiently informed to learn from the experiences of earlier model builders.

Table 20. Availability of model documentation

Type of documentation	Available?		
	Yes	To a certain extent	No
(1) Documentation about structure and limitations	30	8	0
(2) User manual, testing data	6	23	9
(3) Documentation enabling one to replicate the model	15	18	5

8 Concluding Remarks

This general overview reveals that there is a large variety of model structures in the survey. We have found, for most of the aspects of model structure, that most of the models are not particularly sophisticated; indeed it appears that most models are only sophisticated in a small number of respects while the remaining parts are modeled in an ordinary and simple way (see also Chapter 12). Not all relevant aspects of the models have been covered in this overview. In the following chapters we will therefore pay special attention to some of these.

At several places in this chapter we have indicated models with distinguishing features in order to help the reader to find his way when he is particularly interested in them. We are aware that we may have been biased in these references. The main reason for this bias is simply that for some models much more documentation has been available than for other models. This means that we may have overlooked some interesting features of models that are not so well documented. This again underlines the importance of adequate provision of model documentation.

References

d'Amours, A., G. Simard, and F. Chabot-Plante (1975), CANDIDE-R, in *L'Actualité Economique*, 51, 603-625.

Chaubey, J.N. (1979), *A Plan for the Validation of MREEED, Multiregional Policy Modeling Project* (Boston University Press, Boston).

Fromm, G., W.L. Hamilton, and D.E. Hamilton (1975), *Federally Supported Mathematical Models: Survey and Analysis* (Data Resources Inc. and Abt Associates, Inc., National Science Foundation, Washington, DC).

Glickman, N.J. (1977), *Econometric Analysis of Regional Systems* (Academic Press, New York, NY).

Ledent, J. (1981), Statistical Analysis of Regional Growth: Consistent Modeling of Employment, Population, Labor Force Participation, and Unemployment, *IIASA Working Paper* WP-81-128 (International Institute for Applied Systems Analysis, Laxenburg, Austria).

Polenske, K.R. (1980), *The US Multiregional Input-Output Accounts and Model* (Lexington Books, Lexington, MA).

Sanderson, W.C. (1980), Demographic Simulation Models: Their Usefulness for Policy Analysis, *IIASA Report* RR-80-14 (International Institute for Applied Systems Analysis, Laxenburg, Austria).

Treyz, G.I. (1980), Design of a multiregional policy analysis model, in *Journal of Regional Science*, 20, 191-206.

CHAPTER 3

STRUCTURE ANALYSIS OF SPATIAL SYSTEMS

Peter Nijkamp
Piet Rietveld

1   Introduction

Spatial systems, especially in a multiregional context, are usually display-
ing complex structures. The number of linkages in such systems may be very high,
particularly when a multisector and dynamic structure is taken into consideration.
In many disciplines (e.g., economics, sociology and biology), attempts have been
made to disentangle and/or to reduce the complexity of systems. General systems
theory (cf. Mesarovic and Takahara 1975) has developed several tools to treat and
characterize complicated patterns and interactions (*inter alia*, by means of notions
like hierarchical linkages, feedback relations and structural stability; see also
Carlsson 1981). All these concepts serve to get more insight into the interwoven
set of relationships in complex systems.

In the social sciences especially, much attention has been devoted to causality
analysis, which aims at identifying the direction of influence or qualitative structural relationships between elements or components of a system. Some common methods
in empirical research in the social sciences are:

cross-lagged panel analysis (based on correlations among variables measured
        at different times; cf. Pelz and Andrews 1964);
estimation of simultaneous equation systems (based on two-stage least-squares
        methods for nonrecursive equations; cf. Heise 1975);
nonexperimental research (by means of ordinary least-squares methods for re-
        cursive systems; cf. Blalock 1964).

In economic research causality analysis has also played an important role (see
Simon 1953, Wold 1954). Recent attempts to deal with causality structures in spatial systems can be found in Blommestein and Nijkamp (1981) and Rietveld (1981).

It may be clarifying to make a distinction between *structural* causality and
relational causality. Structural causality focuses the attention on the major
structures and components of a system in order to identify the existence of feedback or hierarchical patterns among units, main blocks or subsystems of the system
at hand. In this respect, the notion of bottom-up versus top-down structures may
be relevant. The same holds true for demand-supply patterns. Structural causality patterns are general features of models (either unspecified or estimated), so
statistical and econometric aspects of models are not particularly important. Relational causality is oriented toward the analysis of individual or complex relationships in order to investigate the direction of causality among variables (for
instance, does infrastructure lead to higher regional growth or does regional growth
lead to a better infrastructure endowment?). It is evident that relational causality focuses the attention more on actual *statistical/econometric* aspects of relationships and on the *identification* of impact patterns (cf. also Granger 1969, Sims
1972). This kind of causality plays an important role in specifying relationships
and estimating econometric linkages. It should be noted that relational causality
may be important in both individual relationships and sets of relationships.

Clearly, these notions of structural and relational causality are not entirely
independent. For instance, an entirely recursive structure (also at the level of
individual equations) may be a feature of a pure top-down structure (and of course

also of a bottom-up structure). Each structural causality pattern (at the level of systems components or units) has implications for the relational causality pattern (at the level of inclusion of variables in individual equations). In the next three sections some aspects of relational and of structural causality will be dealt with.

2 Relational Causality

Economic models may be based on several kinds of relationships (see Paelinck and Nijkamp 1976):

(a) definitions (e.g., regional balance of trade)
(b) identities (e.g., regional input-output conditions)
(c) equilibrium conditions (e.g., equality of supply and demand on a regional labor market)
(d) technical relationships (e.g., regional production functions)
(e) behavioral relationships (e.g., regional investment functions)
(f) institutional relationships (e.g., regional tax relationships)
(g) empirical relationships (e.g., a logistic regional growth curve).

Relational causality analysis attempts to find out whether a certain variable (or a set of variables) exerts a significant impact on other variables. This implies in more precise terms that the aim of relational causality analysis is to identify whether--given a formal structure for a system--statistical and/or econometric inferences can be drawn regarding the pattern of influences among variables. Consequently, this causality is essentially a property of a structure model: it characterizes the formal directions of impacts among variables in relationships.

On the basis of a systems theoretic approach, one may state that a necessary condition for causal links is the existence of a *stimulus-response* link between cause and effect variables. The existence of such a link should be based on a theoretical and/or empirical justification.

It is clear that the above relationships (a)-(c) cannot be regarded as causal relationships. The remaining relationships (d)-(g) may reflect causal linkages (depending on the recursive structure of the relationship concerned). It should be noted that explanatory relationships (for instance, a relationship between modal choice on the one hand and income level and/or social attitude on the other) are necessarily causal. However, causal relationships are not by definition explanatory relationships; for instance, Kondratieff cycles reflect a causal linkage between economic prosperity and time dynamics, but do not imply an explicit explanation of the existence of long waves.

Usually, the following conditions are assumed for the existence of relational causality (cf. Harvey 1969, Wold 1954):

(i)   a *functional* (nonreflexive, asymmetric and transitive) relationship between stimulus (cause) variables and response (effect) variables, based on a theoretical justification and a consistent dependence structure (according to several authors (Lazarsfeld 1954, Leitner and Wohl-schlägl 1980), a causal order implies that cause variables are realized prior to the effect variables, so that the direction of impacts is irreversible);
(ii)   an *association* among cause and effect variables, on the basis of a testable (statistical or econometric) relationship which validates the assumption of a cause-effect linkage (for instance, by means of correlation analysis, significance tests, etc.);
(iii) a *predictability* of effects, after a stimulus has taken place (based on controlled or noncontrolled experiments), apart from random or disturbance factors;
(iv)   *lack of spuriousness*, so that a causal relationship does not vanish, when the (partial) impact of other variables on this relationship is exactly determined.

The notion of asymmetric relationships has always played an important role in causality analysis. Simon (1953) also notes there is *no necessary* connection between asymmetry in (causal) relationships and asymmetry in time. It should also be noted that the validity of causal relationships may be supported by expert knowledge or by statistical and/or econometric techniques, but there is no unambiguous proof of the existence of a specific causality pattern.

Assume, for instance, a set of spatial phenomena A, B, and C (for example, regional infrastructure, regional unemployment levels, regional activity rates). The spatial configuration *per se* of the observations on these phenomena does not allow us to differentiate between, for example, any one of the following three causal orderings of these spatial phenomena (regardless the number of realizations): $A = f(B)$; $B = f(A)$; $A,B = f(C)$; etc. Thus, several causality patterns may be consistent with a set of events A, B, and C. In consequence, a causal relationship does not only take for granted a functional relationship among cause and effect variables, but also a more precise presentation of the kind and direction of the impacts, so as to obtain a testable causality relationship. Such a relationship may be either deterministic or probabilistic.

It should be noted that causality is very hard to prove: statistical methods (such as correlation and association analysis) indicate only the existence of a statistical link among variables. Therefore, a theoretical and methodological foundation of causal inferences is necessary. In this respect, statistical and econometric results only serve to make causal inferences more plausible or justifiable. It should be added that the concept of relational causality is only meaningful in the specific statistical and econometric framework of a model or of a relationship; it does not necessarily prove real world impact patterns (cf. also Simon 1957).

Finally, in a *spatial* system the relational causality patterns are even more difficult to prove due to the existence of simultaneous reverse directions of spatial impact patterns (see also Section 3). Such phenomena can be studied by means of *spatiotemporal cross correlation* analysis or *cross spectral* analysis, but, especially in the framework of a simultaneous equations system, much research still needs to be done (cf. Cliff and Ord 1973, Hordijk 1979, Nijkamp 1979, Folmer and Nijkamp 1982).

3 Relational Causality in a Spatial Context

The notion of causal links in spatial and/or dynamic systems has led to the intriguing question of whether there exists a basic difference between causality in spatial and temporal models (see Blommestein and Nijkamp 1981). It has been mentioned by several authors (cf. Blalock 1964, Harvey 1969, Bennett and Chorley 1978), that the notion of time is crucial for analyzing, understanding, and interpreting causal orderings. *Time-based systems* usually share the following properties:

$$asymmetry: \qquad E_1 = T_1(E_2) \rightarrow E_2 \neq T_2(E_1) \quad ;$$

$$transitivity: \quad E_1 = T_1(E_2) + E_2 = T_2(E_3) \rightarrow E_1 = T_3(E_3) \quad ,$$

in which E_i denotes an event i, and T_i is a (time-based) transformation operator. The first property plays an especially important role in the solution of many causal inference problems; for example, in Simon's method of drawing causal inferences from correlation data (see Simon 1953, 1954).

For purely *space-based* systems the properties of asymmetry and transitivity are often not valid. The well known *spatial simultaneity* problem--i.e., spatial events are associated, but cannot be ordered--is a typical illustration of this proposition. The problem of spatial simultaneity arises very clearly in the following statistical problem regarding spatial autocorrelation: the log-likelihood function corresponding to the linear regression model, $y = X\beta + u$ with autocorrelated errors $\underline{u} = \rho W \underline{u} + \underline{e}$ (where ρ denotes an autocorrelation parameter, W is a temporal or spatial lag-operator, and $\underline{e}$ is a vector with white-noise error terms); $\underline{e} \simeq$ NID$(0, \sigma_e^2)$; can be written in a concentrated form as (see Hepple 1976)

$$L_c = -\frac{M}{2}\left[(\ln 2\Pi + 1) + \ln\left(\frac{\underline{u}'V^{-1}\underline{u}}{|P|^{2/M}}\right)\right] \tag{3.1}$$

in which $P = I - \rho W$, $\underline{u} = P^{-1}\underline{e}$, $V^{-1} = P'P$, M is the sample size. If the above mentioned model is a spatial econometric model, W denotes a spatial lag-operator--or contiguity matrix--with typical elements $w_{rr'}(w_{rr'} \geq 0; \Sigma_{r'}\ w_{rr'} = 1)$ for regions r and r'. Since both $w_{rr'}$ and $w_{r'r}$ will probably be nonzero (especially if the spatial units r and r' are adjacent), P will, in general, *not* be a triangular matrix $\left(\lim_{M\to\infty} |P|^{2/M} \neq 1\right)$. This leads to complicated econometric estimation problems, and to difficult statistical test methods as well.

With reference to these problems, Bennett (1979) discusses three methods of resolving the question of the causal ordering of spatial phenomena:

(a)   the use of exogenous *a priori* information (e.g., technical, behavioral, or institutional information);
(b)   the estimation of the simultaneous structure of the spatial system;
(c)   the use of Markov properties for spatial equilibrium fields.

These three methods will now be briefly discussed. Let us again assume the existence of three different spatial events A, B, and C. The first approach is successful if it is possible to postulate the hypothesis that A causes B, or B causes A. Actually, the formulation and "solution" of this problem is formally equivalent to constructing a set of hypotheses H on a complex system so as to arrive at propositions relative to links among elements of the system. This approach implies essentially that *a priori* the causal structure is *given*. Clearly, in a purely inductive system, this is not a feasible approach. If one wishes to test (in a statistical sense) the set of hypotheses H, it is necessary to turn to the *second* approach, i.e., to estimate the simultaneous structure of the observed spatial phenomena. However, compared with time-series analysis, this is a rather complex undertaking.

The *third* approach deals with the application of Markov properties in spatial equilibrium situations. This is a highly restrictive approach, as it implies essentially the assumption of time reversibility (cf. Preston 1974). Furthermore, this assumption is very unlikely to be fulfilled in spatial behavioral processes.

Given the foregoing discussion, one may conclude that there is formally no essential difference between the notion of causality in temporal and in spatial systems, provided the above mentioned conditions for causality are fulfilled. Both notions are in agreement with the "classical" concept of causality, as this concept is independent of both the explicit time pattern and the functional form of the relationships (see also, for a discussion of this concept, Basman 1963). However, the operationalization of this concept is--due to the problem of spatial simultaneity--more complex in purely spatial systems and in spatiotemporal systems.

After this discussion of relational causality and its spatial aspects, the attention will now be focused on structural causality, as structural causality especially may serve as a tool to characterize the composition of complex multiregional systems.

4   Structural Causality

Structural causality deals with *impact patterns among components* of a whole system. The attention is not focused on individual causal linkages, but on the *structure* of a system. Clearly, this is codetermined by the relational causality, but the main aim of structural causality analysis is to identify regularities in the main structure of an entire system. This means that structural causality analysis may be regarded as a generalization and extension of relational causality, but with several specific features. Structural causality is a property of a system (cf. Rietveld 1981).

Consider the following linear model:

$$A_0 \underline{y}_t + B\underline{y}_{t-\tau} + C\underline{x}_t = \underline{c}_t \tag{4.1}$$

where $\underline{y}_t$ is a vector with I endogenous variables in time period t, $\underline{y}_{t-\tau}$ is a vector with I lagged endogenous variables (with a lag τ), and x is a vector with N exogenous variables. A_0, B, and C are matrices of order $(I \times I)$, $(I \times I)$, and $(I \times N)$, respectively; $\underline{c}_t$ is a constant. According to Simon (1953), the causal structure of this model is defined by the form of the matrix A_0 (see also Fox $et\ al.$ 1966). The model is completely $recursive$ when A_0 is a strictly $triangular$ matrix. In that case, the first endogenous variable can be determined by the first equation in (4.1). Given the value of the first endogenous variable, the second equation (4.1) can be used to determine the value of the second endogenous variable, etc. In recursive models, it is meaningful to say that the endogenous variable y_i is caused by the preceding endogenous variables (as well as by lagged endogenous and exogenous variables).

Strict triangularity of the A_0 matrix is a strong assumption in many cases. Therefore, Simon (1953) also considers block triangularity.

$$A_0 y_t = \begin{bmatrix} A_{11} & 0 & 0 \\ A_{21} & A_{22} & 0 \\ A_{31} & A_{32} & A_{33} \end{bmatrix} \begin{bmatrix} \underline{y}_{1t} \\ \underline{y}_{2t} \\ \underline{y}_{3t} \end{bmatrix} \tag{4.2}$$

where A_{11}, A_{22}, and A_{33} are square matrices. In this case the endogenous variables contained in $\underline{y}_{1t}$ can only be determined in a simultaneous way. The notion of causal ordering can be maintained, however, since for (4.2) it can be said that the elements of $\underline{y}_{2t}$ are caused by the elements of $\underline{y}_{1t}$, etc.

So far we have discussed only causal links in linear models. It appears to be easy to extend this analysis to nonlinear models. Consider the following series of equations:

$$\begin{cases} h_1(\underline{y}_t, \underline{y}_{t-\tau}, \underline{x}_t) = 0 \\ \vdots \qquad\qquad \vdots \\ \vdots \qquad\qquad \vdots \\ h_I(\underline{y}_t, \underline{y}_{t-\tau}, \underline{x}_t) = 0 \end{cases} \tag{4.3}$$

where the arguments of the I functions have the same meaning as in (4.1). Let $b_{ij} = 1$ when the variable y_{jt} plays a role in h_i, and $b_{ij} = 0$ when this variable does not play a role in h_i. Then the b_{ij} form together an $I \times I$ matrix B_0.

A model is a $simultaneous\ equation$ model, when B_0 cannot be partitioned into a block triangular matrix. Otherwise, when B_0 can be partitioned in a block triangular way, i.e.,

$$B_0 = \begin{bmatrix} B_{11} & 0 & 0 \\ B_{21} & B_{22} & 0 \\ B_{31} & B_{32} & B_{33} \end{bmatrix} \qquad Y_t = \begin{bmatrix} \underline{Y}_{1t} \\ \underline{Y}_{2t} \\ \underline{Y}_{3t} \end{bmatrix} \tag{4.4}$$

it is meaningful to say that the elements of $\underline{y}_{2t}$ are caused by $\underline{y}_{1t}$, etc.

In a multiregional context, the analysis of spatial causality patterns is even more complicated due to the existence of spatial spillover and interaction effects. In such cases, the causal structure of a spatial system depends on the shape of the multiregional structure matrix A_0. Then a recursive *spatial* structure would imply spatial dominance relationships (e.g., in a center-periphery sense). Another causality pattern in a multiregional system may emerge if for each individual equation a spatial cross section relationship holds but if simultaneously all these individual relationships display a recursive structure.

In Blommestein and Nijkamp (1981), an attempt has been made to define structural causality in a more formal way. Consider the following general (linear or nonlinear) model:

$$\underline{h}(\underline{y},\underline{x}) = \underline{0} \tag{4.5}$$

which is a condensed representation of (4.3). In this latter system, the causal structure is already given if a set H of hypotheses does exist that defines a partition $\underline{z} = \underline{y} \cup \underline{x}$ and a set of binary relations $h_j R z_k$ ($h_j \in H = \{h_1, h_2, \ldots, h_J\}$; $z_k \in \underline{z} = \{z_1, \ldots, z_I, z_I + 1, \ldots, z_{I+N}\}$; R stands for: "relationship j contains variable z_k") (see Gilli 1980).

As causal order does not necessarily require information about the sign of the cause-effect structure, the *calculus of qualitative relationships* (Samuelson 1947) can also be used in a meaningful way. In consequence, causality analysis can also be carried out at the level of nonmetric variables, so that the analysis of causal structures can also be dealt with in the framework of *soft econometrics* (see Nijkamp and Rietveld 1982).

Several methods have been developed in the literature to assess the order of magnitude of structural causality in a complex system. Some of these methods have been designed in graph theoretic approaches (which is another way of representing complex systems in a systematic way). By studying the number of edges and nodes from a qualitative or structural point of view, several causality measures can be identified such as direct causality, indirect causality, and mutual causality (see also Blommestein and Nijkamp 1981). Related approaches might be found in computational efforts (via successive permutations) to restructure matrix systems so as to achieve a maximum agreement with triangular systems (e.g., via a Steward algorithm). Then the degree of triangularity may be regarded as a measure of pure structural causality, and of hierarchical causality as well. Evidently, the calculation of such causality measures in multiregional models would require a full presentation of these models. Unfortunately, this information is not always available.

A good illustration of the difference between relational and structural causality can be found in the theory of economic policy designed by Tinbergen (1956). He makes a distinction between the *analytical* problem and the *policy* problem. The analytical problem deals with real impact patterns in an economic model (from exogenous and/or instrumental variables to endogenous and/or policy variables). Hence this problem is related to relational causality patterns. The policy problem is seemingly a reverse problem: it aims at finding the proper values of instruments so as to achieve a set of predetermined values of policy targets. From a structural point of view, this is an inverse qualitative pattern, though evidently the real world direction of influence takes place according to the impact patterns of the analytical problem. Thus the policy problem may be regarded as a structural causality phenomenon.

Two aspects of causality analysis in a spatial setting still remain to be discussed: causality in a bottom-up/top-down structure and demand-supply patterns. These elements will be discussed in the next few sections.

5 Causality Structures and Regional National Linkages

Usually, three types of multiregional models are distinguished from the view-point of national-regional linkages: (1) top-down models; (2) bottom-up models, and (3) regional-national (or hybrid) models. These types can be defined as fol-lows (see, for example, Courbis 1980, Glickman 1981, Lakshmanan and Jourabchi 1981):

(1) in a *top-down* model, the levels of the national variables are first deter-mined, then the levels of the regional variables are determined in accordance with the additivity condition, so that their sum (or average) is equal to the national aggregate;
(2) in a *bottom-up* model, the regional variables are first determined; the national variables follow as resultants of a sum (or an average) of the regional vari-ables;
(3) in a *regional-national* model, the levels of the regional and national vari-ables are determined simultaneously; such a model is characterized by regional-national interactions.

For ease of presentation we will use the following abbreviations for these three model types: TD, BU, and IRN (I refers to "interactive"). We will use the follow-ing notation for a presentation of the causality structure of these model types. Let x_i^r denote the ith variable of region r ($r = 1,...,R$). The corresponding na-tional variable will be denoted by x_i. Exogenous variables will be denoted by a superscript, e.g., $\bar{x}_i$ indicates that x_i is exogenous. Figure 1 contains some ex-amples of the three model types. In Figure 1, an arc from x_i to x_j means that the model has been specified such that x_j is a function of x_i.

$$
\begin{cases}
x_3 = f_1(x_4, \bar{x}_1) \\
x_4 = f_2(x_3) \\
x_3^r = f_3(x_3, x_4^r, \bar{x}_2^r) \qquad r = 1,...,R \\
x_4^r = f_4(x_4, x_3^r) \qquad r = 1,...,R
\end{cases}
\tag{5.1}
$$

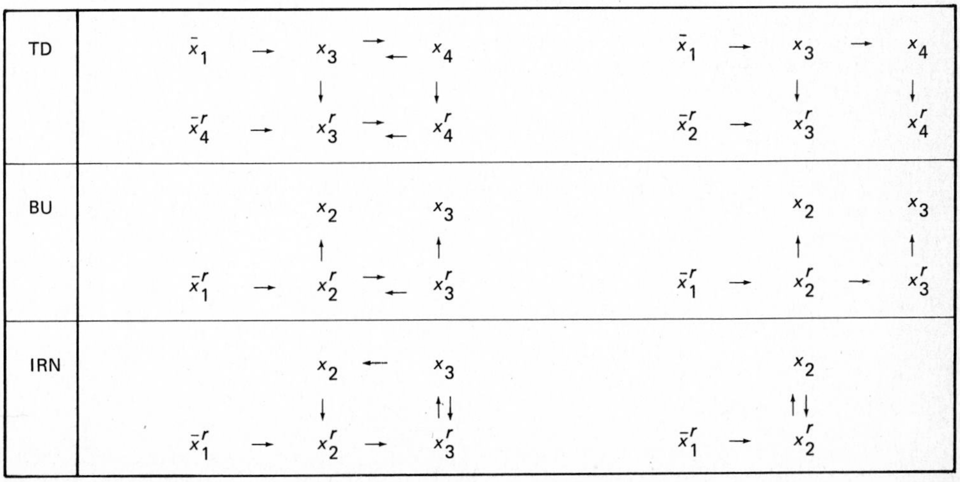

Figure 1.   Examples of top-down, bottom-up and interactive regional-national models

The causality structure of this model can be studied by means of the matrix B_0 as defined in (4.4):

$$B_0 = \begin{bmatrix} 1 & 1 & 0 & 0 \\ 1 & 1 & 0 & 0 \\ 1 & 0 & 1 & 1 \\ 0 & 1 & 1 & 1 \end{bmatrix}. \tag{5.2}$$

In this case, B_0 has a block triangular structure, which indicates that the national variables x_3 and x_4 are determined before their regional counterparts x_3^r and x_4^r.

In this paper we will not discuss at length the advantages and disadvantages of the three model types. For such a discussion we refer the reader to the publications mentioned earlier in this section. Instead we will indicate how the 50 multiregional economic models included in the Appendix can be classified by means of the model types distinguished above.

An important property of TD models is that they can be fed with exogenous national variables generated by macroeconomic models. This is an attractive property when one has confidence in the ability of macroeconomic models to generate reliable outcomes. An obvious disadvantage is that in a TD model the national variables are not affected by the regional distribution of activities. Hence TD models cannot be used to study trade-offs between national efficiency and interregional equity.

The survey includes nine pure TD models: NRWF, MIO, REM, REGAM, WREM, LURE, MULTIREGION, MAG, and INTEREG. The average size of these models (measured according to the number of regions, sectors and/or equations) does not differ much from the average size of the whole set of models included in the survey. Some models are among the smallest (e.g., MIO), others are among the largest (e.g., MULTIREGION). Most of the TD models are rather partial: the focus is on either the labor market, or the production system. Exceptions are NRWF, REM, and MAG.

A pure *BU approach* in multiregional economic models is only rarely found. One should be aware, for example, that when a model contains regionally invariant variables (e.g., prices, interest rates) as exogenous or endogenous variables, it cannot be classified as a BU model in a strict sense. Obviously, in such a case the appropriate national variable does not follow as a resultant from the corresponding regional variables. Models that approach the BU type to a large extent are REMO, LPFM, GISSIR, BACHUE, IRUD, NRIES, ECESIS, NRPEM, and EPAM. These models are characterized by a relatively small number of regions that have been distinguished (2-10). Exceptions are NRIES and ECESIS with 51 regions. Also the number of sectors in these models is smaller than average. One would expect that in BU models much attention would be paid to interregional linkages to compensate for the lack of national-regional linkage (see Chapter 4). A close inspection of these models shows that this does not hold for all BU models. In some of them (BACHUE, ECESIS, and EPAM) interregional relationships receive indeed rather extensive attention, but there are also two BU models (LPFM and EPAM) in which interregional relationships are not specified at all.

It is interesting to reflect on the question of whether a bottom-up model would yield superior results for macroeconomic variables compared with a macroeconomic model. Aggregation theory sheds some light on this question (cf. Theil 1954, Green 1977). Consider the following linear models:

$$\begin{cases} x_2^r = a^r + b^r \, \bar{x}_1^r \\ \\ x_2 = \sum x_2^r \end{cases} \qquad r = 1,\ldots,R \tag{5.3}$$

and

$$\begin{cases} x_1 = \sum \bar{x}_1^{r} \\ \\ x_2^{r} = a + bx_1 \end{cases} \qquad r = 1,\ldots,R \quad . \qquad\qquad (5.4)$$

The BU model and the macroeconomic model are represented by (5.3) and (5.4), respectively. It is a well known fact from aggregation theory that when there are no restrictions on the distribution of the $\bar{x}_1^{r}$, it is a necessary and sufficient condition for (5.3) and (5.4) to yield identical outcomes for x_2, that

$$b^1 = b^2 = \cdots = b^{r} \quad . \qquad\qquad (5.5)$$

This conclusion means that--given the specification of (5.3) and (5.4)--a bottom-up approach is superior to a macroeconomic approach apart from the rather exceptional case when (5.5) arises.

One should be aware that this conclusion has been derived under rather restrictive assumptions. One assumption is that the quality of the data at the regional and national level is equal. This is not a realistic assumption: in general, data at the national level are more reliable and recent; besides, time series in general are over a longer period at the national than at the regional level. Another assumption is that (5.3) and (5.4) have been appropriately specified. In a study of individual investment behavior, Grunfeld and Griliches (1960) found that predictions based on a BU model were less reliable than predictions based on a macro approach. One of the explanations given for this phenomenon is that (5.3) has been misspecified. It assumes that behavior at the disaggregate level is not influenced by variables at the aggregate level. As far as we know, the latter issue has not been systematically investigated in the context of multiregional modeling. This is a regrettable situation, since such an investigation may shed new light on the specification of national-regional relationships.

Interactive regional-national models form an interdependent system of national and regional variables. The survey includes eight models of this type: HESSEN, RENA, MACEDOINE, REGINA, RNEM, SMOPP, SYREN, and MREEED. These models differ considerably in size. RENA and MACEDOINE are below average. MREEED and SMOPP are among the largest. The scope of IRN models is clearly larger than that of the other models. The following key variables are endogenous in almost all models: production, employment, investments, and prices (wages). We may conclude therefore, that the level of integration in these models is not only high in view of regional-national linkages, but also in view of interrelationships between the main economic variables.

6 Noninteractive Regional National Models

In the discussions about the ways in which national-regional linkages can be modeled, it is usually assumed that with the three types mentioned in Section 5 (BU, TD, and IRN), the possibilities are exhausted. This assumption is not correct. It is possible to define a model type that combines a BU and a TD approach but which is not characterized by regional-national interactions. An example of such a model, which will be called noninteractive regional-national (NIRN) can be found in Figure 2.

Thus the causal ordering of variables in a NIRN model reads as follows:

(1) the levels of a subset of national variables are determined;
(2) the levels of the corresponding regional variables and of additional regional variables are determined;

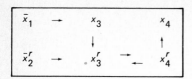

Figure 2.   Example of a noninteractive regional-national model

(3)   the levels of the national variables corresponding with the additional
       regional variables determined in step (2) follow as resultants.

This introduction of a new model type does not arise from an academic interest to
develop an exhaustive and mutually exclusive set of model types. The newly introduced model type has a high practical importance. It appears that around 50% of
the models belong to the class of NIRN models. We will first briefly discuss two
examples of NIRN models; MORSE and IDIOM.
       The MORSE model has been developed for Sweden. In the model, national con-
straints are imposed on energy consumption, and the growth of capital stock. Regional constraints are imposed, e.g., employment and consumption. Given these (and
additional) constraints, MORSE is used as a programming model to determine the spatial pattern of production and investments that gives rise to maximum values for
national policy objectives. Once the regional production levels are determined,
the national level follows as a resultant. In MORSE, a TD approach is applied to
some production factors, while a BU approach is employed for production. There
are also models with a reversed structure: IDIOM is an example of such a model.
       In IDIOM, a model developed for the USA, the level of final demand (except for
consumption) in national sectors is exogenous at the national level. Given these
final demand levels, national production is determined. Regional production levels
are obtained by partitioning. In the next step, regional employment is determined,
which yields national employment as a resultant. A similar approach (TD for production or final demand and BU for factor demand) can be found in REGION, FRET, MEPA,
RDM, BALAMO, and DREAM. Other examples of NIRN models included in the survey that
have not yet been mentioned are IMPE, MEEEI, TLM, SERENA, BREIN, KIM, NORD-SUD,
IIOM, FLEUR, REGAL, MFM, SYREN-OPT, SCIIOM, MRIO, MRMI, OTSIS, and IIOMSK.
       In several cases NIRN models are considered by the appropriate model builders
as pure TD models. They are presented as in Figure 3 where no attention is paid
to the possibility of determining the national aggregate x_4.

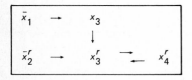

Figure 3.   Example of a disguised NIRN model

       This lack of attention may be due to two reasons:

(1)   One is only interested in the regional levels of x_4 and not in the national
       level;
(2)   One may have reasons to doubt whether the multiregional model yields reliable
       outcomes for the national aggregate x_4.

The latter reason is explicitly recognized in the MAG model, where the national
aggregate x_4 is confronted with the outcome for x_4 from the driving macroeconomic
model. Then the regional values x_4^r are revised, so that ultimately the aggregate

of the x_4^n agrees with the value from the driving model. This is why MAG may be classified as a pure TD model.

There is certainly reason to consider NIRN models as a welcome complement to a driving national model. NIRN models do not only generate a regional partitioning of the national variables, they may also generate national levels of variables for which a BU approach is more appropriate. The latter especially holds true for variables referring to markets operating at the regional level: housing, regional services, labor supply, unemployment, and (in some countries) wages.

The NIRN model type can be considered as a version derived from IRN by imposing a simplifying assumption, namely the absence of a feedback from the national variables determined in the third step on the national variables determined in the first step. Thus the NIRN type is less general than IRN, which may be a disadvantage. The obvious advantage of NIRN models over IRN models is that their causality structure is more transparent since their basic structure is more in accordance with recursiveness than that of NIRN.

7 Demand and Supply in Multiregional Economic Models

An important aspect of the causality structure of multiregional economic models concerns the role of demand and supply variables. The extent to which model outcomes are driven by variables from the demand and/or supply side is an important determinant of the purposes for which a model can be used. For example, a model that is driven exclusively by demand variables is not very useful when one wants to study the effects of a reduction in the supply of production factors (e.g., energy). We will introduce the following definitions for an adequate analysis of supply and demand orientation in a model.

A model is *demand oriented* when the level of regional production is determined by final demand components without being influenced by supply variables. This condition will be called condition D. In some models (e.g., labor market models) final demand is not specified, so the definition of demand orientation has to be extended as follows. A model is demand oriented when condition D holds and/or when the level of use of regional production factors is determined by the level of regional production without a causal link from the regional production factors to the regional production level. Figure 4 contains some examples of demand oriented models.

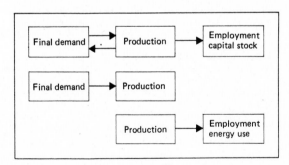

Figure 4.   Examples of demand oriented models

A model is *supply oriented* when the level of regional production is determined by the supply of one or more production factors without being influenced by demand variables. Figure 5 presents an example of a supply oriented model.

A model has a *mixed supply-demand* orientation when the level of regional production is determined by both supply and demand variables. When a model only describes a labor market system it is defined as a model with a mixed supply-demand orientation when the level of employment is determined by both supply and demand variables. The causality structure of models with a mixed supply-demand orientation is illustrated in Figure 6.

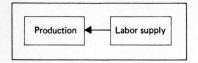

Figure 5. Example of a supply oriented model

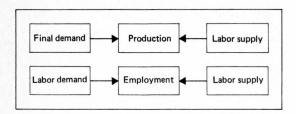

Figure 6. Examples of models with a mixed supply-demand orientation

When we classify the 50 multiregional economic models contained in the survey, we arrive at the following distribution:

(1)   (mainly) demand oriented models   :   17
(2)   models with a mixed supply-demand orientation :   30
(3)   (mainly) supply oriented models   :   2
(4)   not applicable   :   1

Table 1 indicates the model type for each model separately. The number of supply oriented models is much smaller than the number of demand oriented models. Yet, it is not warranted to say that there is in general a neglect of the supply side in multiregional economic models. In more than 50% of the cases both the demand and the supply side play a substantial role.

An especially interesting approach to supply-demand considerations is contained in REM, REGINA, and MREEED. In these models, a supply oriented approach is applied to some national market industries (e.g., manufacturing). In these industries, national investments are distributed among regions according to the regional investment opportunities by a TD procedure. Given the regional investment volumes in these industries, the other regional factor demands and the regional production volumes in these industries can be determined. These production volumes are an important determinant of the regional production in the other industries. Obviously, this approach is essentially based on the distinction between basic and nonbasic sectors. Other models in which this distinction plays an important role (but where the investments in the basic sector are not treated explicitly) are REGAM, LURE, and MAG.

When we compare the results of this section with those of the two preceding ones, the most striking findings are that six of the seven IRN models have a mixed supply-demand orientation and that both supply oriented models have a BU structure. The rather general notion that models in which use is made of input-output analysis are characterized by a demand orientation is not confirmed for the models contained in the survey. It appears that the proportion of models in which use is made of input-output analysis is approximately equal for demand oriented models and models with a mixed supply-demand orientation. The hypothesis that models with a mixed supply-demand orientation are predominantly econometric models is confirmed for this survey: 21 of the 30 models with a mixed orientation are econometric models, whereas only seven of the 17 demand oriented models have been estimated by means of econometric methods.

Table 1. Supply and demand in multiregional economic models

Mixed supply-demand oriented models	(Mainly) demand oriented models	(Mainly) supply oriented models	Not classified
HESSEN	IMPE	IRUD	MIO
NRWF	RENA	NRPEM	
REM	SERENA		
REGAM	BREIN		
MEEEI	KIM		
TLM	NORD-SUD		
MACEDOINE	IIOM		
REGINA	LPFM		
RNEM	LURE		
WREM	REGION		
FLEUR	REMO		
MORSE	SCIIOM		
REGAL	MRIO		
GISSIR	IDIOM		
BACHUE	NRIES		
MFM	OTSIS		
SMOPP	IIOMSK		
SYREN-OPT			
FRET			
MAG			
MULTIREGION			
MREEED			
MRMI			
MEPA			
ECESIS			
MFM			
BALAMO			
EPAM			
INTEREG			
DREAM			

References

d'Amours, A., G. Fortin, and G. Simard (1979), CANDIDE-R: Un modèle national régionalisé de l'economie canadienne, in R. Courbis (ed.), *Modèles Régionaux et Modèles Régionaux-Nationaux* (Cujas, Paris), pp. 175-184.

Basman, R.L. (1963), The causal interpretation of nontriangular systems of economic relations, *Econometrica*, 31, 439-448.

Bennett, R.J. (1979), *Spatial Time Series* (Pion, London).

Bennett, R.J., and R.J. Chorley (1978), *Environmental Systems: Philosophy, Analysis and Control* (Methuen, London).

Blalock, H.M. (1961), *Causal Inference in Non-experimental Research* (University of North-Carolina Press, Chapel Hill, CA).

Blommestein, J.H., and P. Nijkamp (1981), Soft spatial econometric causality models, *Research Memorandum* 1981-20 (Dept. of Economics, Free University, Amsterdam).

Carlsson, C. (1981), Solving complex and ill-structured problems, in P. Nijkamp and J. Spronk (eds.), *Multiple Criteria Analysis* (Gower, Aldershot, Hants.), pp. 53-86.

Cliff, A.D., and J.K. Ord (1973), *Spatial Autocorrelation* (Pion, London).

Courbis, R. (1980), Multiregional modeling and the interaction between regional and national development: a general theoretical framework, in F.G. Adams and N.J. Glickman (eds.), *Modeling the Multiregional Economic System* (Lexington Books, Lexington, MA), pp. 107-130.

Folmer, H., and P. Nijkamp (1982), Linear structural equation models with spatial autocorrelation, *Research Memorandum* (Dept. of Economics, Free University, Amsterdam.

Fox, K.A., J.K. Sengupta, and E. Thorbecke (1966), *The Theory of Quantitative Economic Policy* (North Holland, Amsterdam).

Gilli, M. (1980), CAUSOR--A Program for the Analysis of Recursive and Interdependent Causal Structures, *User's Manual* (Département d'économétrie, Université de Genève).

Glickman, N.J. (1981), Using empirical models for regional policy analysis, in A. Andersson, M. Albegov, and F. Snickars (eds.), *Regional Development Modeling: Theory and Practice* (North-Holland, Amsterdam), pp. 79-98.

Granger, C.W.J. (1969), Investigating causal relations by econometric models and cross-spectral methods, *Econometrica*, 37(3), 424-438.

Green, H.A.J. (1977), Aggregation problems of macroeconomics, in G.C. Harcourt (ed.), *The Microeconomic Foundations of Macroeconomics* (MacMillan, London), pp. 179-194.

Grunfeld, Y., and Z. Griliches (1960), Is aggregation necessarily bad?, *Review of Economics and Statistics*, 42, 1-3.

Harvey, D. (1969), *Explanation in Geography* (Edward Arnold, London).

Heise, D.R. (1975), *Causal Analysis* (Wiley, New York).

Hepple, L.W. (1966), A maximum likelihood model for econometric estimation with spatial data, in I. Masser (ed.), *Theory and Practice in Regional Science* (Pion, London).

Hordijk, L. (1979), Problems in the estimation of econometric relations in space, *Papers of the Regional Science Association*, 42, 99-118.

Lakshmanan, T.R., and M. Jourabchi (1981), *Investment Supply Model: A Preliminary Formulation*, Department of Geography, Boston University, Boston, MA (mimeograph).

Lazarsfeld, P.F. (1954), Interpretation of statistical relationships as a research operation, in P.F. Lazarsfeld and A. Rozenberg (eds.), *The Language of Social Research* (Free Press, Glencoe), pp. 115-125.

Leitner, H., and H. Wohlschägl (1980), Metrische und ordinale Pfadanalyse, *Geographische Zeitschrift*, 68(2), 61-106.

Mesarovic, M.D., and Y. Takahara (1975), *General Systems Theory* (Academic Press, York, NY).

Nijkamp, P. (1979), *Multidimensional Spatial Data and Decision Analysis* (John Wiley, Chichester/New York, NY).

Nijkamp, P., and P. Rietveld (1982), Soft econometrics as a tool for regional discrepancy analysis, *Papers of the Regional Science Association* (forthcoming).

Paelinck, J.H.P., and P. Nijkamp (1976), *Operational Theory and Method in Regional Economics* (Saxon House, Farnborough, Hants.).

Pelz, D.C., and F.M. Andrews (1964), Detecting causal priorities in panel study data, *American Sociological Review*, 29, 836-848.

Preston, C.J. (1974), *Gibbs States on Countable Sets* (Cambridge University Press, Cambridge).

Rietveld, P. (1981), Causality Structures in Multiregional Economic Models, *IIASA Working Paper*, WP-81-50 (International Institute for Applied Systems Analysis, Laxenburg, Austria).

Samuelson, P.A. (1947), *Foundations of Economic Analysis* (Harvard University Press, Harvard).

Simon, H.A. (1953), Causal ordering and identifiability, in W. Hood and T.C. Koopmans (eds.), *Studies in Econometric Method* (Wiley, New York, NY), pp. 49-74.

Simon, H.A. (1954), Spurious correlation: a causal interpretation, *Journal of the American Statistical Association*, 49, 467-479.

Simon, H.A. (1957), *Models of Man* (Wiley, New York, NY).

Sims, C.A. (1972), Money, income and causality, *American Economic Review*, September, 540-552.

Theil, H. (1954), *Linear Aggregation of Economic Relations* (North-Holland, Amsterdam).

Tinbergen, J. (1956), *Economic Policy: Principles and Design* (North-Holland, Amsterdam)

Wold, H. (1954), Causality and econometrics, *Econometrica*, 22, 162-177.

CHAPTER 4

INTERREGIONAL LINKAGES IN MULTIREGIONAL ECONOMIC MODELS

Folke Snickars

1 Background and Scope

A study of the treatment of interregional linkages is a self-evident element of any effort to survey the current trends in multiregional economic (ME) modeling. In view of increasing international interdependencies it is appropriate to extend comparisons to the treatment of international linkages.

In national economic models the regional dimension is implicitly accounted for by the magnitude of those economic sectors that have the role of bridging not only intersectoral but also interregional supply-demand relationships. The transport sector will therefore have a relatively more dominant position in a geographically extended country that shares other economic characteristics with a geographically small nation. Similar relationships may hold for commercial and construction activities. International trade and international factor movements are never regarded as being strongly affected by the reality of spatially extended economies, yet such functional relationships occur, for instance, in regions and nations where economic integration is not congruent with political subdivisions.

In ME models the national dimension is often used as a checkpoint of the realism of regionally based calculations. Although any functional region is a small, open economy, the substitution between interregional and international trade is often neglected altogether. It is in the light of these observations that we wish to review the treatment of international and interregional links in the same context. However, it should be noted that such an integrated view is not taken in most of the ME models surveyed here.

The FLEUR and SCIIOM models treat the EEC area and the US-Canada relationships, respectively, and thus combine national and international perspectives. Our arguments should therefore be looked upon as recommendations for future developments rather than criticism of current models. Space gives rise to place-bound and relative location advantages for regional production and consumption systems. In an existing interregional production system the spatial component gives rise to flows of materials, production factors, services, and information that move the system towards equilibrium. These equilibrating processes operate at different geographical levels and in different time perspectives.

The evolution of the production system is governed in part by another aspect of space: its generation of location factors. This does not imply that only space itself comes into play here. The geographically distributed aspects of the current production system enter into investment decisions of firms, migration decisions of households, and policy decisions of the public. This double aspect of space is central in our subsequent analysis: space as a carrier of location factors versus space as an arena where real time economic processes have to operate.

A survey of interregional linkages is the same as a comparison of how economic processes in contiguous and more distant regions influence one another. The information demands exerted by a complete interdependency analysis are high. Later, we will deal with various proposed ways of coping with this problem in a theoretically and practically reasonable way in ME models.

2 A Categorization of Interregional Linkages

2.1 Linkage types

We need to elaborate a frame for analyzing the types of linkages between regions that are deemed relevant in current ME models. In Figure 1 we have summarized a standard ME model in terms of its main building blocks.

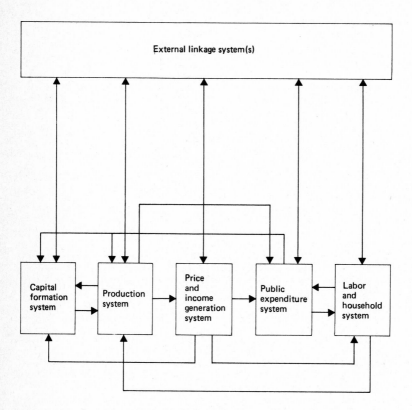

Figure 1. Scheme of a standard ME model and its subsystems

Most of the current ME models are built around a core consisting of a production submodel. That production submodel may be of input-output type as represented by the REGINA and REGIS models built by Courbis and Cornilleau (1978). It may also be econometric and put less emphasis on real intersectoral linkages; e.g., the MAG model of the US.

The production submodel is generally tied to a price and income generation submodel which is often closely related to a public expenditure and public transfer submodel. Models that are especially strong in this respect are the Belgian SERENA model and the large-scale NRIES model of the US. Very few of the currently existing models treat the public sector as a body for providing public goods, but see, for example, the BALAMO and REGAL models for exceptions--here the demand aspect is strongly stressed instead.

Considerable attention is normally devoted to labor supply and household consumption submodels. In some cases these two aspects of the population and its welfare development are treated in separate submodels. Such is the case in the recently proposed Yugoslavian model BACHUE and several versions of the MEPA model (see Treyz

1980). Other modelers treat the consumption aspect superficially and elaborate on the labor market aspects (see e.g., the REGAM, WREM, MULTIREGION, LURE, LPFM, and REMO models).

The production factor market is often strongly related to the production sub-model, at least as far as the short-term aspects are concerned. Among the models in the survey, the REGION and SMOPP models are especially detailed in treatment of factor inputs in the sense that commodity input structures are utilized instead of intersectoral technology links. In the MREED and MEEEI models, as well as in the MORSE model, energy inputs are among the primary production factors.

A weak point in many of these models, concerning their treatment of inter-regional linkages, is the form of their supply functions for capital, labor, and energy, as well as their dynamic trajectories. A standard assumption is to treat investments among the exogenous variables. Capital stocks are often neglected altogether.

The MREED, MORSE, GISSIR, HESSEN, and DREAM models are unusual in the treat-ment of the relationship between capital and capital formation. In several other models investments are modeled directly, without any explicit link to the capital (e.g., the RENA, REM, MRMI, and MEPA models). Only one model in the survey, SERENA, adopts the vintage approach to production theory put forward by Johansen (1972), and developed by, e.g., Johansson and Strömqvist (1981). With their neglect of capital formation many West European and North American large-scale models are more useful for short-term policy analysis than for longer-term projections.

The intraregional economic processes depicted within the submodels discussed above extend to other regions. The links between regions within the subsystems vary in strength depending on the time perspective adopted. Even though there is a short-term macrobehavior of the investment market that may look similar to the production and consumption market development, their microlevel properties are quite different. Other factors are more relevant for investment decisions than for deci-sions about purchases of intermediary products. We have stated some types of inter-regional linkages between regionally separated production and consumption systems in Figure 2.

The current ME models at most focus on intermediary inputs, energy inputs, and production sales when dealing with direct interregional links. In some cases labor commuting is modeled but the interregional mobility of equipment capital (e.g., transport and construction equipment) is hardly ever modeled (see, however, the REMO model). Income transfers are normally only modeled indirectly, e.g., via commuting as well as financial flows. Pollution and wage formation influences are modeled at the regional level in the HESSEN and REGIS models respectively.

The most common aspect of longer-term interregional interaction is labor migra-tion. New technology, and entry and exit processes that give rise to industrial relocation are treated by indirect methods. This holds true even for residential and transport investments in spite of their considerable dependence on regional factors. In the INTEREG model interregional spillovers are introduced, stemming from transport system bottlenecks. In the REGAL model interregional labor and cap-ital inertias are confronted with one another by investigating the trade-off in terms of measures of information gain when minimizing interregional labor and capi-tal mobility, respectively.

In spite of the prospect of analyzing the existing body of ME models from the point of view of a whole set of linkage types, the above arguments indicate that the interregional (and international) trade flows of goods and services as well as migration flows are often the most elaborate ones. In the following we will there-fore focus on these aspects of our sample of 50 models and discuss their properties, mainly concerning ourselves with commodity and factor linkages between regions.

2.2 Linkage structures

In Chapter 3 the causal structure of current ME models was reviewed. The no-tions of top-down and bottom-up approaches to structural relationships were dis-cussed and considerably extended. We will return to this analysis in this section but phrase our arguments in terms of interregional rather than intersectoral link-ages.

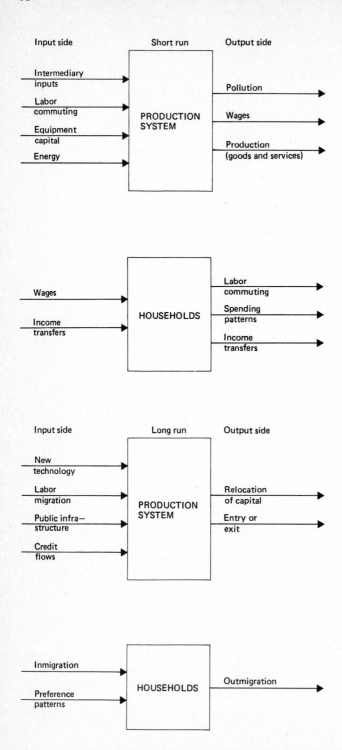

Figure 2.   Some economic linkages between a region and its exterior

Thus we start from the established paradigm, saying that the functional relationships between spatial units can be modeled from two opposite viewpoints in ME
models. The first approach, which is in line with the actual working of the regional economic system, is to analyze and model the mutual relationships between
regions. The other approach is to disregard this detailed information and adopt
a market perspective, letting interregional relationships be introduced implicitly
by clearing the economic system at the national level. The specification of a
level of clearance implicitly assumes perfect market adjustments at lower levels,
if no explicit microresponse functions are given. Even though that approach may
not be consistent with agent behavior at the microlevel, it may still be a good
representation of overall macrorelationships.

We will now extend the classification given in Chapter 3 in the direction of
interregional links and restrict this classification to situations where national
and regional levels can be distinguished. The national level is a single entity
whereas there should be at least two regions at the lower level. Thus, we do not
treat the case where the national level is not present at all, i.e., not even as a
body for aggregation of regional information. The categorization we have adopted
also applies to any two-level configuration so that the top level may be either a
group of regions or a group of nations.

The discussion here deals with the interregional links in the economic system.
However, in view of the various ways in which the intersectoral relationships within the regional models or within the national-level models are treated, it is not
possible to achieve a classification in terms of external linking mechanisms only.

The classification of models given here is simple; however, it is based on a
rather thorough investigation of the properties of 50 currently existing ME models.
We have attempted to group these models according to their overall profiles for
treating external linkages. For larger-scale models especially it is often difficult to select a particular class in the scheme.

We will start the investigation with the least interlinked modeling attempts,
illustrating our points with a two-region system (see Figure 3).

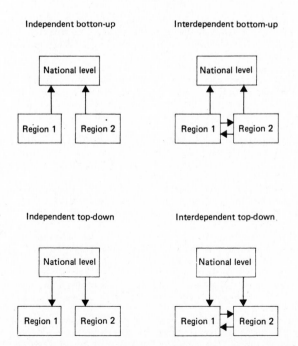

Figure 3. Split of bottom-up and top-down models according to regional linkages

In relation to earlier classifications, we wish to distinguish two types of bottom-up and top-down models. The distinction between independency and inter-dependency is based on the presence of direct links between individual regions. For short- and medium-term models interdependency means that interregional trade of commodities is modeled with an explicit mention of origin and destination region. Models that distinguish between interregional and international trade but do not identify sender and receiver regions are thus classified as independent. Both model types are bottom-up if they do not keep track of the consistency of these trade patterns at the national level and top-down if they do. The flows may also be commuting ones. This means that the scale of the individual region has an in-fluence on the appropriateness of a particular way of modeling interregional inter-actions.

For medium- and long-term models the emphasis in the term interdependencies is shifted towards factor mobility considerations. Thus, even though a medium- or long-term model is of the limited-information input-output type, it is still war-ranted to call it interdependent if labor migration is treated in a region-to-region fashion. Here we need to make another remark on factor mobility. What we just said about migration is an example of a behavioral model of migration where it is tacitly assumed that labor mobility is not perfectly elastic, but that it responds to labor market disequilibrium by either increasing the disequilibrium conditions (which may be the case in those countries where labor migration is more influenced by social or environmental factors than economic factors) or decreasing them, but at a certain rate, as given by the response functions.

Perfect mobility between regions will be looked upon here as an independent treatment of interrelations between regions. This is because there is no explicit representation of the direct links between individual subregions. Assumptions of perfect mobility of this type are generally introduced by equations aggregating supply and demand of production and its factors. The models are bottom-up if these aggregations are of simple type, without exogenous restrictions emerging out of a national equilibrium analysis. In top-down models the national supply and/or de-mand are completely inelastic.

The bottom-up scheme applies to the situation where a national aggregation of regional models is performed, and even to the case where there are a few restric-tions acting at the national level. It also applies where no national model exists at all but where there is a very explicit treatment of, for instance, interregional trade. An example of such an interdependent bottom-up model is GISSIR.

At the other end of the scale as regards the strength of the national level in a multiregional model we find the top-down models. As indicated above a national-level model (or other type of analysis) severely restricts the operation range at the regional level. Not all variables need to be constrained but the majority should be to warrant the term top-down model.

In one sense the interdependent top-down model may be seen as a further refine-ment of an interdependent bottom-up one. What we mean by this is simply that the case implies that the latter model has been complemented with a national-level model or analysis that constrains the options at the regional level further.

With the independent top-down model the situation is not quite the same, at least if we look at the examples provided in the current survey. Independent top-down models are quite common among the less sophisticated attempts to break down results of national-level analyses to the regional level (WREM, LURE). In such allocation models the necessity of having an identification of all the individual links between regions is not evident. However, some important examples of inter-dependent top-down schemes are provided by the hierarchical models. There the trade patterns are derived according to the regional distribution of production, and the national and regional technology development. The Australian INTEREG model and the Canadian FRET model (in its simplest form) are both of the hierarchical type.

We pointed out earlier that many recent ME models fall into a category between bottom-up and top-down models. Following the terminology of Courbis (1982) one might term these models "regional-national". The order of the words could also be reversed since we do not wish to distinguish between regional-national and national-regional models here (such a distinction would imply that the emphasis in the

modeling was on one of the two levels). Since we are dealing with ME models it is
self-evident that we must adopt a larger regional emphasis. Another reason for not
pursuing these arguments further is that our classification pertains to interrelations between regions and between regions and nation rather than to intersectoral
links within each individual region. At the same time it should be noted that we
do not strive for a general structuring of the models in top-down or bottom-up
terms. Even though it might be meaningful to classify the treatment of intraregional links between industries and other sectors in the same fashion we will not
pursue this here. An example of such an interrelation between sectoral and regional
specifications is the notion of local, regional and national industries as well as
basic-nonbasic subdivisions of the economy.

It is clear from the survey that several models have quite incomplete descriptions of the economic system at either the national or the regional level. In the
causality analysis in Chapter 3 the terms noninteractive and interactive were used
to distinguish models with an incomplete national model from models having such a
module. We will borrow the terminology employed in Leontief models and call the
two classes of models formed when distinguishing the degree of interaction between
elements of the economic system "open" or "closed". An open regional-national model
then has an incompletely integrated description at *either* the regional *or* the national level. Since we are focusing on ME models the lack of interaction should
not be significant at the regional level if the model is to be included in the
survey. However, it should be fruitful to attempt to distinguish between open and
closed specifications of the national level in the regional-national models.

We are now in a position to extend our classification scheme further, with
four new classes of models. The first pair of models is formed by identifying sufficient absence of interaction among sectors at the national level. The second pair
emerges when such interaction exists in the models (see Figure 4). The further

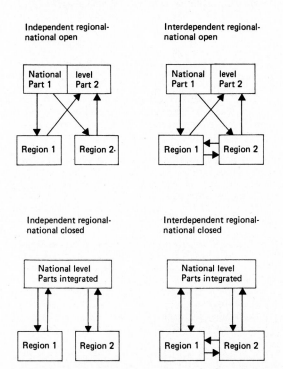

Figure 4.   Split of regional-national models according to the degree of regional
            linkages

subdivision of regional-national models into independent and interdependent ones is
of course based on the same criteria as in the former cases.

It is worth stressing again that one reason for adopting the structure of an
open model of regional-national type might not be related solely to the lack of a
macromodel at the national level; it might also be the case that some markets (private and public services, housing, etc.) may be more properly modeled at the regional level. Therefore, there is no reason to aggregate the results of this market clearing again to the national level, to clear it over again just to make the
outcome consistent with a national calculation. It is only when the regional-
national model builder also controls and can manipulate the national-level model
that iterations towards consistency may be performed.

A subdivision of model structures of the type suggested here has to be adapted
to the current state-of-the-art in modeling, otherwise some of the classes might
simply be empty by definition. An extended version of the REGAL model included in
the survey is an example of an interdependent regional-national open model. It is
interdependent since interregional trade is treated--although in a hierarchical
way. It is regional-national since export sectors are treated by a top-down method,
whereas the national employment in public and private service production is obtained
from aggregating regional information. The links between export sectors and service
ones at the national level are not cleared.

The last pair of model types, which may also be looked upon as the most ambitious one, is formed by the regional-national closed models. These models may or
may not contain direct links between individual subregions. We need not stress
further the properties and characteristics of these quite fully fledged model types.
It may be noted that the REGIS model would be more appropriately placed in the left
than the right category among the closed regional-national models; the reason for
this is its lack of treatment of interregional trade. However, the model does contain explicit migration links and also wage spillover effects from the Paris region
to the rest of France.

2.3   A possible model classification

We will now make an attempt to provide a classification of the 50 models included in the survey along the dimensions sketched here. This is a difficult task
for at least two reasons: one is that the level of documentation is quite uneven;
the other is that, especially for the more comprehensive models, elements of several
types of linkage treatment are included. In the classification below we will use
liberal judgment of the model properties, both as regards the degree of openness of
the models and as concerns whether the linkages between individual regions are
short-, medium- or long-term.

Table 1 shows that only ten of the 50 models can be classified as independent
models. Almost half of the models are interdependent through trade flows only.
Among the models that are not interdependent through trade but through factor mobility several are partial models, for instance focusing on the migration of labor or
commuting between regions. The HESSEN model, which contains a pollution submodel,
and the MACEDOINE model, which treats unemployment influences, are exceptions in
this respect.

Among the models containing both trade and factor mobility the FLEUR model is
the most difficult to classify because of its leaning towards analysis of location
factors. In a way the FLEUR model of the EC is reminiscent of the American MRMI
model although the latter does not contain explicit accessibility measures to factor
markets. The sample contains only two models that might be termed complete in the
sense that they contain both trade and factor flows, and also are built around
closed models, in the sense we have defined here, for the national and regional
levels, i.e., the French REGINA model and the SMOPP model used in territorial planning in the USSR.

We also see from Table 1 that the majority of the models in the sample have
been classified as regional-national open models. One-third of all the models in
the survey are regional-national open and interdependent through trade. This means
that they do not contain a complete description of the economic system at the national level, although they do purport to model regional-national links.

Table 1. Classification of models along linkage dimensions

Indirect linkages between regions	Type of linkages between individual subregions			
	Independent	Interdependent (trade)	Interdependent (factors)	Interdependent (trade and factors)
Bottom-up	NRPEM (Fukuchi) LFFM (Engelbrecht) 2	GISSIR (Andersson) NRIES (Ballard) 2	REMO (Schubert) IRUD (Kulikowski) 2	BACHUE (Macura) ECESIS (Isserman) EPAM (Fukuchi) 3
9				
Top-down	WREM (Elias) REM (van Hamel) 2	MIO (Carlberg) MULTIREGION (Bjornstad) INTEREG (Batten) 3	NRWF (Schönebeck) LURE (Snickars) MAG (Glickman) REGAM (Suyker) 4	
9				
Regional-national (open)	IMPE (Birg) REGAL (Granholm) MFM (Mizera) IDIOM (Dresch) BALAMO (Kawashima) TLM (Hafkamp) 6	MEEEI (Muller) BREIN (Brauers) KIM (Brauers) NORD-SUD (Martellato) IIOM (Gordon) MORSE (Lundqvist) REGION (Bjerkholt) FRET (Los) SCIIOM (Hoffman) MRIO (Polenske) MRMI (Harris) MEPA (Treyz) RDM (Suzuki) DREAM (Sharpe) IIOMSK (Bigsten) OTSIS (Kim) 16	SERENA (d'Alcantara) 1	FLEUR (Molle) 1
24				
Regional-national (closed)	SYREN (Granberg) MREEED (Lakshmanan) 2		HESSEN (Thoss) RENA (van Rompuy) MACEDOINE (Despontin) RNEM (Arora) 4	REGINA (Courbis) SMOPP (Baranov) 2
8				
50	10	23	11	6

If we take a closer look at these models it appears that interregional input/
output analysis is the common factor. Three models stand out as exceptions from
the more or less standard fixed-coefficient treatment of trade. They are MEEEI,
MRMI, and MEPA. A special study of these differences will lead into the more technical matter of how different model builders have attempted, among other things,
the circumvention of the heavy data demands of a more disaggregated trade analysis.
This topic will be developed further in the next section.

3 Trade and Factor Mobility in Multiregional Economic Models

3.1 Interregional trade

The models we are reviewing are normally not used as illustrations of theoretical arguments but are instead directed towards applications. These applications
range from *ex ante* policy analysis to economic forecasting. Therefore, the presentations of the models more often refer to practical considerations when adopting
a certain modeling approach than to alternative economic theories. However, we
can basically find the following theoretical variants of trade modeling in current
practice:

(a) general equilibrium models, including discussions of comparative advantages;
(b) linear programming models;
(c) interregional input-output models (economic-base, Chenery-Moses, Isard, balanced
     Leontief);
(d) gravity and entropy models, including transport network considerations;
(e) econometric models, using accessibility and potential concepts.

In the general equilibrium oriented models reference is made to the Heckscher-
Ohlin theories of the effectiveness of international and interregional trade. Trade
occurs simply because all parties involved in the trading process gain from such an
exchange of goods and services due to the relative rather than absolute production
costs within regions or nations. The multiregional models strictly adopting this
framework often treat only surplus interregional trade (and such factor movements
as migration). One reason for this is that the theory excludes so-called crosshauling of products. Thus, the equilibrium theory presupposes a perfect functioning of the trade market. Among other things, this would imply that any change in
comparative advantages immediately gives rise to a chain of changes in the trade
patterns, i.e., no trade inertia can exist. Among current models adopting this
framework fairly strictly for interregional trade is the REGIS model and also, in
principle, any model that treats trade in the independent fashion discussed here.
The hypotheses are much more commonly used in national models.
Linear programming may either be used as a means of producing a transport equilibrium or to yield cost-optimal shipment patterns. It is surprising to see that
this method of treating interregional trade is used in the two largest models available, i.e., the US model MRMI and the USSR model SMOPP. In the MRMI model the resulting trade flows are not used *per se*. Instead, the shadow prices of production
and consumption are taken as proxies for the influence of transport costs on total
regional production costs. The USSR model works with a specially designed commodity
classification to optimize the costs for transporting bulky and heavy input materials and goods through a coarse national transport network.
Whereas the general equilibrium models are closely related to nonlinear production theory, the interregional input-output models are prime examples of linear
activity analysis. The linearity and fixed-coefficient assumptions are extended
in space by various simplifying techniques. This approach leads to a rigidity in
the spatial interdependencies that is quite opposite to the comparative cost concepts employed in general equilibrium oriented models. Input-output models disregard supply shortages. This assumption is even stronger at the regional level,
because of the uneven geographical distribution of production capacities in the
current production system. The IDIOM, BALAMO, BREIN, and KIM models show examples
of the classical Leontief treatment of interregional and intersectoral dependences.

The developers of the GISSIR and NORD-SUD models, however, attempt to extend inter-regional trade relationships towards combined trade-location equilibria by intro-ducing nonlinear functional forms and price information.

In fact, the gravity and entropy models are not particularly unlike the inter-regional input-output models discussed above. We might make the distinction that gravity models are still fixed-coefficient models in which trade patterns have been explicitly related to transport costs: see the well known US MRIO model and the West German MIO model. Recent developments in entropy modeling include a more de-tailed treatment of the transport market. In the FRET model and the recent develop-ments of Boyce and Hewings (1980) the results from urban transport modeling of zone-network interactions are brought to bear on interregional shipment flows even for different transport modes.

There are very few models in which an attempt is actually made to trace the direct interregional linkages by econometric techniques. As we will see below, this is not quite the case for migration flows. However, most so-called bottom-up models make use of econometric techniques to estimate net or gross total product flows from one region to the rest of the country or to the world market. In the regression equations accessibility and potential variables are constructed as proxies for the relation between the region and its input and output markets. Examples of this procedure are provided by the NRIES, FLEUR, and RDM models. In the MREEED model these types of accessibility measures are used as determinant factors for the inter-regional distribution of investments.

3.2 International trade

There are basically four different ways in which international trade is treated in current ME models. The export and imports may be:

(a)   excluded altogether;
(b)   fixed shares of national totals derived by national economic models;
(c)   endogenous via fixed coefficients (most often for imports);
(d)   endogenous via econometrically estimated demand and supply functions.

We remarked above that international trade is a weak point in many ME models. Even the models currently being developed by Treyz (1980) and in the large-scale MIMUS model of the US (see Chapter 13) treat international trade basically as a net entity, exogenously given by a national-level model. The INFORUM model of Almon and Nyhus (1977) is an example of such a national level model.

Complementary imports are products that are basically not produced within the country and thus not in the region under study. These imports may be either raw materials, intermediaries or consumption and investment goods. If the products are also produced within the country the competitive situation determines what share of those imports are produced nationally. The lack of availability of data concerning the import demands of producing sectors normally force regional economic modelers to give only a superficial treatment of the competitive imports (e.g., the NORD-SUD model). This is even more the case when it comes to tracing the re-exports from the import region to other regions in the nation. It is important to discern these flows, in view of the different levels of indirect effects induced by changes in them.

Surprisingly, the treatment of exports is often more crude than import analyses in ME models. There is seldom any possibility of substitution between domestic and foreign demand. The former is often determined by linear model specifications where-as the latter is exogenously given from national considerations.

The most common treatment of international linkages is the regionalization of results of a national economic model (e.g., a model of the INFORUM type as used in the MRMI model). This treatment is more common for exports than for imports. The latter are often treated as supply variables in input-output models and modeled as constant or time-dependent shares of gross sectoral production in the regions. The GISSIR and MORSE models provide examples of balance of payment constraints formulated by means of regionally specified variables. In the HESSEN model built for the region of Hessen in West Germany imports are actually discerned from domestically produced goods and a balance of payments constraint is also used.

The REGINA and REGIS models developed for the French economy employ import and export functions specified directly at the regional level in which domestic and world market prices are allowed to influence the trade pattern. The SCIIO model and the SERENA, MACEDOINE, and FLEUR models also discern main trading partners in the international context. They are thus approaching the tradition of fully fledged international trade models, which is of course to a considerable extent due to the openness of the Belgian and other West European economies. These trends are natural extensions of the current research direction in the field of ME models which should be fruitful both in theory and practice.

3.3 Factor mobility

As mentioned in Section 2, the treatment of factor mobility depends on the regional and time perspectives used. The labor commuting is of course more important for a small urbanized and economically integrated country than for a large one. However, short-term factor mobility need not be concerned solely with commuting but may also be connected to other submarket variables such as occupational groups. The MRIO, MEPA, and SMOPP models are examples of approaches where occupational and sectoral disaggregation are treated simultaneously. Any ME model where the assumption of a skill- and occupation-homogeneous labor supply is used implicitly assumes perfect occupational mobility to act as the primary intraregional equilibrating force. It is only when this process has ended that geographical mobility is considered. Thus the theories of segmented and dual labor markets recently put forward in other branches of economics have not yet been brought to bear in ME models.

A number of models treat capital formation exogenously. Therefore these models have placed capital mobility at a higher level in the model hierarchy; this perhaps may be derived from a national model. There are also theoretical problems related to an endogenous determination of capital development in input-output models. The class of programming models is less affected by such problems. Therefore the HESSEN, DREAM, and MORSE models, as well as the public sector oriented REGAL model, are quite elaborate as concerns capital formation and capital mobility.

As mentioned earlier, migration of labor is the factor movement most often treated by current multiregional models. The applications oriented ones (LPFM, REGAM) basically analyze net migration. A set of econometrically oriented models set out to explain labor migration by differences in labor demand and supply. The RNEM model developed for Italy contains one of the most elaborate econometric migration submodels. Several models that have a demoeconomic orientation treat migration in a more detailed demographical, but less economic, way. Examples are provided by the Norwegian REGION model, which actually contains a large-scale migration submodel, and the REMO and IRUD models, which also treat rural-urban migration.

Very few of the current ME models contain direct interregional trade, factor, or related links other than the examples we have given above. Atmospheric pollution is a prime candidate for treatment by the direct method; however, in the current survey only the HESSEN model treats environmental pollution. In some cases, such as interregional income transfers which are collected and distributed by the public sector and are not related to commuting or service trips, an indirect treatment of interregional links is of course the natural way of modeling. It is evidently not warranted to go into the field of data-demanding modeling of direct linkages between individual regions without strong theoretical or practical reasons.

3.4 Summary overview

In the previous sections we have discussed various aspects of interregional and international linkages in ME models. Different models have been pointed out as exponents of certain favorable characteristics. No single model shares or should share all these characteristics. It is therefore of interest to give a model oriented summary of the external linkage characteristics.

Such a synthesis clearly reveals that the current frontier of applied ME models is extremely diversified. There are a large number of variants of trade (and final demand and income distribution) models built around the core of the original linear Leontief model for intersectoral technical couplings. One current trend is that the external trade linkages are more often modeled endogenously than by fixed-coefficient methods. At the same time, there is a shift away from the full scale international input-output models specified by Isard 30 years ago. There is even a tendency to build ME models around a core of reduced-form input-output relationships, where production or changes in production are related to different sets of demand variables. In these ways trade and transportation are separated more clearly from production technology than in earlier generations of ME models.

Many current ME models treat labor migration in a quite ambitious way. The costs and benefits of other types of factor mobility are not modeled in the same elaborate way. The question might be raised of whether this emphasis is motivated by data availability, theoretical motivation, or a search for policy relevance.

4 Examples

In this concluding section we will give examples of the treatment of interregional and international trade as well as factor mobility in some recent ME models. The choice is made to obtain a coverage of the different approaches.

4.1 Interregional trade

There are at least two different new lines of approach in the field of modeling interregional trade: one concerns the comparative cost adaption of interregional trade flows; the other relates to network models of transport market equilibrium.

We will first give an outline of the core of the MEPA model developed by George Treyz and co-workers. The trade flows are denoted by ${}^{k}r_{i}^{m}$ indicating the proportion of the ith product or service in region m that is supplied by region k. Treyz specifies the following functional form for the flow proportions:

$$ {}^{k}r_{i.}^{m} = \frac{[({}^{k}P_{i} + {}^{k}S_{i}^{m})/Y_{i}^{m}]^{\eta_i}}{\sum_{l} [({}^{l}P_{i} + {}^{l}S_{i}^{m})/Y_{i}^{m}]^{\eta_i}} \quad . \tag{1} $$

Here ${}^{k}P_{i}$ is the average unit cost of producing goods of type i in region k relative to the nation and Y_{i}^{m} is the average cost of purchasing commodity i in region m. In fact

$$ Y_{i}^{m} = \sum_{k} {}^{k}r_{i}^{m}({}^{k}P_{i} + {}^{k}S_{i}^{m}) \tag{2} $$

where ${}^{k}S_{i}^{m}$ is the transportation cost per product unit shipped from region k to region m. The production costs ${}^{k}P_{i}$ relative to the nation are determined by a Cobb-Douglas production function which contains labor $({}^{k}W_{i})$, capital $({}^{k}C_{i})$, energy $({}^{k}E_{i})$, and intermediate materials $({}^{k}Y_{i})$:

$$ {}^{k}P_{i} = {}^{k}A_{i}({}^{k}W_{i})^{\lambda_{li}}({}^{k}C_{i})^{\lambda_{ci}}({}^{k}E_{i})^{\lambda_{ei}} \prod_{j=1}^{n} ({}^{k}Y_{j})^{\lambda_{ij}} \quad . \tag{3} $$

Thus, in (1), (2), and (3) ${}^{k}P_{i}$ and ${}^{k}Y_{i}$ are determined simultaneously, given the magnitudes of other factor inputs. Treyz asserts that the ${}^{k}r_{i}^{m}$ may be estimated directly from observed shipment data.

The central argument put forward in this analysis is that the expression

$$(P_i^k + {}^kS_i^m) / \sum_k {}^kr_i^m (P_i^k + {}^kS_i^m)$$

is a measure of the comparative advantage of region k products in region m. Thus both interregional differences in production costs and interregional transport costs are brought to bear in the complicated but computable trade linkage expressions.

The FRET model developed by Marc Los and co-workers depicts the freight transport sector much more explicitly than other models. It is framed in a strict commodity-industry setting, i.e., trade flows of commodities between regions rather than interindustry flows are at the core of the model. Thus x_{ij}^k denotes the flow of tradeable item k between region i and j. The unit cost of shipping this commodity a distance unit is given by c_{ij}^k. The production level in the freight transport service sector k in region i is F_i^k.

The interesting feature of FRET is that the entities c_{ij}^k and F_i^k are determined through a more detailed network analysis of the freights by shipping mode (road, rail, air, water). This is done in the freight transportation model FRETNET. This submodel has two distinct purposes:

(i) to simulate the freight transport market at a more detailed spatial and commodity level, including the utilization of freight transport infrastructures;

(ii) to determine aggregate transport costs c_{ij}^k and the outputs of the different transport sectors (F_i^k) by province.

FRET therefore copes with the difficult transport sector with considerable elegance.

4.2 International trade

The REGIS model developed by Raymond Courbis is an example of a reasonably detailed and theoretically justified treatment of foreign trade at a regional level. The REGIS model contains four production sectors and a public and private service sector. It is intended that the model should work at a 21-region level.

Imports are treated in one of two ways for the manufacturing sector. If that sector is assumed to be exposed to foreign competition a share ymr_r of the total national imports (YM_j) is used:

$$YMR_{jr} = ymr_r YM_j \quad . \tag{4}$$

Otherwise the following econometric function is postulated:

$$YMR_{jr} = aymr_{jr} \left\{ \frac{DTOT_{jr}}{DTOTO_{jr}} \right\}^{bymr_{jr}} \left\{ \frac{P_j}{PYM_j} \right\}^{cymr_{jr}} \quad . \tag{5}$$

In (5) $DTOT_{jr}$ means total demand for products from sector j in region r and that demand is normalized by the base-year level. Further $P_j/\overline{PYM_j}$ denotes the ratio between domestic and import prices at national level. Equation (5) does not distinguish between intermediate and final uses. Since the elasticity parameters depend on both sector and region it may be assumed that time series data have been used in function estimations. There is also a separate determination of import duties as a share of total imports.

Exports are treated by an additive price-dependent relationship:

$$EXP_{jr} = aexr_{jr} + bexr_{jr} PEX_j^{cexr_{jr}}$$ (6)

where PEX_j is a national export price index. Equation (6) assumes that only a proportion of the exports are price-dependent.

In addition to these equations there are national sums corresponding to (5) and (6), both endogenous. Thus, foreign trade is actually specified completely in regional terms in the REGIS model, which is a very unusual property in current modeling practice.

4.3 Factor mobility

The migration flows are quite elaborate in many multiregional models. Again, the REGIS model is a good example of an advanced, yet readily understandable, modeling attempt. In fact, labor migration is the only explicit link between regions in the REGIS model. The gross flows $FMIG_{rs}$ have the following form:

$$FMIG_{rs} = fmig_{rs} - afmig_1 (EMPT_r - \underline{EMPTO}_r) + afmig_2 (EMPT_s - \underline{EMPTO}_s) \quad ,$$

$$r \neq s \quad . \tag{7}$$

$EMPT_r$ and $\underline{EMPTO}_r$ denote the total labor demand in the run year and the base year, respectively. Thus, the migration stream from region r to s increases if labor demand goes down in r and increases when it goes up in s.

Foreign migrants are treated separately. However, the model contains only net balance arguments in this section, i.e.,

$$SMIGXR_r = smigrz_r + asmigrz_r (EMPT_r - \underline{EMPTO}_r) \quad . \tag{8}$$

The trend in the net balance is corrected by the supply-demand balance in region r. This treatment of foreign factor flows is thus much less elaborate than in the current models of foreign product trade.

The MORSE model developed by Lars Lundqvist is elaborate as regards both commodity balances and interregional linkages, national-regional relations and production factor mobility. It gives an illustration of the less tight supply-demand relationships that are necessary in a mathematical programming framework.

The model distinguishes between production levels and production capacities. Thus, both a varying capacity utilization and a varying labor utilization are possible within bounds:

$$c_{irt} X_{irt} \leq C_{ir}^0 (1 - \delta_i)^t + (1 - \delta_i)^{t-1} I_{ir1} + \cdots + I_{irt}$$ (9)

$$\bar{L}_{rt} \leq \sum_i l_{irt} X_{irt} \leq \bar{\bar{L}}_{rt} \quad . \tag{10}$$

Here c_{irt} and l_{irt} are capital/output and labor/output ratios, respectively, for sectors, regions, and time periods. In this dynamic model the current capacity in (9) is built up from depreciated investments in earlier time periods. Since

Lundqvist uses a coarse sectoral subdivision, equation (9) in fact allows for a substitution within the capital stock. Equation (10) allows an even larger degree of mobility of the labor force. Thus, although no direct interregional linkages among factor stocks are introduced, the model still allows for considerable factor mobility, unlike many other ME models.

5 Conclusion

We had three aims in writing this chapter. One was to give an overview of the results of the comparative study of ME models relating to the treatment of interregional linkages. A second was to classify the treatment of domestic and foreign trade, as well as some aspects of factor mobility, in these models. The results indicate a large diversity of approaches, complementing the technical linkage core represented by linear input-output structures. The third aim was to give some examples of the new trends in the treatment of region-external linkages in ME models. The results indicate a development away from fixed-coefficient treatment of interregional trade, towards an integration of interregional and international trade modeling and towards an extended treatment of capital and labor mobility.

Acknowledgments

Piet Rietveld, Lars Lundqvist, and Gerard d'Alcantara are thanked for constructive comments.

References

Almon, C., and D. Nyhus (1977), The INFORUM international system of input-output models and bilateral trade flows, *INFORUM Research Report* 21.

Boyce, D., and G. Hewings (1980), Interregional commodity flow, input-output and transportation modeling: an entropy formulation, *Paper presented at the Conference on Multiregion Models, First World Regional Science Conference*, Cambridge, MA, June.

Courbis, R. (1982), Multiregional modeling--a general appraisal, in M. Albegov *et al.* (eds), *Regional Development Modeling: Theory and Practice* (North-Holland, Amsterdam).

Courbis, R., and G. Cornilleau (1978), The REGIS model: a simplified version of the national-regional REGINA model, *Paper presented at the 18th European Congress Meeting of the Regional Science Association*, August 29-September 1, Fribourg, Switzerland.

Johansen, L. (1972), *Production Functions* (North-Holland, Amsterdam).

Johansson, B., and U. Strömqvist (1981), Regional rigidities in the process of economic structural development, *Regional Science and Urban Economics*, 11.

Linneman, H. (1966), *An Econometric Study of International Trade Flows* (North-Holland, Amsterdam).

Treyz, G. (1980), Design of a multiregional policy analysis model, *Journal of Regional Science*, 20.

CHAPTER 5

MEASUREMENT OF THE EFFECTIVENESS OF REGIONAL POLICIES
BY MEANS OF MULTIREGIONAL ECONOMIC MODELS

Peter Nijkamp
Piet Rietveld

1 Introduction

In recent years, policy analysis has increasingly focused its attention on the assessment of impacts of public policies (see, e.g., Pleeter 1980). This development has also taken place in a regional and multiregional context. Multiregional economic models have been developed in many countries during the last few decades. These models contain a more or less comprehensive description of the economic structure of regions, the interrelationships between regions, and/or the interrelationships between regions and the national economy. Some multiregional economic models also contain links to other sectors such as energy, pollution, and demographic developments.

Regional policies deal with problems of interregional equity, efficiency, and unintended or undesirable side effects of spatial developments; consequently, multiregional models are a potentially useful tool in preparing these policies. This paper will be devoted to an analysis of the use of multiregional models in regional policies (see, for an analysis of the effectiveness of policies in a purely regional context, Folmer (1980) for example). We will focus our attention on the extent to which these models have been used to study the effectiveness of regional policies. This requires, of course, a closer examination of the concept of effectiveness in a spatial context. This will be the first subject.

Given the set of multiregional economic (ME) models contained in the Appendix, we will examine how far these models include policy instruments so as to achieve certain policy issues. The choice of instruments and objectives will be based on information provided by the model builders themselves. The presentation will be as follows:

in Section 2 we will discuss the effectiveness concept from a methodological viewpoint;
Section 3 will be devoted to a survey of policy objectives and instruments included in multiregional models;
in Sections 4-6 the effectiveness of some policy instruments (in particular, public expenditures, investment subsidies, and investments in infrastructure) will be discussed, respectively;
Section 7 will be devoted to drawing some conclusions.

2 Measuring the Effectiveness of Policy Instruments by Means of Models

This section will be devoted to an operationalization of the concept of effectiveness of instruments (based on ideas of Kirschen *et al.* 1964 and Tinbergen 1956). The idea underlying this concept is that one should disentangle the effects of policy instruments and of autonomous developments upon policy objectives. This requires a comprehensive representation of an economic system in which a distinction is made between objectives, instruments, and so-called data. Only in this way is it possible to indicate whether a change in policy objectives can be attributed to a certain policy or to autonomous processes.

Consider an economic system that is described by a model with the following types of variables:

$$\underline{w} = (w_1, \ldots, w_J)' \quad : \quad \text{objectives (or goal variables to be maximized)}$$

$$\underline{x} = (x_1, \ldots, x_I)' \quad : \quad \text{intermediary variables (endogenous economic variables, but no objectives)}$$

$$\underline{y} = (y_1, \ldots, y_M)' \quad : \quad \text{instruments}$$

$$\underline{z} = (z_1, \ldots, z_N)' \quad : \quad \text{autonomous variables (data)}$$

$$\underline{v} = (v_1, \ldots, v_H)' \quad : \quad \text{noneconomic side effects (e.g., pollution)}.$$

The relationships between objectives, intermediary variables, instruments, data, and side effects can be represented by means of the simple stimulus-response approach shown in Figure 1.

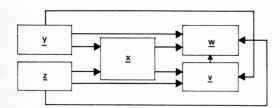

Figure 1. A stimulus-response model for policy analysis

Clearly, in a dynamic context this sytem might contain several feedback relationships. It should also be noted that in a spatial setting this sytem should be extended with spatial spillover effects and spatial interaction linkages (see Nijkamp 1979). Assume that the model concerned consists of a series of K independent equations:

$$f_k(\underline{w}, \underline{x}, \underline{y}, \underline{z}) = 0 \ , \qquad k = 1, \ldots, K \ . \tag{2.1}$$

These equations describe various types of relationships between the variables, such as technical relationships, balance equations, behavioral patterns of various actors, and definitions. Noneconomic side effects are ignored for the ease of presentation. The assumption is made that a clear distinction between objectives, instruments, and intermediary variables can be made. It should be noted, however, that in various cases policy instruments may also have the character of an objective, or vice versa (see also Section 3). This holds especially true in models with various policy levels or with several policy making institutions.

We assume also that the model is *closed*, which means that once $\underline{y}$ and z are known, the values of $\underline{w}$ can be uniquely determined. A necessary condition for such a calculation is that the number of endogenous variables, $I + J$, is equal to the number of equations, K (see Tinbergen 1956). When the model is linear, (2.1) can be rewritten as

$$A_1 \begin{pmatrix} \underline{w} \\ \underline{x} \end{pmatrix} + A_2 \begin{pmatrix} \underline{y} \\ \underline{z} \end{pmatrix} + \underline{c} = \underline{0} \quad , \tag{2.2}$$

where A_1 and A_2 are matrices of order $(K \times K)$ and $(K \times (M + N))$, respectively, and $\underline{c}$ is a vector with K elements. In this case the solution of the model can be explicitly written in the reduced form (provided A_1 is nonsingular)

$$\begin{pmatrix} \underline{w} \\ \underline{x} \end{pmatrix} = -A_1^{-1} A_2 \begin{pmatrix} \underline{y} \\ \underline{z} \end{pmatrix} - A_1^{-1} \underline{c} \quad . \tag{2.3}$$

We define the effectiveness of an instrument m with regard to an objective j, γ_{mj}, as the marginal change in instrument m, holding the other instruments and the exogenous variables constant*, are:

$$\gamma_{mj} = \frac{\Delta w_j}{\Delta y_m} \quad . \tag{2.4}$$

Of course the effectiveness can also be defined in terms of infinitesimally small changes (partial derivatives) in instruments and variables. It is also clear that the effectiveness of an instrument variable is codetermined by the structure and characteristics of the model concerned. When a model is linear, such as in (2.3), γ_{mj} can directly be found when A_1^{-1} and the relevant columns of A_2 are known. Obviously, in the linear case, the value of γ_{mj} does not depend on the values of the instruments and autonomous variables.

When a model is not linear, a straightforward reduced form can only be found in exceptional cases, so another approach has to be adopted. A widely accepted approach is:

(1) determine *reference values* for the instruments and autonomous variables $(\overset{o}{\underline{y}}, \overset{o}{\underline{z}})$ and find by means of some numerical procedure the resulting values of the objectives $(\overset{o}{\underline{w}})$;

(2) formulate a *policy variant* in the following way: let ε_m denote a unit vector of which the mth element is equal to 1 and the other elements are 0, and repeat (1) for the values $(\overset{o}{\underline{y}} + \Delta y_m \varepsilon_m, \overset{o}{\underline{z}})$. The resulting value of the objectives is $\underline{w}_m$;

(3) determine γ_{mj}, the effectiveness of y_m with respect to w_j, as $(w_{mj} - \overset{o}{w}_j)/\Delta y_m$.

When this procedure is repeated for all j and m, we arrive at the impact matrix described in Table 1, which can be considered as the central concept of this chapter.

We will finally discuss two aspects of effectiveness measures that do not usually receive the attention they deserve: *statistical aspects* of effectiveness measures and the way in which *reference values* for $\underline{y}$ and $\underline{z}$ can be determined.

Statistical aspects of effectiveness measures have in general received little attention in theory and practice of modeling. Obviously, this is an unsatisfactory situation, as in economic modeling several sources of uncertainty are present: measurement errors in variables, the stochastic nature of parameter values, omitted and latent variables, specification errors, and uncertainties about the future

---

*For nonlinear models, it may be more appropriate to define effectiveness in terms of elasticities. Another advantage of using elasticities is that it makes the effectiveness measures comparable across all instruments and objectives, as well as across all regions. Note also that an implicit assumption underlying (2.1) is that the *ceteris paribus* condition holds. In some cases, however, this may not be a reasonable assumption, for example when the effects of a policy package consisting of a mix of several instruments have to be studied (synergetic effects).

Table 1.   Impact matrix for M instruments and
           J objectives

Objectives Instruments	w_1 $\cdots$ w_J
y_1	γ_{11} $\cdots$ γ_{1J}
.	. .
.	. .
.	. .
y_M	γ_{M1} $\cdots$ γ_{MJ}

development of autonomous variables. Only recently have the problems of the level of measurement of variables received attention in so-called soft or qualitative econometrics (see Nijkamp and Rietveld 1982).

Even in the case of linear models, it is extremely difficult to draw conclusions in a formal analytical way about the statistical properties of the γ_{mj}. Therefore, Monte Carlo simulations are an obvious alternative (cf. Openshaw 1979), although one should be aware of the disadvantages of these simulations, such as the costs of running a model several times.

From a comparison of *ex post* with *ex ante* effectiveness analyses, it is clear that more uncertainties are involved in the latter than in the former. The additional uncertainties relate to (1) the future values of the autonomous variables and (2) the validity of the model for periods that have not been taken into account during the estimation phase. For instance, one may question the relevance of a symmetric economic behavior in a period of economic growth and of economic decline, especially when these models have been assessed during an economic "upswing" (see Nijkamp 1982a). Both uncertainties may be relevant in multiregional models.

The determination of *reference values* for instruments and autonomous variables is in many cases not straightforward, especially in dynamic models when several periods are involved. Reference values for autonomous variables can be obtained by using other models, extrapolating time series, subjective guesses, or a combination of these (see also Theil 1968). Reference values for instruments are based on the notion of no policy alterations. Such a notion of a reference alternative is not an unambiguous term, however (see for example, Table 2). Table 2 contains (fictitious) data on public expenditures and taxes in previous periods as well as a forecast for the tax base in the next period. Policy 1 is based on extrapolating the trends in the expenditure and the tax rate, while the budget deficit follows as a resultant. Policy 2 is based on a norm for the deficit/tax base ratio (5%) and an extrapolation of the tax rate. In this case the expenditures follow as a resultant. We conclude that in many cases the term "unaltered policy" can be interpreted in several ways (see also De Falleur *et al*. 1975).

Table 2.   Government revenues and expenditures measured in real terms

Period	$t-2$	$t-1$	t	$t+1$ Forecast	$t+1$ Policy 1	$t+1$ Policy 2
Public expenditures	17.0	20.0	23.0		26.0	25.3
Tax rate	0.15	0.16	0.17		0.18	0.18
Tax base	100.0	110.0	110.0	110.0	110.0	110.0
Tax revenues	15.0	17.6	18.7		19.8	19.8
Budget deficit	2.0	2.4	4.3		6.2	5.5

3   Objectives and Instruments in Multiregional Economic Models

        For the purpose of this chapter it is important to indicate first the scope
of ME models.   What kinds of policy objectives and instruments are covered by them?
For an answer to this question we used the responses of the 50 model builders on
the questionnaire concerning ME models mentioned in the introduction to Part A.
One of the questions was: "Which policy goals/objectives are endogenous in the
model (at the regional and/or national level)?"   In 35 cases the response contained
useful information.   In several other models policy instruments and/or objectives
were not dealt with in an identifiable way, so that they had to be left out of consideration.   The frequency distribution of these responses has been represented in
Table 3.
        We conclude that the most important socioeconomic objectives are present in
the table, although the frequencies of economic growth and labor market variables
are clearly higher than those of the other socioeconomic objectives.   Policy objectives from related fields are only present to a moderate extent.   We may therefore
conclude that in a strict sense ME models can only be used to a very limited extent
to analyze the effects of policy instruments on energy, environmental, or physical
planning objectives.   Only when these models are linked with other models (e.g.,
environmental models), is an analysis of effectiveness, in this sense, feasible in
general.
        With respect to the instruments, the following question has been posed: "For
which policy instruments or policy measures can the effects on the policy objectives
be determined (at the regional and/or national level)?."   In 29 cases the response
contained useful information.   The frequency distribution has been represented in
Table 4.
        The main instruments in multiregional models can be found in the fields of
government consumption expenditures, public investments, and subsidies of private
investments.   Other instruments receiving some attention are taxes and employment

Table 3.   Frequency distribution of objectives in 31 ME models

---

Socioeconomic objectives

Income, production, consumption	25
Employment	21
Unemployment	9
Prices, inflation	7
Balance of payment	2
Income distribution	3

Budgetary objectives

Tax revenues, investment costs, budget deficit	4

Facilities

Infrastructure, utilities	4

Energy and environment

Energy consumption	4
Pollution	3

Physical planning objectives

Land use	1
Population distribution	4
Land prices	1
Trip distribution	1

Table 4. Frequency distribution of instruments in 29 ME models

---

Government revenues and expenditures

Consumption expenditures	11
Employment in government services	3
Public investments	17
Flows between national and regional governments	3
Social security payments	1
Taxes	7

Prices

Subsidies of private investments	10
Wage subsidies	1
Average or minimum wage	2
Interest rate	2
Public prices	1
Transportation costs	1
Fuel prices	1

Physical planning

Housing	2

Environment

Pollution standards	4

Other instruments

Limits on productive age	1
Agricultural policies	1
National immigration policies	2

in government services. Relatively little attention is paid to price policies
(apart from investment subsidies) and to instruments from related policy fields
such as physical and environmental planning.

Note that we did not make a distinction between national and regional objectives
and instruments. Instruments may be used at both a national and a regional level,
while also objectives may be specified at both a national and a regional level, leading to complex linkages in a spatial system. So the majority of the objectives may
function at both levels (exceptions are the balance of payment, inflation, and budgetary objectives of the national government), while the same holds true for the
instruments (for example, an investment subsidy may be specified for an individual
region, but it may also be uniformly applicable to all regions). Consequently,
certain impacts can in principle be covered by multiregional models (see Table 5).

Table 5. Impact matrix for regional specific and regional uniform
          instruments and objectives

	Regional specific objectives	National objectives
Regional specific instruments	Λ^{rr}	Λ^{rn}
Regional uniform instruments	Λ^{nr}	Λ^{nn}

The matrix Λ^{rr} indicates the effects of regional policies on regional objectives. The matrix Λ^{rn} indicates the (perhaps unintended) effects of regional policies on national objectives. The matrix Λ^{nn} is the main interest of national policies, while Λ^{nr} describes the (perhaps unintended) effects of national policies on specific regions. When dealing with the performance of a specific region, there is often a tendency to focus on Λ^{rr}, but this is not always justifiable. There are several policy fields without an explicit regional orientation that may have strong differential impacts Λ^{nr} (e.g., education, infrastructure, environmental standards, income, and labor market policies). The same holds true for national capacity limits or national price policies.

Top-down models are based on the assumption that the main national variables are given, or at least not determined as endogenous variables, in a multiregional framework. They provide a feasible area within which regional trade-offs and allocations take place, though the regional distribution of activity will not affect the national totals. Hence, these models can only be used to study Λ^{rr} and Λ^{nr}. One might argue that Λ^{nn} is already covered by national models, so that it can be deleted in the context of multiregional models; this, however, is not necessarily true. Multiregional models with a bottom-up structure or with national-regional interactions are in principle also suitable for this purpose and may even be more appropriate than national models in certain cases.

In subsequent sections we will present some numerical results of effectiveness analyses by means of 14 ME models from various countries. We have restricted our attention to these 14 models since with them well documented policy simulations have been carried out. The following models have been included:

Western Europe: REGAM, RENA, MACEDOINE, REGINA, REGAL
USA   : NRIES, MAG, IDIOM, MRIO, MRMI, MEPA
Japan   : RDM, BALAMO, NRPEM

A selection of specific policy areas will be made. Sections 4-6 will be devoted to three main fields of regional policy: government expenditures, stimulation of private investments, and investments in infrastructure. We will mainly pay attention to the effects of these instruments on economic growth, income, and employment. Some models also yield effects on other objectives, but for ease of presentation these effects will not be reported here.

4 Government Revenues and Expenditures

In this section we will present some conclusions of model results and simulations focusing on the effectiveness of policies in which government revenues and expenditures play an important role. In general, it turns out to be almost impossible to draw inferences about the statistical validity of the results, as almost no model provides information on these aspects. For the ease of presentation a representative sample of models will be treated here. The presentation is based on the results of NRIES, MAG, IDIOM, a version of MRIO, and MEPA. All information has been provided by the model builders.

NRIES has been used to analyze the effects of a revision of the financial flows between the national (federal) and regional (state and local) authorities (see Ballard *et al.* 1980). The revised system assumes grants that are proportional to the population of the regions. The sum of the grants remains the same in the reference case and the policy variant. The redistribution of grants may give rise to a considerable increase or decrease of grants (for many regions a change of 10-20%). The long-term effects of the redistribution on *per capita* income in the regions are relatively small (in most cases a change of less than 1%). The interregional inequality in *per capita* incomes, measured by means of the coefficient of variation, decreases from 0.1374 to 0.1359. Since NRIES is not a top-down model, it also yields results for the effects on the national economy. The redistribution gives rise to an increase of 112,000 man-years in the long run, which indicates that high-multiplier states gained more than low-multiplier states.

Another application of NRIES concerns the effects of a uniform increase in federal expenditures (partially covered by some uniform tax increases) on the re- tional economies (see Ballard and Wendling 1980). The national effect is an average employment growth of 1% per year. The regional variations in the effects of the policy package are substantial: when the USA is partitioned into eight clusters of states, the yearly regional employment growth can be calculated by means of the above mentioned effectiveness analysis and varies from 0.2 to 2.8%.

The second model discussed here is the MAG model. The MAG model has been used for an impact analysis of a spatial redistribution of government activity (see Milne *et al.* 1980). In the reference solution, the share of the northern tier of the USA in government production declines from 37.1 to 36.9% in a ten-year period. In the policy variant, an increase of this share to 39.8% has been formulated. The impli- cations of these policies for the gross regional production are represented in Table 6. We may conclude from the table that a redistribution in favor of the northern tier gives rise to a reduction of differences in regional growth rates. The model does not allow an analysis of the impacts on national efficiency, as the sum of the regional variables is made to coincide with forecasts of the national values from the driving national model.

Table 6. Regional impacts of a redistribution of government activity

	Yearly growth rate of gross regional product		
	Northern tier	Rest of the nation	National
Reference solution	2.5	3.3	2.9
Policy variant	2.7	3.0	2.9

The next model discussed in this section is IDIOM. One of the policy simula- tions with IDIOM concerns the direct, indirect, and induced effects of a cut in military exports (see Dresch and Updegrove 1980). The national decrease in employ- ment is 0.7%. When the USA is partitioned into 13 clusters of states, the regional decrease varies from 0.2 to 1.0%. Two compensatory programs have been devised: a public works program with emphasis on the regions that have been mostly heavily affected and a uniform reduction in the labor tax rate. In both cases the decrease in employment can be offset at the national level. When the second compensatory program is employed, regional variations persist, however (the change in regional employment varies from -0.3 to +0.3%). Not surprisingly, it appears that the main industries hurt by the reduction of exports are not the industries benefitting from the compensatory measures. Therefore, the outcomes of the simulations rely heavily on the assumption of a flexible labor market (large occupational mobility and elas- tic supply). This is obviously due to the fact that IDIOM is a demand oriented model.

Now a specific version of MRIO will be discussed. This version has been used to study the effects of various tax and income redistribution measures (see Golladay and Haveman 1977). It is the version developed at the Institute for Re- search on Poverty (IRP). In the IRP version, much attention is paid to income dis- tribution aspects; for example, consumption functions have been specified for seven income classes; labor requirements for 114 occupational categories are included. The model has been used to identify the impacts of a redistribution of incomes by means of family assistance plan and a negative income tax. In a regional perspec- tive, this means that the southern part of the USA received large net transfers at the expense of other parts of the USA. One of the main conclusions of the study is that the transfers lead to a certain reduction in interregional income inequalities, but that the production shifts resulting from the transfers are substantially less equalizing. Due to the interregional trade pattern, a substantial part of consump- tion in the South is produced in other regions. Another conclusion of the study is that the income transfers give rise to an increase of aggregate demand in the national economy (due to differences in the propensity to consume between income classes). In some policy variants an increase of 120,000 jobs has been found.

In this section we will also pay some attention to policy studies with the MEPA model. MEPA was originally designed as a single-region model for Massachusetts (USA), but at present the model is supplemented with a partitioning into five sub-regions (cf. Treyz 1980, Treyz *et al.* 1980, Treyz and Duguay 1980). Although our presentation is based on the single-region versions of MEPA, the model is included here, since it sheds light on important points that are not covered by the other policy studies reported here.

In MEPA a crucial element of the policy simulations concerns the effects on wages and prices. For example, in a study of the effects of an increase in defense-related contracts in Massachusetts, the model gives rise to the conclusion that the total direct and indirect employment effect in the first year is approximately 2.8 times the direct employment effect. In the fourth year, this number has decreased to 1.7. The reason for the decrease is that the direct effect leads to a tighter labor market and hence to higher wages. This gives rise to substitutions between labor and capital and to a reduction of investment in the pertaining region. In another application of MEPA the effects of an increase of welfare payments of $400 million in Massachusetts have been analyzed (see Treyz and Duguay 1980): 50% of the increase is covered by an increase of the personal income tax, and the other 50% comes from federal resources. The short-term effect of the policy is an increase in employment of 16,790 jobs in Massachusetts. The long-term effect (after ten years) is a decrease of 3170 jobs, the reason being the above-mentioned substitution and spatial reallocation effects.

In order to test the sensitivity of the outcomes for the feedback effects from the labor market, MEPA has been rerun with fixed wage levels. In that case, a completely different effect is found, namely an increase in the long-term of 16,760 jobs in Massachusetts. This is a clear illustration of the sensitivity of the outcomes of policy analysis for the structure of the models. These results once more demonstrate the necessity of a careful effectiveness analysis in regional models. These policy exercises and simulations give rise to the following observations.

(1) Some models (NRIES and the IRP version of MRIO) allow one to study the effects of an interregional redistribution of income or government expenditures on national efficiency (cf. the matrices Λ^{rn} in Table 5). The common idea that there is a trade-off between national efficiency and interregional equity is not confirmed by these models. These models give rise to the conclusion that --given the present situation--it is possible to increase both national efficiency and interregional equity.

(2) Uniform policies at the national level may give rise to substantially varying effects for the regions (see NRIES, IDIOM, and the IRP version of MRIO). This is a clear indication that the Λ^{nr} part of Table 5 should not be neglected in regional policy analysis.

(3) In the policy analyses, little systematic attention is paid to the uncertainties in conclusions concerning policy effects. An exception is the experiment with the MEPA model in which the sensitivity for the assumptions of fixed wages is tested.

(4) Some experiments (IDIOM, the IRP version of MRIO) are based on the method of comparative statics. The obvious disadvantage is that it is not possible to assess the magnitude of effects in the short- and the longer-term. As indicated by an experiment with the MEPA model, short- and long-term effects may differ significantly.

(5) IDIOM and the IRP version of MRIO are pure demand driven models. Hence they are based on the assumption that there are no serious bottlenecks at the supply side (e.g., in the labor market). In cases where this assumption is not realistic, one may question whether the outcomes of the simulations are meaningful.

(6) In all cases, the experiments concern *ex ante* analyses of policy measures.

5 Stimulation of Private Investments

The effects of stimulation of private investments form the subject of the present section. Here again, a selected representative sample of models will be discussed. We will present here results for REGAM, RDM, RENA, MACEDOINE, and REGINA.

REGAM has been used for an *ex post* analysis of the effectiveness of regional investment subsidies in the Netherlands*. One important finding is that the effectiveness depends heavily on the macroeconomic conditions. Consider, for example, the effect of a one percent reduction in the price of investments in a region compared to the average price reduction over the regions on the discrepancy between the regional and national growth rate of manufacturing employment. This effect declines from 0.40% a year in the 1950s to about 0.15% a year in the 1970s.

In another *ex post* analysis, REGAM has been used to determine the extent to which investments for which a subsidy has been received would have been realized without a subsidy. In the period 1973-79, 20,000 jobs have been created in connection with subsidized investments. REGAM leads to the conclusion that approximately 9500 jobs (40-50%) would not have been realized without subsidies. In the model no attention is paid to indirect and induced effects. Hence a certain underestimation of the policy effect may have occurred. REGAM is a top-down model, i.e., the regional investment subsidies only influence the regional distribution of employment, but not the national volume. Consequently, the 9500 jobs created in the stimulation regions have been realized at the expense of 9500 jobs in regions without subsidies. In Table 7 the positive, negative, and net effects per region are represented.

The fourth row of Table 7 contains the actual development of industrial employment during the period considered. Clearly the net effects of the subsidies are small compared with the effects of autonomous variables. The investment subsidies influenced only marginally the development of regional employment. The fifth row indicates the development of regional industrial employment that would have arisen if the national rate of decline had applied to all regions in a uniform way. In the sixth row the regional component in the actual development has been presented (row 6 is defined as the difference between rows 4 and 5). When comparing rows 3 and 6, we conclude that part of the relatively favorable development of the south may be ascribed to the investment subsidy. For the north and the east, it can be inferred that the positive net effect of the subsidy is hardly or not sufficient to counterbalance the negative effects of other variables.

The next model discussed is RDM. Suzuki *et al.* (1978) have analyzed, by means of this model, the effects of policies aiming at industrial decentralization by

Table 7. The development of industrial employment and effects of investment subsidies, measured in man years in the Netherlands (1973-79)

Region		North	East	West	South	Netherlands
(1)	Positive effects	3000	2000	500	4000	9500
(2)	Negative effects	500	1500	5500	2000	9500
(3)	Net effects	2500	500	-5000	2000	-
(4)	Total mutation	-15,500	-33,500	-71,500	-37,500	-158,000
(5)	Mutation based on constant employment shares	-15,500	-31,500	-67,500	-43,500	-158,000
(6)	Regional component	-	-2000	-4000	6000	-

*See the official government document, Nota Regionaal Sociaal Economisch Beleid, 1981-85 (1981); see also Van Delft and Suyker (1981).

means of congestion taxes in highly industrialized regions and subsidies in less
industrialized regions. The taxes are imposed on factory floor space in the industrial sector. The taxes and subsidies are included in the model by means of the
variables determining regional investment. The effects of the policy measures are
represented in Table 8, which indicates that the measures lead to a certain dispersion of industrial activity from the main industrial center (Kanto) to the rest of
the country. The measures are not strong enough to prevent Kanto from increasing
its share when compared with the situation in 1970. This conclusion is striking
when one knows that in the reference solution certain dispersion measures have already been taken into account (e.g., a tax on environmental pollution).

Table 8. Impacts of industrial decentralization policies in Japan

Region	Industrial production in billions of yen (and in %)		
	1970	1985 (reference solution)	1985 (policy variant)
Kanto	64,500 (39.2)	160,600 (40.7)	156,400 (39.6)
Japan	164,400 (100.0)	394,900 (100.0)	395,000 (100.0)

Next, the RENA model will be briefly discussed. According to the RENA model
the short- and medium-term effects of an investment stimulation on regional employment are very small (see Bogaert *et al.* 1979). The model users report that this is
due to the fact that in the past investment aid has been used predominantly for a
rationalization of production, instead of for an extension of the production capacity. This behavior in the past has largely influenced the estimation results and
hence the conclusions of the effects of investment aid on employment.

In MACEDOINE, gross investments as such are assumed to be exogenous. Therefore, in a strict sense an analysis of stimulation policies cannot be carried out.
The model is interesting, however, since much attention is paid to investment multipliers in space and time (see Despontin 1980). The short-term multiplier of gross
regional investments on gross regional production varies considerably among the
eight regions: they range from 0.53 to 1.08. This may be due to large differences
in the economic structure of these regions. The corresponding interim multipliers
increase considerably over several years. Eventually, these multipliers decrease
because of substitution processes induced by wage increases. Cumulative interim
multipliers or total multipliers have not been computed. This is related to the
fact that several eigenvalues of MACEDOINE are substantially higher than 1, giving
rise to a divergent system. This result casts doubt on the relevance of the model
in simulations for a long run.

The REGINA model has been used to find the impacts on the national economy of
various regional investment strategies (see Courbis 1979). For each of the five
REGINA regions, a gradual increase of two percentage points in the share of manufacturing investments that the region holds in the total manufacturing investment
is considered for the period 1970-80. This increase is compensated by a decrease
of investments in the other regions with an equal decrease in relative terms for
each of these. This redistribution of investments would give rise to an increase
of approximately 50,000 jobs in manufacturing in the stimulation region. Since
REGINA is not a top-down model, it can be used to assess the effects of the various
alternatives on the national economy. It appears that these effects vary considerably (see Table 9). For example, a stimulation of the Paris region assuming fast
national economic growth gives rise to a decrease in 1980 of 132,000 jobs in the
total employment, while a similar stimulation in eastern and northern France gives
rise to an increase in 1980 of 40,000 jobs. This difference is due to the tight
labor market in Paris and the dependence of wage development in other regions on
the wages in Paris.

Table 9. Effects of regional investment policy (1970-80) on the national economy in
          1980, given alternative assumptions concerning national economic growth

	Stimulation region	Impact on national employment (no. of jobs)	Impact on national price level (%)
Fast national economic growth	Paris	-132,000	+1.3
	Western and south-western France	-31,000	+0.8
	Eastern and northern France	+40,000	-0.5
Moderate national economic growth	Paris	-109,000	+1.2
	Western and south-western France	+9000	+0.1
	Eastern and northern France	+30,000	-0.4

An interesting result of REGINA is that the effects of regional policy depend
heavily on the assumptions about autonomous variables. For example, when a more
moderate national economic growth is assumed, the effects also tend to be smaller
and may sometimes show a change in sign. This is illustrated in Table 9 by the
employment effect of an investment policy in favor of western and southwestern
France which is negative in the strong-growth variant and positive in the moderate-
growth variant.

These policy experiments give rise to the following observations.

(1) The simulation with REGAM is the only *ex post* experiment in this section.
     This experiment gives rise to the conclusion that a substantial part (40-50%)
     of the jobs created in connection with investment subsidies in the Netherlands
     from 1973-79 would not have been created without the subsidies. Another con-
     clusion from REGAM, which is also supported by RDM and RENA, is that the ef-
     fects of subsidies are small compared with the effects of autonomous variables.
     This means that--given the level of subsidies considered--the spatial distribu-
     tion of investments is only marginally influenced by the subsidies.

(2) From the experiments with the REGAM and REGINA models it appears that the effec-
     tiveness of investment subsidies depends considerably on the national economic
     conditions. In periods of fast economic growth, the effectiveness is, in
     general, larger.

(3) In the simulation with REGINA, attention is paid to the effects of an inter-
     regional distribution of investments on the national economy (see matrix Λ^{rn}
     in Table 5). These effects may be substantial.

(4) In three of the five simulations, investments are stimulated by means of sub-
     sidies, which are modeled via the user cost of capital. In the other two
     cases, no indication is given of the means by which the investments are stimu-
     lated; one simply assumes a given shift in regional investments. If one wants
     to study the effectiveness of subsidies in the latter cases, additional infor-
     mation about the influence of subsidies on investments would be required.

(5) All models are based on the assumption that investments resulting from stimu-
     lation measures are--on the average--not different from other investments in
     a certain sector. This assumption may give rise to questionable results. For
     example, a common argument against investment subsidies is that they are used
     by firms that are--on average--less efficient than other firms. This would
     give rise to a higher than average probability that these firms might close
     down within a fairly short period. This argument is not taken into account

in the models. As far as the argument is real, the models give rise to an
overestimation of the effectiveness of investment subsidies.

(6) It is a well known fact that modeling investment behavior is a difficult task
and that statistical tests of estimated relationships in this field often give
rise to less satisfactory results. Therefore, it is disappointing that in the
simulations little attention is paid to the measure of uncertainty of the
outcomes.

(7) In two cases (MACEDOINE and RENA), the economy is treated as one uniform sector.
Consequently, these models are less adequate for an analysis of subsidies to
specific industries.

6 Investments in Infrastructure

    As a final example of effectiveness analysis, the impacts of public infrastruc-
ture will be dealt with. Investments in infrastructure are part of the government
expenditures, which have already been dealt with in Section 4. A separate treatment
of infrastructure investments is justified, however, since these instruments give
rise to effects that are often absent in the case of consumptive expenditures (see
Biehl *et al*. 1982, Nijkamp 1982b). They are not only a component of final demand,
but may also add to regional productivity, and the attractiveness and development
potential of regions for productive or residential purposes. The latter effect will
be called the attractiveness effect. In this section, we will present the results
of BALAMO, NRPEM, RENA, MRMI, and REGAL.
    In BALAMO, special attention is paid to investments in road infrastructure.
The two production factors determining regional production are the regional labor
force and the regional road stock (this is evidently a rather restricted production
theory). The production function has been specified such that considerable substitution possibilities exist between these production factors.
    In one of the simulations (see Kawashima 1977), a 100% growth rate per five-
year period of gross road investment in a particular region is assumed, while for
the remaining regions a 50% growth rate is taken. The gross investments are devoted
to the replacement or repair of the existing stock (depending on the intensity of
use in the previous period) and the extension of the regional road network. In
this simulation the share of the particular region in the total production of min-
eral resources increased from 6% to 20% after six periods*. The reliability of this
result is questionable. The structure of the model is not very suitable for an
analysis of less than 30 years, especially since no attention is paid to the formation of private capital stock.
    In another Japanese model (NRPEM) considerable attention is again paid to the
role of infrastructure. Infrastructure plays a role in the equations explaining the
regional population (social welfare capital) and the regional production levels in
various sectors (collective agricultural, industrial, and tertiary capital). The
elasticities in the production functions are considerable. For example, an increase
of 1% in collective capital for the tertiary sector in a certain region gives rise
to an increase in the regional production in that sector of 0.3% in the same year.
In this model no attention is paid to the role of investments in infrastructure as
a final demand component. Their only function is that they increase the regional
production capacity. This treatment of infrastructure can also be found in BALAMO.
    The impacts of public infrastructure can also be identified in RENA. A result
of the RENA model is that a reallocation of public investments among regions has
relatively small effects on regional growth and employment (see Bogaert *et al*. 1979).
In this model, public investments are treated as an exogenous part of total investments. Hence, their effects on employment can be found in a way similar to the

---

*Note that in this case reference values for the instruments have not been
given (for example by assuming a uniform growth rate of instruments of 50% in all
regions). The reported result for the share of regional production has been compared with the initial situation and not with the result of a reference policy.
Consequently, in a strict sense, this experiment does not give any information about
the effectiveness of the road investments.

procedure applied to private investments (see Section 5). Consequently, the same
explanation of the small extent of the effects can be given here as in Section 5.

The MRMI model has been used extensively for studies concerning the effects of
changes in transportation networks on regional economies (see Harris 1980, Hilewick
et al. 1980). One study has focused on the effects of building and upgrading high-
ways and railroads in Pitt County, a county with approximately 75,000 inhabitants
in North Carolina (USA). The short-term effects of the investments are clearly
positive: during the years of construction, employment has increased by around
1200 jobs. The long-term effects (10-15 years) of improved accessibility are small
and negative: the model indicates a decrease of 40 jobs. This means that in this
case other regions benefit more from increased accessibility than the region of
investment itself. In a similar case study for other counties, a small but positive
long-term effect is found for the region of investment. Obviously, the MRMI model
allows for both a positive and a negative sign of the long-term effects of investments in transportation on the appropriate region. The sign of the effect depends
among other things on the level of congestion in the transportation system, the
existing spatial distribution of activities and the size of the investment relative
to the regional product.

The effects of investments in transportation have been compared with the effects
of investments in the communication sector (printing, computing machines, broadcast-
ing, etc.) in Pitt County. The conclusion is that investments in communications,
aiming at regional self-sufficiency, give rise to a smaller investment sum, but a
larger number of jobs in the medium- and longer-terms. This is partially due to the
relatively low capital intensity of the communications sector. No indication is
given of the means by which such policy measures could cause these investments in
the private sector to be realized (see the fourth observation of the preceding section).

Finally, the REGAL model will be dealt with. REGAL is based on the assumption
that public capital is a necessary condition for production in the private sector.
Public capital is tied to the volume of the private capital stock by the fixing of
minimum requirement parameters. Thus when the regional public capital stock is
fixed, a limit is imposed on the extent to which the regional private capital stock
can be used, and hence on regional production. Hence, when there is a shortage of
public capital, public investments give rise to a proportional increase in production in the private sector. When there is no shortage of public capital, public
investments have no direct effects on the level of production in the private sector.
The following public sectors have been distinguished: child care and basic education, medical services, public administration (national and regional), transport
and communication, housing stock, electricity and water supply, road capital. Regional public capital also plays a role in REGAL in the determination of the regional population. Given the level of regional public services a constraint is imposed
on the total population that can live in a region.

The policy simulations give rise to the following observations.

(1) In two out of the five models (RENA and MRMI), attention is paid to both the
     demand and the attractiveness effects of public investments. In the other
     three models, only attractiveness effects are dealt with.
(2) The attractiveness effects of public capital investments can be modeled in a
     direct and an indirect way. In MRMI the indirect approach is used. The ef-
     fects of investments in transportation infrastructure on regional development
     are modeled by means of the ensuing reduction in transport costs. In this
     case, the question of how transport costs are influenced by the investments
     has to be solved outside the model. In the other models a direct approach is
     used. The public capital stock plays an explicit role in these models, for
     example, via production functions.
(3) In RENA, BALAMO, and NRPEM, substitutability between public capital and private
     production factors (labor or capital) is assumed. This is not the case with
     the REGAL model. In this model the notion of complementarity of private and
     public capital is fundamental.
(4) The level of disaggregation of the public sector differs substantially among
     the models. In RENA disaggregation does not take place; BALAMO only deals

with road stock; in NRPEM four general classes of public capital have been distinguished; in REGAL eight public sectors have been distinguished. Obviously, a low level of disaggregation hampers the analysis of the effects of specific public investment projects.

(5) In all models, attention is paid to the role of public investments for the behavior of private enterprises. Obviously, public capital may also influence household behavior. For example, in REGAL and NRPEM attention is paid to the influence of infrastructure on migration.

(6) The simulation with MRMI indicates that the short-term (demand) effects of investments in infrastructure may be completely different from longer-run (attractiveness) effects. This indicates the importance of a dynamic analysis.

(7) No uniform conclusions can be drawn about the size of the attractiveness effects of investments. MRMI and RENA indicate small effects, whereas the other models give rise to the conclusion that substantial effects will arise.

7 Conclusions

At the end of various sections we have formulated observations that will not be repeated here. We will confine ourselves to some conclusions of a more general nature.

(1) In Sections 4-6, the contributions of about a third of the models included in the survey have been discussed with respect to the problem of instrumental effectiveness. There are various reasons why the other models have not been discussed: some models are not yet fully operational, some are not intended for policy studies, in some cases insufficient documentation is available, etc.

(2) From conclusion (1), we see that ME models do not give definite conclusions with regard to policy debates concerning labor versus capital subsidies, work-to-workers or workers-to-work policies, the role of direct controls, etc.

(3) In some cases, more definite conclusions can be derived from model simulations (see below).
    (a) Given the present level of investment subsidies considered, the effects of subsidies are small compared with the effects of autonomous variables (observation (1) in Section 5).
    (b) The notion that there is a general trade-off between national efficiency and regional equity is not confirmed by the models. In various experiments it appears possible to increase efficiency and equity simultaneously (observations (1) in Section 4 and (3) in Section 5).
    (c) In various model experiments, uniform policies at the national level give rise to substantially varying effects for the regions (observation (2) in Section 4).

(4) In the experiments, insufficient attention is paid to uncertainties concerning instrumental effectiveness. Uncertainties may arise from sources such as the stochastic nature of parameters, specification errors, and uncertainties about the future development of autonomous variables. In some experiments the latter source of uncertainties is treated (observation (2) in Section 5), but the other sources remain almost unmentioned (observations (3) in Section 4 and (6) in Section 5).

(5) Most studies of the instrumental effectiveness of multiregional models are of an *ex ante* nature (observations (6) in Section 4 and (1) in Section 5). This may be a surprise, since there are various reasons why an *ex post* analysis is easier to perform than an *ex ante* one (see Section 2). On the other hand, an *ex post* analysis may clearly give rise to less welcome results for both policy makers and model builders.

(6) Concerning the time span of the policy analyses, we note that in general it does not exceed 15 years. This means that ME models have only been used for short- and medium-term analyses up to now. Another finding is that the short- and medium-term effects of policy measures may differ considerably (observations (4) in Section 4 and (6) in Section 6). This indicates that models that do not allow one to study short- and medium-term effects separately (e.g., static models), are less adequate for certain policy analyses.

References

Ballard, K.P., and R.M. Wendling (1980), The national-regional impact evaluation
  system, *Journal of Regional Science*, 20, 143-158.
Ballard, K.P., N.J. Glickman, and R.M. Wendling (1980), Using a multiregional
  econometric model to measure the spatial impacts of federal policies, in N.J.
  Glickman (ed.), *The Urban Impacts of Federal Policies* (Johns Hopkins University
  Press, Baltimore, MD), pp. 192-216.
Ballard, K.P., R.D. Gustely, and R.M. Wendling (1980), *National-Regional Impact
  Evaluation System* (US Department of Commerce, Bureau of Economic Analysis,
  Washington, DC).
Biehl, D. *et al.* (1980), *The Contribution of Infrastructure to Regional Development*
  (EEC Report, Brussels).
Bogaert, H., T. de Biolley, R. de Falleur, and P. Hugé (1979), L'utilisation du
  modèle RENA pour l'analyse des consequences régionales des choix techniquement
  possible du plan Belge 1976-1980, in R. Courbis (ed.), *Modèles Régionaux et
  Modèles Régionaux-Nationaux* (Editions Cujas, Paris), pp. 123-133.
Bolton, R. (1980), Multiregional models in policy analysis: a survey, in F.G. Adams
  and N.J. Glickman (eds.), *Modeling the Multiregional Economic System* (Lexington
  Books, Lexington, MA).
Courbis, R. (1977), Regional models in French economic planning, in A. Straszak and
  B.V. Wagle (eds.), *Models for Regional Planning and Policy-Making* (International
  Institute for Applied Systems Analysis, Laxenburg, Austria), pp. 117-141.
Courbis, R. (1979), The REGINA model, *Regional Science and Urban Economics*, 9,
  117-139.
Despontin, M. (1980), *Kwantitatieve Economische Politiek vanuit een Besluitvormings-
  optiek* (Free University, Brussels).
Dresch, S.P., and D.A. Updegrove (1980), IDIOM: a disaggregated policy-impact model
  of the US economy, in R.H. Haveman and K. Hollenbeck (eds.), *Microeconomic
  Simulation Models for Public Policy Analysis*, Vol. 2 (Academic Press, NY),
  pp. 213-249.
de Falleur, R., H. Bogaert, T. de Biolley, and P. Hugé (1975), Use of the RENA
  model for forecasting the main lines of medium-term economic policy, in *Use of
  Systems of Models in Planning* (United Nations, NY), pp. 262-288.
Folmer, H. (1980), Measurement of the effects of regional policy instruments, *Envi-
  ronment and Planning A*, 12, 1191-1202.
Fukuchi, T. (1978), Analyse economico-politique d'un développement régional harmonisé,
  in *Collections de l'Insée* (Serie C), 61,227-253.
Golladay, F., and R. Haveman (1977), *The Economic Impact of Tax Transfer Policy*
  (Academic Press, NY).
Granholm, A. (1981), *Interregional Planning Models for the Allocation of Private
  and Public Investments* (University of Gothenburg, Department of Economics,
  Gothenburg).
Harris, Jr., C.C. (1980), New developments and extensions of the multiregional
  multi-industry forecasting model, *Journal of Regional Science*, 20.
Hilewick, C.L., E. Deak, and E. Heinze (1980), A Simulation of communications and
  transportation investments, *Growth and Change*, 11, 16-38.
Kawashima, T. (1977), Regional impact simulation model BALAMO: for government budget
  allocation policy in Japan, in A. Straszak and B.V. Wagle (eds.), *Models for
  Regional Planning and Policy-Making* (International Institute for Applied Sys-
  tems Analysis, Laxenburg, Austria), pp. 152-180.
Kirschen, E.S., J. Benard, and H. Besters (1964), *Economic Policy in our Time*
  (North-Holland, Amsterdam).
Kuenne, R.E. (1963), *The Theory of General Economic Equilibrium* (Princeton University
  Press, Princeton, NJ).
Malinvaud, E. (1968), *Statistical Methods of Econometrics* (North-Holland, Amsterdam).
Milne, W.J., N.J. Glickman, and F.G. Adams (1980), A framework for analyzing re-
  tional growth and decline: a multiregional econometric model of the United
  States, *Journal of Regional Science*, 20, 173-189.
Moore, B., and J. Rhodes (1974), The effects of regional economic policy in the
  United Kingdom, in M. Sant (ed.), *Regional Policy and Planning for Europe*
  (Saxon House, Farnborough, UK).

Nijkamp, P. (1982a), Long Waves or Catastrophes in Regional Development, in *Socio-Economic Planning Sciences* (forthcoming).

Nijkamp, P. (1982b), A multidimensional analysis of regional infrastructure and economic development, *Research Memorandum* (Free University, Department of Economics, Amsterdam).

Nijkamp, P., and P. Rietveld (1980), Towards a Comparative Study of Multiregional Models, *IIASA Working Paper* WP-80-172 (International Institute for Applied Systems Analysis, Laxenburg, Austria).

Nijkamp, P., and P. Rietveld (1982), Soft econometrics as a tool for regional discrepancy analysis, *Papers of the Regional Science Association* (forthcoming).

Nota Regionaal Sociaal-Economisch Beleid, 1982-85 (1981) (Staatsuitgeverij, The Hague).

Openshaw, S. (1979), A methodology for using models for planning purposes, *Environment and Planning A*, 11, 879-896.

Paelinck, J.H.P., and P. Nijkamp (1976), *Operational Theory and Method in Regional Economics* (Saxon House, Farnborough, UK).

Pleeter, S. (1980), *Economic Impact Analysis* (Martinus Nijhoff, The Hague).

Rietveld, P. (1980), *Multiple Objective Decision Methods and Regional Planning* (North-Holland, Amsterdam).

Rietveld, P. (1981), *Causality Structures in Multiregional Economic Models*, IIASA Working Paper WP-81-50 (International Institute for Applied Systems Analysis, Laxenburg, Austria).

Rietveld, P. (1982), *A Review of Multiregional Economic Models*, IIASA Collaborative Paper CP-82-7 (International Institute for Applied Systems Analysis, Laxenburg, Austria).

Suzuku, N., F. Kimura, and Y. Yasuyuki (1978), *Regional Dispersion Policies and Their Effects on Industries--Calculation Based on an Interregional Input-Output Model* (Version II) (Mitsubishi Research Institute, Tokyo).

Tinbergen, J. (1956), *Economic Policy: Principles and Design* (North-Holland, Amsterdam).

Treyz, G.I. (1980), Design of multiregional policy analysis model, *Journal of Regional Science*, 20, 191-206.

Treyz, G.I., and G.E. Duguay (1980), Endogenous wage determination: its significance for state policy analysis models, *Paper presented at the New Jersey State Economic Conference, April*.

Treyz, G.I., R.E. Williams, G.E. Duguay, and B.H. Stevens (1980), An overview of the MEPA model and its use from 1977 through 1980, prepared for a conference, *An Assessment of the State-of-the-Art in Regional Modeling, April*.

Van Delft, A., and W. Suyker (1981), Regional investment subsidies: an estimation of the labor market effects for the Dutch regions, *Paper presented at the XXI European Congress of the Regional Science Association, Barcelona, August*.

Wold, H. (1954), Causality and econometrics, *Econometrica*, 22, 162-177.

CHAPTER 6

MULTIREGIONAL ECONOMIC MODELS IN DIFFERENT PLANNING
AND MANAGEMENT SYSTEMS

Boris Issaev

1   Introduction

The purpose of this paper is to discuss the impacts of different systems of
planning regional development on existing practices in the elaboration and implementation of multiregional economic (ME) models. The main discussion is based on
the experience of the USSR with some references to regional modeling in France under
an "indicative" system of planning.
    Economic modeling in the USSR in the area of regional development is concen-
trated mainly in two kinds of organization: in research institutes of the USSR
Academy of Sciences and of its territorial branches; and in research institutions
of central and territorial planning authorities which are part of the system of
"Gosplan" (the State Planning Commission). A substantial proportion of economic
modeling is carried out in educational institutions (universities and specialized
institutes) but their links with actual planning and management bodies are weaker
than those of research institutions.

2 Regional Planning Systems in the USSR

    The problem of organization of interactions between regions in the socioeco-
nomic development of the USSR, i.e., interregional relations, is important in the
USSR planning system, but this is not a major problem. The main problems of socioeconomic development of the country are decided upon in the center and from the
point of view of interests of the whole nation. A centralized planning and management system is first realized through a sectoral approach. The territorial dimension in national plans is represented by a specific part of the plan, as a set of
documents organized on a territorial basis. In addition, all other parts of the
national plan also have a territorial breakdown, which means that targets are identified by regions and their fulfilment is controlled by regional authorities. The
relations between regional systems and the national economy as a whole are realized
as a dialogue in the course of coordination of central directives and regional plan
targets.
    The fundamental feature of the planning system in the USSR and other socialist
countries is that the term "planning" includes all activities ensuring the fulfilment of the plan targets. A planning system is theoretically the form in which the
socioeconomic system functions, and the organization of objective elements of real
production systems. In market economies the actual functioning mechanism is independent of planning. Therefore, plans are "indicative", in that they are not inherent parts of the real socioeconomic system. This fundamental difference between
socialist- and market-type planning is relevant for all specific modifications of
the forms of planning (goal oriented programs, current overall planning, etc.).
    The scheme of regional development planning and management within the national
system may, in very broad terms be reflected by Figure 1. The development of each
specific regional system in the USSR is actually determined by the state through
two channels:

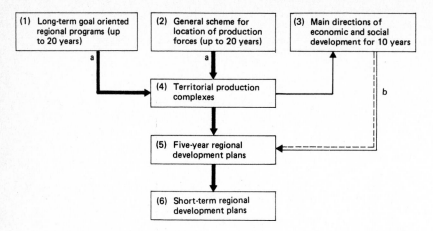

Figure 1. Main elements in regional development planning in the USSR

(1)   predominantly in the framework of territorial production complexes (TPC)
      generated as a form of implementation of a long-term goal oriented program
      (depicted by links a);
(2)   in the framework of current medium- and short-term plans of regional develop-
      ment which are parts of the current national plans (links b).

The synthesizing function for these two channels is contained in the five-year
plans of socioeconomic development of each region. The actual decisions with respect to regional development, use of all kinds of regional and national resources,
and relations of the given region with others, are based finally either on provi-
sions of long-term goal oriented programs or on a general scheme for the location
of productive forces.

      The core problem in each goal oriented territorial program is always important
for the whole nation; therefore, the elaboration of such programs involves interactions between regional and national authorities and the implementation of it affects interregional and regional-national interdependences. The following examples
of core problems may be quoted: oil and gas extraction in western Siberia, erection
of hydropower plants in Bratsk and Ust-Ilimsk, construction of the Baikal-Amur railway line in eastern Siberia, brown-coal extraction in the Kansk-Achinsk area, etc.

      The role of planning, based on long-term goal oriented regional programs (links
a in Figure 1), has drastically increased since the mid-1950s, when the large-scale
development of new energy resources and the building of energy consuming industries
began. It became clear that within traditional forms of current planning these
problems, which had a clear national-regional dimension and were intersectoral in
nature, could not be resolved in a satisfactory manner.

      The development of a long-term goal oriented program began with the existing
level of current planning, where the potential goals may to some extent be taken
into account. Acceptance of the program implies that an actual TPC as a specific
spatial organization of production forces is created. After they reach the maximal
possible level, goal oriented activities of the TPC begin to be replaced by traditional mechanisms determined by the current planning system. But the latter gradually reorients the main goal of the program within the gradually changing structure
of the regional system. Thus, the goal orientation of current planning is increasing. When the goal of the long-term program is achieved, the TPC loses its specific
functions and continues to exist as a set of production and social objectives under
the system of current planning.

      Considering the objective impacts of goal oriented programs in economic model-
ing the following properties of this procedure should be noted:

national criteria behind the main goal;
explicit goal orientation;
scalarized quantification of possible goals;
long-term time horizon and dynamic relations;
hierarchical relations including national level;
focus on main streams of activities leading to achievement of the goal, less
    attention to overall economic balance of the regional system;
explicit distinction between local and central decision making centers in the
    identification of model variables;
predominant *ad hoc* character of main elements and tools of analysis.

The current system of medium-term (five-year) and short-term (one-year) planning (CP) is based on a set of very detailed standardized instructions; it is organized as a dialogue between local and central planning bodies of the goals, formulated in the directions of economic and social development of the country as
suggested by the highest party and state authorities. Plan targets have the status
of legislative solutions; they are compulsory and directly determine economic activities of production units. Regional plans are elaborated for administrative terri-
tories of the USSR (republics and other lower-level areas). Plans relating to
regional development within the whole system of national economic planning are
shown in Figure 2, from which it is evident that regional development planning is
one of the two dimensions of the whole system of planning:

sectoral (from economic units to the industries); and
territorial (from smallest administrative zones to republics).

It is also evident that each regional plan is intersectoral. Orientation of plans
on a system of management is also explicit in this scheme. Addressees of plans are
national or republican ministries or administrative bodies at the lowest level. The
number of current regional planning schemes in the USSR amounts to 191, ranging from
four macroregions down to districts (the largest unit in current regional planning
is the republic). The plans are very wide in scope and contain detailed descriptions of each particular aspect of the regional reality.
    Table 1 shows the coverage of the five-year plans in terms of main groups of
economic and social indicators in some centrally planned economies. Current regional development plans in all countries listed have a very wide coverage, and
are biased towards physical aspects of the economy, strongly emphasized social targets, land and water resources, productive and social infrastructure. In all efforts
to analyze regional inequalities through multiregional modeling, the models should
be linked with the current planning system rather than with long-term goal oriented
programs.
    In centrally planned economies spatial planning documents are elaborated that
determine demand and supply of the most important material resources within each
region, as well as the explicit system of delivery of each item from producer to
consumer. In the USSR the central planning body elaborates balances for up to 2000
kinds of goods. At the level of authorities responsible for actual supply of production units with all kinds of primary and intermediate consumption goods, the
number may amount to more than 13,000. This planning activity at central and local
levels is associated with an elaboration of a matrix of interregional commodity
flows which is used as the basis of transportation planning. Thus, the interregional approach forms part of current practice in the joint planning of material
supply and transportation.
    One important methodological peculiarity of regional planning in the USSR,
which is relevant for the development of multiregional modeling, is the accounting
frame for overall regional plans. This frame is represented in the form of a so-
called "balance of the national economy"; its system of balance-type tables is
elaborated for both national and regional (republic) levels, and regional balances
add up to the national ones. The only exception is the table for financial resources and expenditures which is not elaborated at the republican level. In each
republic the following balances as planning documents are compiled:

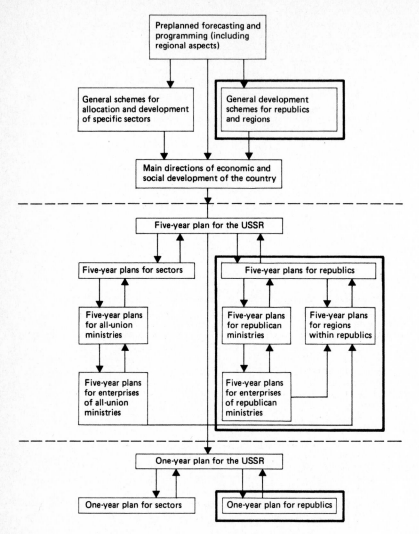

Figure 2. System of plans in the USSR

     balance of production and use of social product;
     balance of production, distribution, and redistribution of national income;
     balance of fixed productive funds;
     balance of monetary income and outlay of the population;
     balance of labor resources.

Balances relating to production activities are established in terms of production sectors based on the concept of "enterprises" (a sectoral approach within each republic).

    Interindustrial flow balances of the Leontiev type are actually elaborated for the plan horizon in every republic, but they are not entered into the formal plan; they serve rather as analytic support for elaboration of production programs for the industrial sector. Balances of social product and national income are not methodologically compatible with input-output interindustry balances.

Table 1. Main groups of indicators in the five-year regional development plans†

Groups of indicators	USSR	Bulgaria	Hungary	DDR	Poland	Czecho-slovakia
Population		x	x	x	x	x
Labor resources	x	x	x	x	x	x
Employment	x	x	x	x	x	x
Payroll for sectors	x			x	x	
Balance of monetary income and outlays of the population	x	x	x	x		
Industrial outputs by sectors	x	x	x	x		x
Agricultural outputs	x	x	x	x	x	x
Agricultural area		x		x	x	x
Forestry		x	x	x	x	x
Volume and structure of capital investments	x	x		x		x
Transport network		x	x	x	x	x
Communications		x	x	x	x	x
Water supply system		x	x	x	x	x
Energy resources		x	x	x		
Storage capacities			x			
Housing stock	x	x	x	x	x	x
New dwellings	x	x	x	x	x	x
Supply of social services	x	x	x	x	x	x
Number of beds in hospitals per 10,000 persons	x	x	x	x	x	x
Number of doctors per 10,000 persons	x	x	x	x	x	x
Number of places in social servicing institutions			x	x		x
Recreation activities, tourism		x		x		x
Education	x	x	x	x		x
Volume of marketable services	x		x	x		x
Retail trade turnover	x		x	x		x
Protection of the environment	x	x	x	x		x

†Table reproduced from Paseczny, L. (1981) *Comparative Analysis of Systems of Regional Planning in Separate Countries* (International Research Institute for Problems of Management, Moscow).

A firm directive from the planning authorities to the model builders demands adaptation of the models to indicator systems provided by official planning regulations and to existing systems of information used for planning. Two computerized systems, now in the course of development at the regional level, substantially determine the requirements of economic modeling:

> the computerized system of planning (ASPR); and
> the computerized system of management at the republican level (RASU).

The first system is based on the direct production of documents for medium- and short-term plans, the second, on the operative monitoring fulfilment of regional plans. This tendency in the development of the system of national and regional planning objectively influences the development of modeling in the sense that models should be finally included into ASPR and should also be based on information available in RASU.

For the relation of multiregional modeling to the current system of medium- and short-term planning (link b in Figure 1), the following should be noted. As compared with the system GOP $\Rightarrow$ TPC, the system CP has no clearly pronounced scalarized goal. The theory of socialism and the pressure of acute economic problems determine the goal orientation of the current regional planning system. In most cases it is not a transition and restructuring, but balanced growth with adjustments towards better solutions to current problems of individual regions. The main criteria behind current planning are volumes of output under resources constraints. Inertia in production activities or levels of output is one of the determinants for plan targets.

In the current planning there is not such a drastically pronounced predominance of national criteria as in long-term goal oriented regional programs. The planning procedure is a dialogue between regional and national levels. The position of a regional partner in this dialogue is determined predominantly by social criteria and achieved level of production as well as by protection of the environment.

As compared with *ad hoc* models that support decision making under long-term goal oriented programs, current planning models should satisfy very severe requirements to be used effectively. These requirements relate to

> degree of integration between different aspects, because planning is integrated;
> interface with users, who should communicate with the model in their own language;
> information;
> standardization, because the models should be included in the computerized systems ASPR and RASU.

3 Multiregional Modeling in the USSR--Main Development Trends

In contrast to the experience of countries with market economies, where development of national planning systems evolved parallel to progress in economic modeling, in the USSR planning has a history of many decades whereas the extensive economic modeling only began in the early 1960s. Historically, input-output models played, in the analysis of integrated regional development, a predominant role that was in fact even more important than in modeling production processes at the national level. This is due to the fact that national macroeconomic and sectoral analysis was traditionally based on the balance of the national economy, which in socialist countries is an equivalent of national accounting. The quality of balances of the national economy at the regional level was not good enough in all republics because the system of indicators was not sufficiently interlinked. The compilation of input-output tables for all republics in 1966 and 1972 strongly stimulated intraregional and multiregional modeling. Now the modified input-output models constitute a methodological basis for regional development modeling. The other most widely used tool in development models is linear programming, which is also traditionally linked with works of Kantorovich.

In the USSR the first optimized multiregional models were developed by Kossov (1963) and Aganbegian (1963). Fundamental problems of a mathematical description of an optimized interregional system were elaborated but there was no empirical implementation of these models. The first experimental multiregional analysis based on a mathematical model was carried out in 1967 by A. Granberg of the Institute of Economics and Organization of Industry in the Siberian Branch of the Academy of Sciences of the USSR. The model is described in Granberg (1973). The name given to this model in the literature is "OMMM", which is the Russian abbreviation for optimized interregional interindustrial model (Granberg himself referred to it as SYREN-OPT).

This first aspect of interregional modeling associated with Professor Granberg is a concept called "interregional interactions". The basic feature of this concept is a regional approach to multiregional modeling in a one-level system (note that SYREN-OPT is discussed elsewhere in this volume).

Experimental work with interregional models has also been done in the Council on Studies of Productive Forces of the State Planning Committee of the USSR (CSPF) in 1971 where another approach to modeling was used. These works, supervised by Nikolaev, had a clear production allocation orientation (see Nikolaev 1971).

The third type of interregional model was theoretically developed and realized in the Central Economics and Mathematical Institute of the Science Academy of the USSR in the period from 1972 to 1980. Theoretical backgrounds were formulated initially by E. Baranov, V. Danilov-Daniljan, and M. Zavelski (Baranov *et al.* 1971); the version of the model implemented by the end of the 1970s was developed by E. Baranov and I. Matlin. The main conceptual peculiarity of this approach is the hierarchical and multiaspect structure of the system obtained. The latest version of this model is called SMOTR (abbreviation of Russian title "Coordination of sectoral and regional decisions"), described in Chapter 11.

Together with the major model products developed under the leadership of A. Granberg and E. Baranov, other original multiregional models should be mentioned:

(i) model "east-west" for distribution of centralized resources between the respective parts of the USSR. The methodological idea of the model consists in an interactive reconciliation between two autonomous LP models through equalization of dual values of common resources in each system (see Granberg and Chernyshev 1970);

(ii) a model with regional response functions (Marjasov and Suslov 1980). In this model structural characteristics of regional systems in terms of input-output relations are replaced by regional functions explicitly linking outcoming parameters with incoming ones that come from the upper level. At the regional level the value of the vector of productive activity of the region is determined so that the maximum of the function is achieved; this depends on two vectors--constraints on national resources and export-import balances.

The model developed by S. Nikolaev dealt with the location of 25 groups of products in five large economic zones. The main features of the CSPF model are:

this is an LP model of input-output type;
only the problem of location of material production is solved under exogenously given growth rates of output and proportions at the national level;
objective function is thus minimum of production and transportation costs at fixed prices, wages, and tariffs;
products considered in the model do not exhaust the whole material production;
no inputs in transportation are taken into account;
the model is static;
final demand in regions and at the national level is fixed exogenously.

This model, although it deals with regional and national economies, could hardly be classified as a multiregional one in the sense stipulated in the introduction to this chapter because the regions here are not considered as decision making centers and only links from the center to regions optimized by the centers' criteria are analyzed. Interregional links are determined in the CSPF model only for the transportation of goods.

The system of models (SMOPP and SMOTR) are clearly ASPR (computerized system of planning) oriented tools of multiregional and multiaspect optimal planning, developed in close contact with regional and central planning authorities and planning research institutions, and experimentally implemented in the computing center of the GOSPLAN.

4 Some Implications of the Centralized System of Planning in the USSR in Multiregional Modeling

All multiregional models considered or mentioned in this chapter have an explicit bearing on the centralized system of national economic planning. The idea of regional development from the "center" is characteristic not only of SMOTR, which, by definition is a national model, but also for SYREN-OPT. The latter, although a single-level multiregional model, is entirely addressed to central planning authorities, providing them with the information about what would happen in regions under different scenarios for national productive policy and how to use regional constraints and organize their mutual relations through flows of goods to get the best common results. SMOTR can more easily include regions as autonomous subsystems having their own decision making centers than SYREN-OPT. The regional blocks in this system are interpreted as representative for independent partners acting on the basis of their own criteria. But this system of models is also addressed to the central planning authority and is not oriented to serve republican planners in their policy formulation as a response to conditions in other regions and to central decisions. Thus, the "central" bias in the best and most elaborate models in the USSR is obvious.

The directive character of the Soviet national planning system is reflected in the predominance of normative regional development models. The preference for linear programming techniques may be also attributed to this factor. It is assumed that whatever optimization criteria were chosen, the authorities would have sufficient means to achieve them in the conditions given by the solution of optimization problems. The model objective functions are not derived from the analysis of the actual motivation of the behavior of socioeconomic actors, but are rather prescribed by the system; models are deterministic.

The direct link between the planning and management system in the USSR and the state of ME modeling is also seen in the degree of challenge. SMOTR has no precedents. Only in a society where the production process is based on state property and is *directly* managed by the state at all levels can these models, which require an enormous amount and variety of data and which link central decisions with details from regional systems, be useful for practical needs.

Considering multiregional models developed and tested in the USSR in the context of actual planning and management of regional development, one should notice that modeling efforts have not yet succeeded in linking intraregional developments with the multiregional environment and central decision making for regions. This link actually exists but in the planning system it is realized through traditional, not model-based, procedures. The multiregional models serve planning needs only for the central authorities.

There are strong efforts to introduce economic modeling into regional planning and management systems and to develop appropriate computerized information systems for regional decision making. It is evident, as Soviet model builders are aware, that the long-term intraregional models supporting regional decision making should be linked with models of the same type as of SYREN-OPT or SMOTR. This is necessary to support the dialogue between regional and national authorities in formulating economic policies and elaborating regionalized plans for national development. This will be done in the context of further extension and improvement of ASPR to integrate regional and national level computerized socioeconomic information systems.

Considering the practical use of existing multiregional models in the planning procedure in the USSR, one should state that multiregional models have not yet entered into current operative use in the planning system. This does not mean that the models are not adequate; it means that further efforts from the two sides are required: from the scientific institutions formulating models and from the authorities responsible for the development of ASPR and computerized information systems.

All models referred to above have been experimentally implemented for the pre-
planned analysis carried out *within planning bodies*. ASPR should be developed to
make it capable of incorporating multiregional models. The intersection of the two
areas above is not properly elaborated as yet (see Figure 3). Tendencies in multiregional modeling reflect this orientation of ASPR. Models tend to operate with
economic indicators that are either direct plan targets or some clear combination
of them. They are also based on the present regionalization of the country in
regional development planning:

15 union republics;
19 economic regions, of which six coincide with union republics or are
combinations of them and 13 republics are subdivisions of the two republics
--Russian and Ukrainian;
four macrozones;

and tend to rely basically on standardized information that is currently used for
planning. There is also a clear tendency (especially in the case of SMOTR models)
to develop an interactive interface of planners with the models in the language of
planners, as well as to create standardized databanks.

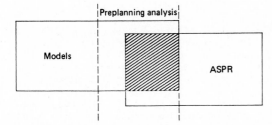

Figure 3.

ASPR has been developed basically as a computerization of work on the elaboration of plans in the framework of existing regulations and instructions for planning
procedures. By definition, the main goal of ASPR is to produce, on the basis of
computerized calculations, an analysis of series of versions of draft plans at all
levels--national, republican, local--and both for sectoral and territorial dimensions of the plan. Functional subsystems of ASPR are oriented towards the elaboration of all parts of the current plan and of long-term goal oriented programs.
Practically, a set of concrete problems is currently being solved in the course of
functioning ASPR. Multiregional models should be one specific set of problems in
ASPR.
As was shown above, the two main multiregional models SYREN-OPT and SMOTR are
based either directly on input-output tables or on their derivatives. This methodological peculiarity of models, which is quite reasonable *per se*, presents serious
problems for integrating models with ASPR. The Soviet system of planning is based
on a large number of so-called material balances for each group of important products. All targets of plans determining what should be produced and delivered and
to whom are precisely addressed to decision making centers--enterprises, ministries,
local and republican authorities, etc. The synthesized targets of the plan as mentioned in Section 2 are elaborated within the accounting frame of the balance of
the national economy, in which sectors and other groups of economic agents are
formed from real units as decision making centers and addressees of the plan. All
these are methodologically incompatible with "pure branches" of input-output models
and with the nonaddressed nature of its indicators and technological coefficients.
Multiregional modeling therefore tends to overcome this methodological obstacle
through the introduction of a clear product dimension into the input-output model,
in which products combine those items that are objects of material balances in the

planning system. In SMOTR, so-called "integrated product value input-output balances" are used, where the product part is detailed and the value part is elaborated
in terms of financial indicators of the traditional form for plans of production
units.

The centralized planning system in the USSR is production-based. Although the
overall goal of production systems is to satisfy the growing material and intellectual needs of the population, the actual plan targets are determined on the basis
of the production levels achieved in each sector and on the direct needs for that
sector's output in other sectors. Thus, the resource distribution approach is predominant in the planning, as is reflected in multiregional modeling. The models do
not describe production response to monetary demand of final consumers, but analyze
the distribution of existing resources among sectors and regions.

From this "direct distribution" approach stems another specific feature of
Soviet multiregional models: they are essentially physical and do not consider
phenomena and behavior generated by monetary factors. Even when financial indicators corresponding to financial parts of the plans are included into the model
(SMOTR), they reveal direct production implications rather than financial and monetary mechanisms which have effects on the behavior of production sectors.

5   Some Comparative References to Multiregional Modeling Under
    "Indicative Planning" in France

A remarkable model product for multiregional analysis has been elaborated in
France by Professor R. Courbis and his colleagues--the model REGINA, although there
are also other models used in regional development planning in France.

It is relevant to compare links between the planning system and regional economic modeling in the USSR with those of France, not only in order to understand
better the existing models, but also to draw benefits from the common experience.
French models are well known in the USSR due to active scientific exchange between
the two countries. Formalized procedures in the French planning system are based
on a set of models including a central real financial model (FiFi and then the DMS)
a model describing the international environment of France (MOISE), models for
administration, for specific sectors, for employment, and for regional development.
(Literature on French models is extensive. An exhaustive bibliography is contained
in Sautter and Baba 1978.)

For regional development planning, three types of analysis are carried out.

(a) *National to regional*--in the course of which the results of calculations
     based on the "central" model are disaggregated by 21 planning regions.
     Analysis is focused on employment distributed by industries and regions.
     No specific models are used; mainly time-series analysis is employed.
(b) *Intraregional*--consisting in simulating developments for each region. Model
     SDR (simulation of regional development) is used to determine for each region
     employment, migration, and equilibrium on the labor market under exogenous
     constraints on production and investment activities. In the regional-national
     dialogues this model has been used for discussion about adaptation of the
     activities of educational institutions to the regions' needs for qualified
     labor and for analysis of the regional demand for housing.
(c) *Integrated national-regional analysis*--the main goal of which is to reconcile
     developments and constraints of five large regions with projections of devel-
     opment estimated for the whole country. The basic tool here is the model
     REGINA, which incorporates the physicofinancial approach characteristic of
     the central models FiFi and DMS, and contains explicit feedbacks from regions
     to the nation.

Fundamental differences in factors affecting multiregional modeling, stemming from
the different types of economy and planning systems, should be pointed out--see
Table 2.

The major feature of the French economic planning system is the "indicative"
character of projections, which are committing only for the expenditures of the

Table 2. Factors of differences in modeling regional development in the USSR and
          France

		USSR	France
(1)	Economy and role of planning	Managed by state through plans whose fulfilment is compulsory. Predominantly administrative management.	Functioning on the basis of market mechanisms with strong regulating functions of the state, realized through financial channels.
		Problems of economic growth and raising living standards.	Typical problems of industrialized capitalist country, open to foreign competition.
(2)	Decision making center	Decision making at all levels is delegated by the state and determined mainly by plans. Extensive system of regional decision making centers. Independent decisions of households.	Decision making at the level of economic units, independent of state and of plans. Decision making for regional planning limited to public sector.
(3)	Coverage of planning	Exhaustive, with main emphasis on physical aspects.	Selective, changing in accordance with actual problems of socioeconomic development. Emphasis on income distribution processes.
		Regional planning focuses mainly on involvement of regional resources in economic turnover.	Main problem is regional development equalization.
(4)	Time horizon	Long-term, medium-term, short-term.	Medium-term.
(5)	Sets of planning tasks	Very extensive.	Very limited.
(6)	Instruments of economic policy	All targets of plan, financial incentives, and administrative decisions.	Limited to normatives of financial nature and to direct expenditures under prerogative of the state.

state. Plan targets are offered to independent decision makers who are guided in
their behavior by the situation of the market. The plan in France is external for
economic activities, whereas in the USSR the plan targets are direct commitments of
enterprises to society whose fulfilment is compulsory. The plan in the USSR is the
only guidance on what and how much to produce, to whom, at what prices to sell, and
from where to get intermediate goods. This guidance is jointly elaborated by all
participants in the production process. From this basic difference stems predominantly the normative character of planning models in the USSR and a descriptive
character in France. Models developed as planning tools in the USSR reflect the
strategy towards economic growth and the approach to planning from the use of resources and production side. French models, including regional models, are aimed
at simulating market mechanisms with the demand for consumption and investments as
determining factors for the level of economic activities. Special attention in

REGINA, as mentioned above, is given to analysis of competitiveness of regional production units. In aiming for perfection in models in the USSR the tendency is towards introducing further detail in models rather than introducing new mechanisms. The main mechanism behind central directive planning is the distribution of re- sources in physical terms. In France, the evolution of models was determined by a striving to understand better the market mechanisms, so that separate physical models have evolved to become integrated real financial models. This has been completed by the introduction of financial and monetary phenomena in the modeling. REGINA has been elaborated to the stage of evolution where the FiFi model was the culminating point in the economic modeling for planning purposes. Now REGINA is criticized for not giving enough attention to flows reflected in the TOF (Table of Financial Transactions in French national accounting).

Models in the USSR describe the national distribution of resources as a result of decisions about the plan. Decisions by production units are implicitly prede- termined by plan targets. Only households have independent behavior, and planning their activities, income, and expenditures involves behavioral functions. In French models, the behavior of economic agents in three markets (goods, labor, and capital) forms the mainstream of analysis.

The different scope of planning in the USSR and France is also reflected in the multiregional models. REGINA is actually the adaptation of a real financial flow model to the regional dimension which has led to a focusing of attention on regional factors. In multiregional models in the USSR, the tendency is to cover all parts of the national plan, which is exhaustive by definition. Social processes are better reflected in Soviet models (SMOTR).

Both in the USSR and France goal oriented programs play an important role in regional development planning, but the content and status of the programs in the actual decision making process is different. In the USSR the programs are not only projections; they are realized through a system of goal oriented activities of the state relating not only to regional production activities, but also to institutional organizations of territorial production complexes. In France programs are goal ori- ented for the expenditure of public funds. They are binding only for the public sector.

There are differences in modeling relating to policy variables and to technical problems connected with them. In the central directive planning system all plan targets may actually be considered as policy variables. Testing them means analyz- ing the response of the whole system to changing each plan target, so that no spe- cial problem of testing policy variables normally arises in multiregional modeling in the USSR. In France, where the choice of policy variables is limited mainly by financial variables, this problem is traditional in model building.

Despite fundamental differences in social organization and in economic planning and management, there are also many common problems in interregional modeling in the USSR and France, especially in the area of modeling social aspects of regional de- velopment, migration, demographic processes, and economic behavior of the population in different economic environments. The scientific exchange between model builders of the two countries is a very important factor in progress in modeling multire- gional interdependences.

References

Aganbegian, A. (1963), Economic-Mathematic Models of Prospective Planning, *Ph.D. Thesis*, University of Moscow.

Albegov, M.M., M.V. Golubitskaja, and D.G. Petuchov (1975), Optimization of Intra- regional Location of Industrial Production, in *Location Models of Production* (Nauka, Moscow).

Albegov, M.M., and I. Solodilov (1970), Problems of Orientation in Location of Sys- tems of Industrial Complexes, in *Economics and Mathematical Methods*, 6.

Baranov, E., V. Danilov-Daniljan, and M. Zavelski (1971), Theoretical and Method- ological Aspects of Optimization Prospective Planning, in *Proceedings of The First Conference on Optimal Planning and Management of the National Economy* (CEMI, Moscow).

Baranov, E., and I. Matlin (1981), *Methodological Principles of Developing a System of Models for Coordination of Sectoral and Regional Decisions* (CEMI, Moscow).

Granberg, A.G. (1973), *Optimization of Territorial Proportions of the National Economy* (Economica, Moscow).

Granberg, A.G. (ed.) (1975), *Interbranch Balances in the Analysis of Territorial Proportions in the USSR* (Nauka, Moscow).

Granberg, A., and A. Chernyshev (1970), Problem of Territorial Planning East-West, in *Izvestia, Siberian Branch of the Academy of Sciences of the USSR*, 6.

Kossov, V. (1963), Economic-Mathematical Model for Location of Production, in *Mathematical Methods and Problems of Location of Industries* (Economizdat, Moscow).

Les Collections de l'INSEE (1978), *La Planification en France et au Japan*, C, 61.

Marjasov, V., and V. Suslov (1980), Use of Resource Functions in Analysis of Territorial Proportions, in *Research in Interindustrial Territorial Proportions* (Novosibirsk).

Nikolaev, S.A. (1971), *Interregional and Intraregional Analysis of Industrial Location* (Nauka, Moscow).

Tsapkin, N. (ed.) (1972), *Planning of the National Economy in the USSR* (Mysl, Moscow).

PART B

TRENDS IN MULTIREGIONAL ECONOMIC MODELING

Introduction

In Part A of this book the current practice of ME modeling has been reviewed from a number of aspects. These reviews and evaluations were chosen to provide a set of cross-national comparisons. What is the current practice concerning the modeling of causality structures? How many models can be classified as truly inter-regional? What variants of modeling interregional trade are present? Is there a common practice of introducing policy levers into the model frameworks? In these reviews we have not attempted to identify and stress nationally motivated differences; instead we have given attention to the role of ME models in different planning and management systems.

In Part B of the book we wished to adopt another perspective. We asked a selection of knowledgeable scientists in the field of ME modeling from different countries to address two related questions. Their first task was to review, from their own personal perspectives, the existing body of ME models in North America, Western Europe, Eastern Europe, and the Pacific area. The second task was to indicate the major development trends, basically by way of examples. Even in this context we wished to refrain from a single-country orientation, although it was inevitable that in some instances the examples relate to experiences in individual countries. A further reason for this is that the presentation of the individual models is in most cases considerably more elaborate here than in Part A.

The authors had access to the material of the comprehensive survey to a varying extent. In some cases, as in the chapter by Uwe Schubert, the discussion might in fact be looked upon as a comparison of the treatment of labor market elements, while in other cases, such as in the chapter by Stephan Mizera, the outlook is specifically country oriented with a strong personal bias. In yet other cases, as in the chapter by Noboru Sakashita, an independent presentation of ongoing research and development is exemplified.

The two chapters covering developments in Western Europe, by Uwe Schubert and Raymond Courbis, are both oriented towards reviewing the current trends rather than giving examples of prospective developments. Schubert approaches the field from the point of view of modern labor market theory. Courbis gives a detailed comparison of experiences in France, Belgium, and the Netherlands, with regard to the degree of endogeneity of basic economic variables (wages, prices, unemployment).

The current trends in Eastern Europe are represented by one paper from Czecho-slovakia and two presentations of ongoing work in the Soviet Union. Stephan Mizera's chapter illustrates the paradigm of building models for planned systems, trying to incorporate econometric relationships into normative contexts. The chapter by Alexander Granberg shows the recent developments of the input-output technique in the Siberian branch of the regional model building family in the Soviet Union. The chapter by Edward Baranov and Igor Matlin gives a clear picture of the high level of ambition of the model development in the central planning system of the USSR. Their model, to some extent even specified mathematically, is the biggest and the most advanced in the whole survey.

Roger Bolton and T.R. Lakshmanan cover the current modeling trends in North America. The emphasis in their chapters is on the US research, but some comments on the Canadian efforts, which are considerable, are also included by Bolton. It is evident from both these chapters that the field of ME modeling is progressing very rapidly in North America at the moment, reflecting a shift in emphasis from urban analysis to multi- and interregional policy analysis.

The development trends in the Pacific Area are covered to a certain extent only in the chapter by Noboru Sakashita, who concentrates rather on some examples of major development projects in Japan, which have to some extent been inspired by access to new sources of input-output data. Due to space limitations, the Australian development work has been left out of the current international overview, although several elements can be found in the Appendix. A detailed review of the Australian research along the same lines as in the current survey can be found in Batten and Sharpe (1982).

We are aware that the choice of contributions to these overviews might imply a slight bias in the representativeness of the statements made and the conclusions drawn. This may be true even for the countries or country groups mentioned explicitly. It is even more so for those countries or country groups for which no research on ME modeling has been included. However, even if the ambition has not been to provide a complete worldwide coverage, we still believe that most of the relevant research has been identified.

Reference

Batten, D., and R. Sharpe (1982), An Overview of Regional and Multiregional Modeling in Australia, *IIASA Paper* CP-82-18 (International Institute for Applied Systems Analysis, Laxenburg, Austria).

CHAPTER 7

THE DEVELOPMENT OF MULTIREGIONAL ECONOMIC MODELS IN WESTERN EUROPE

Uwe Schubert

1 Introduction

It is the task of this chapter to provide the reader with a brief (and hence only superficial) overview of multiregional economic (ME) models available in Western Europe, and to highlight some of their special features. Particular emphasis will be placed on regional labor market problems and on the closely related structures of the population and labor supply models. Some attention will also be given to problems of regional demarcation and to policy aspects of ME models. The analysis will be based in particular on a set of ME models from ten West European countries (see Table 1).

The earliest attempts at quantitative multiregional analysis go back to the 1950s, when the by now "classical" problem of the disparities between the industrialized north of Italy and the rural Mezzogiorno became the focus of research efforts in Italy (Chenery *et al.* 1953, Ferrara 1976, Martellato 1980). An input-output approach was chosen, with the emphasis on the connection between investment, productive capacity and output, and on the final demand side of the interregional trade linkages. Since the labor force, particularly in the south of Italy, was certainly not a bottleneck for economic development, no elaboration of the labor market was attempted.

In the 1960s work on the regional level was started in many West European countries. The starting point seems to have been the already operating national econometric models. In this period of strong economic growth one of the major points of interest was the interregional allocation of resources, the improvement of which, it was hypothesized, should eliminate regional obstacles to national growth. From the evidence accumulated by the author, attempts to disaggregate the national models in the late 1960s seem to have been started in the Netherlands (van Hamel *et al.* 1979), Belgium (Thys-Clement *et al.* 1979), France (Courbis 1979) and West Germany (Thoss *et al.* 1981). In the early 1970s, under the impression of the worldwide stagflation phenomenon, many of these studies included analyses of the price sector of the economy. Courbis (1979) found strong evidence in favor of a "regional" inflation theory, in which the pressure of wage increases emanating from the "overcrowded" Paris region tended to push up production costs in other regions, in some of which employment suffered due to the loss of international competitiveness of the regional economy. Consequently, a negative influence was exerted on aggregate national unemployment figures.

The models created in the 1970s tend to show the influence of the persistent unemployment problems in Western Europe on the one hand, and the influence of the new "demoeconomics" (Rogers and Willekens 1978, Ledent 1980) on the other. Practically all models stemming from the period include an analysis of regional labor markets (or are simply interregional labor market models), where both the demand and supply side are analyzed separately. On the supply side, invariably, phenomena such as interregional migration and regional birth and death processes are investigated and modeled. It seems that the increased mobility of production factors such as capital, labor, and expertise, has led to more emphasis being placed on these points than previously.

Most of the models, particularly those developed recently, show a definite trend towards dynamic approaches. This is particularly true of the input-output type of models which were static in the 1960s and early 1970s. Just as in national modeling, the first step towards economic dynamics is to make the components of final demand endogenous and to apply econometric methods to find their determinants. This is of course particularly relevant in the case of investment (and capital as the connected stock variable) where the next logical step is to formulate production functions based on labor and capital (see, for instance, HESSEN, REGINA, MORSE, REGAL, and SERENA).

West European models reflect a fairly large variety of opinions about the homo-geneity of labor. Practically all models disaggregate labor, but the criteria of disaggregation vary. In some cases this disaggregation is a by-product of a specific approach. In the input-output models labor demand is determined by sector, the the-oretical reason behind this disaggregation is the claimed existence of technological differences. In demographic studies, age and sex groups are often distinguished to help assess stable behavioral patterns. In recent labor economic studies (e.g., Doeringer and Piore 1971, Reich *et al*. 1973) it is strongly suggested that a valid analysis has to take "dual" ("segmented") labor markets into account. This claimed stratification of the labor market can have several causes, one being along "human capital" lines. Educational achievement divides labor into distinct segments, mobil-ity between these strata being very limited. A second cause is more related to the labor demand side. Each economy, so it is claimed, has a "core" group of enter-prises that are large and usually concentrated in a monopolistic or oligopolistic market setting, and a "peripheral" group, in which firms are small and operate in a competitive market situation. The core sector of the economy, which is usually organized hierarchically, offers a large "internal" labor market where prices, costs, etc., it is argued, play no role, as opposed to the "external" labor market follow-ing more closely economic textbook rules. In general, very little empirical, econo-metric work along these lines seems to have been done. This is even more so with multiregional models, where the difficulties are even greater.

Some labor supply submodels have implicitly assumed limited mobility between different types of labor and thus some kind of labor market segmentation. The ear-liest work along these lines is found in Brown *et al*. (1978), where dependent and independent labor is distinguished. In REMO, segmentation is explicitly introduced, where the segments are defined by educational attainment. Mobility between these strata is only possible by means of entering the educational system again.

Another very recent development is the explicit treatment of energy and envi-ronmental quality problems in the framework of interregional modeling (e.g., Lesuis *et al*. 1980). It seems that this topic is particularly important in the most devel-oped, industrialized countries, where migration seems to be sensitive to environ-mental quality differences across regions even when these regions are fairly large. On a smaller spatial scale this phenomenon can already be observed during the "sub-urbanization process" (van de Berg *et al*. 1981). In the countries approaching a "disurbanization" stage of development this factor becomes even important for long-distance moves, while labor market variables tend to lose significance (e.g., REGAM). In earlier development stages, the latter tend to be of some importance (e.g., REMO, REGINA, RNEM, LPFM, etc.). It appears that large and comprehensive models are becoming less common. In particular some of the most recent studies do not attempt to formulate large-scale all-encompassing models, but rather focus on specific prob-lems. Could this be due to a definitely observable trend towards smaller research budgets or is there a real change of opinion?

2 Some Structural Differences and Similarities Between West European
   Interregional Models

Are there features that the models contained in this survey have in common? As mentioned above, practically all studies investigated contain a more or less elaborate analysis of the labor market. Let us hence first look at the structure of a hypothetical labor market model (see Figure 1). Some variant of Figure 1 can be found in many of the papers on which this chapter is based (e.g., Courbis 1979, Engelbrecht *et al*. 1979, van Hamel *et al*. 1979, Thys-Clement *et al*. 1979, Birg 1980, Schuler 1981, Schubert 1981, 1982).

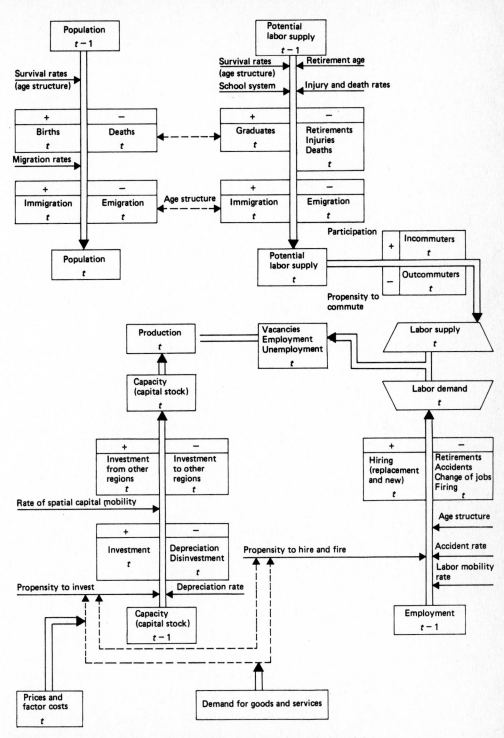

Figure 1. The structure of a hypothetical labor market model

Table 1. Modeling components and basic types of approaches

Country	Model	Labor supply: Population (P) labor supply (LS) submodel?	"Markov" type of constant transition rates	Approach via variable transition rates	"Econometric" type of approach: difference equations	Labor demand: Input-output approach	Labor demand: "Econometric" type of approach
Austria	REMO	yes (LS)		X			X
Belgium	RENA	yes (LS)		X			X
	SERENA	?		?			X
FRG	IMPE	yes (P, LS)	X (population, participation)		X (migration)		
	MIO	no				X	
	HESSEN	yes (P, LS)	X			X	
France	REGINA	yes (P, LS)		X (participation)	X (migration)		X
Italy	RNEM	yes (LS)		(participation)	X		X
	NORD-SUD	no (?)				X	
The Netherlands	REM	yes (P, LS)		X (participation)	X		X
	REGAM	yes (P, LS)		X		X	
	MEEEI	no				X	X
Norway	REGION	yes (P, LS)	X (participation, gross migration)	X		X	
Sweden	MORSE	no (?)	X			X	
	REGAL	yes (LS)				X	
	LPFM	yes (P, LS)	X (population)		X (migration)		X (?)
	GISSIR	no				X	
UK	IIOM	no				X	

The similarity between the population and labor supply models is particularly striking, probably due to the structure of the population accounting systems used for the European censuses, which often constitute the database for the models analyzed. When annual population registers are used, the definitions of the variables are often the same or at least fairly close to the ones used in the census, although there are substantial differences in the modeling approach.

One could distinguish two basic types of methods. One is to formulate the population and labor supply submodels as Markov chains in which transition probabilities ("rates", "propensities") between different "states" of the system have to be formulated. These "states" are often discrete decision alternatives in the microeconomic sense, such as labor market participation or nonparticipation, migration, commuting, and changing profession. These transition probabilities are either treated as constants (or are varied in the form of different scenarios in simulations) or are seen as variables, thus permitting various feedback links in the model. In the Markov approach the dynamics of the system are then fairly straightforward for constant transition probabilities.

The other approach formulates the relevant variables directly (in the form of difference equations) as depending on other endogenous or exogenous variables in the system. As is to be expected, this method is favored by econometricians. Table 1 provides an overview of the population and labor supply submodels and the basic approach chosen. On the demand side of the labor market a frequently used method to determine the level of labor demand is the input-output approach. In these studies the input coefficients are usually assumed to be fixed, although an exception can be found in GISSIR, where the input coefficients are in general variables. The most frequent disaggregation occurs along sectoral lines, but in some cases (e.g., REMO) both a rough sectoral as well as an educational achievement (or professional) breakdown is attempted. In most of the studies labor demand is not treated in a fully dynamic sense, as is often the case in manpower planning models (as indicated in Figure 1), which explicitly consider labor turnover, replacement demand, capacity extensions, etc. (e.g., Scanlon *et al*. 1977, pp. 305-332). The main reason for this is most likely the lack of regionalized data explicitly including these aspects.

A similar situation can be encountered in the analyses of investment. Two considerations usually have to be omitted, i.e., interregional flows of capital and the function of financial intermediaries in the spatial allocation of financial capital. Usually it is (tacitly) assumed that there are no spatial imperfections in the capital markets, that these markets are at least national (if not international) and that there is perfect spatial mobility of financial capital. Additionally it is often hypothesized that loan and credit conditions differ only because of policy measures such as investment subsidies (van Delft and Suyker 1981). Some attempts have been made to investigate the physical and financial capital transfers in connection with investment decisions, the "representative firm" being a multiregional enterprise (see e.g., de Bruyne and van Rompuy 1977, Granholm 1980, Schubert 1981). From an econometric point of view, the lack of interregional capital flow data enforces some kind of indirect "reduced form" approach. Another field still open for interregional modeling is the problem of technical progress and innovation diffusion. Despite the considerable body of literature on this topic, modeling attempts are rare, at least in Western Europe.

Substantial efforts have been made to take the interregional flows of goods and services into account. Many models contained in the survey deal with this problem in some way (e.g., HESSEN, MIO, MEEEI, RENA, and SERENA--for international trade--REGINA, RNEM, NORD-SUD, IIOM, MORSE, GISSIR, REGION, REMO).

Three basic approaches can be distinguished. In the input-output type of models a gravity model is sometimes applied to estimate the commodity flows (e.g., MIO and IIOM). Often constant trade coefficients are also used for this purpose (e.g., REGINA and NORD-SUD). A third approach related to the gravity model, is the utilization of a "demand potential", in which either the total level of demand is based on "space-discounted" regional incomes and prices, or the regional turnover depends on space-discounted regional incomes and production levels (spatial competition); e.g., REMO.

Table 2. Regionalization and data

Country	Model	Number of regions	Size and type of region
Austria	REMO	4	small (counties: core, ring, rural, peripheral)
Belgium	RENA	3	large (Wallonia, Bruxelles, Flanders)
	SERENA	3	large (Wallonia, Bruxelles, Flanders)
FRG	IMPE	79	small (counties)
	MIO	11 (6)	provinces (aggregated provinces)
	HESSEN	5	"planning regions of HESSEN"
France	REGINA	5 × 3	5 large (aggregated provinces); 3 small (rural, medium, urban)
Italy	RNEM	19	large
	NORD-SUD	2	very large
The Netherlands	REM	11	large (provinces)
	REGAM	11	large (provinces)
	MEEEI	2	very large (agglomeration, rural)
Norway	REGION	19	large
Sweden	MORSE	8	large
	REGAL	8	large
	LPFM	24 (300)	small
	GISSIR	8	large
UK	IIOM	11	large

Method of regionalization	Spatial exhaustiveness	Data basis
administrative + cluster analysis	yes	cross sections (1967-75)
administrative	yes	time series (1963-70)
administrative	yes	time series (1960-78)
administrative	yes	census (1961, 1971)
administrative	yes	cross section (1970)
administrative	yes (only for HESSEN)	time series (1960-75)
aggregation of similar regions, size threshold for small zones	yes	time series and cross sections (1959-75)
aggregation of some similar provinces	yes	time series (1951-68)
definition of problem areas and aggregation	yes	cross sections (1969, 1971)
administrative	yes	time series and
administrative	yes	cross sections (1955-80)
definition of problem areas (aggregation)	yes	cross section (1970)
planning regions	yes	cross section
planning regions	yes	point estimates
planning regions	yes	cross section (1975-77)
administrative (counties and municipalities)	yes	cross sections and time series (1970-80)
administrative (counties and municipalities)	yes	cross section (1968)
planning regions	yes	cross sections (1968)

3   Regionalization and Data

As can be seen in Table 2, the majority of models are based on fairly large
regions, such as "provinces" or their equivalents. In two cases (NORD-SUD and
MEEEI) the country is divided into only two regions; in other studies provinces are
aggregated (e.g., MIO and REGINA) to define a "relevant" region. This aggregation
is usually done to arrive at fairly "closed" areas, constituting relatively compact
economies. "Compactness" is usually defined in such a way as to internalize commuting (in some cases an urban area is also a province and the hinterland is added to
achieve compactness; e.g., MIO). The most common method of regionalization, however,
seems to be the use of planning areas and policy responsibilities as regions (usually provinces). Some models use comparatively small spatial units ("counties" or
their equivalents) as "regions" (e.g., IMPE and REMO). In some cases these smaller
regions are then grouped into types of regions (e.g., REGINA, LPFM, and REMO), such
as rural and urban areas. The reason for this procedure is often the lack of time
series, making the use of cross sections mandatory. Instead of assuming the same
behavioral parameters to be valid in the whole country, the data are stratified into
subsamples. It appears that formal, taxonomic algorithms are not frequently used to
define the model regions (see, e.g., Fischer 1981). Two reasons could be behind
this decision. When the basic observational units are only few (such as provinces),
taxonomic algorithms make little sense, as there is practically no allocation problem anyway. If many small units are used, then there is either time series information available that permits the estimation of individual parameters, or in the
cross section case there are intrinsic problems of forecasting. To illustrate this
point, let us consider a region classified as "rural" in the past--its future development, for example, goes in the direction of an (sub)urbanized area. What parameters should be used for forecasting and when should a shift occur?

Even if comparatively large regions are used, the compactness of the described
regional economic system may very well decrease in the course of economic development. Commuting distances tend to stretch with higher development levels and the
overlapping of regions is likely to increase. New growth poles (e.g., in border
regions that disappear with economic integration) have a similar effect; the model
regions should be redefined. In the case of medium-term forecasting models this
problem is not very serious (most model makers define the time scope of their work
as "medium-range"), but for long-run forecasting this difficulty has to be dealt
with. A feasible strategy is to construct the model including a dynamic commuting
submodel with hypothetical parameters utilizing information from smaller-scale
studies, especially with regard to distance elasticity, which should be seen to be
dependent on some development level indicator.

Not much can be said about the data sets utilized from the papers on which the
survey for Table 2 is based. When the regions of the models are large, time series
information seems usually to be available; for smaller spatial units, as well as for
multisectoral models, cross sectional data are generally used as the database.

As far as the parameter estimation techniques are concerned, a wide array of
methods has been used. In the Markov input-output models with constant coefficients,
the usual cross sectional techniques were applied. Some input-output coefficient
matrices were obtained by a spatial or temporal application of biproportional matrix
multiplication methods such as RAS (e.g, MIO). In the case of variable transition
rates the "logit" formulation is sometimes used (e.g., REMO). In the econometric
approaches linear and log-linear functional forms prevail for which various regression techniques are utilized. Due to the sheer size of these studies single-equation
estimation techniques are commonly applied. In the validation phase of the model,
consistency is often achieved by means of various additional calibration techniques;
unfortunately there is not enough information available about these methods in the
papers. Simultaneous equation estimation procedures are sometimes used in submodels
(e.g., REMO and REGINA).

Little can be said about the way models are updated. In input-output models
complete revisions of the coefficients usually occur at large intervals, due to the
scarcity of industrial censuses. A method frequently applied to update coefficients
between the industrial censuses is to use the above mentioned RAS method.

Econometric approaches often have to use proxies for variables that are not (yet) available at the regional level. Considerable progress in this respect can be expected once the public and policy makers realize the value of multiregional models; the necessary data are then more likely to be collected. Analyses based on small regional units often encounter problems in obtaining data from the statistical offices, although they are available. In many countries data that permit conclusions about individual firms or persons may not be released due to legal constraints.

4   Some Observations on Models and Policy

To use the limited space of this chapter as efficiently as possible, I will more or less limit my remarks to labor market problems again. The "classical" instruments of regional economic policy apply mainly to the demand side, where variations in tax rates, subsidies, investment credits, etc., have a direct influence on regional productive capacity via changing investment levels. Government expenditure provides an indirect influence, as the volume of final demand is changed; this change often leads to a change in investment (but not always in employment). This group of variables can be found in most of the models in this survey, the final demand component being more emphasized in the input-output type of models; the other instruments tend to be analyzed in more detail in studies that contain econometrically estimated investment functions. The most commonly analyzed indirect instruments are various tax cut and investment subsidy schemes (see, e.g., SERENA and REGAM). The lack of data on the regional scale seems to present difficulties, especially in the bottom-up approaches. No universal conclusion can be drawn from the evidence in Western Europe as to the success of these policies. It appears that measures to promote investment in peripheral areas are effective when an "autonomous" decentralization trend is already prevalent, which was the case in most of Western Europe in the late 1960s until the mid-1970s. Elasticities estimated on the basis of data from this period could lead to misleading forecasts when the autonomous process changes direction, which could well be the case if the economies of Western Europe experience a longer period of stagnation. Models that predominantly analyze population and labor supply (e.g., IMPE) do not dwell on this subject.

On the supply side there are not many directly applicable instruments. The retirement age is sometimes included as an exogenous variable in this group, and similarly, the obligatory school leaving age (REMO). Another widely discussed instrument at present is the institutional limit on working hours per week. Unfortunately most models compute the labor supply in terms of persons and not working hours, so that an analysis of the impact of such measures cannot be made. In some studies upper and lower bounds on labor supply are introduced, although these of course are influenced by the policies just mentioned (e.g., IMPE and MORSE).

In the group of indirect instruments the most prominent are infrastructure investments. The most common links to labor supply are the migration submodels, but in general, it appears that the influence of differences in social infrastructure upon the migration decision is sometimes overestimated by planners; at least this is the conclusion of many migration studies. It is universally accepted, however, that technical infrastructure, especially the highway and telephone system, are of very high importance for location decisions of people as well as of firms. The "accessibility" of a region is usually found to be a very important determinant in investment, migration, and commuting studies.

A few words should be added at the end of this chapter about the future of regional policy. The "classical" instruments of regional policy, which are usually included in models of regional development, are claimed to have failed by and large to decrease spatial disparities (Stöhr and Tödtling 1978, Stöhr 1981). The suggested counterparadigm favors "selective regional closure" and thus relies on local initiative and resources. Is there a way to formulate models in such a way as to be able to assess the effects of such a policy?

5 Concluding Remarks

This section gives some thoughts about gaps in the theoretical structure that the author subjectively feels deserve some attention in the future.

The question of the "relevant region" and the way to find it, empirically warrants further research. The idea of "functional" regions looks appealing at first glance, but many problems surface when such a functional concept of a region is used. It is clear that fairly wide models contain many different functions, for which the relevant regions differ, and to make life even more difficult, the spatial extents of these functions vary over time (usually endogenously).

Aggregation and disaggregation of relevant variables have to be carefully considered. The widely accepted and practiced disaggregation of economic activity levels by sectors may not always be the most relevant one. This could particularly be the case in labor market related studies, where "segmentation" seems to be a fact.

The effectiveness of regional policy measures in a dynamic and spatial context is by and large an unresolved issue and judgments seem to vary a great deal (see also Chapter 5).

Attempts to use dynamic theories of the firm, in the form of vintage models as well as manpower planning, should be continued and elaborated further. The question of changes in the spatial investment patterns, taking into account the organization of the firms (multiregional?) as well as the market structure seem to be routes already being followed and well worth further pursuit (see also Chapter 16).

References

van de Berg, L., R. Drewett, L. Klaassen, A. Rossi, and K. Vijverberg (1981), *Urban Europe: Elements of a Theory of Growth and Decline* (Pergamon, Oxford).

Birg, H. (1980), The Impact of Settlement Structure on the Tertiary Sector of the Regions of the Federal Republic of Germany, *Vierteljahreshefte zur Wirtschaftsforschung* 3(4), 333–338.

Brown, M., M. di Palma, and B. Ferrara (eds.) (1978), *Regional-National Econometric Modeling--with an Application to the Italian Economy* (Pion, London).

De Bruyne, G., and P. van Rompuy (1977), *Estimation of a System of Non-Linear Investment Allocation Functions* (Centrum voor Economische Studien, Louvain, Belgium).

Chenery, H., P. Clark, and V. Cao-Pinna (1953), *The Structure and Growth of the Italian Economy* (US Mutual Security Agency, Rome).

Courbis, R. (1979), Le modèle REGINA, Modèle du Développement National, Régional et Urbain de l'Économie Francaise, in R. Courbis (ed.), *Modèles Regionaux et Modèles Régionaux-Nationaux* (Editions Cujas, Paris), pp. 87-101.

van Delft, A., and W.B.C. Suyker (1981), Regional Investment Subsidies: An Estimation of the Labour Market Effects for the Dutch Regions, *Paper presented at the 21st European Congress of the Regional Science Association, Barcelona, Spain.*

Doeringer, P., and P. Piore (1971), *Internal Labor Markets and Manpower Analysis* (Heath, Lexington, MA).

Engelbrecht, P.O., L. Johansson, and T. Österberg (1979), Information for Regional Planning Systems in Sweden, *Report to the Council of Europe Seminar on Information Systems for Regional Planning, Madrid, Spain.*

Ferrara, B. (1976), *NORD-SUD, Interdipendenze di due economie* (F. Angeli, Milano, Italy).

Fischer, M. (1981), Eine Methodologie der Regionaltaxonomie: Probleme und Verfahren der Klassifikation und der Regionalisierung in der Geographie und Regionalforschung, *Bremer Beiträge zur Geographie und Raumplanung* 3.

Granholm, A. (1980), *Interregional Planning Models for the Allocation of Private and Public Investments*, Ekonomiska Studier Utgivna av Nationalekonomiska Institutionen vid Göteborgs Universitet 8.

van Hamel, B.A., H. Hetsen, and J.H.M. Kok (1979), Un Modèle Économétrique Multirégional pour les Pays-Bas, in R. Courbis (ed.), *Modèles Régionaux et Modèles Régionaux-Nationaux* (Editions Cujas, Paris), pp. 147-169.

Ledent, J. (1980), A Demoeconomic Model of Interregional Growth Rate Differences, *IIASA Report* RR-80-26 (International Institute for Applied Systems Analysis, Laxenburg, Austria).

Lesuis, P., F. Muller, and P. Nijkamp (1980), An Interregional Policy Model for Energy-Economic-Environmental Interactions, *Regional Science and Urban Economics*, 10, 343-370.

Martellato, D. (1980), Structural Analysis with an Updated Interregional Input-Output Model for Italy 1977, *Paper presented at the 20th European Congress of the Regional Science Association, Munich, FRG*.

Reich, M., D. Gordon, and R. Edwards (1973), The theory of labor market segmentation, *American Economic Review, Papers and Proceedings*, 63, 359-365.

Rogers, A., and F. Willekens (1978), Spatial Population Analysis: Methods and Computer Programs, *IIASA Report* RR-78-18 (International Institute for Applied Systems Analysis, Laxenburg, Austria).

Scanlon, W.S., C.C. Holt, and R.S. Toikka (1977), Extension of a Structural Model of the Demographic Labor Market, in R.G. Ehrenberg (ed.), *Research in Labor Economics, An Annual Compilation of Research*, Vol. I, JAI Press, Greenwick.

Schubert, U. (1981), *Capital Mobility and Labor Demand in Urban Agglomerations During the Suburbanization Process, an Econometric Approach* (Institute for Urban and Regional Studies, University of Economics, Vienna, Austria).

Schubert, U. (1982), REMO, an Interregional Labor Market Study of Austria, *Environment and Planning*, forthcoming.

Schuler, M. (1981), Iteration von Anpassungsprozessen auf regionalen Arbeitsmärkten: Das regionalisierte Bevölkerungs- und Arbeitsplatz-Prognosemodell von Güller, Schuler und Weber, in N. Blattner, D. Maillot, and R. Ratti (eds.), *Regionale Arbeitsmarktprozesse* (Ruegges, Diessenhofen, Switzerland), pp. 192-204.

Stöhr, W. (1981), Alternative Strategien für die integrierte Entwicklung peripherer Gebiete bei abgeschwächtem Wirtschaftswachstum, *DISP 61* (ORL Institut, ETH, Zürich).

Stöhr, W., and F. Tödtling (1978), Evaluation of Regional Policies: Experiences in Market and Mixed Economies, in N.M. Hansen (ed.), *Human Settlement Systems* (Ballinger Press, Cambridge, MA), pp. 85-115.

Thys-Clement, F., P. van Rompuy, and L. de Corel (1979), RENA, a Regional-National Model for Belgium, in R. Courbis (ed.), *Modèles Régionaux et Modèles Régionaux-Nationaux* (Editions Cujas, Paris), pp. 103-122.

Thoss, R., G. Bougioukos, and G. Erdmann (1980), An Evaluation of Spatial Planning Objectives by Means of a Multiperiod, Multiregional and Multisectoral Decision Model--Presentation and Discussion of Certain Results for the State of Hessen, *Working Paper* No. 28 (Sonderforschungsbereich 26 Raumordnung und Raumwirtschaft, Münster, Germany).

CHAPTER 8

INTEGRATED MULTIREGIONAL MODELING IN WESTERN EUROPE

Raymond Courbis

1 Introduction and General Features

While multiregional models using an interregional input-output approach have
been built since the early 1950s, it was only at the beginning of the 1970s that
people began to construct "regional-national" models that combined the "top-down",
the "bottom-up", and the "interregional" approaches (Courbis 1980, 1982a). Since
then, several regional-national models have been built (see the Appendix by Rietveld), but several of them are in fact "non-interactive" regional-national models
for which the national variables (see Chapter 3, p. 35), which are calculated by
aggregation of the regional figures, have no impact on the national ones, on
which the regional variables depend in turn. In such models there are in fact no
regional-national interactions. Following Nijkamp and Rietveld, we shall only
use the term "integrated regional-national model" for those regional-national
models that are interactive, i.e., closed at the national level. For such models
there is a complete interaction between the determination of regional and national
variables.

The first integrated regional-national models were proposed and built in the
early 1970s in Western Europe (in Courbis 1979c a presentation of RENA, REGINA, and
REM 1 is given; see also Table 1); for Belgium, RENA and MACEDOINE; for France,
REGINA; for Italy, the RNEM regional-national model; and for the Netherlands, REM.
(In fact, only the first version of REM is an "integrated" regional-national model.
The second version REM 2 (Van Delft *et al.* 1977) is a top-down model.) More recent-
ly, a simplified version of the REGINA model has been built for France (REGIS) and
a new integrated regional-national model has been built for Belgium (SERENA).

Thus, in the 1970s six integrated regional-national models have been built in
Western Europe: RENA, MACEDOINE, REGINA/REGIS, RNEM, REM 1, and SERENA. (From the
Rietveld 1981 survey it appears that one could also include in this group the HESSEN
model for West Germany, but national feedbacks are quite weak in this model.) However, it is noticeable that only very recently have such models begun to be built
in North America.

This chapter cannot, however, present each of these models in a detailed way;
it will only make comparisons and emphasize the lessons of the West European experience. In Table 1 the general features of these models are given. Except for
RNEM, which considers 19 regions (note that this model did not become operational)
and the Belgian MACEDOINE (a small model designed mainly for academic use), they all
consider only a limited number of regions: three in RENA and SERENA; five in REGINA/
REGIS (seven in the new version of REGIS that is being built at present) and five
for REM 1. Only REGINA introduces a double spatial level with a disaggregation of
each region into three "zones": rural areas; small urban units; large agglomerations (see Courbis 1975b). Such subregional levels allow the taking into account
in REGINA of the impact of urbanization on participation rates, domestic migration
and foreign immigration, wages per capita, investments of local public authorities,
etc. From this point of view, it is interesting to see that in REM 1 investments
of local authorities also depend on the distribution (which is, however, exogenous)
of the population between rural and urban areas, and that RNEM introduces the effect
of urbanization on the labor force.

Table 1. General features of the integrated regional-national models for Western Europe

Country	Model	Number of regions	Number of industries[a]	Use	References Presentation	Utilization
Belgium	RENA	3	1	Has been used by the Belgian Planning Office for the 1976–80 plan	Thys-Clement et al. (1973, 1979)	Bogaert et al. (1974a,b, 1979), de Falleur et al. (1975)
	SERENA	3	7 + public sector	Used since 1980 by the Belgian Planning Office	d'Alcantara et al. (1980), d'Alcantara (1981)	Belgian Planning Bureau (1981)
	MACEDOINE	9	1	For academic use	Glejser et al. (1973), Glejser (1975), Despontin (1981a)	Glejser et al. (1973), Despontin (1981a,b)
France	REGINA	5[b]	10 + public sector[c]	Used mainly by the French Planning Office	Courbis (1972, 1975a, 1979a), Courbis et al. (1980)	Courbis (1978, 1979b, 1982b)
	REGIS	5[d]	4 + public sector	At present, for experiments	Courbis and Cornilleau (1978)	Courbis and Cornilleau (1978)
Italy	RNEM	19	5 + public sector	Has not been operational	Brown et al. (1972, 1978)	–
The Netherlands	REM 1[e]	5	6 + public sector	Has been used by the Dutch Planning Bureau[e]	Van Hamel et al. (1975, 1979)	–

[a] An inter- and multiregional input-output table is only used in REGINA (and a multiregional table for REGIS); a national table is projected in SERENA.

[b] Each of the five regions of REGINA is also divided (for employment, population, migration, and wage bills) into three "zones": rural areas; small urban units; large urban agglomerations; see Courbis (1975b).

[c] Besides the ten productive sectors, REGINA also considers eight nonproductive sectors at the regional level: administration (five), banks, insurance companies, and employment by household.

[d] Seven regions are now considered in the new REGIS version that is currently being built.

[e] While the first version REM 1--which is not used anymore--was an integrated regional-national model, the second version, REM 2, is only a top-down model; see Van Delft et al. (1977).

From an economic point of view, the common characteristic of these models (by definition of "integrated" models) is the combination of "bottom-up" and "top-down" approaches in an interdependent way, but the basic choices are not all the same and we shall emphasize those related to: (i) details of regional analysis and the spatial level at which each variable is first analyzed (Section 2); (ii) determination of production, demand and employment (Section 3); (iii) interregional linkages (Section 4); (iv) national feedbacks and wage determination (Section 5).

For some of the models, the choices made may perhaps be explained by statistical problems. The availability of sufficient and consistent regional data is an important problem for multiregional modeling and that problem is discussed in Section 6. In Section 7, we make a brief comparison of how the models under review have been used for simulations and economic policy. However, all these models are only related to a single country. As the international interdependences are quite important, the building of a multicountry multiregional model is now needed; such is the purpose of the REGI-LINK project we proposed in 1979 for Western Europe; we discuss this in Section 8.

2 The Regional Analysis

Table 2 shows the variables analyzed at the regional level in each of the six models under review. They all analyze production, productive investments, employment, and unemployment at the regional level, but regional demand is only determined in REGINA/REGIS (for which a complete input-output table is projected for each region) and RNEM (where regional production is completely determined by demand). For the other models, this is not necessary because regional production is either obtained by allocating total national production between the regions (RENA and SERENA) or completely determined by supply (REM 1 and MACEDOINE). However, for some industries, REM 1 introduces total regional output as a proxy of regional demand for determining regional production, and MACEDOINE 2 introduces national GNP (or national unemployment for MACEDOINE 1) as an indicator of national demand.

The scope of regional analysis is the largest for REGINA, but this does not mean that this model mainly uses a bottom-up approach; on the contrary, REGINA is a highly integrated model (see Tables 5 and 6, Section 5), and is the only one to make a complete projection of a multi- and interregional input-output table. (This is the same as for REGIS, except that REGIS does not determine interregional flows and consequently considers only a set of regional input-output tables (one for each region). For SERENA, a table is used but it is only a national one.) The REGINA I-O table projection is however only used as a general framework. It does not mean that regional production is *always* determined by an input-output approach; although it *is* (see below) for the "demand located" industries, it *is not* for "supply located" industries for which regional production is determined by supply. In this latter case, the regional input-output table is used to calculate the regional external trade surplus (or deficit). (Also, for REGINA, the regional external trade surplus determines, in turn, the interregional flows, which have a feedback effect on transportation costs.)

Regional variables are often directly determined and, in this case, the corresponding national ones are determined by aggregation (the "bottom-up" approach), but some of the variables are first analyzed at the national level and the regional figures determined by a "top-down" approach. In MACEDOINE and RNEM most of the variables are regionally determined, while it is the opposite for RENA and SERENA. For REGINA/REGIS and REM 1 the approach is more balanced.

An important problem appears here: *at what spatial level* is each variable to be analyzed--at the regional or national level? It seems that choices often have been made for statistical reasons (for example, where RENA analyzes wage dynamics at the regional level, this is not so for SERENA, which would need regional data by sector); perhaps also variables at the regional level are too systematically analyzed (as in RNEM). For the French, however, the relevant level is not arbitrary but depends (see Courbis 1980, 1982a) on the behavior of economic agents and the nature of markets.

Table 2. Variables analyzed at the regional level

Models	Production	Employment	Labor force	Unemployment	Stock of capital	Productive investments	Other components of demand[a]	Wages	Nonwage incomes	Prices
RENA	X	X	X	X	X	X		X^b		
SERENA	X	X	X	X		X		$-^c$		
MACEDOINE	X	X	X	X	X	X	$-^d$	X	$-^d$	X^e
REGINA/ REGIS	X	X	X	X	X	X	X	X	X	$-^f$
RNEM	X	X	X	X		X	X	X		X^g
REM 1	X	X	X	X	X	X	$-^h$	X^i	X	X^j

[a] For more details on the analysis of the regional demand, see Table 4.

[b] Only regional wage rates are calculated: wage bills and salaries are only determined at the national level.

[c] Calculation of wage bills by sector and region is made in SERENA (by assuming an exogenous hierarchy of regional wages per capita for each sector), but it is only made for allocating the total national value by sector among the regions; see Table 3 note (b).

[d] Regional consumption by household and disposable income are calculated in MACEDOINE but they have no feedback on the other model variables.

[e] Index of consumption prices (calculated by an equation combining, in a reduced form, the Okun and Phillips mechanisms).

[f] Only production prices for agriculture are regionally differentiated (but are exogenous); price indices for other products are assumed to be the same for all regions (except house rental in REGINA), but the average indices of aggregates are differentiated according to regional structure.

[g] Regional price indices are determined only by linking them to national ones.

[h] Public investments.

[i] Only regional wage rates are considered (for calculating relative regional costs of capital and labor); wage bills and salaries are not calculated at regional level.

[j] Regional prices of investments (linked to national prices) are calculated for evaluating the relative regional cost of labor and capital.

(1) Variables determined on the basis of a regional market or those resulting
     from the decision of regional agents (production functions, employment and
     labor supply, household consumption, residential investments, local authority
     investments, investments of "located" industries, etc.) should first be deter-
     mined at a regional level and then aggregated at the national level by a
     bottom-up approach. (Or also at an intraregional level such as in REGINA
     where labor force (participation rates, domestic migrations and foreign immi-
     gration) and population are first determined at a "zonal" level--with, how-
     ever, a double-step analysis for interregional migrations--and are then aggre-
     gated for obtaining regional and national figures. This is also partly the
     case in REGINA for wage bills and social security compensations.)
(2) However, a top-down approach should be used for variables determined on a
     national market or by national agents (prices, investments of multiregional
     firms, government demand, interest rates, etc.).

Such an approach at the relevant spatial level is a characteristic of REGINA and
REGIS.

3 Determination of Production, Demand, and Employment

     The determination of regional production appears quite different in the six
models (see Table 3):

(1) In the two Belgian models, RENA and SERENA, regional production is completely
     determined by allocating the total national product among the regions (top-
     down approach)--and this latter is determined at the national level by effec-
     tive demand and foreign trade.
(2) In the Italian model RNEM, on the contrary, the regional total output is
     completely determined by regional demand and regional net imports; it thus
     uses a pure bottom-up approach.
(3) In the Belgian model MACEDOINE, the regional total output also results from
     a bottom-up approach but, in this case, is more strongly determined by supply;
     it depends on the regional capital stock, regional employment, and a proxy
     for national demand (the national rate of unemployment for MACEDOINE 1; the
     total GNP for MACEDOINE 2).
(4) In the French models REGINA and REGIS, and the Dutch REM 1, the determination
     of regional production results from an interdependent approach, combining a
     top-down and a bottom-up approach, taking into account both supply and demand.

     While in the short term a demand oriented approach can be used ("economic-base"
theory), this is not possible for medium-term models such as REGINA/REGIS and REM 1.
One has to take into account that bottlenecks can in fact appear at the regional
level if the level of regional investment is not determined by regional capacity requirements, because investments are either limited for financial reasons, or dependent on the behavior of multiregional firms (and thus on opportunities to invest in
the different regions). This is why, in REGINA/REGIS the builders have distinguished
(as proposed in Courbis and Prager 1971) (i) the "demand located" industries for
which regional production is determined by regional demand and (ii) the "nonrestricted
location" industries that can operate anywhere. For the former, regional production
is determined by regional demand, but for the latter, regional production depends,
in the medium term, on the opportunities to invest in each region. More precisely,
the regional production of nonrestricted location industries is, in the medium term,
determined by the regional stock of capital which, in turn, depends on the regional
location of investments and thus on the location behavior of multiregional firms.
     So, in REGINA/REGIS, regional production of demand located industries is *demand
driven* (and determined by an input-output approach; although one has to take into
account the fact that production of some demand located activities such as services
is also dependent--but weakly--on effective demand in other regions), while regional
production of nonrestricted location industries is *supply determined*. For both,
regional investments are endogenous: for the former they are determined by regional

Table 3. Production determination in integrated regional-national models for
          Western Europe

| Model | Top-down approach | Regional Approach | | | Introduction of regional capital stock |
		Demand oriented	Supply oriented	Mixed	
RENA	X[a]				X[c]
SERENA	X[b]				No (putty-clay functions)
MACEDOINE			X[d]		X
REGINA/REGIS				X	X[e]
RNEM		X			No (demand driven)
REM 1				X[f]	X

[a] Total national added value (which is demand determined) is allocated among regions by a top-down approach, but regional shares of added value depend on regional investments.

[b] Regional added value by industry is calculated first in value terms on the basis of wages and salaries paid by each industry for each region considered and by distributing the national net operating surplus by industry over all regions as a function of their shares in national investments. Then regional added value is calculated in constant prices but the same deflator is used for all regions. Such a treatment is in fact not consistent and it would be better to calculate regional added value in real terms as a function of regional employment by industry (and on the basis of production functions).

[c] Used for calculating regional employment (a function of regional capital stock and of regional rate of utilization of capital).

[d] Emphasizing the impact of regional supply, MACEDOINE also introduces an impact of a proxy for national demand: national rate of unemployment for MACEDOINE 1 (Glejser 1975); total GNP for MACEDOINE 2 (Despontin 1981a).

[e] In the first version of REGINA, capital and labor were complementary production factors but substitutions between them have been introduced in some simulations (see Courbis 1982b).

[f] But uses total regional output as a proxy for regional demand.

production requirements, while for the latter they are first determined and determine, in turn, the regional stock of capital and the regional production (according to the level of regional demand one then determines the total net surplus or deficit of external trade for each region). For the nonrestricted location industries, investments are first determined at the national level and afterwards broken down between the regions according to the location behavior.

Such a distinction between demand located and nonrestricted location industries is extremely important. First, there is an asymmetry between the two groups: an increase in the production of the nonrestricted location industries in one region has a positive leading effect on the regional production of the demand located industries in that region through an increase in regional demand. However, the contrary is not true and the production of demand located industries has no direct effect on the production of nonrestricted location industries (which is determined by supply and not by demand). At the same time, regional production of nonrestricted location industries, and thus regional development, depends directly on the national investment possibilities and national development.

    In the Dutch REM 1, the determination of regional production is quite close to
that in the French REGINA/REGIS. For manufacturing and other footloose industries,
regional production is determined by the stock of capital available for that region
(which depends on the national stock of capital and the opportunities to invest in
the region considered) and the optimal combinations between capital and labor (a
function of the relative cost of labor and capital). Note that the national stock
of capital results from the determination of the national investments which--as in
REGINA/REGIS--depends for these industries on the value of the national profits.
But instead of allocating the national investments among the regions as in REGINA/
REGIS, it is here the national stock of capital. In REGINA and the first version
of REGIS, labor and capital were considered as complementary production factors but
substitutions were taken into account in the simulations where the relative costs of
capital and labor were modified (see Courbis 1982b). As in REGINA, the total national
production in REM 1 is calculated by means of the aggregation of regional production
(as in REGINA/REGIS one determines in fact the national supply, which retroacts on
national development; see below Section 5). For the other industries, such as services and building, which are more demand located, regional production is tied to
the total regional output, which is then used as a proxy for the regional demand.
    According to the specification of production determination in each model, re-
gional demand is (except for productive investments) only analyzed in REGINA/REGIS
and RNEM (see Table 4). For the Belgian RENA and SERENA, which use a top-down approach to determine regional production, as the country is not too large, one can
perhaps assume that regional consumption behavior is uniform. For MACEDOINE, which

Table 4. Analysis of regional demand in integrated regional-national models for
          Western Europe

Models	Final demand				Intermediate demand	Inter-regional flows
	Household consumption	Productive investments	Residential investments	Public demand		
RENA		X				
SERENA		X				
MACEDOINE	$(X)^b$	X				
REGINA[a]	X	X	X	X	X	X^c
REGIS[a]	X	X	X	X	X	Net surplus[c]
RNEM	X	X	X	X		Net imports[d]
REM 1		X	X (exogenous)	X^e		

[a] REGINA and REGIS introduce a regional input-output table but regional demand determines only regional production of demand located industries. For other industries,
  regional production is determined by supply. In this latter case, the regional
  input-output table determines the regional external trade surplus.
[b] If calculated in MACEDOINE 1, household consumption has no feedback on the other
  variables of the model.
[c] In REGINA, regional production and demand are first calculated and then determined,
  followed in turn by the regional surplus and interregional flows. In REGIS, only
  regional surplus is determined.
[d] Net total imports by region are directly calculated by an econometric equation.
  At the national level, the total surplus is determined by aggregation and calculation of total national imports allowing determination of total exports.
[e] Investments of local authorities.

emphasizes the impact of regional supply and national demand, the determination of regional demand is also not necessary (if regional household consumption is determined in MACEDOINE 1, no feedback is introduced into either regional production or the proxy for national demand). However for REM 1, which introduces both regional demand and supply effects, it would be better to consider explicitly regional demand than to use regional product as for regional demand.

In all the models under review, except SERENA, the determination of regional production (or of the regional stock of capital in RENA and REM 1 has a central role because it enables regional employment to be calculated on the basis of the regionally specified production functions. Note that in fact, as labor and capital are substitutable production factors, determining employment on the basis of regional capital stock or of regional production depends more on the reduced forms one has chosen to describe the optimal labor-capital combination. In SERENA, however, regional employment by sector is directly tied to regional investments by a putty-clay approach (which allows one to identify explicitly the creation of the new regional jobs with new investments and the destruction of regional jobs with the scrapping of historical regional investments in each production sector).

For all of the models, the labor force is determined by taking into account the impact of job creation (or of the level of regional activity) on labor supply and by considering migrations (although this is exogenous in SERENA; commuting only is endogenous in RENA). MACEDOINE uses a reduced-form approach and directly determines regional unemployment.

4 Interregional Linkages

Not all of the six models are "interdependent" regional-national models according to the definition of Rietveld and Snickars (p. 54); i.e., models where there are individual links *between* individual regions. The following are indicated in Table 5:

(1) For RENA and SERENA, there is no interregional linkage (except for commuting in RENA).
(2) For REM 1, the only interregional linkage is introduced by migration (on which depends the regional rate of unemployment).
(3) For RNEM there are interregional linkages through migrations, interregional trade (in fact only regional net imports are calculated), and tourism.
(4) For MACEDOINE, three linkages are also introduced: regional unemployment depends first on employment in the bordering regions; regional wage increases (see below) in one region depend on unemployment in that region and in other regions; regional investments depend on the output of other regions (such a relationship can be interpreted as the reduced form of a two-step determination process such as is used in REGINA and REM 1).
(5) For REGINA, four linkages are introduced at the levels of migration (of population and workers), interregional flows, tourism, and wages. (Note that in REGINA, the interregional flows have an impact on transportation costs and consequently on regional costs. Such a linkage however is not introduced in the simplified REGIS version.) As in MACEDOINE, one assumes--but explicitly --that the increase in regional wages is regionally interdependent.

More precisely, in REGINA/REGIS, where the regional rate of increase in wage rates depends on regional conditions (the tightness of the regional labor market), there is also a diffusion process: the labor market of the Parisian region is a leader labor market and the rate of increase in wages in other regions depends on the Parisian one. There is thus a direct interregional linkage for wage increase determination but it is an asymmetric one because the wage increase for the Parisian labor market does not depend on those in other regions. Such a process plays a major role because it reinforces the impact of Parisian wage increases on the average national increase and on unit costs, and thus on prices (and competitiveness and foreign trade) and profitability (and investment possibilities and supply). This is the main reason why, in REGINA, the location of workers and jobs have a great impact on national growth and unemployment (see Section 7). More generally, the

Table 5. Interregional linkages in integrated regional-national models for West-
          ern Europe. Note: MACEDOINE also introduces an interregional linkage
          for regional investments which, for one region, depends on regional output
          in the other regions; but one can interpret such a relationship either as
          the reduced form of a two-step determination process (such as in REGINA/
          REGIS and REM 1) where the regional allocation of total national invest-
          ments would depend on the regional location of effective demand, or as
          describing interregional trade effects.

Models	Migration	Interregional trade	Tourism	Wages
RENA	(commuting)			
SERENA[a]				
MACEDOINE	x^b			x^c
REGINA	X	x^d	X	x^e
REGIS	X	$-^f$	X	x^e
RNEM	x^g	x^h	X	
REM 1	x^i			

[a] Net regional migrations are exogenous and no interregional linkage is introduced
in SERENA
[b] Reduced form. Unemployment in one region depends on unemployment and employment
in bordering regions (but foreign immigration is explicitly calculated).
[c] The rate of increase in nominal wages for one region depends on unemployment in
others; thus there is a regional and a national labor market.
[d] Interregional flows are calculated for equilibrating supply and demand by region;
they have, in turn, an impact on the transportation costs.
[e] The rate of increase in nominal wages for "follower" regions depends on the tightness of the regional labor market and the rate of increase in nominal wages in the
leading labor market (the Parisian region). In the new REGIS version secondary
diffusion effects will also be introduced.
[f] Net regional surplus by industry is only calculated (by differences between regional production and total regional demand) and has no feedback.
[g] Total regional immigration and emigration are only calculated for each region, so
the bilateral flows between the regions are not considered.
[h] Net regional imports by product are calculated for each region and, with regional
demand, determine regional production.
[i] Net migrations are only calculated by region.

determination of regional wage increases is one of the most important channels by
which the national figures can be affected (see Section 5).

5 The National Feedbacks of Regional Variables

     The common characteristic of the "integrated" regional-national models is
(by definition: see Chapters 3 and 4) that these models are "closed" at the national level, i.e., that the national figures calculated by aggregation of regional values affect the national variables on which, in turn, the regional
variables depend.
     These feedback effects vary in importance for the six models analyzed. National
feedbacks of regional variables (see Table 6) are mainly concerned with (i) employment and unemployment which affect on the one hand national unit costs and thus
prices and profitability, and on the other national household income and thus consumption and demand; (ii) investments and productive structures; (iii) total demand;
(iv) production (of "nonlocated" industries); (v) national wages; and (vi) prices.

Table 6. National feedbacks of regional variables[a]

Models	Employment and unemployment	Investments (and capital stock)	Wage rates	Production	Demand (except productive investment)	Prices[b]
RENA	X	X	X			
SERENA	X	X^c				
MACEDOINE	$-^d$			X^d		
REGINA/REGIS	X	X	X	X^e	X	$-^f$
RNEM			X			X^g
REM 1	X	X		X^e	$-^h$	

[a] We consider here only national variables, calculated by aggregating regional figures, that have an impact on other national variables (such as demand or production; costs; income and prices; profits and investments; rate of utilization of capital stock; and competitiveness and external trade) which have, in turn, a direct impact on regional variables. In other words, we only consider regional variables that "close" the model at the national level. This explains why, although obtained by aggregation of regional figures, some variables do not appear for some models (e.g., production and demand for RNEM, prices for MACEDOINE).
[b] We consider here a direct linkage for prices (see note (f)), but in RENA, SERENA, REGINA, REGIS, and REM 1, national prices are in fact dependent on regional conditions, costs, and pressure of demand.
[c] Investments only for SERENA, which introduces putty-clay functions.
[d] In the second version of MACEDOINE, total GNP, as an indicator of national demand, is a determinant of regional production (with regional capital stock). In MACEDOINE 1, national unemployment was considered.
[e] Total national supply is calculated by aggregation of regional production (globally for REM 1; by industry for REGINA/REGIS); so a gap can appear for national demand (for nonlocated industries in REGINA/REGIS). Equilibrium between demand and supply is, in that case, achieved through production prices in such a way that national profits induce sufficient investment. In REGINA/REGIS, for "exposed" sectors (for which prices are imposed by foreign competition), equilibrium between demand and supply is achieved by means of external trade.
[f] National prices for agriculture are determined in REGINA/REGIS by aggregation of regional prices (which, in this case, are exogenous); as is house rental in REGINA if endogenously determined by region, as is possible in the model.
[g] The GNP deflator is directly determined by aggregation of regional deflators and is used for calculating relative regional prices.
[h] Public investments.

   The national feedbacks are the weakest in MACEDOINE; this model is to some extent a bottom-up one and the only national feedback is via national total output (an aggregation of regional outputs--or national total unemployment for MACEDOINE 1) on which depends--with other determinants--regional production. For RNEM, where several variables are also bottom-up-determined and which is a demand model, the importance of national feedbacks is also limited and mainly concerns national inflation (wages and prices).
   In the four other models, RENA, SERENA, REGINA/REGIS, and REM 1, the importance of the national feedbacks is greater, especially in REGINA/REGIS which appears to be the most "integrated" one (see Table 6). In all of them one finds feedbacks concerned with (i) and (ii) (see above) but the most important concerns are supply effects and wage determination (Courbis 1981).

5.1 Supply effects

These concern first the productive structures (and here we notice the elaborate putty-clay formulation of production functions in SERENA, the introduction of factor substitutions in REM 1, the detailed analysis in REGINA--also the sectoral disaggregation in REM 1, REGINA/REGIS and SERENA). Perhaps more fundamental, however, is the impact of supply at the level of nonlocated (footloose) industries in REGINA/REGIS and REM 1. In these models, national production by industry is obtained by aggregation of regional figures, but for "nonlocated" industries there is not an automatic equality between national total supply and demand. A gap may appear, but in both REGINA/REGIS and REM 1, this has a great impact on production prices. If the total supply is too low (or too high), it induces an increase (or decrease) in prices: consequently the profits are increased (or decreased) and, according to the financial investment behavior of firms, it has the consequence of increasing (decreasing) national investment possibilities, and therefore total supply. *Ex post*, the increase in prices is such that total supply and demand (net from imports) are equal. One can also say that, *ex post*, financial investment possibilities are equal to investments required by demand. If, *ex post*, national production is completely determined by national total effective demand and foreign trade, this interactive process of production determination for "nonlocated" industries has, *ex post*, an impact on prices (and also on total investments according to regional differences in productive structures and production functions. (Note that--on production (and exports) prices of a particular industry for REGINA/REGIS, which introduces a disaggregation of prices by product--on aggregate prices of final demand for REM 1, which does not introduce disaggregation by product. For REGINA/REGIS, investments by industry are also related to the profits of each industry while in REM 1 one considers only the total profits of firms.)

In REGINA/REGIS, there is also a second possibility related to "exposed" sectors in which production prices of domestic firms are determined by foreign prices: a gap between supply and demand does not vanish by means of variations in domestic prices, but by external trade (imports are completely substitutable for domestic production). As, in this case, national total investments are completely determined by financing possibilities (and, especially, by self-financing), the total level of national production is completely determined by investments and supply (and the equilibrium between demand and supply is achieved by means of foreign trade). It appears that the distinction between "demand located" and "nonlocated" industries is very important because, for the latter, national feedbacks are introduced into supply.

5.2 Wage determination

All the models except SERENA introduce regional analysis to determine increases in wage rates. A Phillips approach is followed, but important differences appear between the models.

(1) For RENA, increases in regional wages are completely determined (the bottom-up approach) by regional Phillips curve equations, but these equations are independent.

(2) RNEM and REM 1 introduce a national diffusion process (and thus an indirect interdependence between the regions): for one region, an increase in wage rates depends on regional conditions (unemployment) and on national average increases in wage rates. But where this latter results in RNEM from the aggregation of the regional rates of increase, this is not the case for REM 1 which introduces an econometric relationship for directly determining national average increases. For wage determination, REM 1 is thus not correctly specified and here works as a pure top-down model. Consequently, an important regional feedback on national figures vanishes.

(3) For MACEDOINE, the wage increase determination is quite close to RNEM but uses a reduced-form approach that leads to an explanation of wage increases in one region in terms of unemployment (and price increases) in that region and unemployment in other regions.

(4) For REGINA/REGIS, as seen above, there is a regional determination that takes
     into account diffusion effects from the leading labor market.

     For RENA and REGINA/REGIS, national average increase of wage rates, calculated
by aggregation, depends on regional variables according to the nonlinearity of the
relationships and the differences in the coefficients. But in REGINA the national
impact of the leading region (Paris) is reinforced by the diffusion process from
that region to the other ("follower") regions and such a mechanism is very important
for explaining the large effects that a shift in the location of jobs or workers
between the Parisian region and the Province regions has on the national development (see Section 7). For RNEM, although the increase in regional wages depends on
the national level, it is easy to see (Courbis 1980) that the national average increases also depend on regional conditions.
     For the three models, RENA, REGINA/REGIS, and RNEM, national average increases
in wage rates have an indirect impact on regional figures through several channels:
labor costs, prices and profitability, total income, etc. The simulations made with
REGINA/REGIS and also RENA (see below) have demonstrated the importance of such a
mechanism, which affects both production (via prices and investment effects) and
demand. For MACEDOINE, such a feedback is not introduced because the total GNP (or
the national unemployment rate in the first version, both total GNP and national unemployment being calculated by aggregation of regional figures) is the only national
variable that has an impact on regional figures. For REM 1, we have seen that regional wage determination mechanisms cannot have an effect on national development
according to the introduction, in that model, of a national econometric relationship
for the national wages.

6 Statistical Problems

     For regional models statistical problems are more important than for national
models because of the lack of regional data. This can often explain the specifications introduced in multiregional modeling. In general, statistical problems are
not too important for such regional variables as employment and unemployment, and
one can understand why all the models introduce such variables at the regional level.
More important are the problems of obtaining regional data for variables such as the
stock of capital, and of obtaining a consistent set of regional input-output tables.
     No regional data on capital stock were available to the authors of RENA, REGINA/
REGIS, MACEDOINE, and REM 1 and it was necessary for them to make their own estimations (for RNEM and SERENA this was not necessary, since the former is completely
demand driven and the latter introduces a putty-clay approach). For RENA, REGINA/
REGIS, and REM 1, a chronological approach was used, but the methods used for estimation of the value of the regional capital stock for the base year were different.
RENA used a breakdown of a national estimate for 1955; REGINA/REGIS and REM 1 used
an optimization approach (minimization of the differences between regional production functions for a given national value of capital stock). For MACEDOINE, the
estimation of capital stock was done simultaneously with the estimation of the production function but assuming that the nine Belgian provinces had the same initial
input-output ratio (for 1959).
     However, improvements in the estimation of the regional capital stock would be
useful for a better determination of regional production functions and for taking
into account the impact of financial limitations on national and regional investments. Regional data on the capital stock are however not needed if one adopts a
putty-clay approach, such as in the Belgian SERENA.
     Regional data on the rate of capital utilization would also be necessary for a
short-term adaptation of the medium-term mechanisms of REGINA/REGIS or REM 1. One
could, even for nonlocated industries, determine regional production by effective
demand (within the region and outside) but only by introducing the impact of availability of regional capacities on interregional flows (and also on the regional
foreign trade) to allow reconciliation of the economic-base and supply approaches.
     For regional input-output analysis, only REGINA and REGIS introduce regional
tables (see above), but considerable statistical effort by the authors of the model

was necessary for constructing a multi- and interregional input-output table for the French economy (see Courbis and Pommier 1979). However, multiregional input-output tables exist for Belgium, the Netherlands, and Italy (and other European countries such as West Germany and the UK), and one could consider using them to improve the sectoral framework of the regional side. However, one needs improvements and in many cases, time series could be useful for regional production by industry and regional demand by product.

For regional income, if one generally has good information on average increases in regional wage rates (quarterly data for France since 1962), better information than at present would be useful for regional wage bills and the different components of income.

In the supply approach, it would be useful to have data on regional credit markets and regional financing. The national capital market is not completely perfect, and there are also important differences in regional patterns. Improving regional information in that field is necessary; for France a first attempt has been made with the regional financial accounts built at GAMA by Rochoux (1979).

7 Simulations and Utilization

A point of interest in REGINA, RENA, and SERENA, and REM 1 is that they have been used by, respectively, the French Planning Office (Commissariat au Plan), the Belgian Planning Bureau, and the Central Planning Bureau of the Netherlands (see Table 1). Academic (but interesting) simulations have however been carried out with MACEDOINE (in Chapter 5 some of the applications have already been described), but RNEM has not become operational.

For the French economy, REGINA has been used by the Planning Office and other departments for projections and simulations (for the simplified REGIS version, only experimental use has been made). The simulations have demonstrated the usefulness of such a model in the analysis of either the regional impact of national development or the national impact of regional policy. It appears, firstly, that the magnitude of regional inequalities is increased (if no compensatory measures are taken) by a slowing in national growth. But, perhaps more important is the impact of regional factors and regional policy on national development. Let us here give an example: we consider a relocation in ten years of about 30,000 jobs in manufacturing from the Parisian region to the Province regions. For the period 1970-80, such a policy would increase the GDP (+0.55% in real terms), and the national total employment (+71,000 jobs), reduce the inflation rate, improve the external trade balance (+2.9 billion francs) and reduce the public deficit (-3.7 billion francs). More generally, the simulations made with REGINA (mainly on the regional location of manufacturing investments, public demand, and public jobs; on a regionally differentiated reducing of social security contributions; and on some sectoral policies) have demonstrated that regional policy and the regional disequilibria may have an important impact on the national development and that regional policies can be used not only to reduce regional inequalities but also to improve national development.

For Belgium, RENA has also been used for both projections and simulations, but the latter have been more concerned with national policies. As for REGINA, simulations have been made on the impact of the regional location of public investments and regional grants for private investment. However, it appears from the projections that the increase in regional wage rates would become very differentiated, resulting in an increasing discrepancy between the level of wages per capita in Flanders and Wallonia. Such a result has been criticized (Van Broekhoven 1974) and one can see why SERENA introduces only a national determination of wage rates. However, the reason could be that RENA does not introduce diffusion mechanisms (either between the regions, as in REGINA, or on a national basis, as in REM 1 and RNEM).

The new Belgian SERENA model has been used by the Planning Bureau since 1980. The simulations made with this model have analyzed the national and regional effects of regional policies; at the same time it has been used for building national scenarios for a recovery of the Belgian economy, with an analysis of national and regional effects. But due to the general conditions of the new 1981-85 plan, national simulations have been more emphasized. From the projections made, however, it appears that there would be a reduction of the discrepancies in regional unemployment patterns. It appears also that the impacts of national policies are more differentiated by region for SERENA than for RENA. This can perhaps be explained by the fact that SERENA, being a sectoral model, takes into account in a better way the differences in the structure of regional production.

For the Netherlands, the first version of REM, as indicated above, incorporated national feedbacks, but it appears from the simulations made with REM 1 (see Van Delft *et al.* 1977, p. 6) that these effects were weak. We can see consequently why the second version of REM is only a top-down model, but this may not be entirely a good thing. I think that the treatment of national wage determination in REM 1 (a direct econometric relationship instead of a calculation by means of aggregation of regional figures) has weakened national feedback effects (the simulations made with REGINA for the French economy have demonstrated the importance of wage mechanisms).

For Belgium, MACEDOINE has only been used for academic work but these are noteworthy, and attempt an optimal determination of regional policy by using either an optimal control approach or a multiple-criteria approach.

8 The REGI-LINK Project for a Multicountry Multiregion Model
   of Western Europe

As outlined above, one of the main results of the simulations made with REGINA (and REGIS) for the French economy, is that regional factors and thus regional policy have an important impact on national development. In particular, the regional location of activities and people and regional variations have an effect on national competitiveness. From this point of view we must emphasize the empirical finding made by Higgins (1973), who remarked that the position of a country's trade-off curve, relating national inflation to the unemployment ratio, is related to the magnitude of the regional variations; if the magnitude of these variations is high (low), the trade-off curve tends to be high and to the right (close to the axes). This means that, all other things being equal, the higher the regional variations, the weaker is the national competitiveness of the considered country.

Regional factors may also have a national impact via demand effects; the geographical concentration of populations in large urban agglomerations results in an increase in the infrastructure requirements and this has inflationary effects.

We can thus see, as stated in an EEC Commission report (1971) on the impact of the spatial disequilibria, that the differences in the magnitude of regional variations and geographical disequilibria can explain why some EEC countries such as France and Italy (we could also add the UK, which became a new member of the EEC in 1974) have more inflation than other countries, such as West Germany and the Netherlands, and why for the former (or the latter) there is a long-term tendency towards devaluation (revaluation) of their currencies.

As the regional variations *within* a country have an important impact on national growth, external trade balance, and exchange rates of that country, they consequently affect the development of *other* countries. To analyze such international effects, we need to use a multicountry multiregion model, i.e., an internationally connecting system of models from all countries that would analyze each country at a regional level. Such a model would also allow improvement of regional analyses by inclusion of the important effects that national development has on regions.

A multicountry approach might allow one to take into account the impact of the structure of foreign demand on one country's trade balance, such as is done in the Belgian SERENA (d'Alcantara *et al.* 1980), which distinguishes the main trading partners. At the same time, the use of a multicountry, multiregion model would enable one to take into account international feedbacks between countries (and even, if possible, between regions of different countries). It would introduce not only an international linkage (which is quite weak for several multiregional models; see Snickars 1981) of each country's multiregional model, but also a true international interdependency.

Thus it appears that the use of a multicountry, multiregional model would improve both multiregional and national (and multinational) analyses. We proposed such a project for the EEC in 1979 (see Courbis and Cornilleau 1979): this is the REGI-LINK project whose value and feasibility were discussed by an EEC group of experts in October 1979.

The REGI-LINK model should consist of an interconnected system of regionalized models of the EEC countries (or, more generally, of Western Europe if possible). It would be tempting to try to construct a model in which the regions would be directly integrated in a European model, but this would be neither realistic (for statistical reasons) nor desirable (because several markets are in fact more national). Since multiregional models have been built for several European countries (see above), it would also be tempting to try to link these models together, but this would, in fact, be unsatisfactory. The purposes and the structures of these models are quite different: the national feedbacks are too weak for several (except for REGINA/REGIS); the sectoral disaggregation varies; the supply effects are often neglected, etc. Also, the experience of multicountry models suggests that it is interesting to have the *same* structure for each country's model. This allows easier use of the system, and comparisons between results for each country are more significant.

For all these reasons, we proposed the adoption of the same structure for each country's model and, more precisely, the adoption of that of REGIS (the simplified version of the French REGINA) which appears significantly more consistent and sufficiently integrated, and the use of the REGIS software, which has been written in such a way that it can easily be used for other countries: the computer program is an interactive FORTRAN program and allows for special cases. Discussions by the experts in Brussels on the REGI-LINK project have shown that only a few minor adaptations would need to be made to the REGIS formulation. A "REGIS-type" model would be built for each country, and then the individual models would be linked together.

At the semiglobal sectoral level used in REGIS the project would not come up against too many statistical problems; in particular this is the case for regional data. Multiregional input-output tables are now available for all the largest West European countries and the simplifications made in the REGIS model have been made precisely to avoid any important statistical problems.

The international linkages between the models of individual countries would concern:

(1) Foreign trade (volume of exports and import prices). Two solutions *a priori* can be adopted here: either an international linkage at the level of regions, or at a national level. This would be possible for France because, in this case, there are regional time-series data for foreign trade, with a breakdown by origin and destination for each commodity group, but for several other countries this first solution would be impossible for statistical reasons. One could thus analyze the foreign trade linkage at the national level but, if trying to build a medium-term model, such a solution can be considered as convenient.

(2) Other linkages such as intercountry migration and commuting; international transmission of wage increases for border regions (wage increases in eastern France depend not only on the Parisian region but also on Switzerland and southwest Germany); tourism; and regional location of multinational firms. From this point of view, the regional level of multicountry, multiregion models allows the introduction of more linkages than in a pure multicountry model.

As a decentralized process appears to be the best for building each country's block, all the models would be built by national partners. At present (January 1982), national partners have been accepted to cooperate for Belgium, Finland, West Germany, Greece, Italy, Portugal, Spain and the UK. Thus, work on the REGI-LINK might begin in 1982. At the same time, the basic structure of the REGIS model will be improved.

The REGI-LINK project is certainly ambitious but it now appears feasible, and would constitute a new step in multiregional modeling and an interesting synthesis between the multiregional model and the multicountry model approaches.

Acknowledgments

    The author thanks for their helpful remarks and materials on their models:
G. d'Alcantara, T. de Biolley, M. Despontin, H. Glejser, P. Nijkamp, F. Snickars,
and W.B.C. Suyker.

References

d'Alcantara, G. (1981), Regional Investment, Employment and Growth at the Macro-
    Sectoral Level, *Paper presented at the 21st European Congress of the Regional
    Science Association, Barcelona, Spain, August 25-28.*
d'Alcantara, G., J. Floridor, and E. Pollefliet (1980), Major Features of the
    SERENA-Model for the Belgian Plan, *Brussels, Planning Bureau, Working Paper*
    2279.
Belgian Planning Bureau (1981), Kwantitatieve Bijdrage tot de Economische Politiek
    op Middelange Termijn (81-85), Alternatieven Gesimuleerd met het SERENA-Model,
    Brussels, Planning Bureau, Serena Report 2598.
Bogaert, H., T. de Biolley, R. de Falleur, and P. Hugé (1974a), Etablissement d'une
    Projection Macroéconomique à l'Aide du Modèle RENA, *Recherches Economiques de
    Louvain*, 40(4), 359-391.
Bogaert, H., T. de Biolley, R. de Falleur, and P. Hugé (1974b), Un Exemple d'Utili-
    sation du Modèle Économétrique du Bureau du Plan pour l'Analyse d'Alternatives
    de Politiques Fiscales, *Recherches Economiques de Louvain*, 40(4), 399-424.
Bogaert, H., T. de Biolley, R. de Falleur, and P. Hugé (1979), L'Utilisation du
    Modèle RENA pour l'Analyse des Conséquences Régionales des Choix Économique-
    ment Possibles du Plan Belge 1976-1980, in R. Courbis (ed.), *Modèles Régionaux
    et Modèles Régionaux-Nationaux* (Editions Cujas, Paris), pp. 123-133.
Van Broekhoven, E. (1974), Etablissement d'une Projection Macroéconomique à l'Aide
    du Modèle RENA: A Comment, *Recherches Economiques de Louvain*, 40(4), 393-397.
Brown, M., M. di Palma, and B. Ferrara (1972), A Regional-National Econometric
    Model of Italy, *Papers of the Regional Science Association*, 29, 25-44.
Brown, M., M. di Palma, and B. Ferrara (eds.) (1978), *Regional-National Econometric
    Modeling with an Application to the Italian Economy* (Pion, London).
Courbis, R. (1972), The REGINA Model, a Regional-National Model of the French Econ-
    omy, *Economics and Planning*, 12(3), 133-152.
Courbis, R. (1975a), Le Modèle REGINA, Modèle du Développement National, Régional
    et Urbain de l'Économie Francaise, *Economie Appliquée*, 28(2-3), 569-600.
Courbis, R. (1975b), Urban Analysis in the Regional-National Model REGINA of the
    French Economy, *Environment and Planning*, 7(7), 863-878.
Courbis, R. (1978), The REGINA Model: Presentation and First Contributions to
    Economic Policy, in R. Stone and W. Peterson (eds.), *Econometric Contributions
    to Public Policy* (MacMillan, London), pp. 291-311.
Courbis, R. (1979a), The REGINA Model, a Regional-National Model for French Planning,
    Regional Science and Urban Economics, 9(2-3), 117-139.
Courbis, R. (1979b), Le Modèle REGINA, un Modèle Régionalisé pour la Planification
    Francaise, in G. Gaudard (ed.), *Modèles et Politiques de l'Espace Économique*
    (Editions Universitaires, Fribourg, Switzerland), pp. 225-251.
Courbis, R. (ed.) (1979c), *Modèles Régionaux et Modèles Régionaux-Nationaux* (Editions
    Cujas and CNRS, Paris).
Courbis, R. (1980), Multiregional Modeling and the Interaction between Regional and
    National Development: A General Theoretical Framework, in G.C. Adams and N.J.
    Glickman (eds.), *Modeling the Multiregional Economic System* (Heath, Lexington,
    MA), pp. 107-130.
Courbis, R. (1981), The National and Multinational Impact of Regional Policy, *Paper
    presented at the 28th North American Meeting of the Regional Science Associa-
    tion, Montreal, Canada, November 13-15.*
Courbis, R. (1982a), Multiregional Modeling: A General Appraisal, in M. Albegov,
    A.E. Andersson and F. Snickars (eds.), *Regional Development Modeling: Theory
    and Practice* (North Holland, Amsterdam), pp. 59-78.

Courbis, R. (1982b), Measuring Effects of French Regional Policy by Means of a
    Regional-National Model, *Regional Science and Urban Economics*, 12(1), 1-21.
Courbis, R., J. Bourdon, and G. Cornilleau (1980), *Le Modèle REGINA, GAMA Report
    for the French Planning Office 321* (Economica, Paris), to be published.
Courbis, R., and G. Cornilleau (1978), The REGIS Model, A Simplified Version of the
    Regional-National REGINA Model, *Paper presented at the 18th European Meeting
    of the Regional Science Association, Fribourg, Switzerland, August 29-
    September 1.*
Courbis, R., and G. Cornilleau (1979), Propositions pour l'Élaboration d'un Modèle
    Communautaire Régionalisé: REGILINK, *Paper presented at the Experts Group on
    Building a Regionalized EEC Model* (Commission of European Communities, Brussels)
    (GAMA Working Paper 270).
Courbis, R., and Ch. Pommier (1979), *Construction d'un Tableau d'Échanges Inter-
    Industriels et Inter-Régionaux de l'Économie Française* (Economica and Documen-
    tation Francaise, Paris).
Courbis, R., and J.C. Prager (1971), Analyse Régionale et Planification Nationale:
    le Projet de Modèle REGINA d'Analyse Interdépendante, *Paper presented at the
    Joint French-U.S.S.R. Conference on the Use of Models for Planning, Paris,
    October 11-15* (published in *Collections de l'INSEE*, R(12):5-32).
van Delft, A., B.A. Van Hamel, and H. Hetsen (1977), Een Multiregionaal Model voor
    Nederland, *Paper presented at the meeting of the Dutch Group of the Regional
    Science Association, Rotterdam, April 5* (Central Planning Bureau, The Hague,
    Netherlands) (Occasional Paper 13).
Despontin, M. (1981a), Kwantitatieve Economische Politiek vanuit een Besluitvormings-
    optiek, *Ph.D. Dissertation* (Free University, Brussels).
Despontin, M. (1981b), Dynamic Optimization in a Multiregional Econometric Model for
    Belgium, in J.P. Brans (ed.), *Operational Research '81* (North Holland, Amster-
    dam), pp. 209-220.
EEC (1971), Politique Régionale et Union Économique et Monétaire. Les Déséquilibres
    Géographiques Face à la Réalisation des Équilibres Économiques Fondamentaux,
    Directorate of the Regional Policy Working Paper XVI/137/71 (Commission of the
    European Economic Community, Brussels).
de Falleur, R., H. Bogaert, T. de Biolley, and P. Hugé (1975), L'Utilisation du
    Modèle RENA pour la Prévision des Lignes de Force de la Politique Économique
    à Moyen Terme, in *Utilisation des Systèmes de Modèles dans la Planification*
    (United Nations, European Economic Commission, Geneva), pp. 268-293.
Glejser, H., G. Van Daele, and M. Lambrecht (1973), The First Experiments with an
    Econometric Regional Model of the Belgian Economy, *Regional Science and Urban
    Economics*, 3(3), 301-314.
Glejser, H. (1975), *MACEDOINE, un Modèle Régional de l'Économie Belge* (Planning
    Bureau, Brussels).
Van Hamel, B.A., H. Hetsen, and J.H.M. Kok (1975), Un Modèle Économique Multirégional
    pour les Pays-Bas, in *Utilisation des Systèmes de Modèles dans la Planification*
    (United Nations, European Economic Commission, Geneva), pp. 212-267.
Van Hamel, B.A., H. Hetsen, and J.H.M. Kok (1979), Un Modèle Économique Multirégional
    pour les Pays-Bas, in R. Courbis (ed.), *Modèles Régionaux et Modèles Régionaux-
    Nationaux* (Editions Cujas, Paris), pp. 147-173.
Higgins, B. (1973), Trade-Off Curves and Regional Gaps, in J.N. Bhagwati and R.S.
    Eckaus (eds.), *Development and Planning: Essays in Honour of Paul Rosenstein-
    Rodan* (MIT Press, Cambridge, MA), pp. 152-177.
Rochoux, J.Y. (1979), Analyse Régionale des Opérations Financières, *Doctorate Dis-
    sertation, GAMA, University of Nanterre, October.*
Snickars, F. (1981), Interregional and International Linkages in Multiregional
    Economic Models, *IIASA Working Paper* (forthcoming) (International Institute
    for Applied Systems Analysis, Laxenburg, Austria).
Thys-Clement, F., P. Van Rompuy, and L. de Corel (1973), RENA, un Modèle Écono-
    métrique pour l'Élaboration du Plan 1976-1980 (Planning Bureau, Brussels).
Thys-Clement, F., P. Van Rompuy, and L. de Corel (1979), RENA, a Regional-National
    Model for Belgium, in R. Courbis (ed.), *Modèles Régionaux et Modèles Régionaux-
    Nationaux* (Editions Cujas, Paris), pp. 103-122.

CHAPTER 9

SOME DEVELOPMENTS IN MULTIREGIONAL MODELING IN EASTERN EUROPE

Stephan Mizera

1 Initial Development of Multiregional Models in Eastern Europe

Economic modeling in East European countries is aimed at improving the national planning system, its mechanisms, and the solution of tasks at all stages of the national economic plan. A number of models have been developed to prepare and evaluate planning documents and, by ensuring that consistency is achieved between national and regional plans, they make a significant contribution to the formulation of development objectives.

Economic models of single regions, such as those constructed by Jemelianov and Kushnirski (1974), Mizera (1970) and Fundarek (1975) were among the first to be employed. They focused on problems similar to those dealt with in national economic models, but in contrast with the latter, regional models emphasize the treatment of specific territorial features of the national economy, i.e., they contain variables representing, for example, links between regions and the national economy, the openness of the regional economy, and regional responses to national economic development policy.

In the 1970s several multiregional models were developed and made operational (see, e.g., Baranov and Matlin 1976, Macura and Popovic 1977, Hoffman 1978). These models can be classified according to their method of calculation, their intended applications, and their spatial-structural features. Within the first group, there are econometric models (Jemelianov and Kushnirski 1976, Mizera 1980), and input-output models (Baranov and Matlin 1976, Macura and Popovic 1977, Zabák 1974). In addition, depending upon the application, it includes descriptive and analytical models characterizing the existing system, forecasting models, and programming models.

The time lag in the development and application of multiregional models can be attributed to several factors. The principal reason is that in most East European countries the methods used in economic planning have tended to concentrate on sectoral and enterprise aggregations at the national level, with regional aggregation made only as a secondary territorial cross section of national, sectoral, and enterprise planning and decision making. Another reason may be the difficulties inherent in fitting the model structure and input data to actual conditions. The majority of planned economies lack statistical information on regional and interregional flows of goods and services.

2 Multiregional Models of the Czechoslovak Economy

To give a general idea of the development and application of multiregional economic (ME) models in East European countries, in this section a brief description of three multiregional models of the Czechoslovak economy is given (Hoffman 1978, Mizera 1980, 1981). These models were developed and applied as components of national economic model systems.

2.1 Multiregional forecasting model for the development of the Czechoslovak economy

The purpose of this multiregional forecasting model is to provide information for long-term planning of the Czechoslovak economy. It is an econometric forecasting model of multiregional economic and social development covering a period of 10-15 years (Mizera 1980).

The model is divided into nine relatively independent segments: population; labor resources and their allocation; basic production (industry, agriculture); auxiliary production (construction industry, transportation, communications, commerce, research); services (community and social security services, education, entertainment, health care); investments and capital resources; monetary income and expenditure of the population; balance quations; aggregated indicators representing the structure of regional development. These segments are used to calculate the values of more than 400 indicators of the socioeconomic development in four regions, taking into account intra- and interregional commodity and capital flows, as well as migration and commuting. The solution of the regional development problem is based on the assumption that the primary goals relate to the national economic development program, the allocation of investment to industry, and the regional allocation of labor (top-down process). Regional service development resulting from national economic policy for the regions is a secondary objective.

The calculation process in the model is iterative and operates as a relatively closed cycle for individual time periods. Continuity is assured by means of endogenous variables shifted over time or by exogenously determined values. Interregional and regional-national linkages are achieved through the use of exogenously determined variables in regression equations, through the adherence of the internal balance to some predetermined indicators of national economic development, and through the interregional allocation and distribution of resources.

2.2 An econometric model

This model is designed to forecast the development of key national indicators of sectoral and regional development in Czechoslovakia, using extrapolation and normative calculation procedures (Mizera 1981). It contains three subsystems: a macroeconomic model of national development; a submodel of the development of industrial sectors; and a regional development model.

The macroeconomic model contains 66 equations and seven segments (population, labor resources and their allocation; productivity, income and cash income and expenditure of the population; utilization of national income; capital formation and renewal investment; reproduction of the basic means of production; development of the productive sectors of the national economy; nonproductive labor). The purpose of this model is to analyze the influence of national economic development on two macroregions (Slovak and Czech Socialist Republics) and to determine the global constraints on regional and sectoral development in the two macroregions.

The submodel of the development of industrial sectors consists of 44 equations and three segments: industrial sectors of national importance (mining--iron and nonferrous metals, engineering, fossil fuels, electricity); industrial sectors of regional importance (pharmaceutical industry, forestry, building materials, pulp and paper, glass, ceramics and porcelain, textiles, leather and rubber, foodstuffs, clothing); and centrally managed industry. This submodel is used to analyze the consumption structure in industrial sectors. A stochastic structural balance approach (comprising regression equations in which the explanatory variable is the production of the sectors with the greatest contractual activities, as determined by the input-output table) is taken in the segment that includes industries with intraregional linkages, whereas in the segment including national economic sectors regression relationships dividing regional production according to its dependence on regional resources are used.

The regional development submodel is divided into seven segments: population; labor resources and their allocation; basic production (industry, agriculture); auxiliary production (building, commerce, regionally managed transportation); nonproductive activities and services; investments and basic production means, income

and expenditure of the population. This submodel contains a total of 263 equations
for four regions. Its purpose is to translate development objectives formulated at
national level into a macroregional context. It should also provide a framework
for regional development planning that takes into account regional conditions and
requirements as well as constraints from the national level. In the calculations,
the model is treated as a coordinated system in which the iterative process is carried out in individual segments without considering their relation to particular
submodels. The structure of the segments and equations takes account of the links
of practical planning methods to the available statistical information on national,
sectoral, and regional economic and social development. There is a two-way feedback flow in the solution process, i.e., bottom-up and top-down, which always corresponds to the prevailing national or regional feedback in individual segments.

2.3 A national decision making model

The national decision making model is used to find the values of the most
important regional indicators, which will then serve as constraints on national
plan fulfilment (Hoffman 1978). Input data on regional income, the renewal of regional investment, as well as capital formation and nonproductive consumption in
two macroregions, labor and capital flows, and equalization of their socioeconomic
level is required. In addition, certain parameter values, such as the depreciation
rate, the age structure of the population, production efficiency, and the extent of
labor-capital substitution should be predetermined.

The point of departure for studying the interrelations and characteristics of
the two macroregions is an examination of the demand for service provision. This
should determine the extent to which this sector should be developed within each
region over the period under analysis. In order to achieve the national socioeconomic goals, it is necessary to increase the national income, capital accumulation
in each macroregion, interregional transfers of capital, shifts in the regional
shares of national income expenditure, etc.

3 Characteristics of Multiregional Models in Eastern Europe

ME models developed in the USSR and their implementation are discussed in
Chapters 6, 10, and 11 of this book. Here, only some general considerations are
presented relating to approaches and specific emphases to modeling imposed by a
sectorally oriented centralized planning system.

ME models operating in planned economies are an integral part of the planning
system, which has a direct influence on their structure, objectives, and methodological base. They are employed at every stage of the planning process and include
information on the spatial aspects of national economic development. For this reason they are used to translate centrally determined objectives into a regional context. The time period covered by an ME model generally ranges from five years
(medium-term) to 15 years (long-term).

Multiregional problems are incorporated into national economic models in one
of two ways, usually by employing a relatively independent model to solve such problems and to link this to other components of the system, either by means of a defined
set of inputs and outputs, or by informal methods. This approach involves the complete integration of regional problems within the national economic models, so that
multiregional problems form an integral element of the overall model structure.

The spatial subdivision of the country is of decisive importance for the planning system, but also for the internal structure of multiregional models. In
general, administrative and political units constitute the basic structure for the
multiregional division of the centrally planned economy. Such a division of the
country directly affects the size of the models and their degree of detail. For
microregional applications, detailed information is included, since political and
administrative regions have a certain degree of autonomy. This spatial division
of the country also influences national level sectoral relationships within the
model and is a factor governing the openness or closedness of intraregional units.
In multiregional models a distinction is made between the sectors managed at national, regional, and local levels.

Several methodological approaches are employed to examine regional development problems. The choice of approach is to a great extent dependent upon the type of mathematical calculations used. Econometric models use direct methods of adjustment such as simple corrections of mutually interrelated indicators, as well as normative balance methods based on simple balances and on interregional structural balances. In optimization procedures, indirect reconciliation methods are used, based on the dual assessment of regional resources or on their integrated spatial distribution.

Multiregional models achieve a spatial-temporal compatibility through the comprehensive balancing of supply and demand at the regional level by aggregating direct and indirect demands of a certain type. This balancing principle is applied to solve the problem of resource distribution at the regional level (programming function) or as a means of determining the difference between the overall resource requirements for development and the existing allocation of resources in space and over time (evaluative function).

The planning approach is to balance the demand for and supply of resources over time and in space at all levels of the planning hierarchy individually and between levels. Various goals and targets are used to express demand in quantitative terms. Planning calculations are made in varying degrees of detail and at several levels of aggregation, i.e., at national, regional, and sectoral levels. Cause-effect relationships between economic indicators with varying degrees of aggregation are represented in quantitative terms by specific dynamic normatives that fluctuate according to the type and number of indicators included in the model and over time.

At the national level, multiregional models generally include indicators representing the aggregated production of the national economy (production, plus the generation and use of national income), resources production and development, labor and population growth, improvement in living standards, etc.

At the regional level, the main sectoral indicators (industry, agriculture, construction, transportation and communications, and commerce), the main service indicators (education, health care, other services) and aggregated national economic indicators of the region under analysis (population, labor resources and their allocation, natural and economic resources, basic indicators of living standards) are included. In addition national data, although disaggregated, are important. The greatest degree of detail occurs in those indicators representing the lowest level of the planning hierarchy, i.e., the subregional level.

There are two types of links between the elements of multiregional economic models: (i) a link reflecting the effect of national economic development on a given region or group of regions, and (ii) a link between subregional elements. In most of the above models, it is assumed that there is a top-down linkage in which primary changes in the dynamics of development of the region arise as a result of national development objectives either in correspondence with the existing distribution of resources or with the interregional allocation of the means of production and labor. In econometric models, these changes are represented by regression functions in which the indicator representing the estimated regional share of total national production depends, for example, on the regional proportions of those indicators on which the explanatory variable depends. In other models, such changes are effected by means of elasticity coefficients that express the relative change in a given indicator of the region as compared with the relative change of the same indicators at the national level or by the use of exogenously determined normatives. Consistency is achieved by a gradual resolution of conflicts made directly in the optimization models or by dual assessments of a global solution. Intraregional relationships are determined by the same type of procedures as used in national models.

4   Concluding Remarks

ME models have an important role to play in aiding planners to achieve consistency in the formulation and implementation of national and regional economic programs.

Further development will be focused on the problems of integrating these models into national economic model systems. Direct and indirect feedbacks from the regional and subregional levels to the national level will be incorporated to register the effects of national plans on regional development. It is important to develop multiregional models that can be applied on several levels to solve a variety of economic problems. Their information base should comply with the principles governing the existing planning system.

Another line of development should also be pursued to improve the implementability of these models; this requires a strengthening of the links between economic and physical planning. A more detailed picture of spatial interrelationships and a more specific identification of the economic effects of this arrangement of economic and social processes should result from such a development.

References

Baranov, E.F., and I.S. Matlin (1976), About Experimental Implementation of a System of Models of Optimal Perspective Planning, *Economics and Mathematic Methods*, 12(4).

Fundárek, M. (1975), Long Term Forecasting Model for the Economy of Slovakia, *Research Paper* 56 (VVS, Bratislava).

Hoffmann, P. (1978), Decision Model for Two-Regional System of National Economy, *Research Paper* 62 (Research Institute of Regional Economic Planning, Bratislava).

Jemelianov, S.S., and F.I. Kushnirski (1974), *Modelling the Indicators of the Development of the National Economy in the Soviet Union Republics* (Ekonomika, Moscow).

Kolek, J. *et al.* (1976), *An Improved Econometric Model of Middle-Term Analyses and Forecasts of the Slovak Economy* (Research Computing Centre, Bratislava).

Macura, S., and B. Popovic (1977), Economic-Demographic Model BACHUE in Jugoslavia, *Population and Employment Working Paper* 55 (International Labour Office, Geneva).

Mizera, St. (1970), Econometric Model of Slovak Economy, *Research Paper* 49 (Research Institute of Regional Economic Planning, Bratislava).

Mizera, St. (1975), Econometric Models and their Application in the Analysis and Projections of Economic Development, *Research Paper* 97 (Research Institute of Regional Economic Planning, Bratislava).

Mizera, St. (1980), Multiregional Forecasting Model for Development of National Economy, *Working Paper* 121 (Research Institute of Regional Economic Planning, Bratislava).

Mizera, St. (1981), Econometric Model of the Sectoral and Regional Development of the Republic, *Research Paper* (Research Institute of Regional Economic Planning, Bratislava).

Zabák, Z. (1974), The Two-Regional Structural Planning Balance Model of the Czechoslovak Economy, *Research Paper* 88 (Research Institute of Regional Economic Planning, Bratislava).

CHAPTER 10

EXPERIENCE IN THE USE OF MULTIREGIONAL ECONOMIC MODELS
IN THE SOVIET UNION

Alexander Granberg

1 Introduction

The importance of the role of interregional models in the study and planning
of the national economy of the USSR is due to the vast size of the country, the
extraordinary diversity of physical conditions and socioeconomic development trends
of particular regions, and the existing national-political structure of the planned
management system. In the Soviet economy the interdependence of national and regional development is continually being strengthened by means of interregional economic interaction.

The conditions for applying interregional models in the USSR are determined
by specific features of the existing state planning system, as described in Chapter
6. The economic and social development plans and preplanning documents at the upper
territorial hierarchy level are already worked out for 15 republics and 19 economic
regions for periods of up to 20 years. Thus interregional models elaborated in the
USSR should involve up to 26 regions at the first level (13 republics and 13 economic regions being part of the Russian Federation and the Ukraine), and should be
adapted to specific long-term (10-20 years), medium-term (five years), and short-
term (one year) planning problems. This chapter summarizes the experience of the
Institute of Economics and Organization of Industrial Production, Siberian Branch
of the USSR Academy of Sciences (IEOIP) in the building and use of interregional
models of the national economy.

2 Main Types of Models

2.1 Interregional input-output models

The IEOIP studies the economy using three types of interregional input-output
models (SYREN): (i) models of the interregional input-output balance; (ii) interregional optimization models with a global (scalar or vector) optimality criterion;
and (iii) models of economic interaction of regions with local optimality criteria.
The third type can be also classified into the group of two-level models (national
economy and regions)--see below.

Models of the interregional input-output balance. These models are usually
reduced to simultaneous algebraic equations with a sole solution with a given set
of structural parameters. The model formulated by Chenery and Moses is the most
widely used one in the USSR, largely because of its small information requirements.
Interregional input-output balances were drawn up on the basis of this model for
two zones of the Soviet Union (zone I, the Russian Federation, and zone II, the
other 14 republics), for three Transcaucasian republics, for five republics of the
zone of Kazakhstan and Central Asia, and for seven territorial units of the Far East.
The IEOIP also used modified input-output models involving, within the simultaneous
equations, interrelationships of production, private consumption, and incomes of
the population as well as equations for noncompetitive imports.

The main shortcoming of the balance models is that they include many exogenous
parameters of the national economic territorial structure (e.g., trade coefficients
in the model by Chenery and Moses), and so this restricts their applicability for

planning purposes. Therefore, in studies conducted in the IEOIP (for example, the planning of the interregional distribution of investments) for a planned period, the balance model is used mainly to check the consistency of more complex interregional models (see below and Section 2.2).

Interregional input-output optimization models (SYREN-OPT). A SYREN-OPT type model can be regarded firstly as a specialized model at the national economic level --a tool for centralized preplanning and planning substantiations of territorial proportions--and secondly as a form for synthesizing regional models and coordinating regional designs.

A basic SYREN-OPT model (Granberg 1973, 1975a, 1976) involves regional balances of sector outputs, transportation, labor resources; constraints for particular groups of endogenous variables (for the last year of a plan period), and regional and national balances of investments (for the whole plan period, e.g., 10-20 years). Regional outputs, consumption, interregional deliveries of outputs (for the last year), and parameters of an investment growth (for the whole plan period) are the main endogenous variables.

The objective conditions of the basic SYREN-OPT model are formulated as follows: we have to maximize the consumption level of the nation (z), given certain ratios of regional consumption levels ($z^r \geq \lambda^r z$). In the simplest case z and z^r characterize consumption and nonproductive accumulation (with constant prices). For each vector λ^r satisfying $\lambda^r > 0$, $\Sigma \lambda^r = 1$, the model produces a development variant for the regions and of the nation that is Pareto-optimal: it cannot be improved in the interests of one or several regions without adversely affecting the well being of at least one of the rest. By varying the components of vector λ^r, one always obtains Pareto-optimal solutions which, however, contribute to a differing degree to achieving the goals of national social policies and to meeting the interests of particular regions.

2.2 Models of two-level systems for the national economy and regions

Within the planning management system the first-level regions (republics and economic regions) are, in accordance with the principle of democratic centralism, subjects of centralized planning, and economic units with their own interests and comprehensive economic rights. The modeling of two-level systems of the national economy and the regions emphasizes such aspects as the coordination of national economic and regional interests, the optimal distribution of economic resources, the coordination of regional designs, the interdependence of national economic and regional conditions, and the allocation of functions between national and regional bodies of planning management.

Model of optimal interregional allocation of centralized resources. The principle of coordinating autonomous regional decisions by controlling the allocation of centralized resources was tested with the problem "west-east" within which the USSR is divided into two zones (Granberg and Chernyshov 1970). A development variant providing the highest standard of living with given investment limits and under the condition that the interzonal exchange targets are fulfilled is found on the basis of a special model for each zone. The investment limits and interzonal deliveries are varied within the process of iterations so that the total living standards could be improved, given the ratios of the zonal levels. An algorithm based on equalization of dual prices of the same resources and of the products in exchange is used to find a global optimal plan.

Models of optimal economic interactions of regions with local optimality criteria (SYREN-INT). These models coordinate regional solutions by means of a built-in mechanism of interregional economic relationships. A model with the following structure was tested (Rubinshtein 1976). Regional models include in addition to the conditions of SYREN-OPT the trade balance equations; and output export-import balances are common to all regions. The living standard is maximized for each region (a global objective function is not included in the model conditions). Regional solutions are coordinated by choosing the exchange prices of products and correcting the interregional trade balance in value terms.

The existence of equilibrium points belonging to the Pareto set was demonstrated; equivalence conditions for solutions to SYREN-OPT and SYREN-INT were obtained. The equilibrium solution can be "moved" along the Pareto boundary by choosing the trade balance values (in value terms).

National economic model with response functions for regions. The main idea of this model is that the structural models of the regions are, within the system of interactions entitled "national economy regions", replaced by functions showing the explicit dependence of the model output parameters on the input ones (Marjasov and Suslov 1980). The general methodology for building "response" functions of a region to stimuli from the national economic level is based on experimental design theory.

3 Role of Interregional Models in Decision Making

The task of a model at the preplanning stage is largely not to find the sole best development variant (univariant forecast), but to find the mechanism of inter-sectoral and interregional interactions, the quantitative value of dependences and interdependences of major factors, and to identify stable dynamic and structural patterns of movement towards the optimum system of national economic territorial proportions.

The active use of interregional models within the process of designing state plans requires a restructuring of planning technology and a modernization of the models.

At present there is a discrepancy between the potential of interregional models and the routine of territorial planning at the upper level. The national economic plan and the regional plans (of republics and economic regions) have different indi-cator systems, so that it is impossible to present a national economic plan as a synthesis of regional plans--it cannot be broken down into regional plans. The linkages "from bottom to top" within the system of planning and informational link-ages insufficiently affect the formation of the national economic plan, which is approved prior to the regional plans. The role of planning of interregional link-ages is inadequate. It is impossible to evaluate directly the effect of different interregional integration variants.

On the other hand, the experimentally tested SYREN-type models are as yet un-able to answer some practical questions because: (1) the level of detail is insuf-ficient (e.g., the highest number of regions is 11 at present); (2) they do not deal with some regional development variables covered by state plans; and (3) it is dif-ficult to use these models under the current annual planning scheme. These diffi-culties can be overcome by adapting the models and the actual decision making tech-nology. The use of interregional models will allow the coverage of territorial planning at the upper level to be widened, and territorial planning to be integrated into the planning of the national economy.

An interregional model can be employed at the initial stages of the elaboration of a national economic plan, initially for studying the effect of regional factors on the national economic development trends, working out a general concept of the territorial distribution of productive forces (in particular, of potentialities of an accelerated development of the eastern regions of the USSR possessing significant natural resources), and evaluating possibilities and effects of equalizing regional development and welfare levels. For these purposes it is sufficient to use a highly aggregated model.

The emphasis at subsequent planning stages moves to the field of substantiating in detail the production development and location within sectors and regions, the deployment of transport, interregional linkages, etc. Much more detailed interre-gional models should be employed for this purpose. Finally, an interregional model can, at the concluding stages of the formulation of the national economic plan, serve as a tool for generalizing and testing summary socioeconomic, sectoral, and regional designs with regard to balance. A disaggregated interregional model can involve a great number of national economic, sectoral, and regional conditions, al-though it should not be considered as a "supermodel" to replace summary (pointwise) national model. A model has a great number of direct linkages and feedbacks with other models; therefore, its potentialities are most comprehensively employed within the framework of multilevel systems of national economic planning models.

The most complex problem for the more efficient use of interregional models in planning is the creation of the database. A substantial advance in this field has been made in the USSR. Input-output tables have been set up for all 15 republics for 1966, 1972, and 1977, and similar tables are being constructed for ten economic regions of the largest republic--the Russian Federation--but this work is not yet a regular scheme. Forecasting models as generalizations of input-output models (Granberg 1975b, 1979) are being built in most republics and in a number of regions of the Russian Federation. This has created good informational and organizational conditions for building interregional national economic models by synthesizing regional models.

The role of statistical data for modeling the planning decisions for 10-20 years to come must not be overestimated, however. Statistical forecasting of input-output coefficients with three statistical observations does not produce good results. The USSR has some experience; it has engaged 300-400 scientific research institutions to draw up a matrix of national economic models using technological and economic design methodology. Essentially, this work can also be done for the regions. Improving the system of regional statistical and planning information resolves the main problem of adapting interregional models to more detailed and more specific planning tasks. Clearly, it would be wrong to think that the creation of more perfect data is a primary prerequisite for modeling rather than for planning. In fact the use of models, while widening and regulating the composition of planning problems, only intensifies the work on improving information that is undoubtedly needed for planning itself. The interests of "planning" and "modeling" are combined within the automated system of planning computations (ASPR) created by the USSR state planning committee (see Chapter 6).

The ASPR covers a summarizing and functional subsystem--the "Territorial Plan". Interregional models are assumed to be the main elements of this subsystem of planning. One model has already been implemented at the head computing center of the USSR, Gosplan.

4 Experience in Modeling Interregional Interactions in the Soviet Economy

4.1 Analyzing and optimizing territorial proportions of the national economy

Studies for 1966-75. Optimization models of the SYREN-OPT type were tested for the first time by IEOIP for a ten-year period (1966-75), broken down into 16 sectors of material production and ten economic zones of the USSR. For the subsequent decade work was carried out on updating information and computing new variants of the long-term territorial proportions of the USSR. A detailed analysis of the main variants of these territorial proportions for 1966-75 computed by an optimization model is given in Granberg (1973, pp. 117-191). A number of stable qualitative specific features of optimal solutions were revealed; in particular, a notable differentiation was seen in the growth rates of most sectors by zone, and of different sectors within each zone, as well as a deepening of the specialization of the zones. On the whole, economic growth forecasts up to 1975 proved to be too optimistic (incidentally, this was also true of most other long-term forecasts made in the early and mid-1960s). To a much greater extent the forecasts of structural shifts within the system of territorial proportions of the national economy were borne out.

Some outcomes of optimization computations that were first considered false or fortuitous were recognized later. The recommendations concerning the optimal interval within which the development rates of Siberia and the Far East should be greater than those of the rest of the Soviet economy, the necessity for the narrower specialization of a number of regions, the possibility of a preferential development of the mining industry in Siberia, and the need to reduce the growth rates of light industry, etc. were the first to be accepted.

As the analysis of the problem "west-east" showed, the effect of the two Soviet macrozones on the value of the national economic objective function is substantially higher than the share of the zones in GNP and in the national income (2-2.5 times higher for the "east" zone). It was stated that the two zones and the national economy essentially benefit from the territorial division of labor. By a series of computations a range was outlined within which the zones might be interested in output exchange and a range of compromises (the Pareto set).

A simplified version of the interregional optimization model of the national economy was also employed to make an economic-mathematical analysis of the established system of territorial proportions of the USSR for 1966 (republican and regional input-output tables were constructed for that year). The findings of the analysis are shown in Granberg (1975b, pp. 282-297). The most important finding of the analysis seems to be the determination of dual prices of production capacities (marginal output volumes) which classify bottlenecks in production development and location, and reveal the most efficient directions for short-term investments to expand output.

Studies for 1976-90. The computations were mainly carried out with SYREN-OPT for 16 sectors and 11 regions, and a problem with 48 sectors was also tested. Prior to this a considerable amount of work was carried out on the creation of a database for 1975. Direct data and extrapolations of the data of input-output tables were supplemented by the findings of the simulation technique, i.e., missing variables were found with the aid of interregional models.

In modeling territorial proportions for 1976-90 most attention was paid to the problem of the interdependence of national and regional economic factors. Methodologically, the emphasis was placed on the scenario technique; most scenarios were employed to analyze situations occurring due to assumptions for the dynamics of the efficiency of the main production factors (labor, capital investment) and for the growth rates of productive capital investments, i.e., the scenarios of the social production intensification process were the most thoroughly analyzed.

Optimization computations indicated a large dependence of the future territorial proportions on the national income growth rate (gross product) and on the national production efficiency trends up to 1990--for which there existed much uncertainty. Under these conditions, it seems that an isolated quantitative forecast of even the main territorial proportions loses its value to a great degree. The general remarks on the basis of the computations were therefore formulated as optimal intervals of elasticities of regional growth in output in relation to the national rates, and as optimal intervals of regional shares in the national output and investments.

IEOIP is at present preparing the data and software to carry out, with the aid of a group of SYREN-type models, an analysis of development trends of territorial proportions of the USSR for 1961-80 and to study the main directions of changes in territorial proportions for 1981-2000.

4.2 Modeling economic development of the Russian Federation (two-zone analysis)

The leading role in the Soviet national economy is played by the Russian Federation which has about 60% of the country's economic potential. That is why the search for ways of improving the efficiency of the Federation's economy and alternatives for its interactions with the economies of the other republics is of special importance. In modeling the economy of the Russian Federation the principle of two-zone economic analysis is widely employed. This means that the economic situation, the economic development trends, and the outlook of the federation are studied within the framework of a two-zone economic system: zone I is the Russian Federation, and zone II comprises the other republics. The main findings of the study are summarized in Granberg *et al.* (1981), but in this chapter all the types of models considered in Section 2 were used.

The analysis made with the aid of two-zone interregional models indicates that a specific division of labor exists currently in the Soviet economy: the Russian Federation carries a considerable load as regards the creation of the accumulation fund for the second zone, whereas the other republics provide substantial amounts of material and labor input and capital investment for the consumption fund of the Russian Federation. The development of the territorial division of labor promotes labor saving in the federation, but it increases the demand of the republics for productive investment.

The following conclusions were drawn from the analysis of development prospects and interactions of the two zones carried out with the help of the models. As far as major "extensive" variables are concerned, the Russian Federation's share will

not change essentially in future five-year plan periods. Growth rates of the gross
output and national income will be similar in the two zones, although they may be
a little lower in the Federation. There is no hope that an essential reduction in
the economic growth rates of the Russian Federation could be offset by higher development rates of the other republics. The advantage of the Federation in relation
to most "intensive" synthetic variables is likely to grow, mainly due to the substantial differentiation in the growth rates of population and employment.

In order to offset the effects of a sharp reduction in the further recruitment
of additional labor for the material production sphere in the Russian Federation
it is necessary to fulfil at least two conditions: (i) the labor productivity growth
rates in the republics should be somewhat higher than in the second zone; and (ii)
the republics' share in productive capital investment should be increased, and the
stock of basic production assets should grow somewhat more rapidly.

4.3 Modeling the development of Siberia within the Soviet economy

The striking specialization of Siberia in the national territorial division of
labor and its increasing influence on the national economic development reduce the
potential for an isolated study of the socioeconomic problems of this region. A
national economic approach is needed for an appropriate study, i.e., the examination
of possible development alternatives for Siberia within the integrated national
economy. Such an approach will surely have application in places other than Siberia;
therefore, in a critical analysis of the experience with development studies of
Siberia, it is essential to specify general conceptual principles and methodological
techniques to be employed for similar studies of other regions of the USSR.

Possible variants of the development rates and proportions of the Siberian
economy were studied with the aid of the SYREN-OPT model, with the USSR divided into
11 zones. The most comprehensive description of the studies carried out can be found
in Aganbegyan *et al.* (1980, pp. 9-67).

As emphasized above, the main task of modeling is considered to be the finding
of the mechanisms of interregional interactions and natural development trends of
regions within the planning optimization process of the national economy, and the
use of this knowledge to work out long-term territorial socioeconomic concepts,
rather than to make one forecast of future regional development. Correspondingly,
the development outlook of Siberia within the integrated national economy was modeled
in three stages: (i) analysis of "inert" development variants; (ii) analysis of
"central" variants corresponding to the most likely development assumptions for the
Soviet economy as a whole; and (iii) building and analysis of the Siberian economy's
development variants within the integrated national economy, which correspond to possible future situations which cannot be predicted with certainty.

Inert development variants. In preparing this group of variants the task was
set out as follows: what effects would the extrapolation of certain trends in the
past have on the economy of Siberia and of the USSR? For example, the following
basic assumptions were studied: that the trend towards a reduction in investment
and labor productivity growth rates, paralleled by the continuing increase in the
capital intensity of production, will continue. The variants obtained under this
assumption have some common features. For example, the Siberian economy is developing faster than the nation as a whole, but the economic growth rates of the USSR
essentially decrease. That is why at subsequent stages it is necessary to examine
the variants associated with relieving negative socioeconomic development trends.

Central development variants. The main finding from the analysis of the numer-
ous variants with varying conditions is the following dynamic pattern: the annual
increase in Siberia's national income and gross product should be 1.2-1.4 times
higher than the national average. If Siberia exceeds the optimal growth rate the
national rate will decrease slightly; if the economic growth rate of Siberia is
slower than the optimal, the curve of the optimal national rate tends to decrease
more sharply. Such a response of the national economy to the changes in the development rates of Siberia is due to the mechanism of interregional economic interactions. A reduction in the growth rate of the Siberian economy almost immediately
affects the growth rates of the sectors in which Siberia is particularly specialized.
But since the reduction in the output of these sectors cannot be compensated by an

increase in the output in other regions, this leads to a substantial decrease in the growth rate of the Soviet economy.

A system of shadow prices of the sectoral output, labor resources, capital investments comparing the various inputs and outputs from the standpoint of the national economic efficiency, corresponds to the optimal variants of territorial proportions of the development of the Soviet economy. Shadow prices of Siberian labor resources are higher to a remarkable extent than those in the European regions and in central Asia. This confirms the assumptions about the economic efficiency of a reallocation of the labor force to the eastern regions of the Russian Federation. The rate of reasonable substitution of labor inputs by additional capital investment is, in Siberia, about 25% higher than the national average, which means that it is more profitable to employ more capital-intensive, labor-saving technologies in Siberia.

On development scenarios of Siberia under varying national conditions. Five basic development scenarios of Siberia within the national economy were studied, each aimed at the examination of a particular problem and obtained by generalizing alternative computations, given the variations in (i) the efficiency in the use of fuels, raw materials, and materials; (ii) labor productivity growth rates and the attraction of additional labor to Siberia; (iii) national capital investment resources; (iv) the share of Siberia in the national nonproductive consumption and accumulation funds; and (v) transport services to ensure economic linkages between the various parts of the country.

Some findings concerning the effects of the changes in the efficiency of the production factors should be stressed. As Siberia is the region with the largest labor shortage (in this respect it competes with the Far East only), the increase in productivity results in a relatively higher benefit there, even if the rate is the same as the regional average. This is shown by the fact that the difference in the growth rates of income produced in Siberia and in the whole USSR is somewhat increasing the benefit to Siberia.

Increasing the efficiency of material resource utilization in the national economy does not weaken the position of Siberia within the Soviet economy. This process can slightly slow down the development rates of raw material sectors in Siberia (due to the increase in the export demands this reduction cannot be significant), but at the same time it will contribute to the expansion of production facilities in these regions for comprehensive processing of natural fuels and raw materials (the required labor force will be recruited from mining industries).

The Siberian economy responds to an increase in capital investment efficiency by accelerating the pace of its development (especially if measured in terms of the national income; the growth of the GNP is insignificant). The sectoral structure undergoes a significant change. Computations of the alternatives with varying capital investment volumes confirm that policies aiming at a higher growth rate of capital investments in the Siberian economy and at improving capital productivity in Siberia are favorable for national economic efficiency. The national economic benefit of allocated investments essentially rises if at the same time labor saving policies (including those due to the increase of equipment per worker) and actions aimed at the saving of material resources are undertaken.

5 Concluding Remarks

We consider as most important in the very near future the following directions for study.

(1) Further improvement of the models
    (a) taking into account alternative conditions for the economic mechanism of combining the goals and interests, and of population migration.
    (b) A broadening of the freedom to make decisions in the production and consumption spheres (including alternative technologies and structures).
    (c) The dynamization of models (transferring from a current model with a back recursion SYREN-OPT-2 to a multiperiod model with bilateral linkages of time series).

(d)   Using models with built-in, detailed blocks of sectors, regions, and transportation.

(e)   Taking into account more completely uncertainty of the social, economic, and technical development (in particular, using the methodology of the Siberian Energy Institute, Irkutsk), etc.

(2) Adapting interregional models to the wider sphere of national and regional planning problems to ensure an interactive regime for working with a different model.

References

Aganbegyan, A.G. *et al.* (eds.) (1980), *Sibir' v Yedinom Narodnokhozyaystvennom Komplekse* (Nauka, Novosibirsk).

Granberg, A.G. (1973), *Optimizatsiya Terrotorial'nykh Proportiy Narodnogo Khozyaystva* (Economica, Moscow).

Granberg, A.G. (1975a), The Construction of Spatial Models of the National Economy, in A. Kukliński (ed.), *Regional Development and Planning: International Perspectives* (Sijthoff-Leyden), pp. 189-200.

Granberg, A.G. (ed.) (1975b), *Mezhotraslevyye Balansy v Analize Terrotorial'nykh Proportsiy SSR* (Nauka, Novosibirsk).

Granberg, A.G. (ed.) (1976), *Spatial National Economic Models* (Novosibirsk).

Granberg, A.G. (1979), On Using Input-Output Models Studying the Territorial Proportions of the USSR, in A. Kukliński and O. Kultalahti (eds.), *Regional Dynamics of Socioeconomic Change* (Tampere, Finn), pp. 69-82.

Granberg, A.G., and A.A. Chernyshov (1970), Zadacha Optimalnogo Territorialnogo Planirovaniia "Zapad-Vostok", in *Izvestia Sibirskogo Otdelenia* (Academy Nauk SSR, Social Sciences Series, 2(6)).

Granberg, A.G., V.S. Zaykin, and V.Ye. Seliverstov (1981), *Rossiyskaya Federatsiya v Obshtchesoyuznoy Ekonomikye (Mezhotraslevoy Analiz)* (Nauka, Novosibirsk).

Marjasov, V., and V. Suslov (1980), Use of Response Functions in Analysis of Territorial Proportions, in *Research in Interindustrial Territorial Proportions* (Novosibirsk) (in Russian).

Rubinshtein, A.G. (1976), Modeling of the Economic Interaction of Regions and Problems of Effect Distribution, in A.G. Granberg (ed.), *Spatial National Economic Models* (Novosibirsk), pp. 33-68.

CHAPTER 11

A SYSTEM OF MODELS FOR COORDINATING SECTORAL AND REGIONAL DEVELOPMENT PLANS

E.F. Baranov
I.S. Matlin

1   Introduction

A primary aim of long-term planning is to coordinate the solution of social and economic problems of both national and regional economies. Substantial efforts in this field have been made in the course of the elaboration of systems of models for sectoral and regional coordination. In this chapter special attention will be paid to the systems of this type developed at the Central Economic and Mathematical Institute (CEMI) of the Academy of Sciences of the USSR.

Research into such systems began in the USSR in the late 1960s and early 1970s, at which time concepts were formulated that allowed the construction of the experimental version of the system (Baranov and Matlin 1976, Baranov et al. 1975, 1980). New theoretical results were also given by Danilov-Daniljan and Zavelski (1975a,b).

The successful results from the simplified version of the model system (Baranov and Matlin 1976) stimulated further efforts to continue the experiment on a more complicated system. Correspondingly, the sectoral and regional model coordination system (SMOTR) was elaborated for application at the preliminary stages of long-term planning, i.e., to prepare the main indicator variants aimed at achieving the desired social and economic development towards national plan targets, as well as the coordination of sectoral and regional plans.

2   General Presentation of the SMOTR System

The SMOTR system was developed according to the following basic principles (Baranov 1975, 1980, Baranov and Matlin 1976, Baranov et al. 1971, Danilov-Daniljan and Zavelski 1975a,b, Fedorenko 1972, 1979):

(i)   It is oriented towards the maximum achievement of the whole complex of national economic targets, including the most significant aspects of the functioning of the socialist economy (i.e., further development of the socialist productive relations, growth of welfare, etc.).

(ii)   It aims to provide an adequate description of the complicated hierarchy of plan targets of socialist society and its separate groups on the basis of both decomposition and composition approaches.

(iii) It attempts to incorporate options of the most efficient directions of scientific and technological progress.

(iv)   It aims to achieve consistency in planning in physical and value terms.

Three types of coordination are foreseen:

coordination of sectoral and regional development policies;
coordination of disaggregated indicators with aggregated national economic indicators;
coordination between all the main functional aspects of the plan (i.e., labor force, finance, standards of living, foreign trade, etc.), as well as their coordination with production planning and capital investment subsystems.

143

The determination of the plan's fulfillment of the social and economic goals is performed via an iterative composition based on regular data exchange between models of different levels and aspects of the economy, an application of the available statistics along with low-priced and easily obtained data to existing soft- and hardware, and by introducing the system into the computerized system of the USSR Planning Committee and State Planning Committees of the republics. This is facilitated by using the adopted nomenclature indexes, economic indicators, and estimates. Particular use is made of aggregated dynamic value (18 sectors) and disaggregated physical (260 commodities) input-output classifications, in an attempt to trace out the dynamic development of the economy based on the long-term (10-15 years) plan.

Today the application of the system of models as a tool for simulation of plan consequences is regarded to be of paramount importance. It may also be used as a tool to improve the interconnections between economic indicators and the main social and economic plan targets together with resources.

SMOTR has been developed to estimate basic national economic proportions and to coordinate sectoral and regional plans on three hierarchy levels (see Figure 1):

(1)   the higher level is represented by a national economic model in which 18 sectors are distinguished and where various social and economic plan targets are specified at the national level;
(2)   the second level is constituted by a national economic model in which 260 commodities are specified and where the outcomes of both sectoral and regional plans play a role;
(3)   the third level is composed of sectoral and regional models specified at a disaggregated level.

SMOTR comprises the following functional blocks: population and labor force; income and consumption; public sector; finance; foreign trade; natural resources.

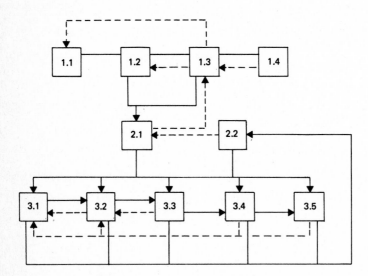

Figure 1.   General outlook of the SMOTR system without isolating functional blocks. Continuous line--direct links; dotted lines--feedback links. (1.1) General macroeconomic system; (1.2) Basic national plan targets; (1.3) Simulation dynamic input-output model (18 sectors); (1.4) Input-output model with sectoral production functions; (2.1) Dynamic input-output model in physical units and in value (260 commodities); (2.2) Central model; (3.1) Sectors and multisectoral complexes (excluding construction); (3.2) Construction block; (3.3) Regional block; (3.4) Transportation block; (3.5) Material supply block

These blocks provide data for the estimation of (a) goals at both national and regional levels; (b) correlation between planned development and natural resources;
and (c) particular aspects of the coordination of value and physical proportions
of social and economic development. Calculations on the basis of SMOTR are iterative in character, aimed at the coordination of development proportions defined on
all three levels.

3 Presentation of some Submodels of the System

3.1 Models at the first level

SMOTR may be referred to as a "top-down" model because it operates down from
the upper-level national plan targets worked out on the basis of resolutions adopted
by the congresses of CPSU, governmental decrees, and the main economic and social
indicators of the national development for a 10-15 year period. A more detailed
elaboration of plan targets requires the application of aggregated macroeconomic
parameter calculations. For this purpose it is planned to include in the first
level a separate econometric forecasting model for the more detailed substantiation
of admissible limits by interconsistent changes of the main plan targets (Yaremenko
et al. 1975, Yaremenko 1981, Ershov and Levchenko 1981).

The dynamic input-output model (Matlin 1980) used on the first level can
verify the fulfillment of plan targets within the planned period and if necessary
can correct them. If the targets are achievable, the trajectories for their implementation may be chosen. The procedure is carried out by means of a man-computer
dialogue with the dynamic input-output algorithm which explicitly includes capital
investment lags.

3.2 The second level of SMOTR

To operate on the second level means to disaggregate the plan targets and proportions of 18 branches down to the level of disaggregated product classification
and to adjust them by means of iterative aggregation. The general idea of the
iterative aggregation method for the static input-output model is presented in Figure 2, where I,K is the index of aggregated products and i,k the index of detailed
products. In the iterative process, the following condition is given: the solution of the aggregated input-output model is equal to the aggregated result of the
detailed model solution.

A modification of the dynamic input-output model in physical units and in value
is used here as a disaggregated model. Comparison of coefficient matrices of the
traditional model and the input-output model in physical units and in value (in a
static version) is shown in Figure 3. The advantages of the second model lie in its
more compact presentation of structural parameters and in the possibility of output
coordination in aggregated and detailed nomenclature. The equation system of the
input-output model in physical units and in value is the following:

$$\sum_{j=1}^{260} a_{ij} x_j + \sum_{l=1}^{18} \tilde{a}_{il} X_l + y_i = x_i \qquad i = 1,\ldots,260 \quad ,$$

$$\sum_{j=1}^{260} P_{lj} x_j + \alpha_l X_l = X_l \qquad l = 1,\ldots,18 \quad .$$

At the initial iteration this model defines initial tasks and constraints over the
sector allocation optimization models confined to national economic plan targets.

In the following iterations a special central model is applied aimed at estimating the adjustment of sectoral and regional solutions to national plan targets

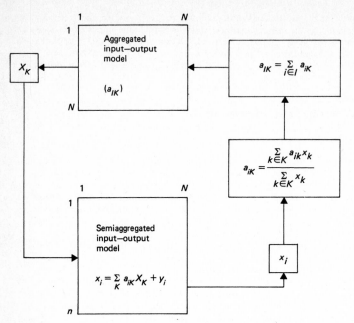

Figure 2.   Iterative aggregation scheme

(a)

Commodities

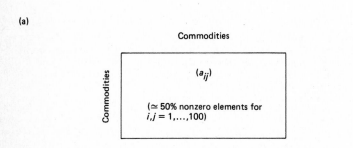

(b)

Commodities ($i, j = 260$)	Industries ($k, l = 18$)
$(\bar{a}_{ij})$	$(\tilde{a}_{il})$
Most important a_{ij} in physical terms ($\simeq 2-3\%$ nonzero elements)	Rest of intermediate demand in physical terms
(P_{kj})	α_l
Price of commodity i produced in industry k	Share of rest of output industry l in value

Figure 3.   (a) Traditional input-output model; (b) input-output model in physical
            units and in value.

(Baranov *et al.* 1975). Section 3.6 gives a more detailed description of the central model. In case it is necessary to correct national objectives the central model provides a feedback onto the disaggregated dynamic input–output model. By means of aggregation, a national economy model is built by repetition of the procedure described previously.

3.3 Sectoral models

The estimations on the third level start with the sector (or intersectoral complex) allocation optimization models which focus on the optimal spatial allocation of production. The optimization criterion is aimed at the minimization of production costs related to labor, investments and intermediate consumption, services to other industries, and transport. In the initial version of the model system (Baranov and Matlin 1976), a standard industrial model was used (see Table 1).

Table 1. Structure of the standard industry model

I = set of intermediate goods

N = set of natural resource types

L = set of labor force types

T = set of planning period years

I_j = set of most important intermediate goods consumed by production of j

I_r = set of goods that most use transport services

I_{kj} = set of capital goods invested in production of j

Objective function

$$\sum_{t,h} \left(\sum_{i \in I_j} P_i(\cdot) a_{ij}^h(t) + \sum_{i \in I_j \cap I_r} P_{ri}^h(t) a_{ij}^h(t) + \sum_{i \in NUL} U_i^h(\cdot) a_{ij}^h(t) \right.$$

$$\left. + \sum_{i \in L} w_i^h(t) a_{ij}^h(t) \right) \bar{x}_j^h(t) + \sum_{t,h} \sum_{i \in I_{kj}} P_k^h(\cdot) \bar{K}_{ij}^h(t) E(t) \to \min$$

t = year, $t \varepsilon T$

h = region, $h \varepsilon H$

$P_i(\cdot)$ = "price" of good i

$$P_i(t,n) = P_i(t,n-1) \left(1 + \frac{\sum_{h,j} a_{ij}^h(t) [\bar{x}_j^h(t,n) - \bar{x}_j^h(t,n-1)]}{\sum_{h,j} a_{ij}^h(t) \bar{x}_j^h(t,n-1)} + \frac{\sum_{h,j} a_{ij}^h(t) \bar{x}_j^h(t,n-1)}{\sum_{h,j} \bar{x}_j^h(t,n-1) P_j(t,1)} \right)$$

Table 1. *Continued*

---

n = number of interior iteration

$P_i(t,1)$ = from the central model.

$P_{ri}^h(t)$ = "tariff" for transportation of good i (from transportation block)

$U_i^h(\cdot)$ = "rent" for using resources of type i

$$U_i^h(t,n) = U_i^h(t,n-1) \left(1 + \frac{\sum_j a_{ij}^h(t) [\bar{x}_j^h(t,n) - \bar{x}_j^h(t,n-1)]}{\sum_j a_{ij}^h(t) \bar{x}_j^h(t,n-1)} + \frac{\sum_j a_{ij}^h(t) \bar{x}_j^h(t,n-1) U_i^h(t-1)}{\sum_j \bar{x}_j^h(t,n-1) P_j(t,1)} \right)$$

$U_i^h(t,1)$ = from the regional block

$w_i^h(t)$ = wage rate

$P_k^h(\cdot)$ = construction "rent" (from construction block), calculated analogously
        to $U_i^h(\cdot)$

$E(t)$ = rate of efficiency of investment (from central model)

Constraints

$$\sum_h \bar{x}_j^h(t) = V_j(t) \quad , \quad t \in T \quad , \quad V_j(t) \text{ from central model}$$

$$\sum_h a_{ij}^h(t)\bar{x}_j^h(t) + \sum_h \bar{K}_{ij}^h(t) \leq F_i(t) \quad , \quad i \in I_j \cup I_{kj} \quad , \quad F_i(t) \text{ from central model}$$

$$\frac{1}{\lambda_j(t)} \bar{x}_j^h(t) \leq \tilde{N}_j^h(t) + \sum_{\tau=1}^{t-1} \Delta\bar{N}_j^h(\tau) + \Delta\bar{N}_j^h(t) \quad , \quad h \in H$$

$\lambda_j(t)$ = rate of capacity use

$\Delta\bar{N}_j^h(t)$ = increase in capacity

$$\bar{K}_{ij}^h(t) = \sum_{\tau \geq t} b_{ij}^h(t) v_j^h(t,\tau) k_i^h(\tau) \Delta\bar{N}_j^h(t)$$

b_{ij}^k = capital coefficient

$v_j^h(t,\tau)$ = distributed lag coefficients

$k_j^h(\tau)$ = investment capacity per capita

$$\sum_h \sum_{i \in I_{kj}} \bar{K}_{ij}^h(t) \leq K_j(t) \quad , \quad K_j(t) \text{ from central model}$$

The multilevel character of the planning structure is clearly reflected in the price information (derived from the central model), which is used in the objective function. Traditionally, the model aimed at searching for the spatial allocation for the new enterprises. Today, the special emphasis lies not on the extent but on the intensity of production. This has led to some evident changes in the approach to industry models, where the technology reflecting the variety of possible implementations of industrial resources is of particular importance.

At the present stage of the development of SMOTR it is inadequate to describe all the sectoral complexes in a homogeneously detailed manner; to complete the system, all the sectoral models should be present. As a compromise, the sectors are subdivided into two groups: one demanding a typical treatment, and the other demanding a special treatment.

In typical models the production functions are used for an aggregated description of labor and capital stocks as basic resources. Production functions may obviously be built only for the aggregated sector classification, which leads to the two-level structure of the sector models: the upper level is represented by an aggregated product allocation model (A); the lower level is represented by a disaggregated corresponding model (B) in physical units.

One nonlinear constraint and a nonlinear criterion are introduced into model A together with constraints on the admissible substitution of resources; this is similar to the treatment by Ershov and Levchenko (1981). The constraint guarantees the equality of the sum of regional gross output with the aggregated sectoral output derived from the aggregated input-output model. The corresponding production functions describe the sectoral gross output by region, which means that the only variables within the model will be output, capital stocks, and labor force. The cost indicators applied in model A are aggregated from the iteration of model B. Model A solutions serve as constraints for model B to find the optimal allocation of labor resources and of new capacities for the sector as a whole and for separate regions. Tasks for the commodity output in disaggregated form for the whole national economy are introduced into this model from the disaggregated model of the upper level. As production functions cannot be applied to model B the labor intensity coefficients and investment per unit of capacity have to be modified by the solutions of model A. The optimization criteria in both models are similar. The iterative process in the typical sectoral model continues up to the stabilization of the transmitted parameters.

Currently two sectors have been marked out as nontypical in the modified system, ferrous metals and agriculture, but we will not give a description of these models in this chapter. Neither will we do so for the construction and material supply blocks (see blocks 3.2, 3.3 and 3.5 in Figure 1).

3.4   The transportation model

Transportation block calculations have to be carried out on the basis of regional model calculations after import and export indicators are defined (Kovshov 1979). The principal relations of the main transportation model are as follows:

$$\sum_{h' \in H} x^i_{hh'}(t) = V^i_h(t)$$

where

$$V^i_h(t) = \text{export of good } i \text{ from region } h$$

$$x^i_{hh'}(t) = \text{flow of good } i \text{ from region } h \text{ to region } h'$$

$$\sum_{h \in H} x^i_{hh'}(t) = W^i_{h'}(t)$$

where

$$W^i_{h'}(t) = \text{import of good } i \text{ to region } h'$$

$$x^i_{hh'}(t)x^i_{h'h}(t) = 0 \qquad \text{(no crosshauling)}$$

$$\underline{x}^i_{hh'}(t) \leq x^i_{hh'}(t) \leq \bar{x}^i_{hh'}(t)$$

$$\bar{x}^i_{hh'}(t) = \min_{\tau < t} x^{i\tau}_{hh'}(t)$$

$$x^{i\tau}_{hh'} = \text{forecast of flow based on } ex\ post \text{ data}$$

$$x^i_{hh}(t) = 0 \quad .$$

Objective function

$$\sum_{h,h'} c^i_{hh'}x^i_{hh'}(t) \to \min \quad .$$

In the transportation model various modes of transport are distinguished (train, ship). The material supply proportions should be based on shipping which provides the general idea of the most efficient forms of supply development for the future as well as the development of the network of storehouses. Because of this the material supply model should be treated after the transportation block.

·3.5 Regional models

A complex of problems on the optimization of the industrial allocation with maximization of regional plan target implementation is treated in the regional SMOTR system block. Being complicated, the calculations are carried out by stages.

Part 1 is aimed at studying the regional industrial aspects of the plan, where the necessary level of achievement of regional plan targets will naturally be a constraint. It is not easy to formulate the optimization criterion for this model; the calculations should be based on various objective functions (minimum total production or transportation costs, rationalization of labor force distribution, security of certain environmental quality levels), followed by the results of the corresponding iterative procedures.

Part 1 is subject to the following constraints:

(a) on the labor force within aggregated sectors (established in the functional block "Population and labor force");
(b) on intersectoral natural resources consumption: water, etc. (calculated within the "Natural resources" block);
(c) on regional construction capacities (construction block);
(d) bilateral constraints over the regional output by industries (for this purpose we use simulation modeling of industry);
(e) on conditions for regional plan target implementation (from part 2, at the first iteration--by expert estimation).

   The estimated production structure should be included into part 2 for the optimization of the production structure and regional economic development trajectory
which maximizes the degree of feasibility of the plan targets. Regional and national
model systems in this case may be similar (Matlin 1980), but may still account for
further specific regional targets.
   As the regional model is based on optimization, all plan targets should be
transformed into one particular dimension. Weighted coefficients for such a reduction may serve as indicators characterizing the degree of deviation of the normative
regional targets from their average. Using simulation techniques the central model
defines resources for social development of the region.
   Part 2 of the regional model is a two-stage system. At the initial stage the
optimization models are solved with the use of the above criteria confined to constraints on:

(a)   intersectoral natural resources (water, etc.);
(b)   labor force;
(c)   functional dependences linking variables with the indicators of the optimiza-
      tion criterion (based on "incomes and consumption" and "public sector" data);
(d)   the balance of the main regional economic and social development fund initially
      derived from the central model (given by experts at the first iteration); it
      may be reduced in case of deviation of the solution of part 2 from the sectoral
      model solution; the degree of decrease of the regional fund depends on empir-
      ically defined control parameters;
(e)   balance of the additional regional social and economic development fund as
      function of the main fund which can be decreased if the solutions to part 2
      deviate from the solution of part 1; the level of such decrease depends on
      the control parameters;
(f)   balance of the consumption of locally produced commodities which is nonoptimized
      within sectoral allocation models;
(g)   limit for investments for the development of the local industries.

   The maximization of the main and additional social and economic development
funds of the regional economy should be incorporated into the objective function
of part 2:

$$\sum_t \left(\sum_p \alpha_p^h(t)\, G_p^h(t) \; + \; \alpha^h(t)\, B^h(t) \right) \;\to\; \max \quad ,$$

where

$$G_p^h(t) = \text{goal indicator}$$

$$\alpha_p^h(t) = \text{weight of goal } p$$

$$B^h(t) = \text{regional, social and economic development fund}$$

$$B^h(t) = \tilde{B}^h(t) - \beta^h \sum_{j \epsilon I_h} P_j(t)\, [\bar{x}_j^h(t) - \overset{\circ}{x}_j^h(t)]^2$$

$\tilde{B}^h$ is from the central model, and β^h, from simulation experiments, is a fine for
deviation of regional production structure from the solutions of sectoral models (denoted by bar) in territorial aspects (denoted by ring).
   At the second stage of part 2 the total regional production and consumption are
estimated on the basis of solutions received at the initial stage (Baranov and Matlin
1976). The corresponding calculations are carried out on the basis of the regional
input-output model in physical units and in value. Regional production and consumption indicators define the import-export indicators as the initial data for the
transportation block.

3.6 The central model

The central model aims at checking the coordination between sectoral and regional solutions and national plan targets. The structural parameters are represented in the central model by the vectors of production, material resources consumption for current purposes, and investment by sector and intersectoral complex
(with the optimized development and allocation plans), and by region for the other
types of industry (industrial indicators are represented by +, consumption by - in
Figure 4). Moreover, the structural parameters comprise vectors of resources necessary for transportation and material supply block functions, and also for the implementation of regional social and economic goals (Figure 4). The right-hand sides
of the constraints comprise indicators of resources for implementation of national
objectives which are analyzed as exogenous inputs within SMOTR.

	Sectoral and intersectoral complexes	Input—output for regional oriented production	Demand of transportation and supply blocks	Regional private and public consumption
Commodities	$\pm A_{iq}$ $A_{iq} = \sum_h \left(\vphantom{\big|} \mathring{x}_i^h(t) \right.$ $- \sum_{j \in q} (a_{ij}^h(t) \mathring{x}_j^h(t)$ $\left. + \mathring{x}_{ij}^h(t)) \right)$	$\pm A_{ih}$	$- A_{ir}$	$- y_{ih}$

Figure 4. Central model scheme

The variables of the model are indicators for the coordination of sectoral
plans or projects and regional social and economic programs with regard to the optimization criterion of the central model (Baranov *et al.* 1975, Baranov and Matlin
1976). These are performance indicators. It is assumed that the system is consistent when the variables are equal to 1 or deviate from 1 within admissible limits.
If the variable is greater than 1, then the objectives set in the plan are underestimated and vice versa.
The central model is subject to the following constraints:

(a) production and consumption of commodities;
(b) capital investment for sectoral development (intersectoral complexes) and for
     the implementation of regional socioeconomic programs;
(c) relations describing the dependence between regional goal indicators and a
     vector component of regional socioeconomic programs (within the following
     blocks: "income and consumption", "public sector").

The maximization of the degree of implementation of regional, social, and economic
programs is taken as the objective function. In this case, two systems of weight
coefficients are used to characterize the degree of deviation of the particular
goal indicator: on the *national* economic level: the deviation from the normative
value (derived from part 1); and on the *regional* level: the deviation from the
national average. The greater the deviation, the greater are the weighted coefficients.

The mathematical form of the main relations in the central model is given below.

Objective function

$$\sum_{t,h,p} w_p^h(t) \left(G_p^h(t) - \tilde{G}_p^h(t) \right)^2 \to \min$$

$G_p^h(t)$ = pth goal indicator for region h

$w_p^h(t)$ = weight of goal p

Constraints

$$\sum_q A_{iq}(t)\lambda_q(t) + \sum_h A_{ih}(t)\lambda_h(t) - A_{ir}(t)\lambda_r(t) - \sum_h y_{ih}(t)\bar{\lambda}_h(t) \le \tilde{G}_i(t) \quad ,$$

λ = indicator of degree of coordination of corresponding sector with goals

$$\sum_q B_{iq}(t)\lambda_q(t) + \sum_h B_h(t)\lambda_h(t) + B_r(t)\lambda_r(t) + \sum_h B_h(t)\bar{\lambda}_h(t) \le K(t) \quad ,$$

where $K(t)$ is derived from the aggregated input–output table, and

$$G_p^h(t) = f\left(y_{ih}(t), \bar{B}_h(t) \right) \quad .$$

Various objective indicators are correlated with various production goals estimated from the central model, derived as the iteration process continues, and the corresponding information is transmitted into the sectoral (intersectoral complex) models and regions. Correction methods verified during the preceding experiment may be applied here (Baranov and Matlin 1976). For example, the parameters transferred from central to sectoral models are calculated as shown below.

$$V_i(t) = A_{iq(i)}(t)\Gamma_i(t)\lambda_{q(i)}(t)$$

$q(i)$ = good produced by industry i

$$\Gamma_i(t) = \frac{-\sum_{q \in q(i)} A_{iq}(t) - \sum_h A_{ih}(t) - A_{ir}(t) + \sum_h y_{ih}(t) + \tilde{G}_i(t)}{A_{iq(i)}(t)}$$

$$P_i(t,n) = P_i(t,n-1)\Gamma_i(t)$$

$$K_j(t) = B_j(t)\lambda_j(t)\frac{K(t)}{\sum_j B_j(t)}$$

$$U_i(t,n) = U_i(t,n-1) \; \frac{\sum\limits_{j \in I_h} a^h_{ij}(t) \bar{x}^h_j(t)}{\sum\limits_{j \in I_h} a^h_{ij}(t) \overset{o}{x}{}^h_j(t)}$$

n = iteration index

$\overset{o}{x}{}^h_j(t)$ = value from solution of regional model.

The structure and coordination procedures of SMOTR will be improved in the course of further experimental application.

4 Concluding Remarks

Among the most significant and as yet unsolved problems in SMOTR is how one can take into account location economies related to the use of infrastructure. At present, this is not taken into account because of the exogenous character of capital investments per unit within the sectoral models.

This problem contains a serious obstacle: experience in the field of agglomeration effect modeling is inadequate, based on complicated heuristic procedures, and is confined to specific industrial sectors. It is assumed that similar approaches on the regional level will be impossible. A fruitful way to proceed might be the estimation of econometric relationships between the regional capital investments per unit and the regional agglomeration level indicators on the one hand, and the level of industrial infrastructure development on the other.

References

Baranov, E., V. Danilov-Daniljan, and M. Zavelski (1971), Theoretic and Methodological Aspects of Optimization of Prospective Planning, in *Proceedings of the First Conference on Optimal Planning and Management of the National Economy* (CEMI) (in Russian).

Baranov, E., V. Danilov-Daniljan, and M. Zavelski (1975), A System of Optimal Perspective Planning, in A. Kuklinski (ed.), *Regional Disaggregation of National Policies and Plans* (United Nations Research Institute for Social Development, Regional Planning, Geneva), Vol. 8.

Baranov, E., and I. Matlin (1976), About Experimental Implementation of a System of Models of Optimal Perspective Planning, in *Economics and Mathematical Methods*, 12(4), (in Russian).

Baranov, E., I. Matlin, and A. Koltsov (1980), Multiregional and Regional Models in the USSR, in F.G. Adams and N.J. Glickman (eds.), *Modeling the Multiregional Economic System. Perspective for the Eighties* (Heath, Lexington, MA).

Danilov-Daniljan, V., and M. Zavelski (1975a), Socioeconomic Optimum and Territorial Problems of National Economic Planning, in *Economics and Mathematical Methods*, 12(3), (in Russian).

Danilov-Daniljan, V., and M. Zavelski (1975b), *System of Optimal Prospective Planning of the National Economy* (Nauka, Moscow) (in Russian).

Ershov, E., and N. Levchenko (1981), Structural Proportionality of National Economy and its Macroeconomic Analysis, in *Economics and Mathematical Methods*, 17(4), (in Russian).

Fedorenko, N. (ed.) (1972), *Problems of Optimal Functioning of the Socialist Economy* (Nauka, Moscow) (in Russian).

Fedorenko, N. (1979), *Some Problems of Theory and Practice in Planning and Management* (Nauka, Moscow) (in Russian).

Kossov, V. (1973), *Input-Output Models* (Economica, Moscow) (in Russian).

Kovshov, G. (1979), Transport System of Models for Perspective Planning of the Economy, in *Matekon*, 15(2), (in Russian).

Matlin, I. (1980), An Overall Model of the Economy within Optimal Long-Term Planning, in *Matekon*, 16(2), (in Russian).

Yaremenko, J. (1981), *Structural Change in the Socialist Economy* (Mysl, Moscow) (in Russian).

Yaremenko, J., E. Ershov, and A. Smyshlaev (1975), Model of Interindustrial Interdependencies, in *Economics and Mathematical Methods*, 11(3) (in Russian).

CHAPTER 12

THE DEVELOPMENT OF MULTIREGIONAL ECONOMIC MODELING IN NORTH AMERICA:
MULTIREGIONAL MODELS IN TRANSITION FOR ECONOMIES IN TRANSITION

Roger Bolton

1 Introduction

In this paper I aim to provide a general overview of multiregional modeling in
North America, emphasizing the various contexts, the achievements, and the research
remaining to be done. I shall not give any extensive description of individual
models. There is ample information about specifics in the Rietveld survey contained
in this book (Chapter 2), in my own previous papers on the subject (Bolton 1980a,b,
c,d,e, 1981), and in other sources (e.g., Adams and Glickman 1980). It would be
inefficient for me to discuss the many details that can be readily found in those
sources. I plan to concentrate instead on what I see as the "big picture", and also
on some very recent developments. In doing that, however, I will try to supply
enough specific references and critical comments on the various models to whet the
reader's appetite for deeper exploration, if he is not familiar with the various
models in North America.

I will spend a good deal of time at the beginning of the chapter on the several
contexts of multiregional modeling research in North America. I distinguish the
forecasting and policy analysis context, the theoretical context, and the data and
computational capacity context. Then I will describe briefly the broad features of
the operational models in the US and Canada (the Rietveld survey includes no model
for Mexico, and the only one I know about for that country is a multiregional agricultural sector model, which is not encompassing enough to merit discussion in this
context (Goreux and Manne 1973). After commenting on the gaps that remain, I will
describe some innovative ongoing efforts, and close by pointing out the most important directions for future research.

2 The Larger Contexts of Multiregional Modeling

The three contexts that are important are the forecasting and policy analysis
context, the theoretical context, and the data and computational capacity context.
I will review each of them in turn, but it is obvious that they are interconnected.

2.1 The forecasting and policy analysis context

This is, I feel, the most important context (note that this is an expanded and
revised version of earlier discussions in Bolton 1980b,e, 1981). The needs for
multiregional models in forecasting and policy analysis have become even greater in
recent years in both the US and Canada. The theoretical context is also important,
but less so, in the sense that operational multiregional modeling has not forged
much new economic theory, or even new regional science theory. The third context,
data and computational capacity, is important, but I see it as responding to forecasting and policy analysis needs rather than leading them.

The regional structures of the US and Canadian economies are changing rapidly
and are creating new political pressures and alliances. The central governments
need better tools to *predict* the consequences of technological and global market
changes (this is the *forecasting* context) and to *analyze* the effects of *policies*.
In the US, we have continuing frostbelt-sunbelt shifts, although the 1970s changes

157

in world energy markets have tended to add a new East-West conflict which cuts
across the sunbelt-frostbelt one. A combination of developments has put extreme
downward pressure on the labor markets and local public sectors of the older "core"
regions, the northeastern and midwestern manufacturing belts. Those regions must
adjust to the downward pressure in one way or another. The crucial question is not
whether the fundamental technological and world market forces can or should be reversed; clearly they will not be reversed in an economic and political system in
which government intervention of the kind that would be required is not traditional,
and where the sense of place or region has usually been subordinated to the goal
of an integrated national economy; the question is rather how fast the adjustments
will be allowed to take place, and what will be the effects on individuals now
caught temporarily or permanently in the declining regions.

In the US, then, a fundamental role for multiregional models is to translate
major long-term structural changes into impacts on individuals and the distribution
of income in the lagging regions, including the distributional impacts of changes
in the public sector. But we also need them to analyze the changes taking place in
the rapidly growing regions. There are many manifestations of rapid growth that our
models should help us anticipate. But there are two particular angles that tend to
be largely ignored. First, the changes in industrial and demographic structures in
those regions will affect their fortunes far into the future; they will affect the
specialization and diversification of income sources and tax bases, which will become relevant at that inevitable time in the future when wholly new economic forces
emerge. Secondly, the adjustment to rapid growth in those regions, particularly in
their labor markets, will affect the adjustment in lagging regions. An important
point here is that the more elastic the supply of labor in the growing regions, the
longer it will be before increases in wages eliminate their present labor cost advantages, and the longer and more difficult will be the adjustment process in the
lagging regions (my co-authors and I stress the importance of elasticity of labor
supply in Jackson *et al.* 1981).

If the nation as a whole grows slowly, and is plagued by frequent recessions,
then the regional imbalances caused by other factors are aggravated greatly. The
slowing of national population growth means that migration is now the major component of regional population growth or decline. Obviously a multiregional model,
and a sophisticated one at that, is essential to analyze interregional migration
and the interrelationships between migration and the labor markets that migrants
leave and enter. There is ample room for improvement here, in both modeling and
data. In the shorter run, American (and Canadian) national policy makers will continue to have difficulty resolving the inflation-unemployment dilemma, and the end
of the business cycle is not in sight. Both secular and cyclical declines in the
growth rate of real output have disproportionate effects on older heavily industrialized regions (US Advisory Commission on Intergovernmental Relations 1980).
The increasing integration of the US economy into the larger international economy
has also created pressure points in some regions. Macroeconomic and international
developments sharply raise the need for multiregional models to include good *national*
macroeconomic models. Integration of national and regional models is just beginning
and regional and national model builders need to do much more in cooperation with
each other.

In lagging regions, the adjustment process will force some combination of the
following results: reduced (relative to national average) wages; reduced consumer
prices (as in housing, which is inelastically supplied, and in labor-intensive services whose prices will be lower if wages are lower); unemployment; lower level of
public services. The exact combination that results has important implications for
the welfare of individuals, the distribution of income by income class, the public
sector, and the ability of the region eventually to re-establish a competitive
position in national and world markets. *How* the adjustment takes place will influence how *long* it takes and it will also affect the new equilibrium positions toward
which the regions move. It will also profoundly affect the distribution of income
within the regions. Multiregional models have been able to analyze the distribution
of income between regions in the nation, but they should be able to do more; they
should be able to analyze each region's internal distribution of income. Only very
recently have they been able to do so. The importance of the subject is shown by

Harrison's recent evidence on the internal distribution of earned income in New England, a region that is probably farther along in the required transition than any other in the US. Inequality has increased significantly as a result of a long period of slow growth and of the gradual replacement of some export industries by others (1981).

As I indicated above, what happens in the labor markets and local public sectors of expanding regions is also important. We have long been concerned with modeling how regions of a national economy influence each other, and we have concentrated on trade and transportation. Now, with the structural changes and the required adjustments, interregional migration and the connections between regional labor markets are becoming increasingly important, and it is incumbent on multiregional modelers to shift their attention onto them.

In Canada the mixture of problems is a bit different. The Maritimes have lagged behind the nation for a long time; Ontario, where manufacturing is important, is more prosperous but may become vulnerable to slower growth and international competition in the future; in Quebec there is strong separatist sentiment; in Alberta new energy developments are creating enormous natural resource rents. William Alonso has often said that the re-emergence of Ricardian rent is a major new force in regional economics and in regional policy. Nowhere is this more true than in Canada, although it is not a trivial force in the United States either. The importance of resource rent, along with the other problems I mentioned, makes good modeling essential in Canada. Unfortunately, as far as I can determine, the field is much less developed there than in the US and Western Europe.

The uses of resource rents, including how they are divided between Canadian individuals, foreign investors, provincial governments, and the national government, is perhaps the most important economic regional question in Canada. It has jumped ahead of concern with depressed areas on the national agenda. The political situation is one of serious constitutional debate on the powers of provincial and central governments. The situation is less extreme in the United States, but the economic and political implications of resource rents are serious enough. In both countries there is a new element in the policy analysis context, and modelers must adapt and innovate to help policy makers cope with it. The rents will do more than raise the incomes of the resource-rich regions; the uses to which they are put will change the basic economic structures of the regions. Two modeling angles are especially important here: (a) the impact of energy development may be so great that structural equations econometrically estimated from historical data may not capture the behavioral responses, particularly in the local public sector; (b) the adverse terms-of-trade effect on consumers in energy importing regions is hard to capture in models that seldom have specific commodity prices in them (see my comment (Bolton 1980d) on both of these problems as presented by a NRIES simulation reported by Ballard and Gustely 1980).

I have dwelt long on the forecasting and policy analysis context, but I hope that in doing so I have pointed out some directions in which modelers should move. National and regional economies must adjust to fundamental new forces; so must modelers. It is no longer sufficient to get the interregional trade flows right or to track down all the direct, indirect, and induced demands. Of course, some things I have referred to were raised to the point of national concern in North America only recently; inevitably models lag behind, due to lags in data and funding. The lack of good data is still a fundamental limit on the quality of analysis of some aspects. But the recent developments do point the way. Also, by the way, data availability is not a wholly exogenous variable in that larger model of social science research that explains the pace and direction of multiregional modeling. Demands for better data will help produce better data.

2.2 The theoretical context

Our modelers have not developed much wholly new theory. Most features of even the newest models are familiar to one trained in economics or regional science some time ago. The main achievements recently have been a general "tightening" of econometric specifications and a catching up with microeconomic theory. An example is the explicit use of production functions and labor demand functions derived from

modern microeconomic theory. New production functions are being used, as for example in the work by Lakshmanan (1981); he was conscious of the need to use a model
to *test* the validity of different functional forms, not merely to use it to make
predictions based on one functional form.

Another example is a sophisticated departure from simple export-base theory.
Modelers allow part of any industry, even services, to be export oriented, and make
the export fraction of an industry's output depend on the region and perhaps on the
state of demand. Treyz and Stevens have been leaders in this direction (Treyz 1980,
Treyz *et al*. 1980a,b). A third example is the use of "leading region" models of
interregional wage determination models, similar to the use of leading-sector wage
determination models in national macroeconometric models (Milne *et al*. 1980). I
could give other examples of tightening up of specifications.

However, there are four ideas that are rather new, and that are on the border-
line between "tightening specifications" and more original contributions. They are:
the development of some "bottom-upness" and the integration of regional and national
models; a new approach to transportation; a proposal for a new overall design of an
integrated model and a new way of organizing the researchers building the model; an
approach to the labor market that is less conventional than the usual neoclassical
one. All four ideas are still in early stages of development as far as *operational
regional* models are concerned, and some are merely proposals.

A. *Bottom-up models*. Bottom-upness is a widely recognized development and
there are other papers on the subject in this volume. I have discussed the subject
elsewhere (Bolton 1980a,c, 1981, Bolton and Chinitz 1980). Bottom-upness must be
relative; I believe there are only a few pure bottom-up models (see Chapter 3).
But a hybrid model that combines some top-down and some bottom-up features is attractive, and it will be a popular approach in the future. Such a model is called a
"regional-national" model, to emphasize that the results for the nation are determined simultaneously with, and not independently of, the results for each of the
nation's regions. At the moment, there is only one operational model in North
America with substantial bottom-up characteristics; that is NRIES, the US Bureau of
Economic Analysis (BEA) model developed by Ballard and others (see Ballard and
Gustely 1980, Ballard and Wendling 1980, Ballard *et al*. 1980). BEA continues to
use, develop, and improve NRIES (Ballard and Wendling 1980, Kort and Cartwright
1981), but it has made slow progress because of budget cuts by recent administrations
in Washington. The new work at BEA concentrates on improving the NRIES national equations, which have appeared weak and which have been criticized, and on adding a residential and nonresidential construction sector in each state (Kort and Cartwright
1981, Kort 1981). The construction equations will be likely to have specifications
similar to those given by Conway and Howard (1980) in their model for the state of
Washington.

The profession would benefit if the NRIES work were faster. It is a pioneer
model in North America, and although it has weaknesses, we would learn from improving it. The multiregional modeling fraternity is very much in need of experience
in using a regional-national model to analyze American and Canadian problems, and
it needs experience in integrating national models with regional models in ways that
foster progress in building both. NRIES is the only bottom-up model available for
such experimental development; others are proposed (see discussion below and Chapter 13), but funding is very uncertain and even if funded they will not be ready for
experiments until well into the future. NRIES is available now and is fully documented. Its small national sector is in some ways a weak point, but on the other
hand, it offers the advantage of easier experiments in integrating a national model
with many regional models in a hybrid blend of top-down and bottom-up. We shall
have to wait at least a couple of years before any alternative is available, and
that will inevitably delay the accumulation of experience with regional-national
interdependence.

B. *Overall design of models*. It is stretching a point to call model design
a theoretical development, but one recently proposed design is for a new blend of
existing theories so new as to be different in kind. I refer to the design by Isard
et al., which Lakshmanan elaborates in Chapter 13. Isard proposes to assemble several specialists, each of which would build one "module" in the combined system, and
then to rely on teamwork by the specialists to integrate their modules into a smoothly working system. The proposed model includes these modules:

(i)   a national module, which will be an existing national macroeconometric model (with an embedded input-output model to convert demand components into industry outputs), *modified* to reflect bottom-up principles for many variables;

(ii) a microsimulation household behavior and labor supply module, following the Poverty Institute (University of Wisconsin) version of the multi-regional input-output (MRIO) model (see Golladay and Haveman 1977) and the multiregional policy impact simulation model (MRPIS) effort at Boston College and MIT (on which more below);

(iii) a comparative cost, linear programming, input-output industrial complex module in order to capture, among other things, the special effects of energy prices and energy supplies and pollution;

(iv) a factor demand module, which continues Lakshmanan's use of modern pro-duction functions and duality theory to explain demand for labor, new investment, and energy (1981);

(v)   an innovative transportation module.

The transportation module deserves special discussion, and it is one of the four developments I promised to discuss. It is based on a recent paper by Boyce and Hewings (1980), who propose a new way to combine input-output and transportation and commodity flow models. They avoid the extremes of least-cost optimum allocation models and instead allow crosshauling. Indeed, they *posit* some amount of cross-hauling, and use it as a constraint on the location of new capacity and the movement of goods (the amount of crosshauling is represented by an entropy measure developed by Wilson 1970). Crosshauling reflects, first, the aggregation in production and transportation flow *data*, and, second, some inefficiency in the real world which is induced by uncertainty, lagged adjustments to changing prices and costs, and regula-tion. Boyce and Hewings make specific the input-output relationships and the cross-hauling as constraints that the model solution must satisfy. Something like this is already incorporated in the Canadian FRETNET model discussed below. The Boyce-Hewings module would also allow for congestion of transportation routes, which is desirable in models of situations like a bumper crop of grain moving into export markets or congestion at coal terminals.

The integration of these modules into a single model will be challenging. The present proposal describes each module in detail, but does not spell out the precise ways in which inconsistencies among them will be resolved in the process of integra-tion. That is a topic of research. Incorporation of substantial bottom-up features into the national module will be especially difficult; it will require resolution of discrepancies between the national variables from the off-the-shelf model and the national variables implied by the regional models, on an iterative basis.

The reliance on a separate specialist for each submodel contrasts sharply with the previous American experience, in which one or a very few persons built an entire model. Ben Chinitz and I, in our earlier surveys of the field (Chinitz and Bolton 1978, Bolton 1980a,b,c, Bolton and Chinitz 1980) were struck by the uneven emphases within each model. Typically a model goes into much detail in a few aspects, but is rather ordinary and simple--indeed simplistic--in other important aspects. That reflects the particular interests of the individuals who built the models. Isard's team promises more even attention. Of course, that *might* raise problems of integra-tion more serious than the present unevenness! The proposal, however, is similar to the work on the Brookings national model in the 1960s, and one must say in retro-spect that the Brookings work achieved notable results in integrating separate ap-proaches.

One wonders if the modular system can be extended so as to make different ex-perts' modules *interchangeable* (Bolton and Chinitz 1980, Bolton 1981). For example, there might be two different national models. Model X might be especially suited for short-run macropolicy analysis, model Y for long-run growth and structural change analysis. Model X would be more detailed in the monetary and financial sectors, in inventory investment, and in the international exchange rate; it would model the "multiplier" process in detail. It would be used to simulate the effects of reces-sions and countercyclical policy, or perhaps an energy crisis. Model Y would have changing input-output coefficients and would model the capacity effects of invest-ment and population change.

Another example: expert A and expert B might each build a household behavior-labor supply model, with different degrees of disaggregation, different policy handles, and different labor market theories. One might be coupled with the national model X and used in cyclical analysis; the other might be coupled with national model Y and used in long-term growth and migration analysis.

This scheme of course would be expensive, and it would tax coordination resources to the limit. But the cost would be reduced somewhat if the modules had independent lives of their own and were usable outside the multiregional system in question.

C. *Labor market*. Most regional models use a rather neoclassical model of the labor market, where the wage level (relative to the nation) clears the market. Thurow (1975) has argued an alternative theory, the job competition or labor queue theory. In it, even *relative* wages are rather rigid and do not adjust to clear labor markets when supply or demand changes. Rather, employers use various nonprice (nonwage) rationing devices to allocate the job slots to workers (random selection, discrimination by background characteristics, or changes in "entry requirements").

The alternative theory has got great attention in microeconomic analyses of income distribution, but it has not yet penetrated multiregional modeling. However, the MRPIS project is committed to using the theory (Social Welfare Research Institute 1981) and has already completed some simulations with it. In MRPIS, jobs are allocated to available workers in a "hierarchical assignment" procedure. Based on extensive microdata, the modelers estimate the number of workers in a region who have experience in an industry-occupation group for which labor demand rises, but who are less than fully employed at the going wage rate. Those people are grouped into categories, such as: full-time, full-year, part-time, part-year; involuntarily unemployed; discouraged worker; voluntarily unemployed (not participating in labor force). If labor demand for an industry-occupation group increases, the additional hours of work will be assigned to the groups in some specified order. For example, one might assume that hours worked increase first for full-time, full-year workers, until no more overtime hours are available from them; then to part-time workers; then to involuntarily unemployed; then finally to discouraged workers and to voluntarily unemployed. And one might want to assign these added hours *without* assuming that the relative wage in the region rises. If no more hours are available from those groups, the modeler might allow the relative wage to rise until workers in *other* industry-occupation groups, or even workers in other regions, were induced to move into the industry-occupation-region group where demand is high. Thus, migration would be allowed for, but only in some specified sequence of assignment of added hours. The same sort of hierarchical assignment, but not necessarily symmetrical, would be used to determine which workers lose hours and jobs when demand falls.

In later stages of development, age, sex, and education classes can further subdivide the labor force status groups. If this approach works, it will be a rather rare example of regional modeling moving apace with national modeling. It is interesting to note that this approach is not now contemplated in the proposed Isard model. On the other hand, the MRPIS plans do not now have some of the features contemplated by Isard *et al.*, such as a hybrid top-down, bottom-up national model.

Where do we need more theoretical development? Among the many areas, I think five can be picked out. As I discuss below, there definitely is work going on in these areas both in established models and in newer ones.

(1) *Public sector modeling*. Above I noted that the public sectors in both declining and growing regions are critical in determining the impacts of structural change on the real incomes of individuals. So far, multiregional models have done little with the public sector except to simulate tax bases and public employment. When discussing regional change in the US, we often adjust personal incomes to reflect the nominal state and local tax burden. However, no one has modeled definitively how the *benefits* of public sector operations affect individuals' decisions to migrate, or firms' decisions to invest. Now, with migration such a dominant factor, we need to make progress on this front.

(2) *Environmental modeling*. It is important to know the effects of other variables on environmental quality, and the effects of environmental quality on individual utility functions, for the same reasons as in the above.

(3) *Investment and capital stock*. Both investment and the supply effects of
    capital stock are important. Data and theory need improvement. Investment
    is still exogenous in many regional models. In particular, we have not really
    decided how we should model investment in a bottom-up context. If investment
    responds to full utilization of existing capital stock and also to profits of
    firms, then investment in the nation, even investment by national firms, must
    be a bottom-up variable. But there is resistance to this idea.

(4) *Regional money and credit markets*. Modelers, like other regional economists,
    usually assume that capital is sufficiently mobile to make interest rates
    uniform across regions. But we know that this is not really so for small
    business and for housing loans. There are persistent interregional differ-
    ences in interest rates for some loans; L'Esperance (1981) noted that there
    are differences in banks' attitudes toward risks.

(5) *Transportation*. It is surprising that regional scientists and regional econ-
    omists have seldom included transportation explicitly in their operational
    multiregional models. They model employment in transportation, but not the
    physical movement of goods or capacity limits on routes or modal choices by
    shippers. Models project the location of production without regard to whether
    there is enough capacity in transportation systems; they project network changes
    on the assumption of fixed patterns of industrial location. The MRMI model and
    the Canadian FRET models are the only notable exceptions.

2.3 Data and computation capacity contexts

    The low cost of computation has encouraged extensive simultaneity and also very
large microdatabases. NRIES is a good example as far as simultaneity is concerned.
Both the low cost of computation and the availability of very detailed microdata
shaped the MRPIS project staff's decision on the labor market. Low computation cost
is also essential for more disaggregated analyses of transportation, as in the existing MRMI model and the Canadian FRET and FRETNET, and in the Boyce-Hewings proposal.
    Microdata are a very significant development. The MRPIS effort, by the way,
is an interesting example of the happy combination of important innovations in *all
three* of the areas of theory, data availability and computation capacity, and the
increasing demands for income distribution results in the policy analysis context.
    Where do we need more data? Almost everywhere, of course. What are the pri-
orities? We still do not have gross output by industry and region in the US; we
do have it in Canada. In the US we must either estimate time series by the weak
Kendrick-Jaycox method or link regional employment directly to national output or
national employment. Ballard based the NRIES equations for output on new, but still
unpublished, time series developed by the Bureau of Economic Analysis; we can only
hope the series will become more widely available if they are of good quality.
    We need better data on regional investment and capital stock, and on regional
money and credit markets. One could hope for a microdata set on investment by firms
and, less importantly, on banking and other lending institutions. Banking data are
probably available in the files of the Federal Reserve System in the US; it is not
clear how much it would cost to bring them into usable form.
    A couple of years ago I would have said capital stock data were the most impor-
tant, but now I am more impressed with our needs to model long-term structural adjustments than to model "impacts", so I put migration data equal to capital stock
data. Our migration data are not very good. Even the US Continuous Work History
Sample (CWHS, sometimes called the longitudinal employer-employee data), has proved
to have serious snags. The researchers in the Census Bureau economic-based demographic projections project ECESIS (from the Greek word for "movement of a living
being into a new habitat") concluded that the CWHS data were so weak that they could
not rely on them for estimation of historical functions (Isserman 1980, Isserman
et al. 1981). This example shows that some microdata sets are less useful than we
had hoped.

3 Review of Existing Models

Shortage of space requires me to be sketchy. In addition to the Rietveld survey, further details and references are available in Bolton (1980a,b,c) and Bolton and Chinitz (1980). I review the US models first (I am concentrating on fully operational models here, so will not comment on Treyz's proposed design, which is in any event only multiregional *within* one state: Massachusetts).

We have three input-output models. IDIOM is a Leontief "balanced" model, which has no explicit interregional trade and which assigns to each region a constant share of a national market industry, rather than making the share a function of comparative costs or the origin of demand. MRIO, the Polenske interregional trade model, has been used in many applications and is notable as a part of the Poverty Institute model. There are theoretical questions about the MRIO specification of constant interregional trade patterns. It remains fundamentally weak in practice, in any event, because it has had to rely on outdated 1963 trade coefficients. In light of changes in industrial structure and the process of import substitution in the noncore regions since 1963, the model would surely err in estimating the effects of national policies on core and noncore regions. It would overestimate the import leakage out of noncore areas and overestimate interregional export demand in core areas. However, MRIO is to be part of the new MRPIS model, so new 1977 interregional trade coefficients are being estimated for MRIO, as part of the MRPIS project. When that updating is completed, MRIO will suddenly become a potent competitor again.

The Poverty Institute (PI) model has MRIO as its core, but aggregated to 23 regions. It adds a household income and consumption module in order to convert tax and transfer policies into consumer demand by industry. By making consumer demand endogenous, it adds a lot. But the PI model makes only the first round of consumption changes endogenous--only the consumption changes caused directly by a tax or transfer change--so it does not simulate the full multiplier process. It also adds a labor demand and household income module to convert the MRIO industry outputs into an income distribution. Both of these modules that PI added to MRIO are pioneering uses of microdata simulation in the multiregional modeling field; the Poverty Institute's concern with income distribution is itself a pioneering development. None of these models has endogenous investment or government spending; none has an explicit transportation model; none has any labor market supply or migration equations.

There are several econometric models. Harris's MRMI forecasting model relies on location rents, as determined by a linear programming optimal transportation and production allocation scheme, as a basic force in changing regions' shares of national industries. The formulation assumes that higher location rents attract investment and thus increase capacity output; the location rent enters directly into regional share equations for capacity output of an industry. It has labor market supply and demand and migration submodels. Two weaknesses of the original version of the model were the heavy reliance on synthetic data and the reliance on cross section regressions on 1965-66 changes in variables. They have been remedied to some extent by a recent reestimation of the model with pooled cross section and time series data for 1970-74.

MULTIREGION, an econometric model developed at Oak Ridge National Laboratory (ORNL), is a very long-term model and is used at ORNL for population projections and energy analysis. It has only employment and population as basic variables, and not income, but it is notably disaggregated in population (11 age-sex cohorts). It relies heavily on the "potential" concept from gravity models to predict changes in employment shares and in-migration. Transportation is not explicitly modeled, but truck travel time between regions is used in calculating economic potential (with different elasticities for different commodities). A shortcoming is that travel time up to 8.3 hours has a negative effect on potential, but all regions further away than 8.3 hours are completely ignored and receive a weight of zero. This does not seem correct for many high-technology industries in which there are established supplier networks stretching from coast to coast. It has a labor market, with the employment/population ratio rather than the wage rate as the clearing mechanism; but labor is the only factor of production. The model is long-term. The industry share specifications weaken its use for the long-run structural change analysis we need. However, it is the one model in the current inventory explicitly designed for long-run structural analysis.

NRIES, developed at the US Bureau of Economic Analysis, is the only model with substantial bottom-up features. It also uses economic potential variables, but it relies solely on purely geographical distance and a uniform elasticity of -1 for all goods. The top-down part of the national model is very small and is recognized as weak in, for example, the monetary and financial sectors. Transportation is not explicit, but there is a labor market supply and demand submodel. Microdata are not used, but the model does use unpublished BEA data on gross output by industry and region, so labor demand can be dependent on regional gross output.

Two other operational models are worth mentioning. The Milne-Adams-Glickman (MAG) model is a top-down model with only nine large regions (the US Census regions) instead of the state or substate regions found in all the other models, and it has only six industries. Each region's share of a national industry is based on the region's relative labor and energy costs in a logit transformation; labor demand functions are derived from CES production functions. There is a labor demand and supply model, with a "leading-region" wage determination process in manufacturing: the mid-Atlantic and East North Central regions are the pattern setters.

The Chase econometrics model is proprietary and only Chase and its clients know much about it. A region's share of industry output depends on its relative costs of energy, labor, and taxes, and, interestingly, on the national capacity utilization rate in manufacturing. Labor demand, supply, and migration are all endogenous.

All of these models except NRIES are top-down in the most important sense: they do not allow any feedback from the regions to the national economy. However, IDIOM and the PI model are bottom-up in a certain restricted sense. The income-consumption coefficients and the output-employment coefficients can be allowed to differ from one region to another, so that total aggregate demand and total employment in the nation are determined endogenously and simultaneously with the regional employment and income results. This kind of bottom-up effect reflects the dependence of certain national totals on the sectoral and regional *composition* of demand in a fixed-coefficient model. Such a bottom-up effect is very different from one in which regional labor markets impinge on each other--one in which wages or employment conditions in one region effect those in others--or in which the national total of investment, for example, depends upon the state of demand in various regions.

Finally, I mention again ECESIS, the US Census Bureau's population projection model. It is not a fully fledged multiregional economic model, for it specializes in population alone. But it is noteworthy for the attempt by official population projectors to incorporate economic variables, chiefly economic potential, rather than relying only on extrapolations of previous trends, to project migration (Isserman 1980, Isserman *et al*. 1981).

In Canada, we have first Canada's interprovincial input-output model, which is basically a MRIO model adapted to Canada's rectangular input-output accounting system. The agency is also working on a two-region model of North America, in which the US and Canada are the two regions, and which would link up the two national input-output tables. If completed it will be noteworthy as one of only two models *of* North America, as opposed to the other models which are merely *in* North America! Of course, the US and Canada are rather aggregated "regions".

The detailed Canadian model called FRET (Forecasting Regional Economies and Transportation) was designed to analyze the interdependence between transportation systems and regional development (Los 1980). It is a combination of two models: a multiregional model called Transport Oriented Multiregional Model (TOMM) and a very detailed freight transportation modal choice and cost model called FRETNET. The two models are run together as a mathematical programming model. Both use as much spatial and commodity data as are available; in TOMM the regions are provinces and the industries are quite aggregated; in FRETNET there are 64 areal "zones" in Canada, nine in the US, and nine in the rest of the world, and there is much more commodity detail. Because FRETNET simulates transportation between some Canadian regions and some US ones, it is the second model *of* North America.

TOMM simulates interprovincial trade flows and provincial output and employment by industry. It takes as input FRETNET's determination of interregional transportation cost for various commodities, and it uses the transportation costs, wage rates, labor productivity, and product prices to determine the optimal location of production. Capacity constraints and labor supply constraints can be entered exogenously.

Inputs other than transportation are used in fixed proportions in the usual input-output way, but, unlike in MRIO, interregional trade is not determined by fixed trade coefficients but rather by the optimal production patterns of the combined FRET model. Prices are assumed to be uniform across Canada for traded goods, but they can vary regionally for nontraded goods. The model is a static programming model; it could be used recursively over several simulation periods, if one entered the wages, labor productivity, product prices, and capacity and labor supply constraints exogenously for each period.

In the mathematical programming solution, the objective function is a weighted sum of three terms: (a) gross profit of all nontransport sectors in all provinces, defined as value of sales minus cost of labor and value of all intermediate inputs except transportation; (b) the transportation cost of all traded commodities; (c) an "information term" similar to the one in the Boyce-Hewings approach. If a positive weight is put on the third term, the results reflect inertia in the system and all other factors that cause the actual production and transporation pattern to differ from the optimal one, including aggregation in the data. At present, it is not clear how the three weights will be determined. Presumably, if a completely efficient solution is desired, the weights will be unity for each of the first two terms and zero for the third.

Finally, the Institute of Policy Analysis at the University of Toronto has completed the first stages of a new Canadian multiregional model called PRISM (Provincial Industrial Satellite Model) (Dungan 1981). It is a top-down model designed to be driven by a national model called, naturally, FOCUS. The model is somewhat similar to MAG, but so far it is simpler. Sectors are divided into traded goods (primary products and most manufactures) and nontraded goods; the provincial shares of traded goods are exogenous, based on trends or explicit scenarios. The share of each nontraded item is determined in this way: in each year, the province's share of a sector changes by some proportion (<1) of the change in the province's share of total national gross domestic product. This is similar to the relationship in some other models where what would be called "local" industries depend on total regional output.

Employment is determined by simple share equations, with exogenous adjustments for relative productivity changes. Population is so far exogenous, but there are simple participation equations relating the labor force to the working-age population. A province's share of national wage income changes in proportion to its share of employment, so the regional wage structure does not change. Milne has expressed the goal of adding endogenous wage determination, using the leading-region idea; incidentally, he believes an important chain of effects is from midwestern US automobile and other manufacturing industry wages to similar industries' wages in Ontario, and then from Ontario to the rest of Canada. This illustrates yet another possibility for US-Canada interaction. Milne also hopes to add some bottom-up determination of national variables.

On surveying the whole array, it is clear that we have made lots of progress. We have large-scale consistent models that give intuitively plausible results, especially for the short run (some have a tendency to predict excessive divergence of regional growth rates when used for long-run simulation). Some integrate input-output with econometric equations for consumption demand and for labor market variables, which is a very notable achievement. For all its disadvantages, input-output modeling has great advantages in that it distinguishes among direct, indirect, and induced demands. That accounting scheme is very useful in modeling certain kinds of impacts, such as of national defense expenditures or changes in export demand induced by international trade policy; both defense and trade policy are newly important examples of eligible candidates for analysis. I think there is a presumption that regions are more vulnerable to shifts in demand if they specialize in direct rather than indirect production in the industries whose demand might shift.

Incorporation of microdata is an achievement; so is the development of a regional-national model with both top-down and bottom-up features. There are good starts in modeling the labor market behavior which I have argued is especially important. The weaknesses in the present array are clear from my selected comments earlier on the three contexts of modeling: forecasting and policy analysis, theory, and data.

4 Ongoing Developments

Curtis Harris has recently made several important changes in MRMI and he and his associates are at work on still more changes. He has revised the endogenous investment equations (Nadji and Harris 1982); his model has of course long been unique in the multiregional field in having endogenous investment. Unlike most national and single-regional modelers, Harris does not make investment depend on lagged output in the region. For a region, he argues convincingly, desired capacity output depends on profitability (location rent in his model) and investment depends on the change in the desired capacity output and depreciation of existing capital stock. Lagged output is not a good proxy for expected future demand or profitability in a region, and Harris's model recognizes better the indivisibility of investment, the totally new investment in a region by an industry that has not been there before, and production for export demand. However, Harris's production function is much simpler than in some other models--he assumes the ratio of capital to capacity output in all regions is equal to the national ratio. His procedures also require intricate estimates of some parameters--utilization rates and depreciation rates--not found in standard regional data.

Harris is also estimating 1972 commodity flows between regions, and he plans to use those data in the future to estimate regional input-output coefficients and regional shadow prices. His team has also added pollution emission coefficients to the model, using the more reliable parts of the US Environmental Protection Agency's Strategic Environmental Assessment System model (SEAS) and other sources (McConnell *et al*. 1981). They hope later to add industrial pollution control costs to location rent, to add damage functions to affect labor migration, and to integrate emission levels with dispersion and diffusion models to predict ambient concentrations. Finally, an associate is developing a state and local government model; it would link economic variables to tax bases so that revenues can be projected (determined by the identity, revenues equal endogenous tax bases times some exogenous tax rates), and would also use a median voter, linear expenditure system model to project expenditure (Uyar 1981).

MREEED (see Lakshmanan 1981) is a notably complicated and sophisticated model. Like most others, it reflects the builder's own interests, and is especially strong on energy and environmental aspects. It uses a more general production function, the translog, than other models, with *seven* inputs (fixed capital, working capital, labor, and four fuels). It will eventually incorporate extensive estimates of capital stock in order to have a lagged adjustment model of demand for new capital. For regions' shares of national output, it relies on both the cost functions derived from the production functions and on the economic potential concept. It makes innovative steps in including pollution emissions and in using a median voter model to predict detailed government expenditures. This model is nearly finished. It is basically a top-down model as far as determination of national totals is concerned; the model is designed to be driven by INFORUM or some other national model.

I have already referred occasionally to two other important efforts. One, by Isard and others, is described by Lakshmanan in Chapter 13. I have already mentioned the overall design of the model and the organization of the research team, and the use of the Boyce-Hewings transportation model, as notable features. The continuation of Lakshmanan's work on flexible production functions and the modification of a national model to reflect bottom-up are others.

I have also referred to the MRPIS model. It is being developed in stages. The builders' first simulations were with the 1963 MRIO, but later ones will use the 1977 MRIO. The household consumption sector is based on microdata on consumer expenditure; it has functions relating marginal expenditures in each region on each of 56 commodities to income. An alignment matrix converts consumption demand by commodity into demand by industry (79 industries) in each region. The consumption sector will "close" the model, improving it over the Poverty Institute version of MRIO (Social Welfare Research Institute 1981).

MRPIS's labor demand model follows the Thurow job competition theory. Industry output variables from MRIO will feed into an industry-occupation matrix to get labor demand by industry and occupation in each region; there will be 79 industries and 51 regions, and a large number of occupations. However, initial simulations are being done with a condensed set of 816 IORs (four industries, four occupations, 51 regions). Migration and mobility between industries and occupations are not yet allowed, but will be introduced later. The staff has completed a simulation of the detailed income distribution effects of a change in defense procurement, and there is a plan to compare a simulation using the 1977 MRIO model with a simulation using the 1963 MRIO; this will be an interesting exercise and will shed light on changes in interregional dispersion of demand and on the diversification of regions.

But like many other models, MRPIS is uneven in its emphasis. There appear to be no firm plans to integrate a fully fledged national model with it, either a top-down or a bottom-up one, until some years in the future, and the labor demand functions are much simpler than in MREEED or in the Isard *et al*. proposal. Until some years in the future factors other than labor will not be considered or will be assumed to be used in fixed proportions with labor. If funding is forthcoming, MRPIS might eventually be as elaborate as the other two models, but in the early stages it concentrates most of its innovations on microsimulation and on the labor market job competition submodel. (Unfortunately, funding was halted, at least temporarily, in spring 1982.)

5 Directions for the Future

Many of my suggestions were really implicit in my earlier discussion.

First, although not most important, it would be helpful to have some models *of* North America: the interdependences in energy, environmental emissions and quality of life, the fortunes of the automobile industry, the process of wage determination--all of these require some simultaneous treatment of the US and Canada in one model. There are other examples for the US and Mexico.

The MRMI, Isard *et al*., MRPIS, and MREEED work are all examples of desirable directions. We need to continue the now established framework of integration of input-output models with econometric equations for final demand and the labor market. For long-run simulation, the reliance on constant coefficients becomes hard to justify--for both technical and trade coefficients--so it is essential to have some work on how to change the coefficients gradually over time in the simulation period if we are to continue to exploit the advantages of the input-output *cum* econometric combination (Kort and Cartwright 1981).

However, econometric models present some inherent difficulties in the new environment of structural change. Structural change by the very term suggests difficulties for econometric specifications. In addition, some of our serious problems will be problems of declining regions, and it is not clear that equations fitted to periods of growth will fit and serve as well: the process of decline is not symmetrical with the process of growth. In decline, the longevity of capital already in place becomes crucial, in addition to the capital added by investment. And in declining regions, the rate of *out*migration is important, but demographers and economists have had trouble explaining outmigration econometrically. It appears that we will need to combine *a priori* specifications with the usual econometric methods, and we can hope that microdata will allow progress on the migration side and perhaps even firm behavior.

We need to continue to explore the alternative approaches to transportation and the labor market which Isard *et al*., the MRPIS group, and the FRET group are pioneering.

Finally, we do need to make more progress on combining top-down and bottom-up features in a hybrid or regional-national model. There are major challenges in the integration of sophisticated and disaggregated national macromodels, with good monetary and credit sectors and commodity prices and endogenous investment, into larger multiregional models. That is important because we know that the national growth rate is one of the most profound determinants of the fortunes of regions, in particular the older industrialized core regions, in the US and Canada. We also know that the effects of explicitly "regional" (or "targeted") policies are often smaller, by far, than the implicit and often unintended effects of national policies designed to deal with other problems that are not specific to regions. This has been found in tax policy, transportation policy, the transfer system, energy policy, etc. Finally, a good regional-national model should be able to analyze hypothetical national policies that redistribute income among regions. The totality of regional effects depends on how redistributive policies are financed, and on the effects of the financing on various national variables. For example, if regional subsidies are financed by Federal taxes the effects on various regions will be different from those if they are financed by deficits or reductions in other expenditures. A good national model is needed to simulate those differences. Thus, it remains incumbent on us to pay careful attention to the *national* model that is connected to our regional models in the multiregional system—more attention, I think, than regional modelers have been accustomed to pay. And it is essential to do this in a way that recognizes the *mutual* feedbacks between the national economy and the regional economies.

Acknowledgments

I wrote this paper while a visiting professor at the Department of City and Regional Planning, University of Pennsylvania. I am of course deeply indebted to Ben Chinitz, with whom I have worked on this subject in the past. I received special help in the writing of this paper from T.R. Lakshmanan, Barry Bluestone, Ben Harrison, John Kort, William Milne, C. Gaston, and Curtis Harris. I received financial assistance from Williams College. I am responsible for any errors of fact or interpretation.

References

Adams, F.G., and N. Glickman (1980), *Modeling the Multiregional Economic System* (Lexington Books, Lexington, MA).

Ballard, K., and R. Gustely (1980), NRIES: A Bottom-Up Multiregion Model of the United States Economy, *Paper presented at NSF Conference on An Assessment of the State of the Art in Regional Modeling* (Harvard-MIT Jt Center for Urban Studies, Cambridge, MA).

Ballard, K., R. Gustely, and R. Wendling (1980), *NRIES: Structure, Performance, and Application of a Bottom-Up Interregional Econometric Model* (Bureau of Economic Analysis, US Department of Commerce, Washington, DC).

Ballard, K., and R. Wendling (1980), The National-Regional Impact Evaluation System: A Spatial Model of US Economic and Demographic Activity, in *Journal of Regional Science*, 20(2), 143-158.

Bolton, R. (1980a), Multiregional Models in Policy Analysis: A Survey, *Research Paper* 30 (Williams College, Dept. of Economics, Williamstown, MA).

Bolton, R. (1980b), Multiregional Models: Introduction to a Symposium, in *Journal of Regional Science*, 20(2), 131-143.

Bolton, R. (1980c), Multiregional Models in Policy Analysis, in F.G. Adams and N. Glickman (eds.), *Modeling the Multiregional Economic System* (Lexington Books, Lexington, MA)., pp. 255-283.

Bolton, R. (1980d), The Public Sector in Regional Models, *Paper presented at NSF Conference on An Assessment of the State of the Art in Regional Modeling* (Harvard-MIT Jt Center for Urban Studies, Cambridge, MA).

Bolton, R. (1981), Industrial and Regional Policy in Multiregional Modeling, in M. Bell and P. Lande, *Regional Dimensions of Industrial Policy* (Lexington Books, Lexington, MA).

Bolton, R., and B. Chinitz (1980), Multiregional Modeling, *Paper presented at American Economic Association meetings, Denver, Colorado, 1980.*

Boyce, D., and G. Hewings (1980), Interregional Commodity Flow, Input-Output and Transportation Modeling: An Entropy Formulation, *Paper presented at the Conference on Multiregional Models, First World Regional Science Congress, Cambridge, MA, 1980.*

Chinitz, B., and R. Bolton (1978), *Multiregional Models in Policy Analysis*, unpublished paper.

Conway, R., and C. Howard (1980), A Forecasting Model for Regional Housing Construction, in *Journal of Regional Science*, 20(1), 1-10.

Dungan, D. (1981), *Introduction to the PRISM Provincial-Industrial Satellite Model (Version PRISM 1)* (Institute for Policy Analysis, University of Toronto).

Golladay, F., and R. Haveman (1977), *The Economic Impact of Tax-Transfer Policy: Regional and Distributional Effects* (Academic Press, New York).

Goreux, L.M., and A. Manne (1973), *Multi-Level Planning: Case Studies in Mexico* (North-Holland, Amsterdam).

Harris, C. (1980), New Developments and Extensions of the Multiregional Multi-Industry Forecasting Model, in *Journal of Regional Science*, 20(2), 159-172.

Harrison, B. (1981), The Impact of the Economic Base Transformation of a Mature Industrial Region, *Paper presented at Regional Science Association meeting, Montreal.*

Isserman, A. (1980), ECESIS: An Economic-Demographic Forecasting Model of the States: Overview of the Modeling Strategy, *Paper presented at American Statistical Association/US Bureau of the Census Evaluation Conference, Washington.*

Isserman, A. *et al.* (1981), Forecasting Interstate Migration in the United States, *Paper presented at Regional Science Association Meeting, Montreal.*

Jackson, G., G. Masnick, R. Bolton, S. Bartlett, and J. Pitkin (1981), *Regional Diversity: Growth in the United States, 1960-1990* (Auburn House for Harvard-MIT Jt Center for Urban Studies, Boston, MA).

Kort, J. (1981), *NRIES Investment Sector*, unpublished memorandum.

Kort, J., and J. Cartwright (1981), Modeling the Multiregional Economy: Integrating Econometric and Input-Output Models, *Paper presented at Southern Regional Science Association meeting, Arlington, Virginia.*

Lakshmanan, T.R. (1981), A Multiregional Model of the Economy, Environment and Energy Demand (MREEED): A Progress Report, *Paper presented at Southern Economic Association, New Orleans, Louisiana.*

L'Esperance, W. (1981), Modeling the Regional Monetary System, *Paper presented at Regional Science Association meeting, Montreal.*

Los, M. (1980), *A Transportation-Oriented Multiregional Economic Model for Canada* (Centre de Recherche sur les Transports, Université de Montréal).

McConnell, V., C. Harris, and J. Cumberland (1981), A Multi-Industry, Multiregional Environmental Model, *Paper presented at Southern Economic Association meeting, New Orleans, Louisiana.*

Milne, W., N. Glickman, and F.G. Adams (1980), A Framework for Analyzing Regional Growth and Decline, in *Journal of Regional Science*, 20(2), 173-189.

Nadji, M., and C. Harris (1982), *Location and Theory of Investment* (University of Maryland, College Park, MD).

Social Welfare Research Institute (1981), *MRPIS: A Research Strategy* (Boston College, Boston).

Thurow, L. (1975), *Generating Inequality* (Basic Books, New York).

Treyz, G. (1980), Design of a Multiregional Policy Analysis Model, in *Journal of Regional Science*, 20(2), 191-206.

Treyz, G., A. Friedlaender, and B. Stevens (1980a), The Employment Sector of a Regional Policy Simulation Model, in *Review of Economics and Statistics*, 62, 63-73.

Treyz, G. *et al.* (1980b), An Overview of the Massachusetts Economic Policy Analysis (MEPA) Model, *Paper presented at NSF Conference on the State of the Art in Regional Modeling, Harvard-MIT Jt Center for Urban Studies, Cambridge, MA.*

US Advisory Commission on Intergovernmental Relations (1980), *Regional Growth* (principal author Janet Pack) (US Government Printing Office, Washington, DC).

Uyar, B. (1981), *Report on the Progress and Future Direction of the State and Local Government Financial Model* (University of Maryland, College Park, MD).

Wilson, A. (1970), *Entropy in Urban and Regional Modeling* (Pion, London).

CHAPTER 13

INTEGRATED MULTIREGIONAL ECONOMIC MODELING FOR THE USA

T.R. Lakshmanan

1 Introduction

The current interest in multiregional modeling in the US reflects, to a large
degree, the growing realization in the policy and modeling communities that the
resolution of emerging major issues of the 1980s and beyond depends, in part, on
our ability to address their distributional implications--in space and among households, firms, and sectors.

Some of these emerging issues pertain to a desired revitalization of the economy suffering from "stagflation", productivity and income declines, and competition
from abroad. Others relate to gathering changes in the policy environment--in business regulation, in incentives available to households and firms, and the need for
environmental protection and energy security. Finally, these issues are emerging
against a backdrop of some broad secular changes in society--changes in birth rates,
in household formation, in female labor force participation, and in the consequent
shifts in consumptive structure: the significant shifts in comparative advantage
between metropolitan and nonmetropolitan areas on the one hand, and among large
regions such as the "snowbelt" and the "sunbelt" on the other (Harrison 1981).

As a variety of policy packages is proposed to improve the productivity of
private and public activities, there is urgent need to understand the multidimensional consequences (for output, employment, productivity, incomes, energy security,
environmental quality, etc.) of these policies. Further, many of the consequences
are likely to be unevenly incident on different households, firms, sectors, and
regions. Consequently, information on these consequences--in terms of their magnitude, type, and distributional detail--must be available for policy makers to facilitate the *ex ante* assessment of and redesign (as necessary) of these policies and
to help in building the socioeconomic coalitions necessary for policy implementation.

However, available multiregional models are largely unequal to the task of providing such information (Bolton 1980). The depiction of limited segments of the
economy, the neglect of the supply side and income distributional effects, and the
few "policy handles" available restrict their utility in integrated policy analyses.
It is in this context that there have recently appeared some proposals for comprehensive models of the economy, termed integrated multiregional models for a variety
of reasons.

First, these models depict and integrate major components of the economy--insti-
tutions (households, business, government) and exhange media (factor and product markets, regional and interregional transportation, and other networks). Second, consistent with this broad definition, the model structure is eclectic, using the
notions of aggregate demand, input-output, neoclassical theory, programming models
and microsimulation modeling. Often a modular design strategy is adopted so as to
be appropriate for integrating the contributions of different investigators special-
izing in specific subsystems and for a preliminary model to be improved over time.
Third, there is an attempt in these models to treat comprehensively the linkages
between regions, and between regions and the nation ("bottom-up" and "top-down").
Fourth, a broad range of policy handles relevant to different sectors of the economy are designed into these models so that not only can sectoral and systemic effects
of policies in one area be assessed, but so also can "interpolicy" effects.

This chapter describes the components of such an integrated model (Section 2), and proceeds to a description of choices made in this framework for operational representation by two different groups. In Section 3, the paper outlines the proposed multiuniversity integrated multiregional model of the US (MIMUS) in which the author is a co-principal investigator. Section 4 discusses some of the conceptual and technical issues in the implementation of the MIMUS model and its potential applications.

2 The Components of an Integrated Multiregional Model

Three classes of issues are emerging in the contemporary public policy agenda of the US. First, there is the growing concern with the state of the economy. The persistence of high unemployment with high inflation is worrisome. The unimpressive progress of productivity and incomes is bringing distribution issues to the fore (in a society where structural income redistribution is difficult). Increasing foreign competition threatens traditional US markets. Consequently, academic and policy communities advance various proposals for economic regeneration in the form of incentives for investment, taxes, etc. To provide *ex ante* assessments on the effectiveness of these proposals, information on their pervasive effects on industrial mix, output, employment incomes, environmental quality, etc., is required. Further, the response of different households and firms to these initiatives will vary with their initial endowment, demand curves, location, etc. The resulting uneven incidence of the policy impacts on individuals and industries in different regions, at a time when populous high-income regions (many metropolitan areas, the northeast) are experiencing stagnation and relative decline, is a major political issue. Consequently, policy-relevant information detailed in terms of region, household type, and industry becomes important.

Secondly, there is a growing notion that the effective performance of many institutions--households, industries, and governmental agencies--is impaired by the existing system of incentives, i.e., economic and social policy instruments. These relate to various economic and social areas in the form of regulations, policies related to taxing, investment, income security, health; education, environmental protection, energy supply, etc. Often policies in one area have adverse effects in another. Thus, one part of the current energy supply incentive system is represented by the considerable resources rents extracted by energy exporting states. This leads to large income transfers from the energy importing states, and an extra rise in input costs and cost of living with long-term competitive disadvantage and decline in these older regions (Lakshmanan 1981). Again, a number of proposals abound in this area about revising the incentive system by greater deregulation, and instituting various growth maximizing incentives. The critical analytical issues in assessing these proposals are: How effective are these proposals in achieving their professed objectives? What effects are these proposals likely to have on other societal goals such as regional equity, environmental protection, energy security, etc.?

Thirdly, secular changes in the form of demographic shifts and emergent technological change are likely to alter in fundamental ways consumption and production structures. The falling birth rates, the changes in household structure, the increasing participation of females in the labor force, may alter the patterns of consumption of food, durables, housing, transportation, etc. At the same time, the high-technology revolution under way in New England and California is being viewed as a restructuring of the workplace (Harrison 1981). In a manner reminiscent of the effects of capital-intensive import substitution industrialization in developing countries, there is a high demand for highly skilled labor, and for low-skill periodic labor, and very little for middle-level skills, with adverse consequences on income distribution. Any analysis of the labor market in this context should explicitly deal with human capital categories.

Our ability to assess the alternative proposals being advanced for addressing these kinds of issues depends on our understanding of the multidimensional consequences on economic growth, equity, and environment. Distributional consequences are particularly crucial. To be successful, national policies must consider potential

regional gains and losses so as to fashion stable political coalitions for policy
formulation and implementation.

If the multiregional modeling community is to respond to the informational
challenges inherent in these emerging issues, its agenda must be broadened. An
idea of such an agenda may be gained from Figure 1, which shows the major components
of a comprehensive multiregional model. These components provide a systemic view
of the potential structure of an integrated multiregional model. The figure applies
to each region of a multiregional model. The extensive linkages among these components and between these components in different regions are via regional and interregional networks of transportation, communication, and monetary flows (Figure 1(a)).
Further, there are flows from the region up to the national model in some cases
(bottom-up) and in others from the nation to the regions (top-down) as seen in Figure 1(b). The purpose of this representation is to sketch in broadly the potential
agenda of multiregional modeling and to provide a framework by which to assess the
kinds of choices made by designers of operational integrated multiregional models.

Three institutions and two media of exchange, or markets, comprise the components or sectors of the comprehensive model. The institutions are households,
businesses or industries, and government. The markets are the factor markets and
product markets that link the institutions and serve as media of exchange. The
exchanges involve not only goods, services, and individuals, but also money and
credit; and these flows take place across *space*. The regional and interregional
transportation and monetary networks determine these exchanges (Figure 1(a)).

The household sector comprises individuals grouped as families, and unrelated
individuals. Traditional governmental activities at the federal, state, and local
levels are categorized into two groups: those that produce goods and services (e.g.,
post office, sewer service, water supply, etc.) and those involving policy making
(regulations, incentives, defense, etc.). The government sector in Figure 1 retains
only the second group of activities or the policy making function. The public enterprises that provide goods and services are included in the businesses or industries
sector.

The industries sector includes all the private and public enterprises in each
of the regions of the US that extract primary resources, and acquire various factor
inputs, corresponding to their technology, to produce various goods and services.
The circular flow depicted inside this sector is intended to indicate the broad
range of interindustry interactions. The value added is distributed partially to
households as wages and interest (retained earnings are also a source of factor
inputs). Taxes are paid out to government and transfers of various kinds are received from the government. Productive enterprises invest or disinvest in order to
increase or decrease production, alter technology, or relocate in a different region
as guided by changing markets, altered relative factor prices, and shifting interregional comparative advantage. Consequently an explicit analysis of comparative
costs, industrial complex analysis, dynamic factor substitution, characteristics of
labor supply, transportation, and other public investments at a regional level is
necessary in order to track the sectoral and spatial changes in production in the
economy and the responses to specific economic proposals.

The size and demographic composition--race, age, sex, family formation--of
households in a region depend upon natural increase, family formation, and interregional migration processes. Diverse households in a region offer labor and capital
to enterprises in return for wages, salaries, and interest. They consume a variety
of goods and services for money and credit, pay taxes, and receive transfers for
which they are eligible. Their participation in factor and product markets depends
upon their assets (physical and human capital), income, savings and consumption
behavior, and some institutional factors (e.g., discrimination in labor markets and
housing). It is only by an explicit regional analysis of these determinants of market participation that it is possible (a) to determine the regional distribution of
income and consumption among categories of households, and (b) to assess the effectiveness of social programs such as those that try to induce among some groups increased labor supply, higher income and household savings, and desired levels of
consumption, etc.

Factor inputs are exchanged in factor markets for factor payments. Current
analytical work on factor markets at the national and regional levels has broadened

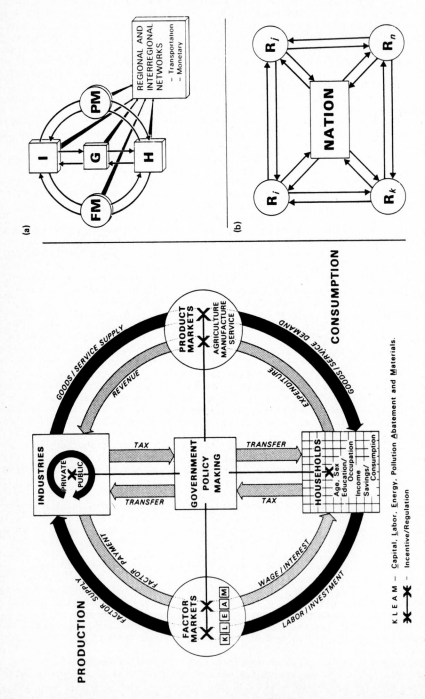

Figure 1. Components of a comprehensive multiregional model: (a) interregional links; (b) national-regional relationships.

traditional orientation to labor and capital to include energy and material inputs
(Hudson and Jorgenson 1974, Lakshmanan 1979, 1981). Such a model permits the determination at a regional level of substitution and complementarities among factor inputs in the face of changing relative factor prices and leads to formulations where
factor inputs and production locations are jointly determined. Since control of
many stationary-source industrial pollutants is national policy, it may be appropriate to incorporate abatement services as a separate input--hence the KLEAM model
in Figure 1. Of course, the separability of pollution abatement (A) services can
be tested by appropriate specification of the form of a production function and
econometric testing. For greater policy power in an integrated multiregional model,
disaggregation of factor inputs into types of labor, capital, energy, and materials
(water, etc.) is highly desirable.

The product market links producers and demanders in the region and in the nation. Products are exchanged for money or credit over a transportation network.
In view of the traditional interest in regional modeling in output determination
and spatial flows, the behavior of different classes of products, agriculture,
manufacturing, and service have been analyzed.

In its policy making role, government determines the incentive system for production and consumption. Thus the incentive/regulation structure affects households
(tax deductions, eligibility for transfer programs, traffic regulations, etc.), industries (investment tax credit, pollution regulations, etc.), and both markets
(labor market regulation, resource rents, financial market regulations, etc.).
Integrated models should incorporate a broad range of these policy measures in the
model. The ability to incorporate such policy handles in the multiregional models
depends upon:

(i)   the consistency between the time regimes of the model and the policies
       in question. A short-term model will be appropriate for assessment of
       regional effects of expenditure policies, and monetary policies. If
       the objective is to assess economic development agency (EDA)-type
       public investment programs a medium-run model is required;

(ii)   the behavioral specification of the model. The assessment of govern-
       ment expenditure policies would require an input-output model compo-
       nent. On the other hand, the medium-run model above will require
       behavioral specification of capital formation in relation to supply
       costs and output level; and

(iii) of course, availability of appropriate data.

In addition to the coverage of all the major institutions and markets in the
economy, our integrated multiregional model should explicitly deal with linkages
between the sectors and markets. First, there is the need for full specification
of a *multimodal* transportation system in a manner wherein not only the transportation consequences (mode and route choice, link costs, travel time, delays, congestion, and commodity flows) of production and consumption, but also the consequences
of transportation networks on the scale and location of production and consumption
can be assessed. In spite of the pervasive interest in transportation and location
among regional scientists and economic geographers, a specification to permit two-
way relationships between transport and economic activities has not been available
until recently to interregional modelers (Boyce and Hewings 1980).

Secondly, the two-way informational and decision flows--"top-down" and "bottom-
up"--between national and regional models must be specified in a hybrid approach,
an illustration of which appears in Figure 2. Some national economic variables are
exogenous, while others are endogenous. Among the latter some are spatially uniform
and others spatially variant. The former group of endogenous variables (e.g., investment in some manufacturing process) can be specified in a top-down format, while
the latter group (e.g., housing investment) can be determined at regional level as
a function of regional demand and supply variables and selected national variables
and summed up. The key point is that the design of an integrated multiregional
model should build in these two-way relationships between regions and nation.

Set against these impressive requirements for multiregional modeling, designers
of operational models abstract and simplify. In the interests of manageability,

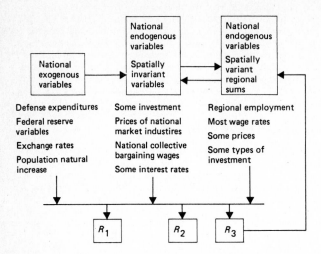

Figure 2. Hybrid approach: an illustration.

cost-effectiveness, and intelligibility, modelers sacrifice comprehensive detail
and seize upon strategic elements of Figure 1. However, there has been a growing
tendency in the last half-decade or more to cover the economy more comprehensively.
At the same time, the modeling structure tends to be eclectic, combining different
techniques such as input-output, econometric modeling, Keynesian notions, neoclassical theory, gravity modeling, household microsimulation, etc. Further, newly available databases and imaginative use of existing databases have helped.

    Such an integrative approach is evident in five multiregional models of the
US--of which only the two most recent models approach the scope of integrated multiregional models sketched here. The three other models, while less ambitious, were
early attempts at comprehensive, eclectic interregional modeling (Golladay and
Haveman 1977, Lakshmanan 1979, 1981, Treyz 1980).

    One contribution of Golladay and Haveman's model lies in its comprehensive
coverage of industries and households by imaginative links between Polenske's multiregional input-output model and a microsimulation of households so that labor supply,
income distribution, and consumption effects of welfare reform policy and the consequent indirect and induced interregional effects can be estimated. The Treyz model,
while traditional in scope, is noteworthy in its eclectic use of regional economic
theory--input-output accounting, neoclassical theory, location theory--and in use
of new databases so as to specify carefully investment, labor markets, and lag
structures of variables. The distinguishing features of the Lakshmanan model are
its efforts to incorporate significant details on energy use and environment, and
some methodological innovations from mainstream economic theory (multiple-factor
substitution, flexible production functional forms, median-voter model for public
expenditure determination, etc.), in multiregional modeling.

    The two multiregional models that hold promise for policy analysis in the con-
text of the emerging issues of the eighties and beyond are:

    (i)   the Multi-Regional Policy Impact Simulation Model (MRPIS)--designed
         by researchers from Boston College, the Massachusetts Institute of
         Technology, and SWRI *et al*. (1981). (See this book, Chapter 12.)

    (ii) the Multiuniversity Integrated Multiregional Model of the US (hence-
         forth MIMUS) designed by a multiuniversity team (Isard *et al*. 1981).

3   The Multiuniversity Integrated Multiregional Model of the U.S.

A multiuniversity team plans to build models of various subsystems of the economy and link them to one another and to a national econometric model (NATLEC) to yield an integrated multiregional model (Figure 3). The Wharton model will probably be NATLEC, and will provide national magnitudes of components of final demand, material prices, output, employment, investment, and financial market variables. The regional components of MIMUS are as follows:

(i)   CICIOP. This module provides locational studies through comparative cost, and industrial complex analysis of key industrial sectors, and through combining input-output and linear programming models determines output, value added by sector, and the optimal pattern of energy production, conversion, and interregional transmission.

(ii)   FACTIN determines (a) the demand for capital, labor, energy, and materials (and categories thereof) using dynamic versions of flexible cost forms such as translog, and (b) region investment supply by sector.

(iii) REGLEC (multiregion econometric module). This determines equilibrium labor supply, demand, and unemployment and wage rates. Potential extensions include regional government sector and household sector output.

(iv)   DEMO. A microsimulation model of the household sector providing disaggregated labor supply, and associated elements of household income, expenditures, and savings.

(v)   TRANS. This allocates interregional commodity flows over different links and by modes, using a dispersion constraint that results in crosshauling of aggregated commodities.

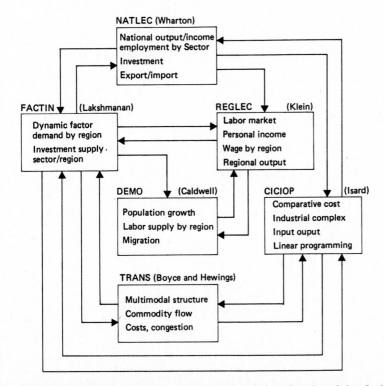

Figure 3. Multiuniversity integrated multiregional model of the US (MIMUS)

Given the scope, variations in spatial scale, and variations in behavior specification of these modules, intermodule links are crucial. The outputs of one module
are used in another. Consistency checks between variables generated in the "hybrid"
fashion and between variables of different levels of disaggregation at the micro
and macro portions of the model are required. In practice, some link modules--some
of an accounting nature, some of a behavioral type--will be developed. Significant
technical knowledge may accrue to the modelers during these specifications of intermodule links in MIMUS.

3.1 CICIOP

One purpose of this module is to conduct locational studies of industries,
such as iron and steel, aluminum, and petrochemicals, by comparative cost and industrial complex techniques (Isard *et al.* 1959). The second is to use an input-
output and programming model to focus on energy issues. In order to focus upon
particular regional and national policy issues, the set of energy sectors is removed
from the standard structural matrix of the interregional input-output submodel, and
following a procedure developed by Brookhaven National Laboratory, a set of energy
product sectors is defined. The redesigned input coefficients matrix becomes

$$
A = \begin{bmatrix} A_{SS} & A_{SP} & 0 \\ A_{PS} & 0 & A_{PN} \\ A_{NS} & 0 & A_{NN} \end{bmatrix} \tag{1}
$$

where S represents energy supply sectors, P, energy product sectors, and N, nonenergy sectors.

The energy product sectors are dummy sectors, which convert energy resources
into energy product used to satisfy locally (i) intermediate demand from the energy
supply sectors (reflected in the technical coefficients A_{PS}) and the nonenergy sectors (reflected in A_{PN}), and (ii) final demand. The only inputs used by these dummy
sectors are energy resources, reflected in A_{SP}. As a consequence, the submatrices
A_{PP} and A_{NP} are zero. Finally, the nonenergy sectors use inputs from the energy
product sectors and themselves, as recorded in A_{PN} and A_{NN}. Their outputs are delivered to the energy supply sectors (reflected in A_{NS}) and nonenergy sectors (reflected
in A_{NN}) as well as to final demand.

The particular sectoral structure of this submodel implies an iterative solution
method. Given the final demand vector Y_N covering all regions, first the output X_N
of the nonenergy sectors is determined, where $X_N = (I - A_{NN})^{-1}Y_N$ and I is the unit
vector; second, X_P of the energy product sectors is determined where $X_P = A_{PN}X_N + Y_P$,
in which Y_P is the final demand for their output; third, X_S of the energy supply
sector is determined via a linear programming submodel detailed below; fourth, A_{SP}
is determined from the results of this submodel, taking into account final and own
demand for the output of these sectors; fifth, a revised projection is made of the
output $\bar{X}_N$ of the nonenergy sectors where $\bar{X}_N = (I - A_{NN})^{-1}(Y_N + A_{NS}X_S)$; sixth, a
revised projection of output $\bar{X}_P$ of the energy product sectors is made where $X_P =
A_{PN}\bar{X}_N + Y_P + A_{PS}X_S$; and so forth until the output vectors upon which the submodel
converges can be approximated.

The interregional linear programming submodel is a standard "transportation
problem" model applied to resource allocation. It starts from energy resources
extraction, and conversion of the raw resource into a more marketable product (the
intermediate energy forms).

$$
\sum_{j=1}^{P} c_j z_j \qquad\qquad j = 1,\ldots,mn \ ; \qquad p = mn \tag{2}
$$

$$\sum_j \frac{1}{e_{uj}} z_j \leq S_u \qquad\qquad u = 1, \ldots, n \qquad\qquad (3)$$

$$\sum_j d_{vk} z_j \geq D_v \qquad\qquad v = 1, \ldots, m \qquad\qquad (4)$$

$$\sum_j f_{wj} z_j \leq B_w \qquad\qquad w = 1, \ldots, r \qquad\qquad (5)$$

where

z_j = a shipment along path j connecting a source u with a destination v

c_j = cost at destination v of the unit of energy shipped along path j

e_{uj} = efficiency of conversion into intermediate energy form, taking into account energy use by energy source (A_{SS})

S_u = energy supply capacity at source u

d_{vj} = the energy efficiency of the end-use device

D_v = demand at destination v, equivalent to X_P, each v being a demand of a particular region for an energy product

f_{wj} = coefficient of emission of pollutant w per unit of shipment (inclusive of production) along path j (to be disaggregated by relevant local area)

B_w = binding magnitude on emission of pollutant w by all shipments (to be disaggregated by relevant local area)

plus additional constraints pertaining to extraction, transportation, and infrastructure capacities, and to satisfactory achievement of other objectives relating to other policy issues. When the z_j are appropriately summed by source, and the sources appropriately aggregated in terms of the given set of regions, the required X_S of the input-output submodel are obtained. CICIOP will provide regional-sectoral outputs, regional-sectoral demands, industrial structure of regions, sectoral labor requirements, energy shadow prices, and unadjusted interregional sectoral flows.

3.2 FACTIN

In the first part, drawing heavily upon Lakshmanan (1979) and Lakshmanan *et al.* (1981), and in line with recent developments in microeconomic theory, this submodel uses flexible functional forms for estimating cost functions. A concave, twice-differentiable production function at the state and regional levels in the manufacturing sector is assumed:

$$Y = F(K, L, E, M) \qquad\qquad\qquad (6)$$

where

$$K = K(k_1, k_2, \ldots)$$
$$L = L(l_1, l_2, \ldots)$$
$$E = E(e_1, e_2, \ldots) \qquad\qquad (6a)$$
$$M = M(m_1, m_2, \ldots)$$

Here output is related to four factors--capital (K), labor (L), energy (E) and materials (M); hence the name KLEM production function.

If input prices and output levels are exogenous, the production structure in (6) can be equivalently described by a cost function that is also weakly separable and of the form (in the translog case)

$$\ln C = \alpha_0 + \alpha_y \ln Y + \sum_i \alpha_i \ln P_i + \frac{1}{2} \beta_{yy} (\ln Y)^2 + \frac{1}{2} \sum_i \sum_j \beta_{ij} \ln P_i \ln P_j$$

$$+ \sum_i \beta_{yi} \ln Y \ln P_i \qquad\qquad (7)$$

where $i,j = K,L,E,M$, and the P_i are factor prices.

If (7) is differentiated with respect to input prices logarithmically, the derived demand equations can be obtained:

$$\partial \ln C / \partial \ln P_i = (\partial C / \partial P_i) P_i / C = \alpha_i + \sum_j \beta_i \ln P_j + \beta_{yi} \ln Y \quad . \qquad (8)$$

From Shepard's lemma, $\partial C / \partial P_i = X_i$ is the cost minimizing quantity of input i. Since the cost function is linearly homogeneous in prices, $C = \sum_i P_i X_i$. Substituting gives:

$$\partial \ln C / \partial \ln P_i = P_i X_i / \sum_i P_i X_i = S_i$$

or $\qquad\qquad\qquad\qquad\qquad\qquad\qquad\qquad\qquad\qquad\qquad\qquad\qquad\qquad\qquad (9)$

$$S_i = \alpha_i + \sum_j \beta_{ij} \ln P_j + \beta_{yi} \ln Y$$

where S_i is the cost share of factor i. For one component factor, if we assume S_{ei} is the share of fuel i (with price P_{ei}) in the aggregate energy cost share S_E, then by similar reasoning about cost minimization and homotheticity of the P_E function, we have

$$S_{ei} = \sigma_i + \sum_j \gamma_{ij} \ln P_{ei} \quad . \qquad\qquad (10)$$

The demand equations for the factors are

$$D_i = S_i Y P_y / P_i \qquad\qquad (11)$$

where D_i and S_i are the demand and share of total costs for factor i.

Initially, we estimate the instantaneous adjustment model in (8)-(11). Then we attempt dynamic versions of the model in two stages--first a partial adjustment model, and then a fully dynamic adjustment model.

In dynamic models, in general, there is an assumption of an optimal or "desired" level of any input $X_i^*(t)$ at any given time t, to which the firm adjusts over some period. The process of adjustment of input levels over time may be represented as

$$X_i(t) = \lambda_i (X_i^*(t) - X_i(t)) \qquad\qquad 0 \le \lambda \le 1 \qquad\qquad (12)$$

where $\dot{X}_i = dX_i(t)/dt$. The static model is the case when $\lambda = i$ 'for all i.

A partial adjustment mechanism will be used initially. However, this version does not in itself provide a structural model of the firm that is consistent with profit maximizing behavior.

Rigorous descriptions of the dynamic adjustment process are available (Eisner and Strotz 1963, Lucas 1967, Treadway 1971, 1974). In the Treadway model, the firm uses a vector $\bar{\omega}$ representing the cost of current services of each resource stock, and a vector $\bar{g}$, representing the market price of additions to each stock. The cost of adjustments to new levels of input stocks is viewed as the sum of the market price of the input and the cost of allocating resources to the process of adjustment in terms of output foregone.

Berndt *et al.* (1977, 1979) adopted Treadway's internal adjustment cost concept but maintained the distinction between variable and quasifixed inputs in developing a model in which the firm minimizes the present value of an infinite stream of production costs. In addition to determining the optimal or desired level of quasifixed inputs, this model determines an optimal partial adjustment parameter (λ_i in (12)).

In our treatment we propose to try initially a quadratic functional form, although we may experiment with other functional forms later.

A second part of the FACTIN module consists of an investment supply submodel. The regional investment model differs from the traditional specifications in two ways (Lakshmanan 1981). First, regional supply of investment is viewed as determined by both supply and demand side factors. Second, two specifications are provided depending upon the way the relationships between national and regional variables are viewed in an industry.

In the first class of industries, outputs and prices are determined in national markets and technology is easily spatially transferable (e.g., multiplant manufacturing industries, energy industry). National capital formation is viewed as determined in response to national capital market variables. A top-down spatial allocation of this predetermined investment to regions, based on regional comparative costs, follows. The spatial allocation of investment is viewed as one of qualitative choice and specified as a multinomial logit model. The arguments of this function are relative regional profit rates, access to inputs, access to markets, production capacity, local taxes, quality of life, and amenity factors.

As contrasted with the above top-down approach, a "hybrid" approach (assuming two-way relationships between national and regional variables) is utilized for the second class of industries. Thus in industries such as retail, housing, and service industries, oriented largely to regional markets, regional investment is specified in terms of regional demand and supply determinants and selected national variables. National investment in such industries will be aggregations of investments by region.

3.3 REGLEC

By explicitly deriving equilibrium prices, supplies, and demand, this module contributes crucially to the integrated model. Drawing heavily upon the work of Fromm *et al.* (1980), a submodel may be constructed to consist of: (i) a labor demand equation for each sector and age-race-sex class in each region. The labor demand function may be derived from a Cobb-Douglas production function, and as such is an alternative to the approach followed in the FACTIN module and to the input-output approach in the CICIOP module, which generates labor requirements by sector and region; (ii) a labor supply function and an unemployment function, each by region and demographic class; (iii) a population and migration function by region and demographic class; and (iv) an equilibrium condition that ensures that the wage rate (by region and age-sex-race class) equates total regional supply and demand for each demographic class.

The labor supply function essentially relates the fraction of a population of a demographic class that is employed (effective labor supply) to: (i) after-tax wages modified by the ratio of wages to the amount of public assistance or unemployment compensation available; (ii) the current unemployment rate; and (iii) the previous-period unemployment rate, a lagged effect.

The labor supply specification is unconventional in that it expresses age-race-sex-specific jobs *per capita* rather than employed persons *per capita* (the employment rate). This specification, in effect, combines an expression of multiple job holding with an expression of the decision to accept employment, thus permitting the determination of a labor market equilibrium without having to reconcile census employment (employed persons) with Bureau of Labor Statistics employment (jobs filled). Formally,

$$\lg \left(E_d^J / N_d^J \right) = A_0 + A_{1d} \lg \left[1 - TY^J \left(W_d^J \right) \right] \left(W_d^J / S_d^J \text{ or } C_d^J \right) + A_{2d} \lg \left(U_d^J / N_d^J \right)$$

$$+ A_{3d} \lg \left(U_d^J(-1) / N_d^J(-1) \right) \tag{13}$$

where

E_d^J = number of jobs held in region J by d-type people.

$N_d^J, N_d^J(-1)$ = population in demographic class d in region J in the current period and previous period respectively.

$TY^J(W_d^J)$ = effective rate of income tax on a standard d-type person earning W_d^J in region J; TY^J reflects state, local, and federal income taxes, and FICA (fiscal income adjustment).

S_d^J = public assistance entitlements (in dollars per year) in region J of a standard household with head in age-race-sex class d.

C_d^J = unemployment compensation entitlements in region J for a standard person in age-race-sex class d.

$U_d^J, U_d^J(-1)$ = the number of unemployed d-type people in region J in the current and previous period, respectively.

The specification of the unemployment function is in the same spirit as the employment supply function. Willingness to seek work is affected by the relative returns of "working" and "not working". However, whereas the labor supply function contains current and lagged unemployment to capture a discouraged-worker effect, our unemployment function contains current and lagged employment to capture an encouraged-worker effect. Rising employment needs to pull people into the labor force and so increases the number of people seeking work. A time trend is included in the unemployment function to capture, crudely, the effect on measured unemployment of welfare programs that require recipients to seek work. These programs, which require welfare recipients to seek (but not necessarily to accept) work, push up measured unemployment but do not affect incentives to work. The unemployment function is

$$\lg \frac{U_d^J}{N_d^J} = A_{0d} + A_{1d} \lg \left\{ \left[1 - TY^J \left(W_d^J \right) \right] \frac{W_d^J}{S_d^J \text{ or } C_d^J} \right\} + A_{2d} \lg \left(\frac{E_D^J}{N_d^J} \right)$$

$$+ A_{3d} \lg \left(\frac{E_d^J(-1)}{N_d^J(-1)} \right) + A_{4d} T \tag{14}$$

where

$$U_d^J = \text{the number of persons in region } J, \text{ and age-race-sex class } d$$
$$\text{who are unemployed (out of work and seeking work).}$$

The wages that follow from market clearing between the sum of the demand for labor
from a particular demographic class over all sectors in the region and the supply
of labor in that class are used as inputs in the flexible functional form factor
demand equations of the FACTIN module. Also, they may be considered as macroinputs
into the household formation and migration (and possibly expenditures and savings)
submodels of the DEMO module. From this labor market submodel the wage income by
region is determined by simple aggregation over demographic groups. Combining such
with the nonwage income that can be derived from CICIOP (via regional disaggregation
of NATLEC (national economic) magnitudes) yields personal income by region for use
in CICIOP and FACTIN.

3.4 DEMO

This module deals with the household sector in a microanalytic framework (Orcutt
et al.1980) and provides explicit analysis of the changes in population of a system
(its breakdown by region, age, sex, type of occupation, skill, income class, etc.),
household formation, migration, and other important factors.

A description of any component in the household sector would include a listing
of its own input, status, and output variables along with those relationships that
are used in updating status variables and in generating output variables. The behavioral relationships used to generate values of the updated status variables and
of the output variables, given the predetermined status variables and the input
variables, are called "operating characteristics of that component". In microanalytic modeling, populations both actual and synthetic are given sample representations. Public-use samples drawn from real populations are a major source of
data.

The DEMO module involves a population growth submodel for each region. In this
submodel a sample population at time t is subject to a *micropass* program, that is,
it is subject to: (1) incrementing of each family and each person, i.e., updating
of age; and then to probabilities of: (2) home leaving; (3) divorce; (4) giving
birth; (5) death; (6) first marriage; and (7) remarriage; all of items (2-7) are
identified probabilistically as functions of (8) education (move to next level,
graduate, retained at current level); (9) the family moving; if it moves, the
probability that it migrates; and if it migrates, the family's region, SMSA city
size and whether its members live in a central city or a suburb of an SMSA (the
family's new location is recorded as well as last year's region and SMSA size);
and (10) being disabled. To yield labor supply and its characteristics, each person over 13 years of age passes through a *labor program* block, which establishes
for him: (11) wage rate; (12) labor force participation; (13) hours in labor force;
(14) fraction of hours unemployed; and (15) earnings.

Families as well as individuals in the sample population are traced. Each
family is passed through the *transfer program* block, which establishes for it: (16)
social security income and contributions: (17) pensions; (18) unemployment compensation; (19) aid to families with dependent children; (20) supplemental security income; (21) food stamps; and (22) total transfer income.

The ninth item of this natural population growth submodel pertains to family
movement, specifying region of origin and destination. For proper multiregional
modeling, however, the migration component must be much more extensively developed
than in the present treatment, in terms of simple probabilities with no identification of the driving forces behind migration. The proposed migration submodel takes
each family and/or unrelated individual and estimates the probability of its leaving
a specific location and terminating at another location in terms of such factors as:
(1) growth rate of region of origin; (2) growth rate of region of termination; (3)
industrial structure of region of origin; (4) industrial structure of region of

termination; (5) wage rates and wage differentials between regions of origin and termination; (6) unemployment rates at regions of origin and termination; (8) housing costs, and other costs of living; (9) environmental and quality-of-life indices; and (10) special characteristics such as presence of a dominating R and D sector or a dominating old declining sector. The relevance and coefficient values of the different variables considered can be inferred from estimations based on historical data sets for each specific region of origin and termination (if available).

Specifically, the migration submodel might proceed as follows.

(i)   Based on a few key variables such as unemployment rate relative to the rest of the US, wage rates relative to the rest of the US, welfare payments relative to the rest of the US, and certain characteristics of the household (whether head unemployed, presence of children, age and past mobility of head), a probability is derived that a particular household will outmigrate from a given region J, or any region in a subset J of regions.

(ii) Given a probability for each household that it will leave the current location, a Monte Carlo procedure is used to select those households that actually leave.

(iii) Given the set of movers, the model then determines for each mover the probability of terminating in any given subset of states, and then each state in this subset, and if necessary, each BEA (bureau of economic analysis) of each state. For example, the probability of a family whose head is 25, black, and unemployed, outmigrating from Mississippi to New York state (or NYC) may be a function of differences in wages, welfare payments, housing costs; and likewise to (a) Illinois (Chicago); (b) the rest of the northern US (east of the Dakotas and Iowa); (c) the rest of the US. In the case of (b) and (c), the probabilities will be crudely disaggregated by states using simple indices like population or employment percentages. Thus if we have ten originating subsets of states (Louisiana, Mississippi, and Arkansas may belong to one), and if each segment from each subset of states moves to five subsets of terminating states, we have 50 equations. In each of these equations there will appear some but not all of the key variables.

3.5 TRANS

A multiregion model that projects output by sector, employment by sector, household consumption, regional investment, etc., has rarely been operated simultaneously and consistently with a model that projects changes in the transportation network flows and costs so that the two-way relationships between location and transportation can be explicitly studied. It is well recognized that the nonlinkage of the transportation system to the employment-production system is a source of major errors in existing models, whether single-purpose or multipurpose. Hence, we consider it essential to integrate the CICIOP framework and a transportation system module to yield simultaneously consistent projections from both, and thereby to provide a basis for evaluating a consistent set of policies for transportation, sectoral development, regional development, energy, etc.

In the first iteration of one integrated multiregional model, the entire input-output framework (the adjusted regional final demand, the interregional sectoral flows, the regional outputs by sector) and perhaps the energy shadow prices from the operation of the programming submodel are input to the TRANS module. Drawing upon the thinking of Boyce and Hewings (1980), the basic transportation cost minimization problem subject to realistic constraints may be set up as follows:

$$\text{minimize } C = \sum_h \sum_J \sum_I x_h^{JL} c_h^{JL} \tag{15}$$

such that

$$\sum_{L} x_h^{LJ} = \sum_{J} a_{hj}^{J} \sum_{L} x_j^{JL} + Y_h^{J} \qquad \text{for all } h \qquad (16)$$

$$S_h \leq -\sum_{J} \sum_{L} x_h^{JL} \lg \left(x_h^{JL} \right) \qquad \text{for all } h \qquad (17)$$

$$x_h^{JL} \geq 0 \qquad \text{for all } h, J, L \qquad (18)$$

where

x_h^{JL} = amount of commodity h shipped from region J to region L

c_h^{JL} = transport cost per unit of h from J to L

C = total system transportation costs on all commodities

$Y_h^{J}, \sum_{L} x_h^{JL}$ = region J's final demand for and output of commodity h, respectively, obtained from the operation that transforms input-output sector outputs to output of all commodity h

S_h = a required level (alternatively, an entropy-type measure) of cross-hauling of commodity h

a_{hj}^{J} = input-output coefficient giving requirements of commodity h for production of one unit of commodity j in region J.

For constraint (16) to be meaningful, two basic assumptions are necessary: (a) each region's producers are indifferent as to the final destination of their output, and (b) each region's consumers (both intermediate and final) are indifferent as to the origin of their inputs. In other words, only transportation costs determine interregional flows, provided the crosshauling constraint (17) is met. Such a crosshauling term is legitimate because (a) commodity flow analysis requires at least some aggregation if it is not to be exceedingly costly; consequently, opposing shipments of distinctly different goods in the same commodity class take place and become recorded as crosshauling, albeit fictitious; and (b) actual cross-hauling of the same commodity may occur because of established trading patterns, lack of information, product differentiation (through advertising, etc.), and other institutional factors. S_h is to be interpreted as a scalar measure of "miscellaneous" spatial interaction and is to be set at one or more reasonable levels in accord with past conditions and data on "crosshauling" and estimates of future conditions.

The model described by equations (15-17) builds upon past attempts to model commodity flows with the transportation problem of linear programming. Our approach avoids the inherent errors introduced into such models through sector aggregation and actual crosshauling that may be undertaken in the future to insure reliability of supply in addition to the reasons discussed above. The use of constraint (17) in this model illustrates the benefits from a multidisciplinary approach to model integration. Constraints of this form are now widely applied in aggregate urban transportation system modeling.

Additionally, a submodel of *network equilibrium* is to be developed within the TRANS module to take into account congestion costs (a function of the link flow on any link) wherein (a) the transportation costs over all paths that are used from each origin to each destination are equal, and (b) no unused path has a lower transportation cost. The problem of network equilibrium for a single mode has been solved mathematically and computationally for large networks.

Moreover, a *modal choice* submodel can be specified as a direct extension of the route choice submodel. If it is assumed that link costs increase with flow, mode routes can be identified for each commodity and origin-destination combination. This type of submodel has already been implemented on urban networks of a size comparable to a large interregional multimodal transportation system. Composite transportation costs across routes and modes may be determined in the manner suggested by Williams (1977). These transportation costs are then in a form satisfactory for use as inputs in the next iteration of the comparative-cost industrial-complex and programming submodels, and, along with the TRANS estimates of flows, for use in revising input-output coefficients in CICIOP.

4 Implementation and Use of MIMUS: Some Issues

MIMUS is quite clearly an ambitious multiregional model, but one whose scope is clearly demanded by the major policy issues of the day. It integrates major segments of the economy: production and locational processes, factor markets, household microbehavior (demographic, migration, labor supply, consumption), energy and environmental sectors, and a transport systems analysis integrated into production and consumption. Future extensions may incorporate a regional governmental sector and further elaborations of the household sector.

An impressive theoretical apparatus has been mobilized in the design of MIMUS. Some of the innovations are in the form of incorporation into multiregional modeling of state-of-the-art mainstream economic theory, while the TRANS module is drawn from recent innovations in economic geography and regional science (Wilson 1970, Boyce and Hewings 1980). Further, a broad range of techniques--input-output econometric modeling, programming, microanalytic simulation, multinomial logit, etc.,-- is being deployed.

In the implementation of this model a number of conceptual, technical, and data issues need to be addressed. Two classes of conceptual issues arise: first, the specification issues inside a module. An example is the formulation of adjustment processes in factor markets and the household sector, such as in the acquisition of industrial energy-efficient capital equipment and household appliances or autos, or labor supply adjustments. In some cases dynamic full adjustment has been specified; elsewhere, work is necessary to move away from static formulations. Second, the articulation of the intermodule links is important. Conceptual consistency may be an issue in the links in some cases, e.g., labor demand is determined by substitution processes in FACTIN and REGLEC, but via the input-output process in CICIOP. It may well be that at some aggregate level of sectors and regions, the input-output representation may be applicable. So, a definition of scale sector regimes may be necessary for establishing consistency.

Three technical areas--functional form specification, econometric estimation, and validation--where multiregional models have been generally deficient need particular attention. In some cases, the use of flexible functional forms in production functions, for instance, has the advantage of generality and the ability to test hypotheses that are often maintained in advance (for abatement or energy)-- e.g., separability, concavity, homogeneity. There is also greater need for careful specification of the error distributions in econometric estimation instead of indiscriminate use of OLS. Further, it must be noted that there is a considerable level of simultaneity in this system. Finally, validation procedures (largely neglected in multiregional modeling) need to be explicitly built in during model development.

The increasing availability of a range of new databases--public-use samples and household survey data on income, education, migration, etc., databases on multimodal networks and flows, new energy data, etc.--is a key factor in the design of this model.

The broad range of policies that can be assessed by MIMUS derives from the incorporation of (a) many policy handles (investment, prices, transportation and other infrastructure, etc.--FACTIN, TRANS, REGLEC), (b) the houshold microsimulator, and energy and environmental policy areas (DEMO, CICIOP, FACTIN), and (c) the proposed articulation of the two-way relationships between national and regional models.

This allows the assessment of not only regional effects of national policies but also the national effects of regional supply (e.g., labor supply, resource shortages) and demand policies. Among the potential policy uses of the integrated multiregional model are:

> the assessment of a whole range of national and regional economic policies--industrial growth policies, alternative international trade scenarios, different "mixes" of macrostabilization policies, changing structure of public programs as embodied in the federal budget, major regional infrastructure development, etc.;
> the assessment of alternative environmental standards and energy development scenarios in terms of economic, environmental, and locational effects; and general issues such as patterns of substitution in society: e.g., locational changes for industries responding to relative factor prices, changes in consumption patterns of households as household formation and female labor force participation rates change.

In all the above cases, it should be noted that MIMUS can provide descriptions of multidimensional policy impacts in their regional, demographic, and income distributional detail.

References

Berndt, E.R., M.A. Fuss, and L. Waverman (1977), Dynamic Models of Industrial Demand for Energy, *Electric Power Research Institute, Palo Alto, CA Report* EPRI EA-580.

Berndt, E.R., M.A. Fuss, and L. Waverman (1979), Dynamic Adjustment Models of Industrial Demand: Empirical Analysis for US Manufacturing 1947-1974, *Electric Power Research Institute, Palo Alto, CA Report* EPRI EY-1613.

Bolton, R. (1980), Multiregional Modeling in Policy Analysis, in F.G. Adams and N.J. Glickman (eds.), *Modeling the Multiregional Economic System* (Heath, Lexington, MA), pp. 255-284.

Boyce, D., and G. Hewings (1980), Interregional Commodity Flows, Input-Output and Transportation Modeling: An Entropy Formulation, *Paper prepared for the Conference on Multiregional Modeling, First World Science Congress, Cambridge, MA, 1980.*

Eisner, R., and R.M. Strotz (1963), Determinants of Business Investment, in *Impacts of Monetary Policy* (Prentice-Hall, Englewood Cliffs, NJ).

Fromm, D., D.C. Loxley, and M. McCarthy (1980), *The Wharton EFA Multiregional Econometric Model: A Bottom-up Approach* (University of Pennsylvania, Philadelphia, PA).

Golladay, F., and R. Haveman (1977), *The Economic Impacts of Tax Transfer Policy* (Academic Press, New York, NY).

Harrison, B. (1981), An Analysis of New England Experience, *Paper presented at the 28th North American Meeting of the Regional Science Association, Montreal, Canada, November 13-15.*

Hudson, E.A., and D.W. Jorgenson (1974), US Energy Policy and Economic Growth, 1975-2000, in *Bell Journal of Economics and Management Science*, 461-514.

Isard, W., E. Schooler, and T. Vietonisz (1959), *Industrial Complex Analysis and Regional Development: A Study of Refinery-Petrochemical Synthetic Fiber Complexes in Puerto Rico* (MIT Press).

Isard, W., D. Boyce, T.R. Lakshmanan, L.R. Klein, and S.B. Caldwell (1981), Integration of Multiregional Models for Policy Analysis, *Research Proposal submitted to US National Science Foundation* (November, unpublished).

Lakshmanan, T.R. (1979), A Multiregional Policy Model of the Economy, Environmental and Energy Demand, *Boston University, Boston, MA Working Paper* NSF 79-1.

Lakshmanan, T.R. (1981), Regional Growth and Energy Determinants, in *Energy Journal*, 2(2), 1-24.

Lakshmanan, T.R., W. Anderson, and M. Jourabchi (1981), Regional Dimensions of Factor and Fuel Substitution in US Manufacturing, *Paper presented at the International Conference on Structural Economic Analysis and Planning in Time and Space, Umeå, Sweden, June 21-26.*

Lucas, R.E. (1967), Optimal Investment, Policy and Flexible Accelerator, in *International Economic Review*, 8, 78-85.

Orcutt, G. *et al*. (1980), *Policy Exploration Through Microanalytic Simulation* (Urban Institute, Washington, DC).

SWRI (1981) (Social Welfare Research Institute, Boston College, Massachusetts Institute of Technology, and Sistemas), MRPIS: A Research Strategy (March, unpublished).

Treadway, A.B. (1971), The Rational Multivariate Flexible Accelerator, in *Econometrica*, 39(5), pp. 845-855.

Treadway, A.B. (1974), The Globally Optimal Flexible Accelerator, in *Journal of Economic Theory*, 7, 17-29.

Treyz, G.I. (1980), Design of a Multiregional Policy Analysis Model, in *Journal of Regional Science*, 20(2), 191-206.

Williams, H.C.W.L. (1977), On the Formation of Demand Models and Economic Evaluation Criteria, in *Environment and Planning A*, 9, pp. 285-344.

Wilson, A. (1980), *Entropy in Urban and Regional Modeling* (Pion, London).

CHAPTER 14

RECENT DEVELOPMENT OF MULTIREGIONAL ECONOMIC MODELS IN JAPAN

Noboru Sakashita

1 Introduction

As a consequence of the abundance of regional economic data, there have been many attempts to build multiregional economic (ME) models in Japan. Exaggerating slightly, we can say that each ministry of the Japanese government with at least a partial relation to nationwide economic activities wishes to possess its own ME model in order to support the implementation of the economic policies under its control.

In this chapter I will discuss two ME models being developed in Japan relating to different national economic or transport plans. The first is the nationwide regional econometric model for the forthcoming (fourth) comprehensive regional development plan (Yonzensoh) which has been under development by the National Land Agency (Kokudocho) of the government since 1980. This model is called the NLA model. The second model discussed here is *the long-range forecasting model of traffic demand* which has been under development since 1980 by the Research Center for Transport Economics, which is closely related to the Ministry of Transportation (Unyusho). We call this model the RCTE model.

I have cooperated with the agencies that developed these two ME models so I am in a good position to review these models. Needless to say, I will do my best to give an objective review of the models as far as possible.

2 The NLA Model

The NLA model is being developed to supply predictive information for the fourth comprehensive regional development plan which will be formulated by the Japanese government in the near future to follow the third plan which was formulated in 1977. As a matter of fact, the third plan was formulated without the support of any econometric models, and in that sense it could be criticized for lacking logical consistency concerning forecast values of different variables. After some discussion of the desirable industrial and regional classifications, the model builders decided to use a 15-industry and a nine-region classification. The model comprises the following main blocks.

2.1 Regional income accounts

The basic framework of the NLA model consists of three groups of major income balance equations. In the model, gross value added and net imputed interest are made up of regional income, fixed capital depreciation, and the net of indirect taxes and subsidies. Some of the entities involved in these balances are exogenous to the system, i.e., imputed interest, and import taxes. The gross regional product is distributed among private and public consumption and investment, and housing investment is separated out as an endogenous variable. No detailed treatment is given to imports and exports.

The third group of balances is made up of personal income balances where a special emphasis is placed on isolating different types of income transfers to households. These transfers include payments to households by government, corporations, and insurance companies. The connection with other regions is given by a variable for net income transfer from outside the region. Some of the transfer variables are also central in the set of policy variables, such as tax rates and social security payments.

2.2 Adjustment of demand and supply

The demand for and supply of a specific industrial product are mutually adjusted by the "degree of operation" variables of that industry in the NLA model. These variables affect employment, private inventory, exports, and the fixed investments of the related industries in the same time period or with some time lag, and, in doing so, work as adjustment factors. This adjustment process is considered, however, not by region and industry, but by industry at the national level.

2.3 Production behavior of firms

For each industry, a production function of the following form is considered (regional and industrial suffixes are omitted):

$$V_t = A_{0t}(\rho_{kt}K_t)^{\alpha}(\rho_{lt}h_t^*L_t)^{1-\alpha} \qquad (2.3.1)$$

where

V_t = gross value added in time period t (t has the same meaning for all variables)

K_t = capital stock

L_t = labor force (employment)

ρ_{kt} = degree of operation of capital stock

ρ_{lt} = degree of operation of labor force (employment)

h_t^* = average working time of labor force.

With the simplifying assumption $\rho_{kt} = \rho_{lt} = \rho_t$ and introducing a factor for technical progress, the final form of the production function will be one of the following equations:

$$(V_t/\rho_t) = A_0 K_t^{\alpha}(h_t^*L_t)^{1-\alpha}e^{\lambda t} \qquad (2.3.2a)$$

$$(V_t/\rho_t) = A_0 v_t^{\beta}K_t^{\alpha}(h_t^*L_t)^{1-\alpha}e^{\lambda t} \qquad (2.3.2b)$$

where v_t = coefficient of value added (gross value added - total output ratio). Data for the degree of operation and that for the working time are obtained industry by industry from the different data sources.

2.4 Investment behavior of firms

Adopting a Jorgenson-type investment theory, the following form for industrial investment is specified:

$$I_t = b_0 + b_1 V_t + b_2 K_{t-1} + b_3 r + b_4\left(\frac{\varepsilon P_{1t}}{P_{vt}}\right) \qquad (2.4.1)$$

where

$$I_t = \text{private investment (regional and industrial suffixes are omitted)}$$
$$V_t = \text{gross value added}$$
$$K_{t-1} = \text{capital stock at the end of previous time period}$$
$$r = \text{rate of discount}$$
$$\varepsilon = \text{land coefficient with regard to investment}$$
$$P_{lt} = \text{price of land}$$
$$P_{vt} = \text{implicit deflator of value added.}$$

In addition, some attempts are made to include wage differentials, agglomeration economies, and urbanization economies in the investment functions as independent variables. The process of capital accumulation is described by the following formula:

$$K_t = I_t + (1 - \sigma)K_{t-1} \tag{2.4.2}$$

where σ = rate of depreciation.

2.5   Demand for labor by firms

As a consistent formulation with the investment function of firms, demand for labor by firms is specified by one of the following equations (regional and industrial suffixes are omitted):

$$\log (\rho_t h_t^* L_t) = a_0 + a_1 \log V_t + a_2 \log (W_t/P_{vt}) + a_3 \log (\rho_{t-1} h_{t-1}^* L_{t-1}) \tag{2.5.1}$$

$$\log (\rho_t h_t^* L_t) = a_0 + a_1 \log K_t + a_2 \log \rho_t + a_3 \log V_t + a_4 \log (W_t/P_{vt})$$
$$+ a_5 t + a_6 \log (\rho_{t-1} h_{t-1}^* L_{t-1}) \tag{2.5.2}$$

where W_t = wage rate.

2.6   Private consumption function

A traditional consumption function is formulated in each region as follows (regional suffixes are omitted):

$$CP_t = a_0 + a_1 (YD/P_c)_t + a_2 CP_{t-1} \tag{2.6.1}$$

where P_c = deflator of consumer goods. The total private final consumption CP_t is divided into the itemized consumptions:

$$\log CP_t^j = b_0 + b_1^j \log CP_t + b_2^j \log (P_c^j/P_c)_t \tag{2.6.2}$$

where

$$CP_t^j = \text{consumption of } j\text{th category, } j = 1,\ldots,5$$

$$P_c^j = \text{deflator of the } j\text{th consumer goods}$$

$$CP_t = \sum_{j=1}^{5} CP_t^j \quad . \tag{2.6.3}$$

2.7   Private housing investment

Private disposable income, deflator of housing investment, land price index, population, number of households, housing stock, age of houses, and the rate of interest are considered as explanatory variables of the private housing investment function.

2.8   Interblock trade functions

Interblock (interregional) trade of commodities is treated by gravity-type equations of the following form:

$$E_{rs} = b_{rs}^0 \frac{X_r^{b_{rs}^1} Y_s^{b_{rs}^2}}{d_{rs}^{b_{rs}^3}} \tag{2.8.1}$$

where

E_{rs} = export of commodities from the rth block to the sth block

X_r = production in the rth block

Y_s = income of the sth block

d_{rs} = economic distance (transport cost) between the rth block and the sth block.

The total export from the rth block and the total import of the sth block are defined by the following equations:

$$E_r = \sum_s E_{rs} \tag{2.8.2}$$

$$M_s = \sum_r E_{rs} \quad . \tag{2.8.3}$$

The trade coefficient between two blocks is defined as follows and is a function of supply capacities and economic distances:

$$t_{rs} = E_{rs}/M_s \quad . \tag{2.8.4}$$

2.9   Interblock population movement

The population movement between a pair of particular blocks is expressed as a function of job opportunities, school opportunities, population sizes, income, accessibility, and amenities.

2.10   Wage determination

A Phillip curve approach is adopted to explain the behavior of wage rates, i.e.:

$$\dot{W} = f(ELDS, \dot{P}_c, \dot{Y}) \qquad\qquad (2.10.1)$$

where

$\dot{W}$ = rate of change of wage rate

$ELDS$ = tightness of labor market

$\dot{P}_c$ = rate of change of consumer goods deflator

$\dot{Y}$ = rate of change of paying ability of the firm.

2.11   Input-output relations

The fundamental framework of input-output analysis in the NLA model is indicated by Tables 1 and 2 in which U is the commodity input matrix (15×15) of the industries, V is the commodity output matrix (15×15) of the industries, and all other variables are column and row vectors (1×15 or 15×1). The row vectors are given using the transpose symbol "'". The symbols are:

(definitional relations)

$$O = Ui + e \qquad\qquad (2.11.1)$$

$$e = f_d + x - m \qquad\qquad (2.11.2)$$

$i = (1,1,\ldots,1)'$ = addition vector

$$q = V'i \qquad\qquad (2.11.3)$$

$$g = Vi \qquad\qquad (2.11.4)$$

$$S = (SB)i \qquad\qquad (2.11.5)$$

$$S* = SB'i \qquad\qquad (2.11.6)$$

$$O - S = q - S* \qquad\qquad (2.11.7)$$

$$g = U'i + y \quad . \qquad\qquad (2.11.8)$$

Table 1. Input-output relations

			Production		Final demand			Output
			Commodities 1 ••• 15	Industries 1 ••• 15	Domestic demand	Export	Import	
Production	Commodities	1 ⠄⠄⠄ 15		U	f_d	x	m	0
	Industries	1 ⠄⠄⠄ 15	V					g
	Value added			y'				
	Output		q'	g'				

Table 2. Refuse and byproducts

		Industries 1 ••• 15	Total	
Commodities	1 ⠄⠄⠄ 15	SB	S	SB = 15 × 15 matrix
				S = 15 × 1 vector
				$S^{*'}$ = 1 × 15 vector
Total		$S^{*'}$		

Equation (2.11.7) implies that there is a difference between the treatment of refuse and byproducts for the commodity disposal table and the V table. For the V table they are added to the diagonal elements of the matrix at the generating sectors, but for the commodity disposal table they are classified into commodity rows.

Technical coefficients
(1) Input coefficients of industries $B = U\hat{g}^{-1}$

$$\hat{g} = \text{diagonal matrix formed by vector } g = \begin{bmatrix} g_1 & \cdots & 0 \\ & \ddots & \\ & & \\ 0 & \cdots & g_{15} \end{bmatrix} \qquad (2.11.9)$$

(the same for other vectors)

(2) Output coefficients of industries

$$C = V'\hat{g}^{-1} \tag{2.11.10}$$

Relation between commodity input coefficients and industry input coefficients.
From equations (2.11.1) and (2.11.7), we have

$$q = Ui + e + S* - S$$

$$= (B\hat{g})i + e + S* - S \qquad \text{(see equation (2.11.9))}$$

$$= Bg + e + S* - S \quad . \tag{2.11.11}$$

On the other hand, from equations (2.11.3) and (2.11.10) we have

$$q = V'i = (C\hat{g})i = Cg \quad . \tag{2.11.12}$$

Therefore we have

$$q = Aq + e + S* - S \tag{2.11.13}$$

$$A = BC^{-1} \tag{2.11.14}$$

from equations (2.11.11) and (2.11.12). Equation (2.11.13) is the basic relationship to obtain the q vector of the V table.

Treatment of imports. Let m_i be the ratio of import to domestic demand (domestic
intermediate demand plus domestic final demand) for the ith commodity, and form a
diagonal matrix $\hat{M}$ composed of $m_i s$ ($i = 1, \ldots, 15$). Then we have

$$m = \hat{M}(A_q + f_d) \quad . \tag{2.11.15}$$

From equations (2.11.2), (2.11.13), and (2.11.15), the solution of q is given by
the following formula:

$$q = [I - (I - \hat{M})A]^{-1}[(I - \hat{M})f_d + x + S* - S] \quad . \tag{2.11.16}$$

Treatment of refuse and byproducts. Assume the following technical coefficients
for the refuse and byproducts:

$$G = SB\hat{S}^{*-1} \qquad \text{(15 × 15 matrix)} \tag{2.11.17}$$

$$d = (D_{iag}V)^{-1}S* \qquad \text{(15 × 1 vector)} \tag{2.11.18}$$

$D_{iag}V$ = diagonal matrix formed by the diagonal elements of V. By equations (2.11.5) and (2.11.17), we have

$$S = SB\iota = G\hat{S}*\iota = GS* \tag{2.11.19}$$

From equations (2.11.18) and (2.11.19), we can deduce

$$S* - S = (I - G)S* = (I - G)(D_{iag}V)d = (I - G)\hat{d}(V_{11}, V_{22}, \ldots, V_{15,15})' \; . \tag{2.11.20}$$

If we define $D = V\hat{q}^{-1}$, then we have

$$S* - S = Hq \tag{2.11.21}$$

in which $H = (I - G)\hat{d}(D_{iag}D)$. Using equation (2.11.21), we obtain the final solution for q as follows:

$$q = [I - (I - \hat{M})A - H]^{-1}[(I - \hat{M})f_d + x] \; . \tag{2.11.22}$$

2.12 Determination of final demand

In Table 3, a set of final demand converters is tabulated. Scalar variables of national totals are defined by block variables that appeared in Section 2.1.

$$CH^k = \sum_{i=1}^{9} CH_i^k \qquad k = 1, \ldots, 5 \tag{2.12.1}$$

households final consumption

$$CH = \sum_{i=1}^{9} CH_i = \sum_{i=1}^{9} \sum_{j=1}^{5} CH_i^j \tag{2.12.2}$$

$$\overline{CNP} = \sum_{i=1}^{9} \overline{CNP_i} \qquad \text{private nonprofit} \qquad (2.12.3) \atop \text{organizations final consumption}$$

$$\overline{CG} = \sum_{i=1}^{9} \overline{CG_i} \qquad \text{government final consumption} \quad (2.12.4)$$

$$\overline{IG} = \sum_{i=1}^{9} \overline{IG_i} \qquad \text{government fixed investment} \quad (2.12.5)$$

$$\overline{IP} = \sum_{i=1}^{9} \overline{IP_i} = \sum_{i=1}^{9} \sum_{j=1}^{14} IP_i^j \qquad \text{private fixed investment} \quad (2.12.6)$$

Table 3. Final demand converters

	Converters (vectors)	National total
Exports	FE	E
Inventory	FJ	J
Private housing investment	FI_n	IH
Private fixed investment	FI_p	IP
Public capital formation	FI_g	$\overline{IG}$
Final consumption by government	FC_g	$\overline{CG}$
Final consumption by private nonprofit organization	FC_n	$\overline{CNP}$
Final consumption by households		
Total	FC_h^n	CH
Miscellaneous	FC_h^5	CH^5
Housing	FC_h^4	CH^4
Heat and light	FC_h^3	CH^3
Clothing	FC_h^2	CH^2
Food and beverages	FC_h^1	CH^1

$$IH = \sum_{i=1}^{9} IH_i \qquad \text{private housing investment} \qquad (2.12.7)$$

Scalar variables of inventory J and export E are determined by the functions at national level. Summing these relations, the domestic final demand vector and export vector are calculated as follows:

$$f_d = \sum_{k=1}^{5} CH^k.FC_h^k + CN.FC_n + \overline{CG}.FC_g + \overline{IG}.FI_g + IP.FI_p + IH.FI_h + J.FJ \quad . \qquad (2.12.8)$$

$$x = E.FE \quad . \qquad (2.12.9)$$

2.13 Determination of industrial value added

The vector of value added coefficients v is calculated from the following equation:

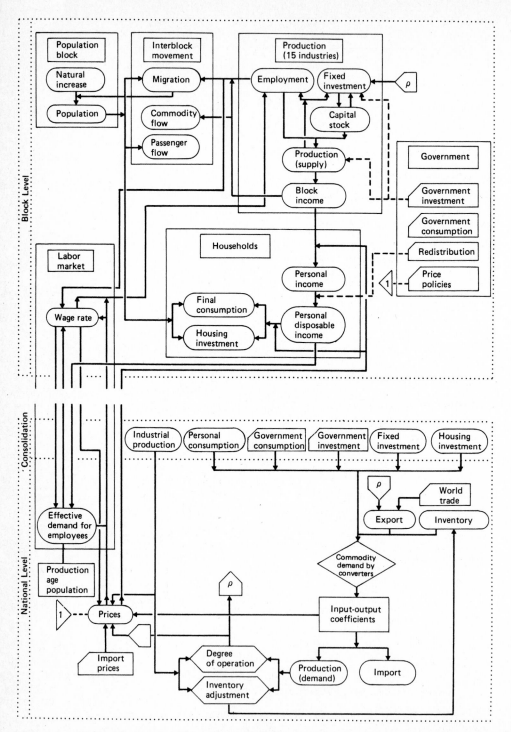

Figure 1. Regional econometric model: outline

$$v = i = B'i \quad .$$

$$\text{(2.13.1)}$$

By equations (2.11.8) and (2.11.9), we have

$$g = \hat{g}B'i + y$$

$$\text{(2.13.2)}$$

from which we can deduce

$$y = \hat{g}(i - B'i) = \hat{g}v = \hat{v}g$$

$$\text{(2.13.3)}$$

and g is derived from q of equation (2.11.22) with equation (2.11.12) as

$$g = C^{-1}q \quad .$$

$$\text{(2.13.4)}$$

The jth components of vector y are directly related to the national total of gross product of the jth industry in all blocks

$$\sum_{i=1}^{9} v_i^j \quad .$$

2.14 Consolidation to the global system

The building blocks described above are consolidated into the NLA model, the outline of which is illustrated in Figure 1. In order to complete the model, a formulation of equations for price determination is needed. The input-output rela-tions are again utilized to deduce price relationships in the model but we omit the explanation of this part. As shown in Figure 1, macroeconomic relationships are formulated for each block (region) together with interblock commodity flows and population movement. Then the final demand sections of all blocks are consoli-dated into the final demand section of the national input-output analysis. In that sense, the NLA model can be taken as a "bottom-up" multiregional model. The vari-ables in the government section of Figure 1 are treated as policy instruments of the model.

So far the final test simulation has been performed for 1971-75, and the per-formance of the model has proved good. The final purpose of the simulation is to forecast the working of the Japanese multiregional economy up to 1995, and the forecast is now in preparation.

3 RCTE Model

The purpose of the RCTE model is to forecast the traffic demand in the form of an origin and destination table for 22 subregions for seven categories of commodi-ties and for passengers, including the modal split between railway, automobiles, shipping, and aviation. The policy variables in the model are the construction plan of trunk line transport facilities, and regional and intertemporal allocation of public investment that includes these transport projects. National level of economic activities is given as a "frame", and the model only concerns regional (eight regions) and subregional (22 subregions) disaggregation of the national totals. A simplified flowchart of the RCTE model is given in Figure 2.

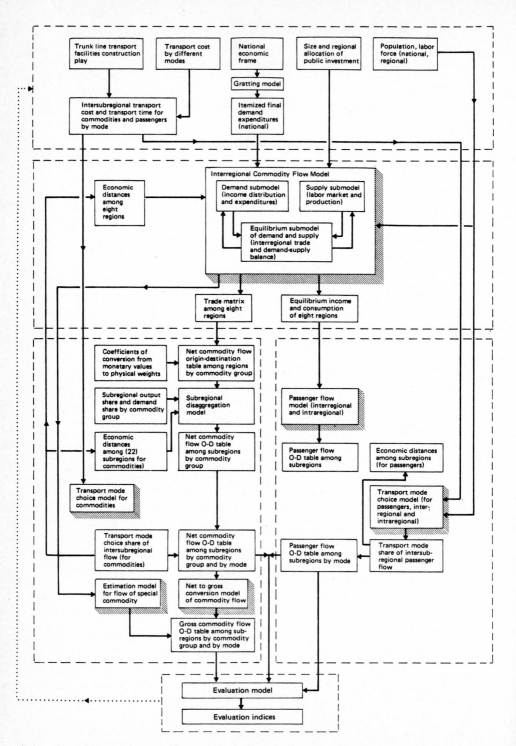

Figure 2. RCTE model: outline

The most important parts of the model are the submodel of interregional and intersubregional trade and those of mode choice for commodities and passengers. Explanations will be given only for these submodels. Let T^{rs} denote the trade volume between regions r and s. T^{rs} is given as a function of the following variables:

$$T^{rs} = f(DK^s, S^r, S^1, \ldots, S^8, d^{rs}, d^{1s}, \ldots, d^{8s}) \tag{3.1}$$

DK^s = total demand for domestic supply of the sth region

$S^i = XC^i - E^i$ = production capacity for domestic demand of the ith region

XC^i = production capacity of the ith region

E^i = exports of the ith region $(i-1,\ldots,r,\ldots,8)$

d^{ij} = interregional economic distance between the ith and jth regions $(i,j = 1,\ldots,r,\ldots,s,\ldots,8)$.

Intraregional trade is explained as follows:

$$T^{rr} = f(KG^r, DK^r, S^r, S^1, \ldots, S^8, d^{rr}, d^{1r}, \ldots, d^{8r}) \tag{3.2}$$

where KG^r = social capital stock of the rth region, and KG^r is introduced to modify the intraregional distance d^{rr} which is hard to define. The balance of supply and demand is given by the following equations:

$$DM^r + \sum_{k \neq r} T^{rk} + E^r = X^r + \sum_{k \neq r} T^{kr} + M^r \tag{3.3}$$

$$DM^r = \sum_k T^{kr} + M^r \tag{3.4}$$

$$DK^r = DM^r - M^r \tag{3.5}$$

where

DM^r = total demand of the rth region

X^r = output of the rth region

M^r = imports of the rth region.

From equations (3.3) and (3.4), we have

$$X^r = \sum_k T^{rk} + E^r \quad . \tag{3.6}$$

The degree of operation R^r is defined by the following formula:

$$R^r = X^r/XC^r \quad .$$

(3.7)

Commodity prices at the origin (PS^r) and at the destination (PD^r) are determined as follows:

$$PS^r = f(R^r)$$

(3.8)

$$PD^r = \sum_s t^{sr} \cdot PS^s$$

(3.9)

$$t^{sr} = T^{sr}/DK^r \quad .$$

(3.10)

Intersubregional trade volumes are calculated by a modification of the Fratar method using interregional trade as control totals.

Explanatory variables of the modal split ratios are transport cost C_i^k and transport time T_i^k by the kth facility for the ith commodity which are consolidated into a general cost $GC_i^k = C_i^k + WT_i^k$ with time-money conversion rate W. The ratio of two modal split ratios (pk'/pk) is considered as a function of the differenc $GC^k - GC^{k'}$ as follows:

$$\log (pk'/pk) = \alpha + \beta(GC^{k'} - GC^k) \quad .$$

(3.11)

A similar treatment is given to the interregional and intraregional passenger flows with a gravity-type total flow submodel.

4 Concluding Remarks

The ME models introduced in this chapter are only two examples of such models being developed in Japan. As stated in the introduction, many ministries and agencies of central government wish to construct their own multiregional models in order to support their demands for the allocation of national budget. Superficially this situation can be seen as a waste of research resources, but such duplication is not so bad from the viewpoint of competitive elaboration of the multiregional model.

The models are becoming larger and more complicated as the demand for detailed predictive information is strengthened. At the same time, the need for a microeconomic theoretical foundation is becoming even more emphasized in all behavioral equations, particularly for investment functions and interregional trade functions. In the near future we can expect the implementation of many forecasting simulations using these ME models in Japan and this will certainly support the formulation of a comprehensive national regional development plan.

PART C

PERSPECTIVES OF MULTIREGIONAL ECONOMIC MODELING

Part C of this volume comprises two chapters indicating the perspectives of multiregional economic modeling. From the several alternative ways of structuring the material we have chosen to separate the discussion of the theoretical prospects of this class of models from the emerging new directions of application.

Thus in Chapter 15 Åke Andersson discusses the potentials for changes in the current mainstream of model structures. He argues that several ME models do not really fulfill the requirement of being multiregional because of their weak linkage structure. In the choice between disaggregation and linearity, and aggregation and nonlinearity, Andersson recommends theoretical developments in the former direction.

Chapter 16 continues a summary of the general discussion held at the IIASA conference that was organized as a stage in the preparation of this volume. Some short written contributions by conference participants to that discussion have been merged with less formal discussion points. The result is a set of claims for a narrowing of the gap between the *ex ante* scope of the models and their *ex post* performance in application. These gaps need to be narrowed as regards relevance to emerging problem areas, model comprehensiveness, model estimation and validation, and model transferability.

The Appendix, which follows directly after Part C, is a basic source of reference both for reading the book itself and for finding further documentation of the models presented. The abbreviations of model names listed in the beginning of the Appendix are generally short forms given by the model builders. In some cases we have invented such short forms ourselves for the purpose of consistency. The model descriptions contained in the Appendix have been authorized by the respective model builders.

CHAPTER 15

POTENTIALS OF MULTIREGIONAL AND INTERREGIONAL ECONOMIC MODELING

Åke E. Andersson

1 Introduction

This chapter discusses some problems of current practice in multiregional and interregional economic model building. The potentials for changes in basic model structure are discussed with a subdivision into aspects concerning:

(a) activities in nodes (regions);
(b) links for communication, transportation, and factor flows between nodes;
(c) principles of determining solutions to a model of a set of nodes interdependently related to each other; and
(d) possibilities of simplification.

2 Common Problems of Multiregional and Interregional Economic Modeling

The basic common problem of multiregional and interregional economic modeling is that of developing a realistic and yet sufficiently simple formal model of the interactions between point economies (nodes or regions) interrelated with each other by discrete spatial links (for transportation or communication); see Figure 1.

The two geographical dimensions are normally collapsed into one spatial dimension, represented by a distance or transportation cost matrix. Similarly, the multitude of economic activities is normally aggregated to a small number of sectors. These sectors are sometimes simplified even further into a Keynesian framework in which sectoral interdependences in flow terms cannot be analyzed, because the basic flow variable is aggregate *value added* and its components are consumption, investment, government, and net export purchases. The interactions are in this case aggregated into a multi- or interregional import/export dependency analysis. Leontief input-output and von Neumann generalized input-output frameworks are, of course, more general than the Keynesian framework. The price of generality is a vastly increased model size in terms of number of variables and relations.

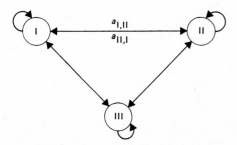

Figure 1. Nodal representation of an economy

My discussion of the modeling problem in this paper concerns *node variables, linking, simplifications of interdependences*, and *model solution principles*. My examples are primarily designed to have a pedagogical and suggestive treatment rather than a deep coverage.

3 Modeling the Nodes

Typical of any regional system is the distinction between activities that take place in a node and those that must be handled on the links for transportation and communication. Typical node variables are: production, consumption, investment, public activity, and resource use.

3.1 Production

Modeling production is a means to find a simplified relation between natural and produced inputs into a production (or transformation) process and the outputs of this process. Two essential *static* principles have emerged. One uses the assumption of the existence of a discrete set of available production techniques in which the output(s) is regulated by fixed proportions of inputs at a designed or freely variable scale of operations. The *problem of substitution* is solved as a problem of an optimal choice of techniques to be used. This principle naturally leads to an interaction scheme of the Dantzig-Wolfe type. Prices are assumed to be system-wide variables. These prices are used as exogenous parameters and determine the choice of techniques in the node through a linear (or sometimes nonlinear) programming model of the production of a subset of commodities of a single node.

An alternative principle of substitution is the neoclassical approach in which the production process is regarded as a black box that can be represented as a production function $f(x) = y$ in which x is a vector of inputs, and y a vector of outputs. The function $f(x)$ is assumed to be differentiable (at least twice) everywhere. An important characteristic of this function is the elasticity of substitution between two of the inputs, say x_i and x_j. The elasticity of substitution can be defined as $\partial \ln (x_i/x_j)/\partial \ln R_{ij}$ where R_{ij} is the marginal rate of substitution between the two inputs. Assumptions about this parameter are crucial in most neoclassical economic modeling. If the elasticity of substitution between two important inputs is assumed to be some constant, the production function for a product y is of the CES or Minkowski form:

$$y = [ax_i^{-\rho} + (1 - a)x_j^{-\rho}]^{-1/\rho} \quad .$$

The elasticity of substitution is $1/(1 + \rho)$. The Cobb-Douglas production function means a further simplification, in which the elasticity of substitution is assumed to be identically equal to 1 everywhere. The assumption that some well behaved production function can model the whole production process of a sector has recently been the object of heavy criticism (Hildenbrand 1981, Puu and Wibe 1980).

Any workable competitive system presupposes a large number of separate production activities producing commodities that are close substitutes for the users. This means that a number of producing units create the output of a sector of a node (region). It is highly unlikely that all such production units were constructed in the same time period. Normally the production units of any sector have come into being at different times, having different fixed production techniques (possibly optimal at the time of construction). Production theory must therefore be *dynamic*, with most of the adaptivity of the producing unit *ex ante* or at the "blueprint stage" (Johansen 1972). *Ex post* adaptivity is only possible at the macro-level where new units come into being through investment and old units are closed down when the marginal cost of production permanently exceeds the marginal revenue. This *vintage approach* to production theory has recently been used in a multiregional dynamic integer linear programming model constructed by Johansson *et al.* (1982) for the Swedish Industrial Board. This model probably means a take off for multiregional and interregional dynamic modeling with proper use of production data for the regions.

3.2 Investment

Two basic principles dominate investment modeling: (a) the principle of marginal efficiency of investment; and (b) the acceleration principle. The first of these makes the crucial assumption that discounted expected revenues of an investment must be larger than discounted expected cost in order to generate an inducement to invest.

A firm is thus assumed to invest in a project with cost I including a fixed staff and other current inputs to be supplied in fixed yearly quantities, if:

$$\int_0^\infty [(p\Delta x(I))e^{gt}]e^{-rt} \, dt \geq I_0$$

p = price of output at time of investment relative to price of labor staff
$\Delta x(I)$ = sales from unit of production represented by investment I
g = expected exponential growth of revenue from the same unit of production
(due to relative price increases of output or disembodied technical growth)
r = rate of discount.

The marginal investment project must therefore fulfil the condition that the investment cost (I) balances the resulting net revenues discounted to infinity. With $r > g$ this implies that the marginal investment should fulfil

$$I = \frac{p}{r-g} \, \Delta x(I) \quad .$$

Assuming a firm i maximizes an infinite stream of profits accruing from a *freely variable investment* cost of the current point of time, the following optimization problem can be formulated:

$$\max_{\{I_i\}} \Pi_i = \left(\frac{p_i}{r-g_i^\varepsilon}\right) \Delta x_i(I_i) - I_i \quad .$$

The condition of a maximum is

$$\frac{d\Pi}{dI_i} = \left(\frac{p_i}{r-g_i^\varepsilon}\right) \frac{\partial(\Delta x_i)}{\partial I_i} - 1 = 0$$

where g_i^ε = *expected* rate of growth of revenue. An implication is

$$\frac{\partial(\Delta x_i)}{\partial I_i} = \frac{r-g_i^\varepsilon}{p_i} \quad .$$

Assuming a vintage Cobb-Douglas production growth function, we have

$$\Delta x_i = k_i I_i^{\alpha_i} \qquad \text{with } 0 < \alpha_i < 1$$

$$\Rightarrow I_i = \left[\alpha_i k_i p_i / (r - g_i^\varepsilon)\right]^{1/(1-\alpha_i)}$$

The consequence of this for investment demand in the presence of interfirm differentials in growth expectations is illustrated in Figure 2.

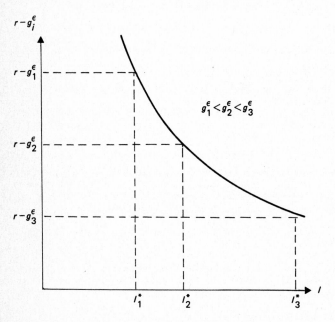

Figure 2. Illustration of investment demand under different growth expectations

The accelerator theory in a crude form states that

$$I = \beta \Delta x \quad .$$

Two interpretations can be given. A nonbehavioral assumption is that there exists a technologically necessary investment/production-increase ratio, $\beta = \partial I / \partial (\Delta x)$. Another interpretation is that $\beta = [p/(r - g^\varepsilon)]/b$, where b is a technological coefficient of the relation $\Delta x = bI$. In this case the conflict between the two investment principles is resolved in a manner similar to the one proposed by Smith (1959), in which the optimization model for the firm is as follows:

$$\min r \int_0^\infty (w_1 x_1 + w_2 \dot{x}_2) e^{-rt} \, dt = \text{cost}$$

subject to $y = A x_1^\alpha x_2^\beta$ = production function; x_1 = flow input; x_2 = stock (capital) input; and y = planned output. The investment in the capital stock function can be deduced to be

$$\frac{d\dot{x}_2}{dt} = I = \frac{w_2}{A(\alpha + \beta)} \left(\frac{w_1}{rw_2} \cdot \frac{\beta}{\alpha}\right)^{\alpha/(\alpha+\beta)} \left(\frac{y}{A}\right)^{[1/(\alpha+\beta)]-1} \dot{y}$$

or $I = k\dot{y}$ if the scale of operations, input prices, and interest rates are constant.

It is clear that we must consider investment theory as an integral part of a vintage approach to regional production modeling, as already outlined above. Each period must in this approach be modeled with time-specific technical information and time-specific expectations of the investment decision makers.

3.3 Consumption

Neoclassical consumption theory is symmetrical to neoclassical production theory. Consumer behavior is assumed to be collapsible into a complete preordering or even into a utility function $u(x - z)$, where x is a vector of consumer commodities and z is a vector of initial stocks of the same commodities; $u(x - z)$ is often assumed to be concave and differentiable (at least twice) everywhere. The consumer environment is assumed to be represented by a budget constraint $p^T x \leq p^I z$. The consumer is then assumed to maximize $u(x - z)$ subject to the budget constraint and the necessary nonnegativity constraints on the variables. It can be shown that this simple system generates consumer response functions $x_i - z_i = E_i(p)$, called "excess demand functions" in which the demand and supply responses of each consumer are uniquely related to the *price vector* observed.

Although commendable for simplicity, this consumer theory is disputable for the structural impotence in a regional and dynamic context. Ample empirical evidence in regional science shows that the scale and internal structure of a region have a considerable impact on human behavior. The scale and structure effects cannot be captured through the price system alone.

In a regional consumption study I have shown that the pattern of education of the employed, the age structure of the population and the density of population must be included together with the price structure in order to generate a reasonable consumption model for dynamic regional analysis. The empirical use of such a dynamic consumption model has not indicated any complications compared with the use of the neoclassical approach (see Andersson and Lundqvist 1976).

3.4 Public activity

The problem of public spending is often confused with the problem of allocation of public goods. The public sector is unfortunately in most cases responsible for production of private as well as public goods. Some examples are given in Figure 3. The definition of public goods follows Samuelson (1954). The problem is made even more complicated by the fact that certain commodities are partly public, partly private. An example is the transportation system, which produces some private service, i.e., passenger kilometers, and some public goods (disservices)--speed, safety, pollution, etc.

	Public sector production	Private sector production
Public goods	Defense	R & D
Private goods	Old-age care	Food

Figure 3. Classification of some public sector activities

Most public spending modeling in the multiregional and interregional context is highly simplified and makes no distinction between production of public and private goods. The standard approach is to use an input-output model in which public activities are represented as a purely consumptive sector. A natural extension of this approach is to represent private goods production by the public sector in the same way as standard private sector production of private goods.

The production of public goods should in principle enter *the response functions* of many actors of the system. This implies the introduction of *nonlinearities* in the production and consumption activities. A standard input-output coefficient of a producing sector (or the household sector) would in this case become a function of the public good volume produced in the node (or even elsewhere):

$$a_{ij}(x_1, \ldots, x_k) = \text{input of commodity } i \text{ in the production of commodity } j$$
$$\text{as a function of the production of public goods } 1, \ldots, k.$$

The value of a certain public good production would then be determined as the negative of the systemwide reduction of cost associated with expansion of public goods production:

$$-\frac{\partial c}{\partial x_k} = -\sum_i \sum_j p_i \frac{\partial a_{ij}}{\partial x_k} x_j \quad .$$

Such a representation of public goods in a regional model does not preclude the existence of an equilibrium. It only implies that we cannot in general assume that an equilibrium can be sustained by a standard competitive price system.

3.5 Natural resource use

In principle nothing has to be said about natural resources in the regional context apart from what has been said in Section 3.1 on production and by Hotelling (1931) and Puu (1977).

4 Interactions on Links

4.1 Trade

Nodes (regions) are related to each other by a number of transport and communication links. A flow of a certain commodity i from region r to region s, x_i^{rs}, can be modeled as a consequence of a simultaneous optimization on a system of nodes. Such an interregional model could take on the following appearance:

$$\text{Maximize total welfare} = \sum_{i,s} U_i^s \left(\sum_r x_i^{rs} \right)$$

subject to: *associated shadow prices:*

$$\sum_x x_i^{rs} = O_i^r(L_i^r) \qquad \textit{Technology} \qquad \lambda_i^r$$

$$\sum_i L_i^r \leq L^r \qquad \textit{"Trapped" resources} \qquad \omega^r$$

$$\sum_{r,s,i} C_i^{rs} x_i^{rs} \leq C \qquad \begin{array}{l}\textit{Transportation}\\ \textit{capacity}\end{array} \qquad T$$

$$x_i^{rs} \geq 0$$

Typical effective conditions of an optimum are:

Trade between nodes.   The marginal utility of trade in commodity i from region r to s is equal to commodity shadow price of i in region r, plus the marginal transport cost of commodity i from r to s evaluated at shadow price of transportation.

Factor use in nodes.   The marginal productivity of the input in production of i in region r is equal to the shadow price of the input/difference between marginal utility in region s and marginal transport cost from region r to region s.

Such a simultaneous treatment of production and resource use in nodes and trade between nodes is not typical of empirically oriented interregional economic modeling.   It is far more usual to subdivide the modeling into one trade and one production model.   The production model is then assumed to be solved for supply S_i^r or excess demand D_i^s and the trade problem is posed for instance in the following way:

$$\text{Minimize } C(x) = \sum_i \sum_r \sum_s C_i^{rs} x_i^{rs} \qquad \qquad \textit{Transport cost}$$

Associated shadow prices   *subject to*

$$\lambda_i^r \qquad\qquad\qquad \sum_s x_i^{rs} = S_i^r \qquad \textit{Supply}$$

$$\eta_i^s \qquad\qquad\qquad \sum_r x_i^{rs} = D_i^s \qquad \textit{Demand}$$

$$x_i^{rs} \geq 0$$

with $x = \{x_i^{rs}\}$.   A typical optimum condition is

$$\frac{\partial C}{\partial x_i^{rs}} = \lambda_i^r - \eta_i^s = C_i^{rs} \quad .$$

The demand shadow price of region s should at the optimum be equal to the supply shadow price of region r plus the marginal cost of transportation from region r to region s.

A feasible multiregional model could be built as a system of node models for supply and demand of each commodity in each node (region) and the balancing of supplies and demands could be achieved through trade as calculated in the trade model (see Figure 4).   A dynamic location model essentially represents a slow-dynamics process, while a transportation/trade model represents a fast-dynamics process. This corresponds to a differential equation problem of the following kind:

$$\begin{cases} \dot{x} = f(x,y) & \text{Location system} \\ 0 = g(x,y) & \text{Transportation system.} \end{cases}$$

There is a paradoxical aspect of transportation systems in this respect.   While transportation flows are almost always in an equilibrium, the transportation network is almost never in an equilibrium.   Shadow prices could serve as linking variables from the trade model to the production models, while quantities supplied and demanded are the linking variables in the opposite direction.

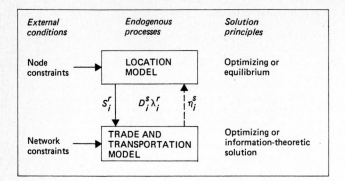

Figure 4. A feasible set-up for a multiregional model system

     Empirically more valid models of trade than the optimizing model are the
information-theory-based models of trade, due to their more efficient use of incomplete data and their ability to represent inertia in trading patterns. The use
of an information-theoretic trade model would not change the linking procedure in
any fundamental way. The iteration procedure could however be smoother, because
of the inherently smooth response surface of information gain models.

4.2 Information flows

     Information flows are extremely important for the functioning of economic sys-
tems*. The structure and efficiency of information flows between actors separated
socially and in geographic space determines the efficiency of market and planning
systems in the short term and the development potentials of all economic systems
in the long term, yet most interregional model builders disregard this important
aspect of real spatial economies. I will not in this context dwell upon different
ways of integrating information flows into regional market analysis; rather, I will
focus the attention on technological development as a spatial phenomenon. I have
discussed in some detail elsewhere the problem of creation and diffusion in space
of knowledge and the consequences for regional growth and distribution paths over
time. In the crudest possible form the model takes on the following appearance:

$$\dot{K}_r = s_r(1 - t_r)F_r\left(K_r, \sum_s e^{-\beta d_{rs}} G_s\right) \quad ; \quad \textit{capital accumulation}$$

$$\dot{G}_r = H_r\left(G_r, s_r t_r F_r\left(K_r, \sum_s e^{-\beta d_{rs}} G_s\right)\right) \quad ; \quad \textit{knowledge accumulation}$$

$$\{r, s = 1, \ldots, n\}$$

where

$$K_r = \text{capital stock of node } r$$
$$G_r = \text{stock of knowledge of node } r$$

-----

*Note that "information" is used here in a way different to that in the dis-
cussion of "information theory", "information gain models", etc.

s_r = propensity to invest in node r

t_r = share of investment going to R & D in node r

d_{rs} = "distance" from node r to node s

F_r and H_r are concave production functions for the standard commodity and R & D.

It has been shown (Andersson and Mantsinen 1981) that an endogenous technological development model of this kind is compatible with steady-state growth paths. The spatial diffusion of technology under conditions of scale economies, however, generates *temporal development lags* for peripheral regions of the kind observed in most developing economies. The same kind of technological development processes can be built into more general models of economic development, like the interregional input-output and von Neumann models. The linearity of those models must then be abandoned.

4.3 Pollution

Flows of pollution between regions are standard phenomena in the development process. Acid rain in Europe is an especially vivid example of this phenomenon. It is no accident that we sometimes speak of information pollution. Pollution flows are from a theoretical point of view very similar to information flows. The object of analysis is of a public nature and dispersion is strongly distance-dependent. It can furthermore be assumed that most of these pollution flows enter the production functions of firms and households as productivity reducing stock inputs accumulated by a spatial discounting process.

4.4 Capital and migration flows

Capital flows have two dimensions--one behavioral and the other technical. The technical part is not fundamentally different from input-output relations and can thus be handled within most dynamic inter- and multiregional programming models (see Lundqvist 1980). Behavioral interregional capital theory is, as a contrast, badly underdeveloped. I believe that an interregional capital flow model can be built along the same lines as migration models built on probabilistic choice theory (McFadden 1978). The condition of choice is the same--a decision maker in a discrete choice situation facing uncertainties in evaluating regional location alternatives. The only fundamental problem facing models of this kind is that of aggregation. Microbehavior predicted by a quantal choice model will not ordinarily be compatible with long-run equilibrium requirements at the interregional level. A possible way of solving this consistency problem with the use of information theory has been proposed by Andersson and Philipov (1982) following suggestions by Snickars and Weibull (1977).

5 How to Close an Interregional or Multiregional System

Four principles of closing an interdependent system have been proposed:

general equilibrium solutions;
social equilibrium solutions;
oligopolistic equilibrium solutions; and
simulation without equilibrium solutions.

The choice between solution criteria is of a paradigmatic nature and cannot be solved in a truly scientific way. Philosophical reasoning is necessary and no absolute truth can exist. The choice options, however, can be described.

A *general equilibrium* is a solution of an interdependent system with *many* response functions in which no decision maker has an incitement to change his decision variable strategy. This means that the general equilibrium concept is useful only if there are identifiable decision rules in the model. It must be stressed that a

general equilibrium has *no* necessary relation to the market economy. The concept
of a general equilibrium is, however, dependent upon an assumption of a multitude
of decision makers.

A *social equilibrium* is defined as a solution such that the system controlling
agency has no inducement to change the actions available. Solving programming and
Tinbergen-type models are standard examples of social equilibrium calculations.
General equilibrium is a necessary but not sufficient condition for a social equilibrium. The choice of a social equilibrium should always be a choice within a set
of general equilibria. Unfortunately, most models of social choice in the regional
context do not reflect this requirement.

Oligopolistic equilibria are general equilibria constrained to conditions of
a limited number (larger than 1) of decision makers. Because of the contingent
nature of decisions, oligopolistic equilibria tend to be *temporary* or *unstable*.
Point solutions are consequently of limited value if oligopolistic equilibria are
determined. Delimiting the possible set of outcomes is then the only reasonable
approach.

Simulation of possible trajectories of a system is a method proposed by many
regional systems analysts critical of any equilibrium paradigm. This attitude does
not preclude modeling, it only precludes calculating system steady-state solutions.
It can also be argued that it precludes most of econometric modeling, because econometric estimation procedures are in most cases built on an assumption of estimation
in equilibrium states or under assumptions of known deviations from an equilibrium
state. Top-down or bottom-up is the spatial counterpart of simulation over time.
It enables the researcher to handle nonlinearities and a large number of variables
at the expense of errors in calculating interdependency effects. In the same way
as simulation models (over time) complicate a proper identification of parameters
(Haavelmo 1947), top-down or bottom-up models complicate a proper identification
of spatial parameters—provided interdependences in reality have importance.

6   Conclusions

Multiregional and interregional models are important to the extent that they
contain the spatial dimension in an essential way. Many of the models used do not
fulfil this requirement because of weak spatial linkage procedures. These models
should also be consistent with the best models of sectoral activities in the nodes
or regions of the spatial networks. In most cases models are built on unduly simplified submodels for households, firms, and the public sector. The lack of dynamics in these submodels is especially embarrassing for our profession. A proper
consideration of vintage theory and theories of endogenous knowledge formation and
diffusion in time and space are especially warranted. If these theories are included, static models and linearity are ruled out. Simplicity is required at the
same time. This implies that the ambition to disaggregate into hundreds of sectors
and regions must be given up.

In the choice between nonlinearity and dynamism versus disaggregation my rec-
ommendation is strongly in favor of nonlinearity and dynamism.

References

Andersson, Å.E., and L. Lundqvist (1976), Regional Analysis of Consumption Patterns,
    Papers of the Regional Science Association, 36.
Andersson, Å.E., and J. Mantsinen (1981), Mobility of Resources, Accessibility of
    Knowledge, and Economic Growth, in *Behavioral Sciences*, 25:5.
Andersson, Å.E., and D. Philipov (1982), Economic Models of Migration, in M. Albegov
    et al. (eds.), *Regional Development Modeling--Theory and Practice* (North-
    Holland, Amsterdam).
Haavelmo, T. (1947), Family Expenditures and the Marginal Propensity to Consume, in
    Econometrica, 15.
Hildenbrand, W. (1981), Short Run Production Functions Based on Micro Data, in
    Econometrica, 49:5.

Hotelling, H. (1931), The Economics of Exhaustible Resources, in *Journal of Political Economy*, 39.

Johansen, L. (1972), *Production Functions* (North-Holland, Amsterdam).

Johansson, B., A. Karlqvist, U. Strömqvist, and F. Førsund (1982), unpublished.

Mansfield, E. (1961), Technical Change and the Rate of Imitation, in *Econometrica*, 29.

McFadden, D. (1978), Modeling the Choice of Residential Location, in A. Karlqvist *et al.* (eds.), *Spatial Interaction Theory and Planning Models* (North-Holland, Amsterdam).

Puu, T. (1977), On the Profitability of Exhausting Natural Resources, in *Journal of Environmental Economics and Management*, 4.

Puu, T., and S. Wibe (eds.) (1980), *The Economics of Technological Progress* (Macmillan, New York, NY).

Samuelson, P.A. (1954), The Pure Theory of Public Expenditures, *Review of Economics and Statistics*, 36.

Smith, V. (1959), *Investment and Production* (Harvard University Press, Cambridge, MA).

Snickars, F., and J.W. Weibull (1977), A Minimum of Information Principle: Theory and Practice, in *Regional Science and Urban Economics*, 7, 137-168.

CHAPTER 16

MULTIREGIONAL ECONOMIC MODELING: PROSPECTS

Boris Issaev
Peter Nijkamp
Piet Rietveld
Folke Snickars

1 Trends in Modeling

Recent developments in both the natural and the social sciences have demonstrated a strong orientation toward quantitative analyses. In many disciplines
modeling efforts have led to new highlights of scientific activity. But at the
same time, many endeavors to model a complex reality by means of a compact set of
formal relationships have led to deceptive results. It is highly interesting to
see that basically parallel developments take place in many scientific disciplines.
After a period of enthusiastic model building and of formal analyses, several doubts
have been expressed regarding the validity and value of these approaches.

This development of intellectual thinking has induced a period of critical
assessment and reorientation concerning prevailing trends in model building. In
many scientific areas the same questions and concerns are emerging. It is, for
instance, striking and interesting that issues such as the desirable size of models
have been discussed--from analogous viewpoints--simultaneously in several disciplines such as economics, demography, biology, and sociology. Large-scale (simulation) models--sometimes put in a dynamic form--had achieved considerable popularity at the beginning of the seventies, but they were at the same time condemned
by empirical scientists claiming that a complex and varied reality could not be
adequately described even in an elaborated closed formal system.

The use of computers has created possibilities for overcoming several limitations inherent in traditional model building; for instance, nonlinearities, thresh-
olds, limits, and discontinuities can now more easily be dealt with. The resulting
gigantic modeling efforts, however, have often been far less illuminating than
anticipated. This, of course, has caused doubts about the usefulness of large-
scale and comprehensive modeling efforts.

The subsequent period of reorientation has imposed a more modest attitude on
model builders in all sciences. A model is no longer meant to describe the whole
world or to solve simultaneously all key questions of our world. Instead, it has
become more common for model builders in many disciplines to address themselves
only to a single or a few key questions, either theoretical or empirical. This
activity rightly puts more emphasis on the problem boundary and the problem identification. Even in that case, large models may be necessary but they are then put
in the perspective of a main focus while allowing interactions to other components
and disaggregations to subsystems. In such cases the analysis of the basic structure of a model is extremely important for encapsulating the essential understanding of fundamental mechanisms at work in our complex world. With respect to this,
structure analyses such as causal pattern analysis, hierarchical structure analysis, redundancy analysis, and decomposition analysis may be very helpful in order
to identify the main structure of complicated models.

The awareness of and insight into the main driving forces in a model also provides several ways of facilitating its use on a computer, validating its assumptions,
excluding redundant variables, identifying more precisely the data requirements, and
increasing its accessibility and transferability.

Thus, the lesson to be drawn from the recent developments in modeling in several disciplines is that *simplicity is not necessarily in contrast with a large
scale*. The number of variables and equations in a model may be extremely high

(including nonlinear dynamics), but a model builder should always strive for a
structure that is manageable and comprehensible by demonstrating the key mechanism
of a system. Only in that manner can modeling activities become successful in
covering the problems of the (probably turbulent) eighties. In the following sections, several key issues in multiregional economic (ME) modeling will be dealt
with from a prospective point of view, based on the lessons we have learned in the
preceding chapters.

2 From Problem to Model

     The preceding chapters have demonstrated that ME modeling has not reached its
final stage, but is still in a state of flux. An evaluation of the practice of ME
modeling is a far from easy task. The diversity of both models and problems pre-
vents us from drawing straightforward and valid conclusions regarding such questions
as: To what degree does current multiregional modeling practice in various countries
address itself to major regional-national economic development problems? Are current
ME models adequate for the problems and the setting for which they have been developed? Are appropriate theories and techniques used in model specifications and/or
solutions? What are the limitations of current ME modeling as aids in decision
making? Which kind of frictions have to be removed in order to increase the practical value of models as tools for policy analysis under the present system of regional management? What new dimensions have to be added to the current modeling
practice in order to provide more perspectives for the future?
     We have attempted to answer some of these questions in the preceding chapters
by considering both different aspects present in the current modeling practice and
prospects for new issues to be dealt with. It is the aim of this concluding chapter to address the issue of prospects of ME models in a systematic way by means of
Figure 1. This figure represents the process of model building as a series of steps
from the observation of a complex reality toward the actual scope of a model. The
figure is built up as a series of shells, the larger ones encompassing the smaller
ones. The picture includes mainly the activities of two actors in the modeling
process: model builders and model users. The outer shells reflect mostly the tasks
of model users, but from the third shell onward the responsibility of model builders
(for instance, for technical aspects or for a validation of the model) becomes more
apparent. These steps will now successively be described.
     The first stage of a modeling process--sometimes even prior to this process--
is the *observation or awareness of a complex world*. This evokes the intellectual
challenge to identify a certain structure, coherence, or regularity in reality or
to attack problems brought to the forefront. The interwoven picture of this complex world, however, cannot be grasped immediately; only certain aspects of this
picture can be understood. There is no holistic science that is able to provide a
comprehensive insight into all aspects of a multidimensional system.

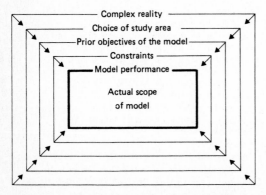

Figure 1. The process of model building

This observation leads us to the next step: the choice of a *specific study area* or *specific problems* we want to focus our attention on. In a regional or urban setting, this specific attention is codetermined by the relevance attached by the model builder (or model user) to these problems. Examples of such problems that might stimulate the process of intellectual challenge and scientific activities at the present are:

(i)   the persistence or emergence of inequality in a system of regions;

(ii)   unexpected impacts and long-run uncertainties arising from structural changes or from the economic recession;

(iii) the effects of regional policy on territorial production complexes;

(iv) lack of effectiveness of economic development and regeneration policies;

(v)   political movements to establish regional autonomy;

(vi) locational effects on the urban and regional level of the rise in energy prices;

(vii) impacts of technological developments and of national policies on the relative competitiveness of regions.

All such problems can never be tackled simultaneously. Therefore, a selection has to be made so as to arrive at a manageable subset of elements from the original set of issues. As mentioned above, the recent tendency is to focus the attention more sharply on a specific well defined study area or on a precisely demarcated set of problems; this is reflected by the second shell of Figure 1.

However, even the identification of relevant problems to be studied does not imply that our scientific tools are appropriate to treat these problems. The diversity of a spatial system cannot be entirely studied in the framework of a formal model. Building a model implies that a stylized picture is made of the structure of parts of reality. Hence, the *formulation of prior objectives of the model* means again that a smaller subset of elements from real world problems will be considered. This is reflected by the third shell of Figure 1. It is clear that the objectives of a model may vary from fairly modest ones (illustration or description) to ambitious ones (forecasting, policy simulation, or policy control). For models that are designed to serve a user who is not familiar with complicated or large-scale modeling activities, there is a tendency toward a "simple is beautiful" view of models. It is indeed striking that the multiregional models that are most frequently used in practice have in general a simple structure (see Chapter 2). In many cases, it turns out to be very difficult to let decision makers express their views on the use and scope of a model (see also House 1977). This situation also explains the popularity of scenario analysis as a learning tool in models for integrated policy analyses (see Nijkamp and Spronk 1982).

The precise formulation of the objectives of a model rests essentially on an interplay between model users and model builders. Model users are inclined to put claims on the objectives of a model from the viewpoint of a range of specific *ad hoc* problems, so that a model is conceived of as a medicine against an entire set of diseases. On the other hand, a model builder will usually aim at developing a model with a high degree of generality without worrying too much about specific applications. Of course, he has to take into account the constraints imposed by data availability, etc. Consequently, the precise formulation of objectives is a task for both types of actors, who are especially operating on a research market (see also Fisch 1982).

The prespecified objectives of the analysis, of course, also determine the structure, contents, and features of the model at hand. Aspects such as the scale and the level of (dis) aggregation will be dealt with in greater detail in subsequent sections.

The formulation of objectives of a multiregional model does not guarantee their fulfillment. In modeling practice the *constraints* which may prevent the model builder from reaching the objectives he had originally in mind may be more conspicuous than the objectives themselves. The emergence of these constraints may *inter alia* be due to lack of appropriate data, limitations inherent in the use of many statistical or mathematical techniques, necessary but inappropriate model specifications, impossibility of taking into account the existence of uncertainties

or unexpected events, rigid institutional or bureaucratic structures, and so forth.
Some of these constraints will be discussed hereafter in more detail. It may suffice for the moment to conclude that the presence of constraints forces the model
builder to focus his attention on a smaller subset of aspects of complex real world
problems, thus arriving at the fourth shell of Figure 1.

Only when all constraints have been taken into account can the *real performance of the model* be investigated, and also validated by means of appropriate
statistical or mathematical techniques. This exercise may lead to a revised specification of the model, to new data requirements and to the consideration of new
constraints, until, after a series of feedback activities, the ultimate model has
been constructed and validated. This interior shell of Figure 1 demonstrates once
more that the actual scope of the model may be fairly limited, at least compared
with the initial objectives of the study or the original pretenses of the model
builder.

We have noted that there is a discrepancy between the prior aims of a multiregional model and its actual scope in practical situations. This discrepancy calls
for methodologies that will remove some of the constraints separating the interior
shell from the third shell of Figure 1. Such methods to bring objective and scope
closer together will be further discussed in the sequel.

3 Constraints on Multiregional Economic Models

In many respects, the eighties seem to call attention to different issues as
compared with the 1970s: sticky economic recession, boost of new technology, energy
scarcity, tight environmental constraints, and sharp conflicts among groups or regions in a society may prevail. All these phenomena have clear regional and urban
dimensions, and ME models may be meaningful tools for analyzing the driving forces
of these phenomena, studying the impacts of new developments, and helping control
undesirable consequences.

Yet there are many constraints in ME modeling that may hamper a fruitful application of these models to urgent contemporary or future problems. Examples of such
constraints are: data availability, lack of appropriate techniques, inappropriate
scale of models, lack of insight into time dimensions, lack of integration or comprehensiveness of relevant aspects, and lack of policy relevance. Another evident
constraint--lack of a proper use of theories--will not be discussed here, as this
was the subject of Chapter 15. The above-mentioned six constraints tend to afflict
many ME modeling efforts, despite the diversity in socioeconomic and political systems and the wide variety of problems to be covered. Several of these constraints
will now be discussed successively, in Sections 3.1-3.6.

3.1 Availability of data

In many studies, a less satisfactory specification or performance of a multiregional model is ascribed to a *weak database*. Though evidently unreliable data
may affect the quality of the results, it is at the same time also true that the
structures of many models presuppose a database that does not fully exist in reality. Model users have to face and accept a situation of inappropriate information
systems and of gaps in statistical data (see also Chapter 2). In this respect,
one may draw attention to meaningful techniques suited for dealing with indirectly
measured variables, latent variables, or multivariate data. It is, for instance,
surprising and also disappointing that operational techniques such as path analysis,
Lisrel methods and partial least squares have hardly found any application in regional modeling. However, some examples of applications of such methods among
others can be found in Wold (1975), Folmer (1980), Leitner and Wohlschägl (1980),
and Folmer and Nijkamp (1982).

In addition to accommodating for *lacking* data, the possibilities of incorporating *qualitative* data have to be mentioned. Qualitative data are measured on a nonmetric scale (e.g., ordinal or nominal). Too often, qualitative data are left out
of consideration, although such data may contain substantial pieces of information.
The recent developments in the area of qualitative (and fuzzy) spatial data analysis

may be a meaningful way of employing all relevant available information as well as possible. Examples of qualitative data methods can be found in e.g., Wrigley (1979), Nijkamp (1982), and Nijkamp and Rietveld (1982).

In an ideal situation, one may expect the availability of a large data set for all relevant variables in an ME model. In reality, however, much information is missing. Examples of information that is often lacking in regional modeling are:

(a)   economic variables: stocks and flows of wealth, real and financial assets, and liabilities; scale and agglomeration advantages; capacity constraints; the value of public overhead capital; distributional effects;
(b)   spatial variables: spatial interactions such as disaggregate migration and commodity flows; spatial spin-off and spillover patterns;
(c)   process and state variables: technical progress, innovation, research and development, infrastructure, communication, energy productivity;
(d)   sociopolitical variables: power groups, decision structures, interest groups, policy controls;
(e)   basic variables: demographic structure, long-run regional dynamics.

In general, *systematic information systems* are a prerequisite for the construction of appropriate ME models. Input-output matrices (especially the commodity-by-industry or rectangular form), capacity and bottleneck variables, social overhead capital and interregional interactions make up basic ingredients of a satisfactory spatial information system. Absence of up-to-date information limits the ability of modelers to adequately represent regional systems. The construction of input-output models based on very old data is not a satisfactory activity, although some models like MRIO and IIOM use 10- to 15-year-old data. Of course, data availability varies from country to country, and often within countries, but one of the crucial gaps is in the area of regional capital stocks and their interregional flows. In the USSR, for instance, compilation of a system of regional input-output tables at regular intervals is a function of the Central Statistical Office of that country. Databases sometimes include investment data for manufacturing, but very little else (except in some countries such as Japan). This implies that a vintage approach is often impossible (see, however, SERENA and Johansson and Strömqvist 1981). This unsatisfactory data situation is regrettable, especially as the movements of capital are very important in long-term regional development in market economies (see also Bluestone and Harrison 1980, Glickman and Petras 1981).

A similar situation exists for interregional *money* flows (social insurances, old-age pensions, entrepreneurial profits, etc.). These flows have a direct distributive impact on a system of regions, while they are neglected in most multiregional models (except in IIOSMK).

In conclusion, firstly, a more appropriate *organization of information systems* is needed in a systematic framework that will permit otherwise incomparable indicators to be statistically interrelated and used in estimating or calibrating ME models (see Garnick 1980). These should avoid the current practice of incoherent and inconsistent regional data that are not comparable from one series to another, from one time period to another, and from one place to another. Secondly, a more efficient and systematic use of existing regional databases in the modeling process is necessary for bridging the gap between prior objectives and posterior scope of a multiregional model.

3.2   Techniques

The *mathematical* and *statistical* problems inherent in a proper estimation and validation of multiregional models should not be underestimated. As indicated in Chapter 2, however, the current practice of ME modeling demonstrates that in general fairly simple tools are used, such as ordinary least-squares procedures.

Recent advances in the area of combined time series cross section analysis have shown, however, that the quality of results may be significantly improved by applying better estimation methods. Unfortunately, many of these modern developments have not been taken account of in multiregional modeling efforts (see Chapter 2). Even the frequently discussed problem of spatiotemporal cross correlation has hardly received any attention in multiregional model building, though in the last decade many publications have appeared in the area of spatial and temporal auto-correlation.

It seems as though multiregional model builders are not entirely aware of the potential of available econometric and statistical techniques. For instance, as indicated in Chapter 2, many existing ME models are restricted to sets of *linear* equations, while in the last decade much progress has been made in dealing with nonlinear systems.

Increased attention in future multiregional modeling should also be given to *convergent algorithms* for solving efficiently dynamic, nonlinear, or large systems, a topic that is a very active research area in modern urban transportation model-ing. Adjustment techniques for regional interaction data (for instance, based on information theory) have not reached their limit potential in multiregional models. So-called KLEM functions (translog functions for dealing with factor substitutabil-ity) were developed in econometrics almost a decade ago, while these functions have only been applied in a few multiregional models, i.e., MEEEI and MREEED (see also Chapter 13). It is also illustrative that in many cases information on the statis-tical reliability of the results of multiregional models is lacking, while a proper documentation of statistical outcomes is necessary for such an evaluation.

In general, a proper and effective use of the existing body of econometric and statistical knowledge may lead to a substantial improvement of the quality of multi-regional models and to a sharpening of their results, so that in terms of Figure 1 the actual scope of models comes nearer to their prior objectives.

3.3 Scale of models

Several general aspects of scales of models have already been discussed, in the first paragraph of this chapter. The appropriate *scale* and *level of aggregation* of a model follow from the purpose of the model at hand. Clearly, a certain scale of a model is not a constraint as such, but choosing a less appropriate one may lead to severe restrictions regarding the interpretation of the model.

Aggregate models do not normally allow detailed conclusions regarding reactions of individual groups or spatial subunits. In addition, very often the behavioral content of an aggregate model is fairly poor, so that there is in general a need for more disaggregated models, especially in policy analysis and evaluation (see also Chapter 2). For instance, an employment policy would require insight into the exis-tence of a duality or segmentation on the labor market. Entirely disaggregated models, however, may become unmanageable in size, as they may become complex con-structs without a clear structure. Large-scale disaggregate models may contain much information, but without a fundamental structure the necessary insight into the basic mechanism is lacking. In this respect, a modular design similar in scale and complexity to large national econometric models such as LINK and INFORUM may be desirable; see also Chapters 13 and 14.

Multiregional models formulated without a reasonably detailed commodity ship-ment/transportation sector must be regarded as generally unsatisfactory from both a conceptual and policy analysis point of view, as the essence of a multiregional system is disaggregate commodity, capital, and population flows (see also the Korean OTSIS model).

Explicit representation of interregional commodity flows raises important issues of model scale and design, as this requires both a fairly detailed defini-tion of regions and an aggregated representation of regional transportation systems and networks. When the regional subdivisions for transportation systems are too detailed for regional economic modeling, a hierarchical modular system of regions and subregions may be desirable. Such a multilevel linkage of components of a sys-tem implies normally a higher degree of systematics and coherence than a set of modules linked in a horizontal way. Apart from multilevel systems analysis, graph theory and path analysis may also be mentioned as meaningful mathematical and statistical tools for detailing with complex interaction patterns. Unfortunately, the above-mentioned techniques have hardly found any application in ME models.

It is clear that any rise in the number of time periods, sectors, regions, or groups of actors will increase the scale of a model, though it will not necessarily

become more complicated. Decisions regarding the scale to be adopted in a model
are clearly the result of the *ex ante* objectives of the model at hand. This can
be illustrated for the Japanese long-run regional planning system, in which public
investments make up a major policy instrument (see also the EPAM and NRPEM models).
In this specific system public investment is disaggregated into four categories,
i.e., basic facilities for agriculture, basic facilities for industry, investments
in the transportation and communication sector, and social overhead capital (such
as schools and hospitals).

In general, when a large-scale model is needed, it is extremely important--
for reasons of operationality and policy support--to build a multiregional model
that is able to describe systematically the *underlying mechanism* of a spatial system. If the scale of a model is becoming too large, a modular structure and decomposition may be a helpful compromise.

In conclusion, the problem of the scale of models may be considered at various
levels. The level of disaggregation may be different among submodels, as long as
they are connected through a common interface which might operate at a more aggregated level. The level of aggregation of presenting policy impacts or model results
can be chosen more or less independently of the level of functional relationships.
Modern computer technology has entailed a higher degree of freedom then earlier in
choosing appropriate scales for different analyses. The old paradigm of "the bigger
the better" does not apply to the field of current ME modeling. By taking account
of the above-mentioned remarks, *ex ante* expectations and *ex post* realization of a
multiregional model may be better reconciled.

3.4 The time dimension

It has already been explained in Chapter 2 that the time dimension in multiregional models depends very much on the specific aims of the model (for instance,
short-, medium, or long-term policy analysis). The majority of current multiregional
models are indeed dynamic in nature, but the specific implications of the aims of the
models for the time dimension and the structure of these models are not so easy to
identify.

A basic problem is, of course, that the time dimensions of the main components
of a whole spatial system do not necessarily run parallel. For example, demographic
modules may relate to long-run changes while unemployment aspects may relate to
short- or medium-term changes. Consequently, a flexible and interchangeable set of
modules for these components may be relevant. This would also guarantee that relevant policy instruments have a position and function in the proper time perspective.

Several aspects of time dimensions have been dealt with in greater detail in
Chapter 2. In general, a *short-term* regional planning model has to describe precisely the determination of prices and the balancing role of prices, the adjustment
mechanism of investments, and the determination of production and consumption levels.
In regard to this model, short-term policy measures like monetary and fiscal policies
and regulations have to be included in a proper way.

In *medium-term* regional planning models, much more attention should be focused
on the way private and public investments are determined, so as to arrive at optimum
investment plans and strategies for different sectors and regions. Thus, in this
case, capital formation in relation to production and final demand and public investment policy deserve much attention.

In *long-term* planning models, locational changes of households and industries
(e.g., shifts in urbanization trends) have to be dealt with. This requires much
more emphasis on the explanation of interregional population movements and of structural migration patterns of firms (including the resulting shifts in service and
commodity flows). In regard to long-run models, appropriate policy measures to be
included are: housing policies, new tax systems, land-use policies, public overhead
investments, environmental regulations or energy policies.

In this way multiregional models should be distinguished--in regard to relevant
policy variables--by the time horizon of the models. Needless to say, in the practice of modeling the availability of data may be an important constraint on the time
perspective of a model, but the above-mentioned suggestions may be meaningful principles for achieving a compromise between *ex ante* pretenses of a model and *ex post*
performances.

3.5 Stability

A specific problem inherent in the time dimension of a model is its *stability* over time (see also the remarks on this topic made in Chapter 2): dynamic input-output models were a first attempt at studying the long-term feasibility and consistency of regional development patterns. Such models have sometimes also been concerned with regional population growth and the associated housing and construction infrastructure. Some examples of this approach can be found in the DREAM and GISSIR models.

However, several dynamic models generate simplistic growth paths. Therefore, one might draw attention to the emerging scientific paradigm of *self-organization* developed by, e.g., Nicolis and Prigogine (1977). The process of self-organization may be closely related to the notion of bifurcations in catastrophe theory (Thom 1975; see also Chapter 1).

Building upon these foundations, Allen (1976) formulated a model in which the change in the population distribution of an area is linked to the employment pattern, and the latter in turn to the population distribution through the concepts of central place theory (Allen and Sanglier 1978). The result was a dynamic model of interacting urban centers, which emphasized the role of transportation in the spatial restructuring process. Although Allen simulated the impact of new economic activities on an urban population, he did not examine the effects of technological innovations on existing economic activities. Nor did he explore the precise nature of the innovative process and the spread of innovative change in a multiregional system.

Batten (1981) has recently formulated some dynamic models of industrial evolution, by allowing the entry and exit rates of firms in an industry to play a similar (but not identical) role to the birth and death rates in a population. Simulations with a model for industrial innovation indicate that such an economic system may undergo a certain self-organization, resulting from the nonlinearities present in the interdependences between various industries. Such nonlinear dynamic models may also be applied to asymmetric regional development patterns (see Nijkamp 1982).

The recent advances in the area of nonlinear dynamics may lead to revitalization of traditional regional modeling. Such a renewal has also been advocated in Chapter 15. A tentative step towards the integration of nonlinear dynamic components in multiregional models might be the inclusion of *technological innovation*. Technological innovation (e.g., introduction of microelectronics or telematics, or a rapid exploitation of coal reserves), may exert a stepwise impact on the industrial structure, which might lead to changes in regional competitive differentials and labor market impacts. In turn, regional employment patterns may then be linked to the spatial distribution of population.

In this way several model builders eventually distinguish between *growth* models, which deal especially with short- to medium-term analyses, and multiregional *development* models, which can examine structural changes in a spatial system such as the industrial effects of structural changes in the long term and the spatial diffusion of innovations. Evidently, multiregional model builders have a long way to go before these new dimensions become fully operational.

4 Comprehensiveness and Integration

The majority of ME models focus attention on traditional economic phenomena such as employment, production, investment, consumption, and interregional trade flows. The problem of spatial equity also receives much attention. There are other cross cutting aspects, however, which are of principal interest in specific policy situations. Six of these aspects will now briefly be treated.

(a) *Urban dimensions*. The impacts of regional developments or federal policies on urban agglomerations can hardly be assessed by means of current ME models. Yet, information on urban repercussions of regional changes may be quite relevant. In respect to this, attention could be given to urban impact analysis (or, more generally, spatial impact analysis) as a method for assessing the foreseeable and expected consequences of regional changes for relevant urban variables

(see Glickman 1980 and Nijkamp 1981). An urban impact module may in principle
be linked as a separate submodule of an ME model.

(b) *International dimensions*. Usually, the international dimensions (including
     Third World aspects) enter a multiregional model via the national system, and
     vice versa. This is indeed a reasonable approach in cases of a fair distribu-
     tion of international impacts over all regions. In specific cases, however,
     one individual region or a set of regions may have strong direct international
     linkages; for instance, a coal-mining area that is exporting almost all its
     production. In these cases, a direct module for international linkages in
     specific regions is desirable, provided the consistency requirement for the
     system as a whole can be maintained (see e.g., NRWF and FRET).
(c) *Environmental and energy dimensions*. Problem driven modeling needs to respond
     to intriguing and urgent policy problems. Especially during the seventies,
     the environmental and energy aspects (e.g., pollution, oil consumption) became
     increasingly important. The use of input-output analysis proved to yield an
     operational contribution to integrating environmental and energy dimensions in
     multiregional models. Here again a modular design with separate satellites can
     be employed, so that environmental and energy aspects are studied in associated,
     more detailed subsystems, but are linked as environmental and energy profiles
     to the relevant regional economic profiles (see Arntzen and Braat 1982).
(d) *Demographic dimensions*. Especially in medium- and long-term models, demographic
     developments may exert a significant impact on the regional economy. The labor
     market, the housing market, and public facilities are directly affected by
     demographic shifts. Fortunately, in the area of demographic modeling many
     successful efforts have been made to build multiregional demographic models
     (see Rogers 1981). A modular linkage of these models with existing economic
     models may lead to a coherent integration of demographic and economic dimen-
     sions in a spatial system (see also the remarks made in Chapter 2).
(e) *Social dimensions*. Social dimensions and distributional issues are among the
     most neglected topics in multiregional modeling. Yet they may be extremely
     important, as they have direct policy repercussions. A good example of this
     is the presence of minority groups and guest workers. The international mobil-
     ity of people has a large impact on the cities and regions of a country, as can
     also be illustrated by German and American experiences. Especially in labor
     market and housing market models, efforts should be made to include such social
     dimensions by trying to build more disaggregated models. Some efforts in this
     direction can be found in the HESSEN model.
(f) *Technological dimensions*. In particular in long-term ME models, shifts in
     technology will cause drastic changes in specific sectors of the regional
     economies. Usually, technology is treated as an exogenous variable, but in
     the long run one may safely assume that technology is also determined by eco-
     nomic developments (boom or recession) or by spatial developments (congested
     settlement systems). The current development in specified microprocessing and
     defense activities have strong regional dimensions. Thus, technology deserves
     more attention in ME models, and more theoretical reflections are needed in
     this respect (see also Chapter 15).

   A closer view of technology would also imply a more appropriate integration of
supply and demand economics in ME modeling. Many current ME models are strongly
demand driven. Especially in long-run analyses, supply conditions (including technology development and public overhead capital) deserve a more appropriate position.
This would also lead to an enhanced use of economic theories in multiregional modeling. In this respect also, elements from polarization theory, location theory, and
agglomeration theory may be brought to bear (Treyz and Stevens 1980).
   We have discussed the prospects of ME modeling as a craft from two perspectives
above. The first one addressed the issue of the most favorable degree of sophistication in the submodels of aspects of regional development already covered in the
existing body of models. Here we have argued that technology and structural change
are catchwords for areas where current ME models need to be made more sophisticated.
The other perspective discussed was that of gauging those claims of extending existing models so as to cover new aspects proposed by model users. The current trend

towards environmental and energy issues is an example of the response to such a
pressure. In this respect, economic contraction is an issue that might be anticipated to become of increasing importance in the 1980s.

5 Policy Relevance

5.1 Use of models

ME models may play a role in regional planning in two ways: (1) as a tool in
an *impact analysis* in order to assess the regional consequences of public policy
measures, and (2) as a tool in *decision making procedures*. Most models focus attention on the first point, while institutional and procedural aspects of such models
in a regional planning context are neglected. This is an unnecessary limitation,
however, particularly because simulation and scenario analyses, learning procedures,
conflict analysis, and interactive multicriteria analyses provide many possibilities
for taking account of institutional aspects of planning and policy making.

Evidently, ME models do not provide appropriate solutions to all kinds of policy questions (see also Chapter 2). There is a diversity of modes of use of such
models in a policy context, such as deriving:

(1) *optimization* solutions: outcomes of an optimization procedure for a system
     of equations describing a multiregional economy by means of one or more well
     established objective functions;
(2) *equilibrium* solutions: outcomes of a simultaneous solution of a set of equa-
     tions describing an equilibrium state of the economy:
(3) *information theoretical* solutions: outcomes of a set of conditions imposed
     on a spatial system in order to identify the most probable solution in a sta-
     tistical sense;
(4) *extrapolation* solutions: outcomes of a statistical or econometric procedure
     by means of which statistical (regression) relationships, fitted to historical
     data, are extrapolated in the future.

The specific kind of solution aimed at depends, of course, on the structure
and the policy aims of the model. It can be seen from the survey in the Appendix
that there is a certain degree of equivalence between the use of some of these
modes, so the choice may also depend on the technical or subjective considerations.

5.2 Models in different socioeconomic systems

ME models are used in various social and political systems; for instance, mixed
and planned economies. Although market economies may also be mentioned and play a
role in assumptions underlying some models, they do not occur in a pure form, so
that it is more appropriate to speak of mixed economies.

A basic problem in designing and employing multiregional models is the fact
that many economies are of a *mixed* type. The standard paradigms in such cases are
usually as follows: a market resource allocation is derived from a model, the market failure (if any) being shown and certain public service needs (e.g., transportation) being derived from the solution. This is done despite the fact that very
often the interaction between the public and the private sector does not appear in
the model, and that the model contains no welfare criterion (see Mills 1975).
Clearly, a difficult issue in economic model building is the interaction between
the public and the private sector, as this requires a careful representation of
exchange markets and policy institutions. This issue should also receive more attention in ME model building; see e.g., the REGAL model.

One role of a multiregional planning model in a mixed economy is to present
two different projection cases: the trend of the economy solely determined by a
free market balancing mechanism (a market oriented trend), and the change in the
trend of the economy caused by regional development policy of government (a mixed
trend).

Among (private) consumers and producers, the imbalance between demand and supply for goods and services may be in the short run partly decreased through changes in prices, inventories, and levels of production and expenditures, in the medium term mitigated through changes of investments (productive fixed and housing investments), and finally in the long run eliminated through changes of location of population and enterprises.

The targets of government development policy are usually multidimensional. For example, a government may be interested in targets of (a) growth or efficiency (maximize real rate of growth), (b) equity (minimize interregional per capita income differences), (c) welfare (increase of per capita or per space endowment of social overhead capital), (d) accessibility (implementation of a good transportation and communication system), and (e) environment (maintenance or improvement of the environmental conditions). When the market oriented trend of the economy contradicts some of these targets, government will undertake a policy action to revise this trend; for example, an income transfer policy in the short run, public investments and special tax and subsidy policies in the medium term, and long-range land-use plans accompanied by adequate financial and legal regulations.

Therefore, the key role of a multiregional model should be to contain adequately the basic balancing parameters or variables of the private sector and also the policy instrument of the public sector, and to calculate the market oriented trend and the mixed trend of the economy. Based upon these projections, the potential growth capacity of the private sector, and the feasibility and effectiveness of a regional development policy, can simultaneously and consistently be assessed in quantitative terms.

In centrally planned economies, the role of ME models is different from that in mixed economies. This may be illustrated by means of the relevance of models in decision making for regional development in the USSR. The modern Soviet planning system puts the following claims on interregional modeling: multiregional models should be elaborated for the whole regional system of the USSR for a period of up to 20 years (divided into five-year periods and, preferably, into separate years of the first five-year period). In a system of planned control, regions are, on the one hand, the objects of centralized planning and, on the other hand, economically detached units, possessing their own planning and control authorities. That is why ME models are used, firstly, as tools for centralized pre-planning studies and for planning the national economy by region, and secondly, as tools for coordinating regional projections and for synthesizing regional models. Development of multiregional modeling should intensify a dialogue between "center" and "regions", among other things by simulating consequences of different planned decisions.

The main difficulty in using ME models in planning practice is a lack of adequate data, especially as far as regional technical coefficients for the planned period are concerned. Currently in the USSR Gosplan, the Automated System of Planning Calculations (ASPC) is being developed, representing a new technology for working out the state plans and controlling their fulfillment under conditions of systematic applications of economic-mathematical methods and computing machinery. In the framework of the ASPC, a definite sequence of planning tasks with its data inputs and outputs corresponds to the models. The ASPC contains also the functional subsystem of a so-called "territorial plan". It is supposed that ME models will become the main elements of this planning subsystem.

5.3 Conflict analysis

A related issue in multiregional modeling is *conflict analysis*. Since a region, as a socioeconomic object, functions within a national system, there are three sources of conflicts, the solution of which determines socioeconomic processes within a given region and the region's relation to the outside world:

(a) *intraregional conflicts*: intraregional criteria and preferences determining decisions of regional authorities for the area of their direct competence and the behavior of regional economic agents;

(b) *interregional conflicts*: open character of regional systems and high sensitivity to events in other regions;

(c) *national-regional conflicts*: national criteria determining decisions taken
at the national level for the given region.

   The relevance of models in a policy context will evidently depend very much
on the way models can take into consideration the above mentioned conflicts. In
nearly all countries there are conflicts that are, in part, intraregional, interregional, and national-regional in content. These conflicts are among the most
important and interesting in our societies. For example, we see political and
economic conflict within a region (central cities versus suburbs), interregional
conflict (the American north versus the south; Dutch- and French-speaking Belgium).
By means of modern conflict analysis (e.g., based on multiobjective decision models)
a systematic formulation of such conflicts might be attained.
   The question is: can models resolve, or even help better the understanding of
these issues? Often regional conflicts have their basis in long-term spatial movements of capital and labor. It would, of course, be extremely valuable if models
could help us with these very important questions in the eighties. Even though
models are very useful for a variety of short-term forecasting and analytic questions, they do not often have the proper sensitivity to answer these very complex
and subtle questions. For example, many models have been built for nonpolicy purposes (e.g., forecasting). They are limited in their area disaggregation, in the
number of variables, are not readily understood by policy makers and citizens, and
lack key components in understanding issues like regional conflicts. Thus much
effort has to be made to link multiregional models in a better way to specific policy issues and conflicts.
   An important question in conflict analysis is the *distribution of decision
making and power in a spatial system*. This is usually again an interface between
the public and the private sector. There is much evidence that multiregional or
multinational companies especially control a substantial amount of the spatial movement of capital and of productive facilities. With regard to this situation, multiregional policy models are only able to represent part of a complex reality, so that
their policy relevance should certainly not be overestimated. It is also clear that
in this area of conflicts among and within regions and of conflicts among various
institutions many links can be established with recent developments in disciplines
such as regional political economy.

5.4 Understanding of models

   A final remark is still in order. Many models developed thus far are of limited use to decision makers for a wide variety of reasons discussed above. Model
builders have not been very good at *communicating* the nature of the models--both
the advantages and limitations--to the public decision makers (see Glickman 1980).
Either the models are presented as "highly complicated" structures, which frightens
decision makers, or the models are presented as "black boxes", which decision makers
often do not trust. It is incumbent upon those who wish to influence political
actions by model implementation to improve the communication of their skills to
decision makers (see also Chapter 2). This also implies that software, documentation, and simulation results should be made available to planners and decision makers
in a comprehensible form. In this sense, ME modeling requires a permanent interaction between model designers and clients so as to increase the relevance of such
models for planning and policy making.

6 Concluding Remarks

   The above sections have been devoted to a discussion of constraints prevailing
in ME modeling. Six major issues were dealt with: the quality of data, the proper
use of available techniques, the scale of a multiregional model, the time dimension,
the integration and comprehensiveness, and the policy relevance. In our view, even
with the *existing body of knowledge and the existing information systems*, *an improvement of ME modeling* is certainly possible. In the preceding sections various ways
have been indicated in which to enhance the effectiveness and usefulness of ME models

It is clear that an ideal model will never be attained (see also Chapter 1). But, given the limitations imposed by data, theory, techniques and policy consider- ations, an optimal use of ingredients for model building has to be made. This is illustrated in Figure 2, where the boxes indicate a quantitative representation of the above mentioned six items (see also Chapter 1, where an analogous attempt at a systematic presentation has been made). Given the *ex ante* aims of the model at hand, one might expect an ideal characterization of the model in the vicinity of the envelope (the envelope representing an optimal treatment of the presence of the six aspects concerned in the model). Of course, one should realize that the regular shape of the hexagon does not imply that all dimensions should receive an equal weighting. In reality, however, the actual scope of the model is much more re- stricted, so that the characterization of these items implies a position nearer to the center of the figure (see the broken line).

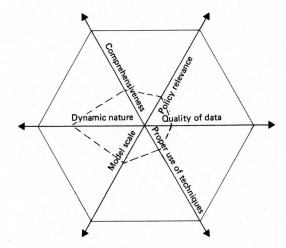

Figure 2. Characteristics of items of a model

The major challenge in ME modeling will evidently now be to improve the quality of models by driving the broken line towards the envelope. This implies that the constraints discussed above should be relaxed so as to attain a situation where the *ex ante* aim of the model does not differ too much from the *ex post* scope.

References

Allen, P.M. (1976), Evolution, Population Dynamics, and Stability, *Proceedings of the National Academy of Sciences*, *USA*, 73, 665-668.
Allen, P.M., and M. Sanglier (1978), Dynamic Models of Urban Growth, in *Journal of Social Biological Structure*, 1, 665-668.
Arntzen, J.W., and L.C. Braat (forthcoming), An Integrated Environmental Model for Regional Policy Analysis, in T.R. Lakshmanan and P. Nijkamp (eds.), *Systems and Models for Energy and Environmental Analysis* (Gower, Aldershot).
Batten, D.F. (1981), On the Dynamics of Industrial Evolution, *Paper submitted to the International Conference on Structural Economic Analysis and Planning in Time and Space, Umea, Sweden*.
Bluestone, B., and B. Harrison (1980), *Capital and Communities* (The Progressive Alliance, Washington, DC).
Fisch, O. (1982), Technological Transfer of Regional Environmental Models, in M. Albegov *et al.* (eds.), *Regional Development Modeling: Theory and Practice* (North-Holland, Amsterdam).

Folmer, H. (1980), Measurement of the Effects of Regional Policy Instruments, in
    Environment and Planning A, 12, 1191-1202.
Folmer, H., and P. Nijkamp (1982), Linear Structural Equation Models with Spatio-
    temporal Auto- and Cross-Correlation, in M.M. Fischer and J. Bahrenberg (eds.),
    Bremer Beiträge zur Geographie, Heft 5, Bremen (forthcoming).
Garnick, D.H. (1980), The Regional Statistics System, in F.G. Adams and N.J.
    Glickman (eds.), *Modeling the Multiregional Economic System* (Heath, Lexington,
    MA), pp. 25-48.
Glickman, N.J. (1980), The Urban Impacts of Federal Policies (Johns Hopkins Univer-
    sity Press, Baltimore, MD).
Glickman, N.J., and E.M. Petras (1981), International Capital and International
    Labor Flow: Implications for Public Policy, *Working Paper* 3 (University of
    Pennsylvania, Department of Regional Science).
House, P.W. (1977), *Trading Off Environment, Economics, and Energy* (Heath, Lexing-
    ton, MA).
Johansson, B., and U. Strömqvist (1982), Rigidities in the Process of Structural
    Economic Change, in *Regional Science and Urban Economics*, 11.
Leitner, H., and H. Wohlschägl (1980), Metrische und Ordinale Pfadanalyse, in
    Geografische Zeitschrift, 68(2), 61-106.
Mills, E.S. (1975), Planning and Market Processes in Urban Models, in R. Gieson
    (ed.), *Public and Urban Economics* (Heath, Lexington, MA).
Nicolis, G., and I. Prigogine (1977), *Self-Organization in Non-Equilibrium Systems*
    (Wiley, New York).
Nijkamp, P. (1981), Urban Impact Analysis: Methodology and Case Study, *Research
    Memorandum* 1981-2 (Free University, Department of Economics, Amsterdam).
Nijkamp, P. (1982), Soft Econometric Models: An Analysis of Regional Income Deter-
    minants, *Regional Studies*, 16(2), 121-128.
Nijkamp, P., and P. Rietveld (1982), Soft Econometrics as a Tool for Regional
    Discrepancy Analysis, *Papers of the Regional Science Association* (forthcoming).
Nijkamp, P., and J. Spronk (1982), Integrated Policy Analysis by Means of Interac-
    tive Learning Models, *Environment and Planning A* (forthcoming).
Rogers, A. (1981), Advances in Multiregional Demography, *IIASA Report* RR-81-6
    (International Institute for Applied Systems Analysis, Laxenburg, Austria).
Thom, R. (1975), *Structural Stability and Morphogenesis* (Benjamin, New York).
Treyz, G.I., and B.H. Stevens (1980), Location Analysis in Multiregional Modeling,
    in F.G. Adams and N.J. Glickman (eds.), *Modeling the Multiregional Economic
    System* (Heath, Lexington, MA), pp. 75-88.
Wold, H. (1975), Soft Modeling by Latent Variables, in J. Gassi (ed.), *Perspectives
    in Probability and Statistics* (Academic Press, London).
Wrigley, N. (1979), Development in the Statistical Analysis of Categorical Data,
    in *Progress in Human Geography*, 3, 315-355.

APPENDIX

A SURVEY OF MULTIREGIONAL ECONOMIC MODELS

Piet Rietveld

Models Included in the Survey

F.R.G.

1	General Information	
1.1	Model Name	IMPE: Interregional Multilevel Population-Employment Model for the F.R.G.
1.2	Model Builder	H. Birg.
1.3	Responsible Organization	German Institute for Economic Research, Berlin (West), F.R.G.
1.4	Publication	(1981) An Interregional Population-Employment Model for the Federal Republic of Germany: Methodology and Forecasting Results for the Year 2000, *Papers of the Regional Science Association*, vol. 47.
1.5	Development Stage	Operational since about 1980.
1.6	Period	Regional data are available from 1961 to 1970; national data are more up to date; the model is meant for the medium and long term: it yields predictions for 1990 with 1970 as the base period.

2	Model Purpose	
2.1	General Purpose	1. Forecasting studies. 2. Analytical studies. 3. Planning studies (*ex ante*).
2.2	Specific Purpose	Generation of reliable forecasts as a basis for investment decisions in the framework of interregional traffic planning.

3	Model Elements	
3.1	Model Size	Regions : 79 (the model also contains partitions into 11 and 2 regions).
		Sectors : 44.
		Exogenous variables : 766.
		Endogenous variables : 753.
		Equations (and inequalities): 2940.
3.2	Exogenous Variables	National: sectoral growth rates of production and employment; foreign migration; mortality rates.
		Regional: natural increase of the initial population stock; upper and lower boundaries for activity rates.
3.3	Endogenous Variables	National: population size, employment, activity rate, unemployment.
		Regional: population size, employment, activity rate, unemployment, in- and outmigration to other regions and countries, commuter balance, number of employees due to the regional share component of shift analysis.

4	Model structure	
4.1	Production Technology	The model does not contain an explicit production function or input-output relationships. Labor is the only production factor considered. The regional demand for labor is determined by means of exogenous national growth rates applied to employment in the base period plus a regional share component.

4.2	Interregional and International Trade	Not present.
4.3	Other Interregional Links	Much attention is paid to migration of labor. The explanatory variables for regional inmigration are the regional increase of jobs and regional outmigration (which can be considered as a proxy for vacant dwellings).
4.4	National-Regional Links	A top-down approach has been adopted for employment and foreign migration, while a bottom-up approach has been applied to variables such as activity rate, unemployment, and commuting.
4.5	Supply and Demand Considerations	Regional labor demand is only marginally influenced by labor supply while, on the other hand, regional labor supply is largely influenced by labor demand. Hence the model is mainly demand oriented.
4.6	Equilibrium Assumptions	On the labor market various processes of supply adjustment have been specified; inter-national and interregional migration, changes of activity rates, commuting. The number of vacancies is zero by definition. The number of unemployed is not necessarily equal to zero.
4.7	Treatment of Prices	Prices do not play a role in the model.
4.8	Dynamics	IMPE is dynamic.
4.9	Functional Forms	All relationships are linear (or have been linearized).
4.10	Solution Techniques	The model has been formulated as a linear programming model, the objective being the minimization of national unemployment. It appears that the set of feasible solutions is very small, which means that the outcomes of the model are rather insensitive for the choice of the objective function.
5	Estimation and Validation	
5.1	Estimation	Behavioral equations have been estimated by means of least squares; to arrive at a non-empty set of feasible solutions, some parameters had to be modified.
5.2	Validation	Econometric test criteria are fulfilled at satisfactory levels. The quality of predic-tions depends heavily on the correctness of the national exogenous variables.
6	Model Use	
6.1	Model Users	The model was designed for (and the results have been used by) the Federal Ministry for Traffic and Transportation.
6.2	Main Applications	Investment decisions for interregional roads and railways.
6.3	Documentation	Structure and limitations: available. User manual, testing data: available to a certain extent. How to replicate model : available.
7	Distinguishing Feature	Use of a programming model for prediction purposes.

F.R.G.

1	**General Information**	
1.1	Model Name	HESSEN: A multiperiod, multiregional, multisectoral decision model.
1.2	Model Builders	R. Thoss, M. Agnew, G. Bougioukos, G. Erdmann, A. Hermann, B. Spiekermann.
1.3	Responsible Organization	Sonderforschungsbereich 26, Raumordnung und Raumwirtschaft, Westfälische Wilhelms Universität, Münster, F.R.G.
1.4	Publication	Bougioukos, G., and G. Erdmann (1980), An Evaluation of Spatial Planning Objectives by Means of a Multiperiod, Multiregional and Multisectoral Decision Model--Presentation and Discussion of Certain Results for the State of Hessen (*Sonderforschungsbereich 26, Raumordnung und Raumwirtschaft, Münster*) Working Paper 28 (in German).
1.5	Development Stage	The model has been operational since about 1976.
1.6	Period	The model is based on data from 1960 to 1975.
2	**Model Purpose**	
2.1	General Purpose	1. Planning studies (*ex ante*). 2. Planning studies (*ex post*). 3. Analytical studies.
2.2	Specific Purpose	To calculate the opportunity costs of socioeconomic targets for regional development.
3	**Model Elements**	
3.1	Model Size	Regions : 6 (5 subregions of the state of Hessen and the rest of the F.R.G.).
		Sectors : 15.
		Exogenous variables : approx. 350.
		Endogenous variables : approx. 1150.
		Equations (inequalities): ≤1330.
3.2	Exogenous Variables	National: expenditures for public finance.
		Regional: population, forecasts (without migration), technical progress.
3.3	Endogenous Variables	National: production, imports, exports, private consumption, public consumption, private investments, public investments, population.
		Regional: *idem* (plus employment and financial transfers between national and regional authorities).
4	**Model Structure**	
4.1	Production Technology	Input-output. Production functions of the Cobb-Douglas type, with capital and labor (and land, in the case of agriculture) as production factors, have been estimated. In the model, a linearized version of the production function is employed.
4.2	Interregional and International Trade	Interregional and international trade are taken into account. For each region the volume of imports and exports to the aggregate of all other regions is determined.
4.3	Other Interregional Links	Interregional migration. (Interregional diffusion of pollution is included in one of the extensions of HESSEN.)

4.4	National-Regional Links	The model uses a bottom-up approach to almost all variables. A top-down approach is applied to the financial transfers between national and regional authorities.
4.5	Supply and Demand Considerations	Regional production is determined simultaneously with the regional supply of production factors and with regional final demand components. Hence, the model is characterized by a mixed supply and demand orientation.
4.6	Equilibrium Assumptions	On the labor and product markets, supply and demand are not necessarily equal.
4.7	Treatment of Prices	Prices are not included.
4.8	Dynamics	HESSEN is dynamic.
4.9	Functional Forms	The relationships are linear (nonlinear functions are linearized).
4.10	Solution Techniques	Linear programming.

5 Estimation and Validation

| 5.1 | Estimation | Coefficients have been estimated by means of OLS. |
| 5.2 | Validation | The model has been simulated for 1970-1985. Simulated growth rates of production volumes are clearly higher than realized growth rates. This is not surprising, since the model aims at describing the most desirable, rather than the most probable regional developments. |

6 Model Use

6.1	Model Users	The model has been used by a national and a regional planning authority, as well as by the model builders.
6.2	Main Applications	Determination of effects of transfers between national and regional authorities, evaluation of effects of infrastructure investments, analysis of consequences of technical change on regional policy targets.
6.3	Documentation	Structure and limitations: available. User manual, testing data: available to a certain extent. How to replicate model : available to a certain extent.

F.R.G.

1	General Information
1.1	Model Name	NRWF: Nordrhein-Westfalen Model.
1.2	Model Builder	C. Schönebeck.
1.3	Responsible Organization	Sonderforschungsbereich 26, Raumordnung und Raumwirtschaft, Westfälische Wilhelms Universität, Münster, F.R.G.
1.4	Publication	Schönebeck, C. (1982), Sectoral Change and Interregional Mobility: A Simulation Model of Regional Demoeconomic Development in North Rhine-Westphalia, *International Institute for Applied Systems Analysis, Laxenburg, Austria Collaborative Paper* CP-82-10.
1.5	Development Stage	The model has been operational since about 1979. A new version became operational in February 1982.
1.6	Period	The model is based on data of 1970. Employment data are of 1961 and 1970.

2	Model Purpose
2.1	General Purpose	1. Planning studies (*ex ante*). 2. Forecasting studies. 3. Planning studies (*ex post*).
2.2	Specific Purpose	Explanation and forecasting of regional development based on attractiveness differentials between regions. Computing the spatial consequences of economic/social/technical change. Computing the effects of public policies on regional development.

3	Model Elements
3.1	Model Size	
	Regions	: 34 labor market regions in North Rhine-Westphalia plus 13 external regions covering the rest of the Federal Republic, the Benelux states and some provinces of France. This model has been linked with a location model for the Dortmund region, consisting of 30 zones. For certain districts within zones land-use models have been developed.
	Sectors	: 40.
	Exogenous variables :	N.A.
	Endogenous variables:	N.A.
	Equations	: the model consists of approx. 4000 FORTRAN statements.
3.2	Exogenous Variables	National: sectoral growth rates of employment, in- and outmigration, fertility, labor force participation, unemployment, productivity, labor demand rates.
		Regional: —
3.3	Endogenous Variables	National: —
		Regional: population, labor force, employment, housing, infrastructure, migration, commuting.

| 4 | Model Structure |
| 4.1 | Production Technology | Exogenous forecasts of sectoral productivity are used. |

4.2	Interregional and International Trade	For each region sectoral input-output market potentials are calculated.
4.3	Other Interregional Links	Interregional migration and commuting have been modeled by means of the entropy model.
4.4	National-Regional Links	The model is top-down.
4.5	Supply and Demand Considerations	Supply and demand relations are modeled for the labor and the housing market.
4.6	Equilibrium Assumptions	Supply and demand are not necessarily equal on the labor and housing market.
4.7	Treatment of Prices	Prices do not play an explicit role in the model.
4.8	Dynamics	NRWF is dynamic.
4.9	Functional Forms	Various forms have been used.
4.10	Solution Techniques	Recursive simulation; simultaneous equations are solved numerically.
5	**Estimation and Validation**	
5.1	Estimation	The model has been estimated by means of OLS.
5.2	Validation	Simulations with the model have been compared with real world data of 1976 and 1979.
6	Model Use	
6.1	Model Users	The model has been used by the model builder.
6.2	Main Applications	N.A.
6.3	Documentation	Structure and limitations: available.
		User manual, testing data: N.A.
		How to replicate model : N.A.
7	Distinguishing Feature	The model performs the upper level of a hierarchical demoeconomic model with three spatial levels.

F.R.G.

	General Information	
1	**General Information**	
1.1	Model Name	MIO: Multiregional Input-Output Model.
1.2	Model Builder	M. Carlberg.
1.3	Responsible Organization	—
1.4	Publication	Carlberg, M. (1979), *A Multiregional Input-Output Forecasting Model: The Case of the Federal Republic of Germany* (Vandenhoeck, Göttingen) (in German).
1.5	Development Stage	Several model versions have been developed, but only the least elaborate one is operational (since 1979). The operational version should be considered as a pilot study.
1.6	Period	Data are mainly based on 1970. The model is meant for the medium term.
2	**Model Purpose**	
2.1	General Purpose	1. Analytical studies. 2. Forecasting studies. 3. Planning studies (*ex ante*).
2.2	Specific Purpose	Analysis of the effects of national and regional economic growth on interregional trade.
3	**Model Elements**	
3.1	Model Size	Regions : 6.
		Sectors : 12.
		Exogenous variables : N.A.
		Endogenous variables: N.A.
		Equations : N.A.
3.2	Exogenous Variables	National: national production, production by sector.
		Regional: production.
3.3	Endogenous Variables	National: —
		Regional: production by sector, interregional trade volumes.
4	**Model Structure**	
4.1	Production Technology	Input-output.
4.2	Interregional and International Trade	Interregional trade is modeled by means of a gravity model.
4.3	Other Interregional Links	None.
4.4	National-Regional Links	MIO has a top-down structure.
4.5	Supply and Demand Considerations	The production levels are determined without explicit references to supply or demand.
4.6	Equilibrium Assumptions	Disequilibria are not taken into account.
4.7	Treatment of Prices	Prices are not included.
4.8	Dynamics	MIO is dynamic.

| 4.9 | Functional Forms | The model contains linear relationships and several iterative bilinear algorithms of the RAS type. |
| 4.10 | Solution Techniques | RAS procedures are used to determine regional production per sector given total regional and total sectoral production volumes. |

5 Estimation and Validation

| 5.1 | Estimation | The gravity parameter of the interregional trade model has been estimated by means of OLS. |
| 5.2 | Validation | The model has been used to generate a prediction for 1980. An explicit confrontation with the actual development in 1980 has not been carried out. |

6 Model Use

6.1	Model Users	The model has been used by the model builder.
6.2	Main Applications	The model has been used to forecast regional development and interregional trade in 1980.
6.3	Documentation	Structure and limitations: available. User manual, testing data: available to a certain extent. How to replicate model : N.A.

NETHERLANDS

1	**General Information**	
1.1	Model Name	REM: Regional Economic Model.
1.2	Model Builders	B.A. van Hamel, H. Hetsen, J.H.M. Kok.
1.3	Responsible Organization	Central Planning Bureau, The Hague, Netherlands.
1.4	Publication	van Hamel, B.A., H. Hetsen, and J.H.M. Kok (1979), Un Modèle Economique Multirégional pour les Pays Bas, in R. Courbis (ed.), *Modèles Régionaux et Modèles Régionaux-Nationaux* (CUJAS, Paris), pp. 147-173.
1.5	Development Stage	REM has been operational since about 1974 but needs updating for use.
1.6	Period	Data are based on 1955-1967. REM is meant for the medium term.
2	**Model Purpose**	
2.1	General Purpose	1. Forecasting studies. 2. Planning studies (*ex ante*). 3. Planning studies (*ex post*).
2.2	Specific Purpose	To generate simultaneous medium-term forecasts of production, employment, labor supply, and unemployment for the Dutch provinces.
3	**Model Elements**	
3.1	Model Size	Regions : 11. Sectors : 7. Exogenous variables : 115. Endogenous variables: 765. Equations : 765.
3.2	Exogenous Variables	National: growth rates of employment and production per sector, labor supply, capital stock (industry). Regional: natural growth of labor supply.
3.3	Endogenous Variables	National: — Regional: production and employment per sector, labor supply (including migration), unemployment, investments.
4	**Model Structure**	
4.1	Production Technology	Cobb-Douglas production functions have been used for several sectors. The production factors are labor and capital.
4.2	Interregional and International Trade	Not included.
4.3	Other Interregional Links	Not included.
4.4	National-Regional Links	In its most recent version, REM is a pure top-down model. In an earlier version, REM was characterized by national-regional interrelations.

4.5	Supply and Demand Considerations	Regional production in the industrial sector is mainly determined by the supply side (capital formation). In the other sectors, regional production is mainly determined by demand.
4.6	Equilibrium Assumptions	Disequilibria occur on the labor market.
4.7	Treatment of Prices	Prices and wages are included. They play a role in substitution processes between capital and labor.
4.8	Dynamics	REM is dynamic.
4.9	Functional Forms	REM is linear.
4.10	Solution Techniques	Standard method to solve a system of linear equations.
5	Estimation and Validation	
5.1	Estimation	OLS, based on pooled cross sections.
5.2	Validation	Simulation runs have been carried out with REM. According to the model builders the validity is sufficient for an analysis of the 1960s and the beginning of the seventies.
6	Model Use	
6.1	Model Users	Central Planning Bureau
6.2	Main Applications	Generation of medium-term forecasts (1975-1980) and analysis of impacts of investment subsidies.
6.3	Documentation	Structure and limitations: available to a certain extent. User manual, testing data: N.A. How to replicate model : available to a certain extent.
7	Distinguishing Feature	Treatment of interrelations between demand and supply of labor.

NETHERLANDS

	General Information	
1	General Information	
1.1	Model Name	REGAM: Regional Labor Market Model.
1.2	Model Builders	W. Suyker, A. van Delft.
1.3	Responsible Organization	Central Planning Bureau, The Hague, Netherlands.
1.4	Publication	van Delft, A., and W. Suyker (1981), Regional Investment Subsidies: An Estimation of the Labor Market Effects for the Dutch Regions, *Paper presented at the 21st European Congress of the Regional Science Association, Barcelona, August.*
1.5	Development Stage	REGAM has been operational since 1981. It is an improved version of a former regional labor market model.
1.6	Period	Data are based on 1951-1980. REGAM is meant for the medium term.

2   Model Purpose

2.1   General Purpose   1. Forecasting studies. 2. Planning studies (*ex post*). Planning studies (*ex ante*).

2.2   Specific Purpose   REGAM has been built to generate forecasts of employment, labor supply, and unemployment for the Dutch provinces for 1980-1985.

3   Model Elements

3.1   Model Size

Regions   : 11.
Sectors   : 6.
Exogenous variables : 465.
Endogenous variables : 1410.
Equations   : 1410.

3.2   Exogenous Variables   National: growth rate of employment per sector; growth rate of labor supply.
Regional: natural growth of population and labor supply, attractiveness of natural scenery.

3.3   Endogenous Variables National: —
Regional: growth of employment per sector, growth rate of labor supply, net migration, rate of unemployment.

4   Model Structure

4.1   Production Technology   No explicit use is made of a production function.

4.2   Interregional and   No explicit attention is paid to interregional or international trade.
       International Trade

4.3   Other Interregional Links   The main explanatory variables of net interregional migration are the situation of the housing market and environmental quality. Labor market variables do not contribute to an explanation of interregional migration.

4.4   National-Regional Links   REGAM is a top-down model.

4.5	Supply and Demand Considerations	On the regional labor market, labor supply and demand are interdependent. Regional unemployment is an important variable in this interdependence: it influences regional labor supply and regional industrial labor demand.
4.6	Equilibrium Assumptions	Unemployment is a key variable in the model.
4.7	Treatment of Prices	Prices and wages are in general not included. The only exception is the variable of price reduction of investment as a result of investment subsidies.
4.8	Dynamics	REGAM is dynamic.
4.9	Functional Forms	REGAM is linear.
4.10	Solution Techniques	A standard approach to solve a system of linear equations can be used.
5	Estimation and Validation	
5.1	Estimation	A weighted least-squares estimation on pooled cross section data has been carried out.
5.2	Validation	The validity of the model has been tested (not published). According to the model builders the validity is satisfactory.
6	Model Use	
6.1	Model Users	Central Planning Bureau.
6.2	Main Applications	Forecasts of the development of regional labor markets for 1980-1985. An analysis of the impacts of investment subsidies.
6.3	Documentation	Structure and limitations: available to a certain extent. User Manual, testing data: N.A. How to replicate model : available to a certain extent.
7	Distinguishing Feature	Treatment of interrelations between demand and supply of labor.

NETHERLANDS

1	**General Information**	
1.1	Model Name	MEEEI: Interregional Policy Model for Energy-Economic-Environmental Interactions.
1.2	Model Builders	F. Muller, P.J.J. Lesuis.
1.3	Responsible Organization	Erasmus University, Rotterdam, Netherlands.
1.4	Publication	Lesuis, P., F. Muller, and P. Nijkamp (1980), An Interregional Policy Model for Energy-Economic-Environmental Interactions, *Regional Science and Urban Economics*, 10, 343-370.
1.5	Development Stage	The model has been operational since about 1972. It is in a continuous process of updating and revision.
1.6	Period	The model is based on data from 1970. It is meant for use in the short, medium, and long terms.
2	**Model Purpose**	
2.1	General Purpose	1. Planning studies (*ex ante*). 2/3. Analytical studies, forecasting studies.
2.2	Specific Purpose	Study of interactions between energy, environment, and the economy.
3	**Model Elements**	
3.1	Model Size	Regions : 2 (the central provinces of the Netherlands versus the rest of the country).
		Sectors : 11.
		Exogenous variables : approx. 60.
		Endogenous variables : approx. 40.
		Equations (inequalities): approx. 50.
3.2	Exogenous Variables	National: —
		Regional: exports abroad, constraints on production, employment, energy consumption, pollution.
3.3	Endogenous Variables	National: —
		Regional: production, employment, energy consumption, pollution, final demand.
4	**Model Structure**	
4.1	Production Technology	Input-output. A production function with fixed technical coefficients has been assumed for the production factors labor and energy.
4.2	Interregional and International Trade	Competing imports originated from the other region are allocated to the regional sector, importing a fixed ratio of total demand for its products (this implies the absence of crosshauling).
4.3	Other Interregional Links	None.
4.4	National-Regional Links	The model has a bottom-up structure.

4.5 Supply and Demand Considerations	Model outcomes depend on demand variables (exports abroad) as well as on supply variables (restrictions on the availability of materials, labor, and energy).
4.6 Equilibrium Assumptions	For all products, demand and supply are equal. On the labor market, excess supply may exist.
4.7 Treatment of Prices	In the model a submodel is included to deal with substitution effects on the production technology due to (exogenous) price changes. The approach in the submodel is based on regional translog price possibility frontiers. Due to weaknesses in the database, the outcomes of the submodel only have a preliminary character.
4.8 Dynamics	MEEEI is static.
4.9 Functional Forms	In the main model, the functional forms are linear. In the submodel they are log-linear.
4.10 Solution Technologies	The model is formulated as a multiobjective programming model with objectives related to employment, energy use, and pollution.
5 Estimation and Validation	
5.1 Estimation	Coefficients in the main model have been obtained by one-point estimates.
5.2 Validation	A validation has not been carried out.
6 Model Use	
6.1 Model Users	The model has been used by a national and a regional governmental agency, as well as at the university.
6.2 Main Applications	Analysis of the interrelations between economic development, air pollution, and energy consumption.
6.3 Documentation	Structure and limitations: available. User manual, testing data: available to a certain extent. How to replicate model : available to a certain extent.
7 Distinguishing Features	Inclusion of energy and pollution. Study of substitution processes in input-output context.

NETHERLANDS

1	General Information	
1.1	Model Name	TLM: Triple Layer Model.
1.2	Model Builder	W.A. Hafkamp.
1.3	Responsible Organization	Department of Economic Statistics, University of Amsterdam, Netherlands.
1.4	Publications	Hafkamp, W.A., and P. Nijkamp (1979), Dilemmas in Environmental Economics, *Canadian Journal of Regional Science*, II(2), 1-22.
		Hafkamp, W.A., and P. Nijkamp (1982), National-Regional Interdependencies in Economic-Environmental-Energy Models, in T.R. Lakshmanan and P. Nijkamp (eds.), *Systems and Models for Energy and Environmental Analysis* (Gower, Aldershot) (forthcoming).
1.5	Development Stage	TLM has been operational from 1982.
1.6	Period	Data are from 1955-1975. The model is meant for the short and medium terms.

2	Model Purpose	
2.1	General Purpose	1. Analytical studies. 2. Educational purposes. 3. Policy planning.
2.2	Specific Purpose	The model simultaneously analyzes the effects of economic, environmental, and energy policy on the economy, the environment, and energy use in a multiregional spatial system. It is used to simulate multidecision makers in their multiobjective decision making procedures.

3	Model Elements	
3.1	Model Size	Regions : 5.
		Sectors : 23.
		Exogenous variables : approx. 90.
		Endogenous variables: 600-2000, dependent on version.
		Equations : 500-1800, dependent on version.
3.2	Exogenous Variables	National: volume of world trade, import prices, exports.
		Regional: labor supply.
3.3	Endogenous Variables	National: (non-)wage income, prices, creation of money, interest rate, imports, consumption (households, government), investments (firms, government), taxes, production capacity.
		Regional: production, final demand categories, labor demand, energy use, emissions of pollutants.

4	Model Structure	
4.1	Production Technology	Production functions include inputs of raw materials, fuels, and intermediary products under capital stock, energy use, and labor demand restrictions.

4.2	Interregional and International Trade	There are no interregional links within the model because of insufficient data on interregional flows of goods and services. International trade is analyzed extensively; there are competitive and noncompetitive imports; some exports are endogenous in the model.
4.3	Other Interregional Links	None.
4.4	National-Regional Links	Labor demand, energy demand, gross production, and total emissions of pollutants are found through aggregation of regional variables. Final demand variables are disaggregated from 4 to 23 sectors through fixed coefficients.
4.5	Supply and Demand Considerations	Price adjustment processes equal supply and demand on commodity markets.
4.6	Equilibrium	Labor supply and demand are not necessarily equal. Deficits on trade account and capital account exist.
4.7	Treatment of Prices	All prices are dependent on exogenous import prices, exogenous world market prices, occupation rate of capital stock, labor market tensions, and tax variables.
4.8	Dynamics	TLM is dynamic.
4.9	Functional Forms	All relations are linear(ized) functions.
4.10	Solution Techniques	The model is solved as a linear programing problem on Apex III.
5	Estimation and Validation	
5.1	Estimation	Relations are estimated through regression analysis, taken from other models, or established as input-output functions.
5.2	Validation	Since the model is not yet completed, general performance over a longer period has not yet been examined. The national part of the model has already been separately in use since 1979 for macroeconomic studies of economic policy in the Netherlands. The regional part of the model is of the input-output type, which is generally acknowledged as a valid form.
6	Model Use	N.A.
7	Distinguishing Features	The model has been built in three stages: first, a simple "common sense" model was constructed; second, a conceptual model was derived (formal, but not quantitative); third, an operational model (TLM) was derived by quantifying the model in the previous stage.
		The model has been built from a perspective of conflicting interests in society. Three layers of the model represent three main objectives of government policy: income, employment, and environmental quality.
		The national part of the model is characterized by a dynamic structure in which the the occupation rate of capital stock plays an important role. Investments are dealt with extensively, as well as the role of the government and of the public sector in general.

BELGIUM

1   General Information
1.1   Model Name   RENA: Regional National Model.
1.2   Model Builders   F. Thys-Clement, P. van Rompuy, L. de Corel.
1.3   Responsible Organization   Belgian Planning Office, Brussels, Belgium.
1.4   Publication   Thijs, F., and P. van Rompuy (1979), RENA, Regional Model for Belgium, in R. Courbis
                                      (ed.), *Modèles Régionaux et Modèles Régionaux-Nationaux* (CUJAS, Paris), pp. 103-122.
1.5   Development Stage   RENA has been operational since 1973.
1.6   Period   The main data are based on 1963-1970.   RENA is meant for the medium term.

2   Model Purpose
2.1   General Purpose   1. Educational purposes. 2. Analytical studies. 3. Forecasting studies.
2.2   Specific Purpose   An instrument in the framework of the 5-year national regional economic plans, espe-
                                      cially for the period 1976-1980.

3   Model Elements
3.1   Model Size   Regions   : 3.
                                      Sectors   : 1.
                                      Exogenous variables : 96.
                                      Endogenous variables: 160.
                                      Equations   : 160.

3.2   Exogenous Variables   National: money supply, government consumption, import prices, world export prices,
                                                 discount rate, social security contributions and transfers.
                                      Regional: population, subsidies, government investment, structural unemployment.
3.3   Endogenous Variables   National: imports, exports, consumption, investments, GNP, tax receipts, profits,
                                                 output, factor prices.
                                      Regional: activity rates, user cost of capital, wages, investment, structural unem-
                                                 ployment.

4   Model Structure
4.1   Production Technology   Production depends on employment and the capital stock.
4.2   Interregional and   International trade is specified in RENA. Much attention is paid to the role of
        International Trade   prices in determining the volume of exports and imports.
4.3   Other Interregional Links   Commuting is taken into account.
4.4   National-Regional Links   The model contains interactions between the national and regional levels. A top-down
                                      approach is applied to regional production. For employment, unemployment, investment,
                                      and wages a bottom-up approach has been adopted.
4.5   Supply and Demand   Regional production is mainly determined by variables from the demand side.
        Considerations

4.6	Equilibrium Assumptions	On the money market, supply and demand are equal by assumption. On the goods market, equilibrium is attained by price adjustments. On the labor market disequilibrium may occur.
4.7	Treatment of Prices	Wages and prices play an important role in the regional investment function.
4.8	Dynamics	RENA is dynamic.
4.9	Functional Forms	Linear and log-linear forms occur.
4.10	Solution Techniques	RENA can be solved by the Gauss-Seidel procedure, after presenting the model in a pseudorecursive form.
5	Estimation and Validation	
5.1	Estimation	RENA has been estimated by means of OLS, two-stage least squares, and restricted least squares.
5.2	Validation	Static and dynamic simulations have been carried out with RENA. The validity of RENA seems satisfactory.
6	Model Use	
6.1	Model Users	The model has been used by the Belgian Planning Office and by the model builders.
6.2	Main Applications	Evaluation of policy measures (subsidies, government investment) for the Belgian Plan 1976-1980.
6.3	Documentation	Structure and limitations: available. User manual, testing data: available to a certain extent. How to replicate model : N.A.
7	Distinguishing Feature	RENA was one of the first operational national-regional models.

BELGIUM

1　General Information

1.1　Model Name — SERENA: Sectoral-Regional Model.

1.2　Model Builders — G. d'Alcantara, J. Floridor, E. Pollefliet.

1.3　Responsible Organization — Belgian Planning Bureau, Brussels, Belgium.

1.4　Publication — d'Alcantara, G., J. Floridor, and E. Pollefliet (1980), *Major Features of the SERENA Model for the Belgian Plan* (Planning Bureau, Brussels).

1.5　Development Stage — SERENA has been operational since 1980.

1.6　Period — SERENA is based on data from 1960 to 1978. It is meant for the medium term.

2　Model Purpose

2.1　General Purpose — 1. Planning studies (*ex ante*). 2. Forecasting studies. 3. Analytical studies.

2.2　Specific Purpose — Prepare the options of the Belgian Plan 1981-1985.

3　Model Elements

3.1　Model Size —
Regions　　　　　　　　　: 3.
Sectors　　　　　　　　　: 7.
Exogenous variables : 75.
Endogenous variables: 800.
Equations　　　　　　　　: 800.

3.2　Exogenous Variables — National: fiscal and parafiscal rates, exchange rate, conventional working time. Regional: population, commuting, employment, investments in public administration.

3.3　Endogenous Variables — National: the complete national accounts, prices, labor supply. Regional: employment, investments, value added (per sector), labor supply, unemployment.

4　Model Structure

4.1　Production Technology — Input-output; "putty-clay".

4.2　Interregional and International Trade — Attention is paid to international trade. Import volumes are, among other items, functions of relative prices. In certain sectors export volumes are determined by foreign demand, in other sectors by profitability conditions given the prices on the world market.

4.3　Other Interregional Links — Some attention is paid to commuting.

4.4　National-Regional Links — A bottom-up approach is adopted for the variables specified at the regional level.

4.5　Supply and Demand Considerations — In most markets the production volumes are determined by variables from the demand side.

4.6　Equilibrium Assumptions — Prices play an important role in determining equilibrium on the markets.

4.7　Treatment of Prices — For all components of demand the corresponding price has been included. Prices play a role, among other items, in the decision to replace production vintages.

4.8	Dynamics	SERENA is dynamic.
4.9	Functional Forms	N.A.
4.10	Solution Techniques	N.A.
5	Estimation and Validation	N.A.
6	Model Use	
6.1	Model Users	SERENA is used by the Belgian Planning Bureau as an official tool for the 1981-1985 Belgian Plan.
6.2	Main Applications	Preparation of the Belgian Plan.
6.3	Documentation	Structure and limitations: available. User manual, testing data: available to a certain extent. How to replicate model : available to a certain extent.
7	Distinguishing Feature	The use of production vintages.

BELGIUM

1	General Information	
1.1	Model Name	MACEDOINE II.
1.2	Model Builders	M. Despontin, H. Glejser.
1.3	Responsible Organization	Free University, Brussels, Belgium.
1.4	Publication	Glejser, H., G. van Daele, and M. Lambrecht (1973), The First Experiments with an Econometric Regional Model of the Belgian Economy, *Regional Science and Urban Economics*, 3, 301-314.
1.5	Development Stage	An earlier version of the model was operational in 1973. Since then the model has been revised and updated.
1.6	Period	The coefficients of the model are based on data from 1959 to 1976. The model is meant for the short and medium terms.

2	Model Purpose	
2.1	General Purpose	1. Planning studies (*ex ante*). 2. Forecasting studies. 3. Planning studies (*ex post*).
2.2	Specific Purpose	Explanation of regional variables by mechanisms on the regional level and not as a disaggregation of national data.

3	Model Elements		
3.1	Model Size	Regions	: 9.
		Sectors	: 1.
		Exogenous variables	: 30.
		Endogenous variables:	63.
		Equations	: 63 (behavioral equations).
3.2	Exogenous Variables	National:	import prices, labor immigration.
		Regional:	gross investments, producer prices, nonwage employment.
3.3	Endogenous Variables	National:	—
		Regional:	gross regional product, employment, labor immigration, unemployment, wages, consumer prices, capital stock.

4	Model Structure	
4.1	Production Technology	A regional production function of the Cobb-Douglas type is used with labor and capital as production factors. In the production function cyclical movements of the national economy and technical development are taken into account.
4.2	Interregional and International Trade	No attention is paid to interregional trade.
4.3	Other Interregional Links	The regional level of unemployment is, among other items, explained by the levels of employment, unemployment and nonwage employment in contiguous regions.

4.4	National-Regional Links	The only exogenous variables at the national level are import prices and labor immigration. Hence MACEDOINE II is very much characterized by a bottom-up approach.
4.5	Supply and Demand Considerations	In the model, the volumes of production and employment are determined simultaneously. Hence, the model is characterized by supply and demand interactions.
4.6	Equilibrium Assumptions	Supply and demand of goods are equal by assumption. On the labor market unemployment may exist.
4.7	Treatment of Prices	Regional wages and consumer prices are endogenous.
4.8	Dynamics	MACEDOINE II is dynamic.
4.9	Functional Forms	The model consists of nonlinear relationships of various forms.
4.10	Solution Techniques	The model is solved by means of the Gauss-Seidel algorithm. In a linearized form it has been used for a series of multiobjective programming experiments.
5	Estimation and Validation	
5.1	Estimation	The coefficients have been estimated by means of OLS and variance components analysis for pooling cross sections and time series.
5.2	Validation	MACEDOINE II has been used to forecast variables in the years 1980-1981. The results are encouraging, according to the authors.
6	Model Use	
6.1	Model Users	The model has been used by the model builders.
6.2	Main Applications	Quantitative economic policy simulations in a multiobjective framework.
6.3	Documentation	Structure and limitations: available. User manual, testing data: available. How to replicate model : available.
7	Distinguishing Features	Application of an econometric model in a mathematical programming context. Modeling of links between contiguous regions.

BELGIUM

1	**General Information**	
1.1	Model Name	BREIN: Belgian Regional and Interregional Analytical Model.
1.2	Model Builders	W.K. Brauers, J. van Waterschoot, P. van Elewijck.
1.3	Responsible Organization	Centrum voor Economische Studiën, University of Louvain, Belgium.
1.4	Publication	Brauers, W.K. (1980), *The Belgian Experience in Interregional Input-Output Tables* Centrum voor Economische Studiën, University of Louvain).
1.5	Development Stage	Operational since 1973.
1.6	Period	An interregional input-output table is available for 1958, 1965, 1970, and 1976. The model is meant for the short term.
2	**Model Purpose**	
2.1	General Purpose	1. Analytical studies. 2. Planning studies (*ex post*). 3. Planning studies (*ex ante*).
2.2	Specific Purpose	To obtain insight into the regional economic structure (regions fixed by law) of Belgium to improve policy formulations.
3	**Model Elements**	
3.1	Model Size	Regions. : 3.
		Sectors : between 46 and 62.
		Exogenous variables : N.A.
		Endogenous variables: between 138 and 186.
		Equations : between 138 and 186.
3.2	Exogenous Variables	National: final demand.
		Regional: final demand.
3.3	Endogenous Variables	National: sectoral production.
		Regional: sectoral production.
4	**Model Structure**	
4.1	Production Technology	Input-output.
4.2	Interregional and International Trade	Interregional and international trade have been modeled explicitly by means of trade coefficients.
4.3	Other Interregional Links	Daily commuting in physical and monetary terms; financial flows.
4.4	National-Regional Links	The model has a top-down structure. Regional value added; production and imports are determined by means of a disaggregation of the corresponding national variables.
4.5	Supply and Demand Considerations	The model is demand driven.
4.6	Equilibrium Assumptions	Demand and supply of goods are not necessarily equal: they may differ because of inventory formation.
4.7	Treatment of Prices	Prices do not play an explicit role.

4.8	Dynamics	BREIN is static.
4.9	Functional Forms	BREIN is linear.
4.10	Solution Techniques	Standard.
5	Estimation and Validation	
5.1	Estimation	Input-output and trade coefficients are based partly directly on statistical data and partly on various data manipulation methods.
5.2	Validation	According to the model builders, BREIN provides insight into the structure of sectors and regions.
6	Model Use	
6.1	Model Users	BREIN was designed for the National Fund for Scientific Research and the Ministry of Economic Affairs. It has been used by a national governmental agency, a private organization, and a university.
6.2	Main Applications	The effects of taxes and government expenditures on the regions.
6.3	Documentation	Structure and limitations: available. User manual, testing data: available to a certain extent. How to replicate model : available.

BELGIUM

1	General Information	
1.1	Model Name	KIM: Short-Term Interregional Model for Belgium.
1.2	Model Builders	W.K. Brauers, J. van Waterschoot, P. van Elewijck, P. Mwebesa.
1.3	Responsible Organizations	Centrum voor Economische Studiën, University of Louvain, Belgium; RUCA, Faculty of Applied Economics, University of Antwerp, Belgium.
1.4	Publication	A first version of the model is operational but publications are not yet available for the general public.
1.5	Development Stage	
1.6	Period	The main national data are from 1952-1977. The main regional data are from 1966-1977. The model is meant for the short term.
2	Model Purpose	
2.1	General Purpose	1. Forecasting studies. 2. Planning studies (*ex ante*). 3. Planning studies (*ex post*).
2.2	Specific Purpose	To give assistance to regional economic policy makers.
3	Model Elements	
3.1	Model Size	Regions. : 3.
		Sectors : 20.
		Exogenous variables : 67.
		Endogenous variables: 124.
		Equations : 124.
3.2	Exogenous Variables	National: final demand, capital formation, employment, imports, time, dummy variables (general).
		Regional: employment, investment, dummy variables for certain sectors and time.
3.3	Endogenous Variables	National: production and value added per sector.
		Regional: production and value added per sector.
4	Model Structure	
4.1	Production Technology	Input-output.
4.2	Interregional and International Trade	Interregional and international trade have been modeled explicitly by means of trade coefficients, corrected over time with Bacharach marginal data.
4.3	Other Interregional Links	Daily commuting in physical and monetary terms.
4.4	National-Regional Links	KIM has a top-down structure. Regional value added; production and imports are determined by means of a disaggregation of national variables.
4.5	Supply and Demand Considerations	KIM is demand driven.
4.6	Equilibrium Assumptions	The supply of goods is equal to demand, by assumption.
4.7	Treatment of Prices	Prices do not play an explicit role.

4.8	Dynamics	KIM is dynamic: it contains lagged explanatory variables and dummy variables in order to incorporate trend breaks.
4.9	Functional Forms	The relationships are linear and log-linear.
4.10	Solution Techniques	Standard.
5	Estimation and Validation	
5.1	Estimation	Coefficients have been estimated, among other items, by means of OLS.
5.2	Validation	N.A.
6	Model Use	
6.1	Model User	National Government: Ministry of Economic Affairs.
6.2	Main Applications	N.A.
6.3	Documentation	N.A.

FRANCE

1		General Information
1.1	Model Name	REGINA: Regional-National Model.
1.2	Model Builders	R. Courbis, J. Bourdon, G. Cornilleau, C. le Van, with contributions from C. Pommier and F. Bourdon.
1.3	Responsible Organization	Groupe d'Analyse Macroéconomique Appliquée, University of Paris X, Nanterre, France.
1.4	Publication	Courbis, R. (1979), The REGINA Model, a Regional-National Model for French Planning, *Regional Science and Urban Economics*, 9, 117-139.
1.5	Development Stage	REGINA has been operational since about 1974.
1.6	Period	REGINA is based on national data from 1959-1975, regional data from about 1962 to 1972 or 1976, and on interregional and multiregional input-output tables from 1969-1970. REGINA is meant for the medium term.
1.7	Related Models	A simplified version of REGINA has been designed: REGIS (Regionalized Simulation Model). Built in 1976-1977, it has been used for experimentation and comparisons. A new version (with 7 regions) is under construction.

2		Model Purpose
2.1	General Purpose	1. Analytical studies. 2. Planning studies (*ex ante*).
2.2	Specific Purpose	Analysis of the interdependence between national and regional development; in particular, analysis of regional impacts of national development and policies, and of national impacts of regional policies and disequilibria.

3		Model Elements
3.1	Model Size	Regions : 5 (with a breakdown of each region in 3 areas in terms of urbanization)
		Sectors : 18 (10 production sectors and 8 service sectors).
		Exogenous variables : N.A.
		Endogenous variables : approx. 8000.
		Equations : approx. 8000.
3.2	Exogenous Variables	National: demographic, variables from foreign countries, national policy instruments. Regional: production and prices of agriculture, natural rate of population growth.
3.3	Endogenous Variables	National: production, demand, consumption, investment, employment, unemployment, wages, prices, income distribution, foreign trade, and more generally the complete national accounts. Regional: employment, unemployment, migration, wages, income distribution, production, investments, capital stock, consumption, public demand, residential investments, interregional trade.

4		Model Structure
4.1	Production Technology	Input-output. Production functions are used with labor and capital as production factors.
4.2	Interregional and International Trade	Interregional trade is modeled by means of interregional input-output analysis and has an impact on transportation costs by industry and region.
4.3	Other Interregional Links	Interregional migration (depends, among other things, on wage differentials and job

4.4 National-Regional Links

creation). Interregional wage linkages (wage increases in peripheral regions depend, among other things, on wage increases in the core region). For almost all variables a bottom-up approach has been adopted. A top-down approach is applied to foreign trade, distribution of profits and investments of state government and free-located industries. The national volume of investments in free-located industries (the manufacturing sector) is distributed among regions according to the regional investment opportunities.

4.5 Supply and Demand Considerations

Certain industries (free-located industries) are supply driven. In these industries regional production is determined by the regional stock of capital. Other industries are demand driven: regional production levels are determined by regional demand.

4.6 Equilibrium Assumptions

In certain sectors, regional supply and demand are equal by assumption. In other sectors regional supply and demand are equal by price adjustment. In yet other sectors equilibrium is attained at the national level by foreign trade. On the labor market, supply and demand are not necessarily equal.

4.7 Treatment of Prices

Wages and prices play an important role in REGINA. The dynamics of regional wages are especially crucial.

4.8 Dynamics

REGINA is semistatic (quasidynamic with a regular path). REGIS will be dynamic.

4.9 Functional Forms

Several forms occur in REGINA.

4.10 Solution Techniques

Numerical methods for solving a system of nonlinear equations.

5 Estimation and Validation

5.1 Estimation

Coefficients have mainly been estimated by means of OLS. In some cases nonlinear estimation procedures or two-stage least-squares methods have been adopted.

5.2 Validation

To a certain extent comparisons between forecasts and results have been made. The validity is--according to the builders--sufficient for projections of main figures and quite interesting for impact studies.

6 Model Use

6.1 Model Users

The model has been used by the French Planning Office, the regional policy governmental agency, several ministries, and the model builders.

6.2 Main Applications

Regional impacts of national scenarios of the French Plan. National impacts of regional policies concerning public and private investments and social security rates. National and regional impacts of large regional projects such as investments in the steel industry, coal mining, tourism.

6.3 Documentation

Structure and limitations: available. User manual, testing data: available to a certain extent. How to replicate model : available to a certain extent.

7 Distinguishing Features

REGINA was one of the first operational integrated regional-national models. The distinction between supply and demand driven industries. The interregional dynamics of wages. Different levels of spatial analysis (national-regional-zonal).

ITALY

1	General Information	
1.1	Model Name	RNEM: Regional-National Econometric Model of Italy.
1.2	Model Builders	S. Arora, M. Brown, M. di Palma, B. Ferrara, T. Furagori, M.J. Hartley, S. Kim.
1.3	Responsible Organizations	State University of New York at Buffalo, U.S.A.; Centre di Studi e Piani Economici, Rome, Italy.
1.4	Publication	Brown, M., M. di Palma, and B. Ferrara (1978), *Regional-National Econometric Modeling* (Pion, London).
1.5	Development Stage	The model consists of series of operational submodels (for migration, prices, labor markets, etc.). The model as a whole is not operational. The submodels were developed around 1972-1973.
1.6	Period	The main data are based on the period 1951-1968. The model is meant for the medium term.

2	Model Purpose	
2.1	General Purpose	1. Planning studies (*ex ante*). 2. Planning studies (*ex post*). 3. Forecasting studies.
2.2	Specific Purpose	To explain the formation, use, and distribution of the components of value added.

3	Model Elements	
3.1	Model Size	Regions : 19.
		Sectors : 6.
		Exogenous variables : approx. 130.
		Endogenous variables: 737.
		Equations :. 737.
3.2	Exogenous Variables	National: interest rate, prices, net imports, government consumption, investments (in one version of the model).
		Regional: government consumption, investments (in one version of the model).
3.3	Endogenous Variables	National: production, consumption, employment, unemployment, taxes, population, wages.
		Regional: production, consumption, employment, unemployment, taxes, population, net imports, prices, wages.

4	Model Structure	
4.1	Production Technology	Factor demand functions are based on Cobb-Douglas and CES production functions with labor and capital as production factors.
4.2	Interregional and International Trade	Interregional and international trade are dealt with implicitly by means of net imports per region that are explained, among other things, by the regional price level relative to the national price level.
4.3	Other Interregional Links	Interregional migration is explained, among other things, by income and urbanization variables.

4.4	National-Regional Links	A bottom-up approach is used for the majority of endogenous variables.
4.5	Supply and Demand Considerations	The model is characterized by supply and demand interactions on the labor and commodity markets.
4.6	Equilibrium Assumptions	Equilibrium exists on the commodity market by price adjustments. On the labor market the existence of unemployment is taken into account.
4.7	Treatment of Prices	Regional prices and wages are endogenous. They give rise to adjustment processes on commodity and labor markets.
4.8	Dynamics	RNEM is dynamic.
4.9	Functional Forms	Linear, log-linear, CES, S-branch.
4.10	Solution Techniques	Most of the submodels have a recursive structure so that the endogenous variables can be found directly.
5	Estimation and Validation	
5.1	Estimation	The following procedures have been applied: OLS, maximum likelihood, Cochrane-Orcutt adjustment, Almon distributed lags, generalized F-analysis.
5.2	Validation	The model as a whole has not been validated.
6	Model Use	
6.1	Model User	The model has been used by the model builders.
6.2	Main Applications	Analysis of the effects of rising energy prices on regional income per worker.
6.3	Documentation	Structure and limitations: available. User manual, testing data: N.A. How to replicate model : available.
7	Distinguishing Feature	This is one of the earliest models with extensive use of bottom-up approaches.

ITALY

1	General Information	
1.1	Model Name	NORD-SUD.
1.2	Model Builder	D. Martellato.
1.3	Responsible Organization	University of Venice, Italy.
1.4	Publications	Martellato, D. (1981), Structural Analysis with an Updated Input-Output Table for Italy 1977, *Ricerche Economiche*, no. 1. Martellato, D. (1981), Consistency and Feasibility in the North-South Model for Italy, *Paper presented at the Structural Economic Analysis and Planning in Time and Space Conference*, Umeå, June.
1.5	Development Stage	The model is still in a development phase, especially as regards regional breakdown.
1.6	Period	The model is based on data from 1969-1977. It is meant for the medium term.
1.7	Related Models	Two other biregional models are being built with a similar approach: VERDI (the Venice region with the Rest of Italy, for 1972, 44 sectors) and TIM (Tuscany-Rest of Italy, for 1975, 31 sectors).
2	Model Purpose	
2.1	General Purpose	1. Analytical studies. 2. Forecasting studies.
2.2	Specific Purpose	The study of dualistic growth phenomena in Italy, and regional impact analysis.
3	Model Elements	
3.1	Model Size	Regions : 2 (the North and the South of Italy). Sectors : 35. Exogenous variables : 70 × 4 final demand components. Endogenous variables: 70 × 3. Equations National: — Regional: final demand.
3.2	Exogenous Variables	
3.3	Endogenous Variables	National: — Regional: production, interregional trade, employment.
4	Model Structure	
4.1	Production Technology	Input-output.
4.2	Interregional and International Trade	For all industries the possibility of interregional trade is taken into account. All sectors of destination within a region are assumed to have the same pattern of imports.
4.3	Other Interregional Links	None.
4.4	National-Regional Links	If the national level is to be made explicit, a top-down approach would be applied to final demand, and a bottom-up approach would be used for the other variables.

4.5	Supply and Demand Considerations	Regional production is exclusively determined by final demand.
4.6	Equilibrium Assumptions	The supply and demand of goods are assumed to be equal.
4.7	Treatment of Prices	Prices do not play a role in the model.
4.8	Dynamics	NORD-SUD is static.
4.9	Functional Forms	NORD-SUD is linear.
4.10	Solution Techniques	Usual methods of solving a system of linear equations.
5	Estimation and Validation	
5.1	Estimation	The input-output and trade coefficients have been constructed by means of usual survey and indirect techniques.
5.2	Validation	The validity of the model has not been tested.
6	Model Use	
6.1	Model Users	The model is used by the model builder, while the related models VERDI and TIM are used by regional planning agencies.
6.2	Main Applications	Analysis of economic integration between North and South in Italy; regional economic impact analysis.
6.3	Documentation	Structure and limitations: available. User manual, testing data: available to a certain extent. How to replicate model : available in Venice for NORD-SUD and VERDI models, available at IIASA for TIM.
7	Distinguishing Features	A version with endogenous investment, shifting trading pattern, shifting technology coefficients and capacity constraints is planned for NORD-SUD. Versions of VERDI and TIM with a new database are also in progress.

U.K.

1   General Information

1.1   Model Name   IIOM: Interregional Input-Output Model for the United Kingdom.

1.2   Model Builder   I. Gordon.

1.3   Responsible Organization   Urban and Regional Studies Unit, University of Kent, Canterbury, U.K.

1.4   Publication   Gordon, I.R. (1977), Regional Interdependence in the U.K. Economy, in W. Leontief (ed.), *Structure, System and Economic Policy* (Cambridge University Press, Cambridge).

1.5   Development Stage   The model has been operational since about 1977.

1.6   Period   The base year of the interregional input-output relationships is 1963. The model is meant for the medium term.

2   Model Purpose

2.1   General Purpose   1. Analytical studies. 2. Forecasting studies. 3. Planning studies (*ex ante*).

2.2   Specific Purpose   To understand and predict some of the broader trends in regional growth performance.

3   Model Elements

3.1   Model Size

Regions : 11.
Sectors : 40 (households are one of the sectors).
Exogenous variables : N.A.
Endogenous variables: 440.
Equations : 440.

3.2   Exogenous Variables   National: exports and investment by sector.
Regional: exports and investment by sector.

3.3   Endogenous Variables   National: gross output and employment income by sector.
Regional: gross output and employment income by sector.

4   Model Structure

4.1   Production Technology   Input-output.

4.2   Interregional and International Trade   Regional trade coefficients are independent of the identity of the purchasing sector. The trade coefficients have been estimated by means of a gravity model.

4.3   Other Interregional Links   Commuting is taken into account because households form one of the sectors.

4.4   National-Regional Links   All endogenous national variables are obtained as the sum of the corresponding regional variables.

4.5   Supply and Demand Considerations   The model is demand driven.

4.6   Equilibrium Assumptions   On the commodity markets supply and demand are equal, by assumption.

4.7   Treatment of Prices   Regional price differences play a role in the construction of the input-output coefficients of some sectors.

4.8   Dynamics   IIOM is static.

4.9	Functional Forms	IIOM is linear.
4.10	Solution Techniques	Usual methods of solving a system of linear equations.
5	Estimation and Validation	
5.1	Estimation	Input-output coefficients are in most cases straightforward proportions of base-year data. Trade coefficients have been estimated via a gravity model.
5.2	Validation	The validity has not been tested.
6	Model Use	
6.1	Model Users	The model has been used by the model builder.
6.2	Main Applications	N.A.
6.3	Documentation	Structure and limitations: available to a certain extent. User manual, testing data: N.A. How to replicate model : available to a certain extent.

U.K.

1 General Information

1.1 Model Name — WREM: Warwick Regional Employment Model.

1.2 Model Builders — P. Elias et al.

1.3 Responsible Organization — Institute of Employment Research, University of Warwick, Coventry, U.K.

1.4 Publication — Keogh, G.T., and D.P.B. Elias (1981), A Model for Projecting Regional Employment in the U.K., *Regional Studies*, 13, 465–482.

1.5 Development Stage — WREM has been operational since about 1978. The model is meant for the medium term.

1.6 Period — Data are based on 1965–1980.

2 Model Purpose

2.1 General Purpose — 1. Forecasting studies. 2. Analytical studies. 2. Planning studies (*ex ante*).

2.2 Specific Purpose — To provide medium-term forecasts of employment by industry group and region.

3 Model Elements

3.1 Model Size —

Regions : 11.
Sectors : 26.
Exogenous variables : 26.
Endogenous variables: N.A.
Equations : N.A.

3.2 Exogenous Variables —

National: employment per sector (generated by a version of the Cambridge Growth Project Model).

Regional: —

3.3 Endogenous Variables —

National: —

Regional: employment per sector, migration.

4 Model Structure

4.1 Production Technology — WREM does not contain production functions.

4.2 Interregional and International Trade — International trade is included in the driving national model.

4.3 Other Interregional Links — An interregional migration model linked to regional rates of growth of employment and regional unemployment is currently being implemented.

4.4 National-Regional Links — WREM is a top-down model driven by a national model. It consists mainly of equations of the type $E_{irt} = f(E_{it}, t)$, where E, i, r, t refer to employment, sector, region, and period, respectively.

4.5 Supply and Demand Considerations — Supply and demand matching occurs within WREM. Interregional migration affects the spatial distribution of unemployment.

4.6 Equilibrium Assumptions — Unemployment may occur on regional labor markets.

4.7 Treatment of Prices — Prices are not included.

4.8 Dynamics   WREM is dynamic.

4.9 Functional Forms   The model consists of linear relationships.

5 Estimation and Validation

5.1 Estimation   The coefficients have been estimated by means of ordinary and two-stage least squares (in some cases with Cochrane-Orcutt adjustments).

5.2 Validation   The model has been used for dynamic simulations. Simulated values have been confronted with actual data.

6 Model Use

6.1 Model Users   WREM is used by the Manpower Services Commission (at the national and regional level), regional authorities, and several corporations.

6.2 Main Applications   Generation of regional employment forecasts for the medium term. Assessment of impacts of alternative locations of London's third airport.

6.3 Documentation   Structure and limitations: available.
User manual, testing data: available to a certain extent.
How to replicate model : available.

7 Distinguishing Features   Interaction with model users: provisional projections of employment by industry and region are provided to regional offices of the Manpower Services Commission, local authorities, public and private corporations for comment. Their feedback is allowed to influence both the national and regional projections and is incorporated into the final set of projections.

E.E.C.

1	General Information	
1.1	Model Name	FLEUR: Factors of Location in Europe.
1.2	Model Builders	W. Molle, J. Paelinck, J.-P. Ancot.
1.3	Responsible Organization	FLEUR is developed by the Netherlands Economic Institute, Rotterdam, for the E.E.C. (Directorate General XVI).
1.4	Publications	Molle, W., and B. van Holst (1976), Factors of Location in Europe, in *Foundations of Empirical Economic Research*, vol. 15 (Netherlands Economic Institute, Rotterdam). Molle, W. (1982), *Industrial Location and Regional Development in the European Community*. (Gower, Aldershot) (forthcoming).
1.5	Development Stage	The project started in 1972. The final report is in preparation.
1.6	Period	The main data are based on 1950, 1960, 1970, 1980. FLEUR is meant for the medium and long terms.
1.7	Related Models	A similar model for Dutch regions is in an intermediate stage of development at the Netherlands Economic Institute: RESPONS deals with 80 regions and 27 sectors. The location factors included are market, availability of labor, cost of labor, industrial sites, accessibility, regional policy, office space.

2	Model Purpose	
2.1	General Purpose	*Ex aequo*: 1. Analytical studies; 2. Projection studies; 3. Planning studies.
2.2	Specific Purpose	To explain and project regional employment by sector in the E.E.C.

3	Model Elements	
3.1	Model Size	Regions : 76 or 100, according to whether there are 9 or 12 E.E.C. members.
		Sectors : 53.
		Exogenous variables : approx. 110.
		Endogenous variables: approx. 4000.
		Equations : approx. 4000.
3.2	Exogenous Variables	National: growth rates of employment by sector. Regional: indicators of transport, labor market, urbanization, regional policy.
3.3	Endogenous Variables	National: — Regional: employment by sector markets (population, gross domestic product).

4	Model Structure	
4.1	Production Technology	The indicator for the presence of markets for inputs or outputs is based on input-output relations.
4.2	Interregional and International Trade	Interregional and international trade are taken into account via the market variable.

4.3	Other Interregional Links	Employment in region r for section j at time t is explained by, among other things, employment in other regions at time $t - 1$.
4.4	National-Regional Links	FLEUR has a joint bottom-up and top-down structure.
4.5	Supply and Demand Considerations	Regional employment is explained by variables from the supply side and the demand side and other variables.
4.6	Equilibrium Assumptions	Equilibrium is assumed on the level of the E.E.C.
4.7	Treatment of Prices	Wages play a role via the labor market variable.
4.8	Dynamics	FLEUR is dynamic.
4.9	Functional Forms	Highly nonlinear.
4.10	Solution Techniques	Iterative.
5	Estimation and Validation	
5.1	Estimation	Relationships are estimated, *inter alia*, by discriminant analysis and specifically constrained OLS.
5.2	Validation	The validation has been carried out for 1950–1960 and 1960–1970.
6	Model Use	
6.1	Model Users	European Economic Community.
6.2	Main Applications	Regional planning; generation of employment projections and regional disparity measures, input in regional labor market model.
6.3	Documentation	Structure : restricted. User manual, testing data: restricted. How to replicate model : restricted.
7	Distinguishing Feature	FLEUR aims at a multiregional-multinational analysis in an international setting.

AUSTRIA

1	General Information	
1.1	Model Name	REMO: A Regional Labor Market Model for Austria.
1.2	Model Builders	U. Schubert, J. Baumann, E. Brunner, P. Hampapa, G. Maier, H. Stoffl.
1.3	Responsible Organization	Interdisciplinary Institute for Urban and Regional Studies, University of Economics, Vienna, Austria.
1.4	Publication	Baumann, J., and U. Schubert (1980), Factors of Regional Labor Force Participation Rates, An Econometric Study for Austria, *Paper presented at the Regional Science Association Conference, Munich, August.*
1.5	Development Stage	Pilot study in development phase.
1.6	Period	Data available: 1960-1975. The model is meant for the medium term.

2	Model Purpose	
2.1	General Purpose	1. Analytical studies. 2. Educational purposes. 3. Forecasting studies.
2.2	Specific Purpose	Experimental study to explore the possibilities of constructing a regional econometric model.

3	Model Elements	
3.1	Model Size	Regions : 4 types of regions (urban core, urban ring, rural, and peripheral areas).
		Sectors : 3.
		Exogenous variables : N.A.
		Endogenous variables: approx. 320.
		Equations : approx. 320.
3.2	Exogenous Variables	National: —
		Regional: school capacity variables, transportation infrastructure variables, social infrastructure variables, regional policy variables: subsidies, etc.
3.3	Endogenous Variables	National: —
		Regional: employment, unemployment, vacancies, investment, wages, population.

4	Model Structure	
4.1	Production Technology	Experiments have been carried out to include a production function in REMO. The production factors are: capital and various types of labor (by qualification).
4.2	Interregional and International Trade	No explicit treatment (at present).
4.3	Other Interregional Links	Migration, commuting, capital movements.
4.4	National-Regional Links	In REMO no explicit attention is paid to the national level of variables.

4.5 Supply and Demand Considerations

In its present form, the model is demand driven: first the levels of regional production and labor demand are determined, after which the effects on regional labor supply are analyzed. In a more definite form supply-demand interactions will be taken into account.

4.6 Equilibrium Assumptions

On the regional labor market several responses to disequilibria are studied: education (in order to improve one's qualifications), migration, commuting, changes in wages and participation rates. Supply and demand are not necessarily equal.

4.7 Treatment of Prices

4.8 Dynamics

REMO is dynamic.

4.9 Functional Forms

Various types, among which logit specifications.

4.10 Solution Techniques

Some numerical methods to solve a system of nonlinear equations.

5 Estimation and Validation

5.1 Estimation

Relations have been estimated, among other things, by means of ordinary and weighted least squares.

5.2 Validation

No validation has been carried out. Consistency of submodels is not guaranteed as partly incompatible data had to be used.

6 Model Use

6.1 Model Users

The model is used by the model builders.

6.2 Main Applications

None.

6.3 Documentation

Structure and limitations: available to a certain extent.
User manual, testing data: N.A.
How to replicate model : available to a certain extent.

7 Distinguishing Features

The labor market is segmented according to educational qualifications. Transition probabilities between various qualifications are variables.

SWEDEN

1   General Information
1.1 Model Name   LPFM: LP Forecasting Model (LP refers to long-range regional development planning).
1.2 Model Builders   P.-O. Engelbrecht, O. Mårtensson.
1.3 Responsible Organization Ministry of Industry, Stockholm, Sweden.
1.4 Publication   Engelbrecht, P.-O., L. Johansson, and T. Österberg (1979), Information for Regional Planning Systems in Sweden, *Report to the Council of Europe Seminar on Information Systems for Regional Planning in Madrid*, pp. 17-21.

1.5 Development Stage   The model has been operational since 1976.
1.6 Period   The main data are based on 1970-1980. The model is meant for the medium and long terms.

2   Model Purpose
2.1 General Purpose   1. Forecasting studies. 2. Planning studies (*ex ante*). 3. Analytical studies.
2.2 Specific Purpose   To forecast employment on 35 (and 7) sectors, and population.

3   Model Elements
3.1 Model Size   Region   : medium term, 24; long term, 24 (and 300 subregions).
                              Sectors   : medium term, 35; long term, 7.
                              Exogenous variables   : N.A.
                              Endogenous variables: N.A.
                              Equations   : N.A.

3.2 Exogenous Variables   National: employment forecasts in certain sectors.
                              Regional: survival and fertility rates.
3.3 Endogenous Variables   National: —
                              Regional: employment, participation rate, commuting.

4   Model Structure
4.1 Production Technology   No explicit use of production functions.
4.2 Interregional and
     International Trade   Not included.
4.3 Other Interregional Links Commuting and migration. Migration is explained by different employment opportunities of the regions.
4.4 National-Regional Links In certain sectors, a top-down approach is used for employment. For other variables a bottom-up approach is employed.
4.5 Supply and Demand
     Considerations   The model is mainly demand driven: regional labor demand is determined independently from labor supply, while labor supply adapts to labor demand.
4.6 Equilibrium Assumptions On the labor market, commuting, migration, and flexible participation rates guarantee equality of supply and demand.

4.7	Treatment of Prices	Prices are not included.
4.8	Dynamics	LPFM is dynamic.
4.9	Functional Forms	LPFM is linear.
4.10	Solution Techniques	Standard procedures to solve system of linear equations.

5	Estimation and Validation	
5.1	Estimation	The majority of the parameters are based on common sense.
5.2	Validation	The validity has not been explicitly tested.

6	Model Use	
6.1	Model Users	The model has been used by the Ministry of Industry, Regional Administrative Boards, private enterprise, and academic researchers.
6.2	Main Applications	Continuous generation of regional labor market forecasts since 1976.
6.3	Documentation	Structure and limitations: available. User manual, testing data: N.A. How to replicate model : available.

| 7 | Distinguishing Features | Regional and sectoral employment forecasts are obtained partly by models and partly by annual surveys and estimates of municipalities, counties, and companies. Thus a decentralized forecasting system is arrived at in which the 24 County Administrative Boards are interconnected in the same time sharing computer system. The model serves to a certain extent as a means of communication between national and regional planning authorities concerning population and labor market forecasts. |

SWEDEN

1   General Information

1.1 Model Name   LURE: Model for Breakdown of Swedish Long-Term Economic Forecasts.

1.2 Model Builder   F. Snickars, B. Tallroth, M. Strandberg, B. Vretblad.

1.3 Responsible Organizations   Ministry of Economy and the Central Bureau of Statistics, Stockholm, Sweden.

1.4 Publication   Snickars, F. (1981), Regional Development Consequences of Different Energy Scenarios. The Case of a Swedish Close-down of Nuclear Power, *International Institute for Applied Systems Analysis, Laxenburg, Austria. Working Paper* WP-81-48.

1.5 Development Stage   The model has been operational since 1978.

1.6 Period   The model is based on time series (2 years for the national variables, 10–15 years for the regional variables). It is meant for the short and medium terms.

2   Model Purpose

2.1 General Purpose   1. Forecasting studies. 2. Consistency checks. 3. Planning studies (*ex ante*).

2.2 Specific Purposes   To find out whether the Swedish economic development will lead to unacceptable imbalance problems in the regional development of employment opportunities. To provide material for planning/forecasting work at the regional, county, and municipal levels in conjunction with the results of the Swedish county planning.

3   Model Elements

3.1 Model Size   Regions   : 8 county groups (or 24 counties).

                       Sectors   : 20.

                       Exogenous variables : 80.

                       Endogenous variables: 320.

                       Equations   : 100.

3.2 Exogenous Variables   National: production and employment by sector, population.
                       Regional: unemployment rates, participation rates (partially), population.

3.3 Endogenous Variables   National: —
                       Regional: employment, labor supply participation rates (partially).

4   Model Structure

4.1 Production Technology   A simplified input-output structure is assumed (basic versus nonbasic sectors).

4.2 Interregional and   Not included.
     International Trade

4.3 Other Interregional Links Gross commuting flows between regions are modeled by Lowry-type relations.

4.4 National-Regional Links   The model has a top-down structure.

4.5 Supply and Demand   The development of nonbasic sectors is determined by the demand exerted by the basic
     Considerations   sectors. The development of basic sectors is determined by trend extrapolation.

4.6 Equilibrium Assumptions On the regional labor market, supply and demand are not necessarily equal.

4.7	Treatment of Prices	Prices are not included.
4.8	Dynamics	LURE is static.
4.9	Functional Forms	Linear relations are used for basic sectors. Nonlinear (ratio-type) relations are used for nonbasic sectors.
4.10	Solution Techniques	Iterative, based on information-minimizing procedures.
5	Estimation and Validation	
5.1	Estimation	Parameters have been estimated by means of linear and nonlinear regression.
5.2	Validation	Estimated parameters have been used to forecast actual outcomes.
6	Model Use	
6.1	Model Users	Ministry of Economy, County Planning Agencies.
6.2	Main Applications	The model has been employed to generate long-term regional economic forecasts, which have been used by, *inter alia*, County Planning Agencies. Further, the model has been used to assess the regional economic impacts of a close-down of Swedish nuclear power.
6.3	Documentation	Structure and limitations: available. User manual, testing data: N.A. How to replicate model : available (in Swedish).
7	Distinguishing Features	Detailed treatment of public sector and labor demand. The model is strongly application oriented.

SWEDEN

1   General Information

1.1   Model Name   MORSE: Model for the Analysis of Regional Development, Scarce Resources and Employment.

1.2   Model Builder   L. Lundqvist.

1.3   Responsible Organization   Research Group for Urban and Regional Planning, Department of Mathematics, Royal Institute of Technology, Stockholm, Sweden.

1.4   Publication   Lundqvist, L. (1981), A Dynamic Multiregional Input-Output Model for Analyzing Regional Development, Employment and Energy Use, *Dept. of Mathematics, Royal Institute of Technology, Stockholm. Report* TRITAT-MAT-1980-20.

1.5   Development Stage   MORSE has been operational since 1980.

1.6   Period   Input-Output coefficients are based on 1975. MORSE is meant for the medium term and to a certain extent for the long term. In its present form, MORSE covers the three 5-year periods from 1975 to 1990.

2   Model Purpose

2.1   General Purpose   1. Planning studies (*ex ante*). 2. Analytical studies. 3. Forecasting studies.

2.2   Specific Purpose   To provide a tool for an integrated analysis of economic, employment, and resource developments in a regional perspective. MORSE should be applicable to feasibility, impact, and policy studies.

3   Model Elements

3.1   Model Size   Regions   : 8.
                                        Sectors   : 9.
                                        Exogenous variables   : 66.
                                        Endogenous variables   : 417.
                                        Equations (inequalities): 498.

3.2   Exogenous Variables   National: balance of payments requirement, upper bounds on resource utilization, lower bound on capital formation rate.
                                        Regional: minimum consumption rate, upper and lower bounds on labor supply.

3.3   Endogenous Variables   National: production, consumption, investments, foreign imports and exports.
                                        Regional: *idem*, plus interregional imports and exports.

4   Model Structure

4.1   Production Technology   Input-output. The production function has fixed technical coefficients. The production factors are capital, labor, and energy.

4.2   Interregional and   All sectors of destination within a region are supposed to have the same pattern of
      International Trade   imports.

4.3   Other Interregional Links   None.

4.4	National-Regional Links	A bottom-up approach is applied to production for the majority of the sectors and consumption. A top-down approach is used for energy consumption, capital formation, international trade, and production in some sectors.
4.5	Supply and Demand Considerations	In MORSE, the values of regional production are determined, *given* the fixed supply of the production factors labor and energy, and given the constraints on minimum consumption. Hence, MORSE has a mixed supply and demand orientation.
4.6	Equilibrium Assumptions	Disequilibrium may occur on the markets of goods and production factors.
4.7	Treatment of Prices	Prices do not play an explicit role in MORSE.
4.8	Dynamics	MORSE is dynamic.
4.9	Functional Forms	The equations and inequalities are linear.
4.10	Solution Technique	MORSE is solved by linear programming.
5	Estimation and Validation	
5.1	Estimation	The interregional transaction table has been estimated by means of an information theoretic approach.
5.2	Validation	Projections for 1975-1980 have been compared with actual outcomes. According to the model builder it is too early to draw definite conclusions about its validity.
6	Model Use	
6.1	Model Users	MORSE has been used by the model builder.
6.2	Main Applications	Assessment of impacts of energy supply systems and oil price increases. Projection of economic development, regional employment, and energy use. Analysis of trade-offs between consumption, employment, and energy use.
6.3	Documentation	Structure and limitations: available to a certain extent. User manual, testing data: N.A. How to replicate model : available to a certain extent.
7	Distinguishing Feature	Treatment of energy resources.

SWEDEN

1	General Information	
1.1	Model Name	REGAL: Interregional Allocation Model.
1.2	Model Builders	A. Granholm, F. Snickars, O. Ohlsson.
1.3	Responsible Organizations	Royal Institute of Technology, Stockholm; University of Gothenburg, Gothenburg, Sweden.
1.4	Publication	Granholm, A. (1981), *Interregional Planning Models for the Allocation of Private and Public Investments.* (Department of Economics, University of Gothenburg).
1.5	Development Stage	REGAL has been operational since about 1979.
1.6	Period	REGAL is mainly based on data from 1975-1977. It is meant for the medium term.

2	Model Purpose	
2.1	General Purpose	1. Planning studies (*ex ante*). 2. Analytical studies.
2.2	Specific Purpose	To investigate the connections between private and public investment allocation in a multiregional context.

3	Model Elements	
3.1	Model Size	Regions : 8.
		Sectors : 21.
		Exogenous variables : 444.
		Endogenous variables : 824.
		Equations (inequalities): 832.
3.2	Exogenous Variables	National: production, employment, and capital stock (in certain sectors); population.
		Regional: lower and upper limits of sectoral employment levels and of population.
3.3	Endogenous Variables	National: —
		Regional: value added, employment, gross investment and capital stock (per sector), population.

4	Model Structure	
4.1	Production Technology	A production function with fixed technical coefficients is used. The production factors are labor and capital.
4.2	Interregional and International Trade	Not included.
4.3	Other Interregional Links	Not included.
4.4	National-Regional Links	For the majority of the sectors the national volume of production, employment, or capital is determined exogenously. Thus, REGAL is basically a top-down model. A bottom-up approach is applied to private and public investments.
4.5	Supply and Demand Considerations	Regional production volumes are determined by variables from the supply side (availability of production factors) and the demand side (demand of firms and households for services of the public sector).

4.6	Equilibrium Assumptions	On the labor market supply and demand are assumed to be equal. Excess supply may exist on the market of goods and services.
4.7	Treatment of Prices	Prices are not included.
4.8	Dynamics	REGAL is static.
4.9	Functional Forms	REGAL is linear.
4.10	Solution Techniques	When the objective function is the minimization of national private and/or public investments, REGAL can be solved by means of linear programming. When REGAL is used for forecasting, use may be made of an extended entropy measure to deal with the problem of inertia of the economic system. In this case, REGAL has to be solved by means of nonlinear programming.
5	Estimation and Validation	
5.1	Estimation	Coefficients are one-point estimates.
5.2	Validation	The validity of REGAL has not been tested.
6	Model Use	
6.1	Model Users	An earlier version of the model has been used by the city of Stockholm.
6.2	Main Applications	Analysis of the optimal regional allocation of population, employment, and private and public investments in Sweden.
6.3	Documentation	Structure and limitations: available. User manual, testing data: available to a certain extent. How to replicate model : available.
7	Distinguishing Features	Detailed account of the public sector: subdivided into 8 sectors. Possibility of using a programming model for forecasting purposes by means of entropy formulation.

SWEDEN

1　General Information

1.1　Model Name　　　　　　　GISSIR: Growth-Inducing Sustainable Structure.

1.2　Model Builders　　　　　A.E. Andersson, L. Lundqvist, H. Persson, F. Snickars.

1.3　Responsible Organization　Ministry of Labor and Housing, Sweden.

1.4　Publication　　　　　　Andersson, A.E. (1979), Integration of Transportation and Location Analysis: A General Equilibrium Approach. *Papers of the Regional Science Association*, vol. 42.

1.5　Development Stage　　　Various versions of the model have been developed since 1974.

1.6　Period　　　　　　　　　The data are based on 1968. The model is meant for the medium and long terms.

2　Model Purpose

2.1　General Purpose　　　　1. Analytical studies. 2. Educational purposes. 3. Planning studies (*ex ante*).

2.2　Specific Purpose　　　To generate integrated location, trade and transportation scenarios for variations in networks, consumption structures, labor productivity, and capital production assumptions.

3　Model Elements

3.1　Model Size　　　　　　　Regions　　　　　　　:　8.
　　　　　　　　　　　　　　　Sectors　　　　　　　:　20-30.
　　　　　　　　　　　　　　　Exogenous variables :　N.A.
　　　　　　　　　　　　　　　Endogenous variables:　240.
　　　　　　　　　　　　　　　Equations　　　　　　:　240.

3.2　Exogenous Variables　　—

3.3　Endogenous Variables　National: growth rates and production structure of sectors.
　　　　　　　　　　　　　　　Regional: production of sectors.

4　Model Structure

4.1　Production Technology　Nonlinear input-output.

4.2　Interregional and International Trade　The sectors of destination within a region are supposed to have the same pattern of imports. Trade coefficients have been estimated by means of a gravity model approach.

4.3　Other Interregional Links　Interregional investment flows (modeled in a way analogous to interregional trade).

4.4　National-Regional Links　The model has a bottom-up structure.

4.5　Supply and Demand Considerations　Regional production levels are determined simultaneously by supply and demand variables.

4.6　Equilibrium Assumptions　Supply and demand of goods are equal, by assumption.

4.7　Treatment of Prices　Prices are not included.

4.8　Dynamics　　　　　　　GISSIR is dynamic.

4.9　Functional Forms　　　Linear and quadratic.

| 4.10 | Solution Equations | The model consists of a system of nonlinear differential equations. After linearization the system is solved by an eigenvalue method. |

5   Estimation and Validation

| 5.1 | Estimation | Coefficients have been estimated by means of information theoretic approaches. |
| 5.2 | Validation | *Ex post* forecasts have been carried out and compared with actual developments. |

6   Model Use

6.1	Model Users	GISSIR has been used by the Ministry of Labor and Housing and by the model builders.
6.2	Main Applications	Evaluation of transportation policies.
6.3	Documentation	Structure and limitations: available. User manual, testing data: available to a certain extent. How to replicate model : available.

7   Distinguishing Features — Endogenous and simultaneous determination of trade and location. Large-scale dynamic input-output model.

NORWAY

1   General Information
1.1   Model Name   REGION.
1.2   Model Builders   O. Bjerkholt, T. Skoglund.
1.3   Responsible Organization   Central Bureau of Statistics, Oslo, Norway.
1.4   Publication   Skoglund, T. (1980), REGION, A Model for Regional Input-Output Analysis, *Articles from
                                        the Central Bureau of Statistics*, no. 122 (in Norwegian).
1.5   Development Stage   The model has been operational since 1979. The coefficients are now being updated, given 1976
1.6   Period   data. The main data are based on 1973. The model is meant for the medium and long terms.
1.7   Related Models   REGION is part of a larger economic demographic model that is at present being devel-
                                        oped at the Central Bureau of Statistics (model builders: P. Sevaldson, S.E. Brun,
                                        K. Ø. Sørensen). In this model (called DRØM), attention is paid to labor supply and
                                        migration, among other things.

2   Model Purpose
2.1   General Purpose   1. Planning studies (*ex ante*). 2. Forecasting studies. 3. Analytical studies.
2.2   Specific Purpose   REGION is meant as a regional supplement to an existing national economic model. The
                                        main purpose is to improve the coordination between national economic planning and
                                        regional planning.

3   Model Elements
3.1   Model Size   Regions   :   19.
                                        Sectors   :   38.
                                        Exogenous variables :   approx. 400.
                                        Endogenous variables: approx. 3000.
                                        Equations   :   approx. 3000.
3.2   Exogenous Variables   National: private consumption, investment, exports, labor productivity.
                                        Regional: consumption and investment capital in central and local government.
3.3   Endogenous Variables   National: production and employment by industry.
                                        Regional: production and employment by industry, private consumption, investment.

4   Model Structure
4.1   Production Technology   Input-output based on a commodity-by-industry approach. Labor is a production factor
                                        in a production function with fixed technical coefficients.
4.2   Interregional and   Interregional flows of commodities are specified in the model. Constant input-output
        International Trade   coefficients have been assumed for interregional flows; the coefficients vary between
                                        commodities, industries, and regions. The production of interregional commodities is
                                        determined by the assumption of constant regional shares for each commodity.

4.3	Other Interregional Links	None.
4.4	National-Regional Links	For private consumption and investment a top-down approach has been adopted. For production and employment a bottom-up approach is used.
4.5	Supply and Demand Considerations	REGION is a demand driven model.
4.6	Equilibrium Assumptions	On the commodity market, supply is assumed to be equal to demand.
4.7	Treatment of Prices	Prices do not play a role.
4.8	Dynamics	REGION is static.
4.9	Functional Forms	The relations are linear.
4.10	Solution Techniques	Usual methods of solving systems of linear equations.
5	Estimation and Validation	
5.1	Estimation	Most of the coefficients are straightforward proportions estimated from the base-year data.
5.2	Validation	Model outcomes have been compared with observed data from 1976. The test results are not satisfactory for all variables, but it is too early to draw conclusions about the validity of the model.
6	Model Use	
6.1	Model Users	The model has been used on an experimental basis by the Ministry of Environment (which is responsible for regional policies).
6.2	Main Applications	An analysis of the regional consequences of different national economic forecasts. Model outcomes have been used as inputs to regional employment forecasts and regional forecasts of energy demand.
6.3	Documentation	Structure and limitations: available. User manual, testing data: available to a certain extent. How to replicate model : available to a certain extent.

YUGOSLAVIA

1	General Information	
1.1	Model Name	BACHUE: Economic Demographic Model.
1.2	Model Builders	M. Macura, B. Popović.
1.3	Responsible Organization	Economic Institute, Belgrade, Yugoslavia.
1.4	Publication	Macura, M., B. Popović, and M. Rašević (1977), BACHUE-Yugoslavia: Regionalized Policy Simulation Economic-Demographic Model of Yugoslavia—Conceptual Basis, Population and Employment, *International Labour Office, Geneva Working Paper* 55.
1.5	Development Stage	The model is operational at the ILO in Geneva. In 1982 it will be transferred to the Statistical Office of the Socialist Republic of Serbia in Belgrade.
1.6	Period	Data are based on 1962-1974. The model is meant for the medium and long terms.
2	Model Purpose	
2.1	General Purpose	1. Planning studies (*ex ante*). 2. Analytical studies. 3. Forecasting studies.
2.2	Specific Purpose	Analysis of the ways in which economic and demographic policies can contribute to a better development of less developed regions and to a more equitable distribution of development benefits between more and less developed regions.
3	Model Elements	
3.1	Model Size	Regions : 8 (socialist republics and autonomous provinces of Yugoslavia).
		Sectors : 21.
		Exogenous variables : approx. 240.
		Endogenous variables: 556 (excluding regional, sectoral, and other disaggregations).
		Equations : 556.
3.2	Exogenous Variables	National: world trade.
		Regional: federal government consumption per person (*ex ante*), mortality, migration abroad.
3.3	Endogenous Variables	National: foreign deficit on current account, national fund for regional development, federal government budget.
		Regional: output, social product, investment, income, personal consumption, imports, exports, social consumption, employment, labor supply, wages, fertility, population, interregional migration, students.
4	Model Structure	
4.1	Production Technology	Input-output. Labor disaggregated by educational level functions as a production factor in production functions (with variable coefficients for less developed regions).
4.2	Interregional and International Trade	Interregional trade is dealt with in the model.
4.3	Other Interregional Links	Population and labor flows.

4.4	National-Regional Links	A bottom-up approach is used for all variables listed under 3.3 as regional endogenous variables.
4.5	Supply and Demand Considerations	Supply and demand variables simultaneously influence regional production levels.
4.6	Equilibrium Assumptions	A supply and demand disequilibrium approach is applied to goods and services, investment funds, and the labor market.
4.7	Treatment of Prices	Wages are endogenous.
4.8	Dynamics	BACHUE is dynamic.
4.9	Functional Forms	BACHUE includes linear, log-linear, double-log, and inverted log relations.
4.10	Solution Techniques	Yearly sequential computations.
5	Estimation and Validation	
5.1	Estimation	The coefficients have been estimated by means of OLS.
5.2	Validation	Based on *ex post* predictions for 1980 and long-term behavior of the main variables.
6	Model Use	
6.1	Model Users	N.A.
6.2	Main Applications	N.A.
6.3	Documentation	Structure and limitations: available to a certain extent. User manual, testing data: N.A. How to replicate model : N.A.
7	Distinguishing Features	Detailed treatment of government sector. Inclusion of education.

CZECHOSLOVAKIA

1	General Information	
1.1	Model Name	MFM: Multiregional Forecasting Model for the Development of the National Economy.
1.2	Model Builder	S. Mizera.
1.3	Responsible Organization	Research Institute of Regional Economic Planning (VÚOP), Bratislava, Czechoslovakia.
1.4	Publication	*VÚOP Research Report* 121 (1980) (in Czechoslovakian).
1.5	Development Stage	The model has been operational since 1980.
1.6	Period	The main data are based on 1970-1978. The model is meant for the long term.

2	Model Purpose	
2.1	General Purpose	1. Forecasting studies. 2. Planning studies (*ex ante*). 3. Planning studies (*ex post*).
2.2	Specific Purpose	Consistent forecasting of socioeconomic development of Slovakian regions.

3	Model Elements	
3.1	Model Size	Regions : 4.
		Sectors : 9.
		Exogenous variables : approx. 140.
		Endogenous variables: 411.
		Equations : 411 (161 of which are regression equations).
3.2	Exogenous Variables	National: population; employment, investment, capital, production, wage index (in certain sectors).
		Regional: migration and commuting balance, agricultural land, medical services, housing stock, development investments in industry.
3.3	Endogenous Variables	National: —
		Regional: population, labor supply, production, investments, average wages, income, expenditures.

4	Model Structure	
4.1	Production Technology	Production levels depend on labor and capital.
4.2	Interregional and International Trade	Not included.
4.3	Other Interregional Links	Not included.
4.4	National-Regional Links	The model has a top-down structure for economic variables and a bottom-up structure for the other variables.
4.5	Supply and Demand Considerations	Certain sectors are supply driven (industry and agriculture). Other sectors are demand driven (construction, commerce, transportation, services).
4.6	Equilibrium Assumptions	Supply and demand of labor and investments are equal, by assumption.
4.7	Treatment of Prices	Wages play a role in the model.
4.8	Dynamics	MFM is dynamic.

4.9   Functional Forms   The equations are linear or log-linear.
4.10 Solution Techniques   The model is recursive, hence it is easy to solve.

5   Estimation and Validation
5.1   Estimation   The model has been estimated by means of OLS and modifications.
5.2   Validation   Computed endogenous variables have been compared with actual data.

6   Model Use
6.1   Model Users   The model has been used by the Slovak Planning Commission and by the model builder.
6.2   Main Applications   Forecasts of socioeconomic development (27 indicators) of regions.
6.3   Documentation   Structure and limitations: available.
                                User manual, testing data: available.
                                How to replicate model : available.

POLAND

1	General Information	
1.1	Model Name	IRUD: Interactive Rural-Urban Development Model (for Notec region, Poland).
1.2	Model Builders	R. Kulikowski, L. Krus.
1.3	Responsible Organization	Systems Research Institute of the Polish Academy of Sciences, Warsaw, Poland.
1.4	Publication	Kulikowski, R., and L. Krus (1980), A Regional Computerized Interactive Planning System, in *Proceedings of Joint Task Force Meeting on Development Planning for the Notec (Poland) and Silistra (Bulgaria) Regions, International Institute for Applied Systems Analysis, Laxenburg, Austria Collaborative Paper* CP-80-9, pp. 102-150.
1.5	Development Stage	IRUD has been operational since 1980.
1.6	Period	The data are based on about 1973. The model is meant for the medium term.

2	Model Purpose	
2.1	General Purpose	Planning studies (*ex ante*). 2. Planning studies (*ex post*). 3. Forecasting studies.
2.2	Specific Purpose	Evaluation of various regional development policies with special attention to effects on migration. Simulation of the decision process concerning the allocation of subsidies by means of gaming.

3	Model Elements	
3.1	Model Size	Regions : 2 (urban and rural).
		Sectors : 1.
		Exogenous variables : 20.
		Endogenous variables: 30.
		Equations : 30.
3.2	Exogenous Variables	National: population subsidies, capital and labor costs.
		Regional: natural development of population, subsidies on capital expenditures, subsidies on aggregate consumption.
3.3	Endogenous Variables	National: —
		Regional: production, personal consumption, aggregate consumption, standard of living, employment, migration, migration costs.

4	Model Structure	
4.1	Production Technology	A Cobb-Douglas production function is used with labor and capital as production factors.
4.2	Interregional and International Trade	Not included.
4.3	Other Interregional Links	Interregional migration is driven by differences in the standard of living.
4.4	National-Regional Links	A top-down approach is used for the subsidies (to be allocated among the regions) and population. For other variables a bottom-up approach is employed.

4.5	Supply and Demand Considerations	Regional production levels are driven by supply variables.
4.6	Equilibrium Assumptions	Supply and demand of goods and production factors are equal, by assumption.
4.7	Treatment of Prices	Prices and wages are exogenous. They influence the substitution among production factors.
4.8	Dynamics	IRUD is static.
4.9	Functional Forms	In IRUD various forms are used: Cobb-Douglas, polynomial and linear relationships.
4.10	Solution Techniques	IRUD can be solved in two different ways. It can be solved as an optimization model. In this case the objective is the maximization of production minus migration costs and the decision variables are the subsidies allocated to the regions for investments or consumption. It can also be solved as a gaming model with three players, the first player allocating the subsidies between the regions and the other players allocating the regional subsidies to investments or consumption. An interactive computer program has been developed so that the game can be played several times in a short period. In both views on the model, use is made of the Newton method in solving nonlinear equations.
5	Estimation and Validation	
5.1	Estimation	Coefficients have been estimated by means of nonlinear regression.
5.2	Validation	Not yet carried out.
6	Model Use	
6.1	Model Users	The model is used by the pertinent regional governmental agency and the Systems Research Institute.
6.2	Main Applications	Effects of urban and rural development policies on migration.
6.3	Documentation	Structure and limitations: available. User manual, testing data: available to a certain extent. How to replicate model : available to a certain extent.
7	Distinguishing Feature	Interactive program for game simulations.

U.S.S.R.

1	**General Information**	
1.1	Model Name	SMOPP: System of Models for Optimal Prospective Planning of the National Economy.
1.2	Model Builders	E.F. Baranov, I.S. Matlin.
1.3	Responsible Organization	Central Economics and Mathematical Institute of the Academy of Sciences of the U.S.S.R., Moscow, U.S.S.R.
1.4	Publication	Baranov, E.F., I.S. Matlin, and A.V. Koltsov (1980), Multiregional and Regional Modeling in the U.S.S.R., in F.G. Adams and N.J. Glickman (eds.), *Modeling the Multiregional Economic System* (Lexington Books, Lexington, MA), pp. 215-220.
1.5	Development Stage	The system of models has been operational since about 1975.
1.6	Period	The system of models is based on data from 1959 to 1972. It is meant for the medium term (10 years).
2	**Model Purpose**	
2.1	General Purpose	1. Planning studies (*ex ante*). 2. Analytical studies. 3. Forecasting studies.
2.2	Specific Purpose	Coherent optimization of sectoral and regional planning under constraints on labor and natural resources, allowing national goals to be reconciled with the social interest of each region.
3	**Model Elements**	
		The system of models includes 1 national model, 16 sectoral models, 24 regional models, 12 transportation models, and 1 migration model.
3.1	Model Size	Regions : 24.
		Sectors : 98.
		Exogenous Variables : N.A.
		Exogenous variables : approx. 140,000 per year considered (the system covers a period of 10 years).
		Equations (and/or inequalities): N.A.
3.2	Exogenous Variables	National: limit to capital investments, supply of specific products.
		Regional: labor supply, rate of growth of social capital.
3.3	Endogenous Variables	National: investments and production levels per sector.
		Regional: investments and production levels per sector, consumption and other final demand components, income, migration, transportation flows.
4	**Model Structure**	
4.1	Production Technology	Input-output. Production factors: labor and capital.
4.2	Interregional and International Trade	For 12 types of goods a transportation model has been included: these are optimization models with the minimization of transport costs as the objective function.
4.3	Other Interregional Links	Interregional migration, explained by, among other things, income and consumption per capita and social capital.

4.4	National-Regional Links	A top-down approach is applied to capital investments and the supply of specific goods. For the other variables a bottom-up approach is used.
4.5	Supply and Demand Considerations	Production/volumes are determined by variables from both the supply and the demand sides.
4.6	Equilibrium Assumptions	Supply and demand of goods are not necessarily equal.
4.7	Treatment of Prices	Prices play a role in the objective functions used in the various programming models of the system.
4.8	Dynamics	The system of models is dynamic.
4.9	Functional Forms	The main relationships are linear. In some cases quadratic objective functions are used in the programming models.
4.10	Solution Techniques	The models included in the system are solved by mathematical programming. Since the models are interdependent, an iterative multilevel programming procedure has to be carried out to ensure consistency between the outcomes of the various models.
5	Estimation and Validation	
5.1	Estimation	Parameters are based on input-output tables, and on OLS regressions applied to time series.
5.2	Validation	Model results have been confronted with actual developments.
6	Model Use	
6.1	Model Users	The system of models has been used by the model builders and by GOSPLAN, the national governmental planning agency.
6.2	Main Applications	The system has been used for checking the consistency of regional and national production programs developed for the Five-Year Plans.
		Structure and limitations: available to a certain extent.
		User manual, testing data: available to a certain extent.
		How to replicate model : N.A.
7	Distinguishing Features	The big size of the system of models. The use of iterative procedures for overall optimization of optimal solutions of particular models.

U.S.S.R.

1 General Information

1.1 Model Name — SYREN models: Synthesis of Regional and National Economic Models

1.2 Model Builder — A. Granberg.

1.3 Responsible Organization — Institute of Economics and Industrial Organization, Siberian Branch of the U.S.S.R. Academy of Sciences, Novosibirsk, U.S.S.R.

1.4 Publication — Granberg, A. (1973), *Optimization of Proportions of Territorial Economies* (Ekonomika, Moscow); Granberg, A. (1976) (ed.) *Spatial National Economic Models* (Novosibirsk).

1.5 Development Stage — The model has been operational since 1967.

1.6 Period — Input-output coefficients are based on 1966, 1972, 1980; other statistical data are based on 1965-1980; planned data are available for the period up to 1990; calculations are carried out for periods of 10, 15, and 20 years.

2 Model Purpose

2.1 General Purpose — 1. Studying trends and prospects of development of the national economy, interregional interactions, particular regions. 2. Including the model in the national economy planning technology.

2.2 Specific Purpose — Studying the Siberian development problems in the U.S.S.R. national economy system.

3 Model Elements

3.1 Model Size (Basic version) —

Regions   : 11.
Sectors   : 16.
Exogenous variables   : 333 per period.
Endogenous variables   : ≥492.
Equations (and inequalities)   : ≥383.

3.2 Exogenous Variables — National: exports, imports, investments. Regional: inventory formation, depreciation of capital stock, transport investments, maximum volumes of primary resources production, shares of consumption, labor resources for the material production, transport expenditures for crosshauling.

3.3 Endogenous Variables — National: Summation of regional variables. Regional: production, consumption, investments, interregional deliveries.

4 Model Structure

4.1 Production Technology — Input-output coefficients vary by region and are forecast for every period.

4.2 Interregional and International Trade — Interregional deliveries are, mainly, exogenous variables; crosshauling may be fixed (assortment exchange within the product group).

4.3 Other Interregional Links — Interregional migration variables are endogenous (their changes are carried out on the basis of analyzing migration costs and shadow prices of labor).

4.4 National-Regional Links — A top-down approach is applied to investments. A bottom-up approach is used for the other endogenous variables.

4.5 Supply and Demand Considerations — Regional production levels are determined by variables from the supply side (labor resources) and from the demand side.

4.6 Equilibrium Assumptions — Supply and demand of goods are not necessarily equal.

4.7 Treatment of Prices — Prices are exogenous. They play a role, among other things, in the transportation and migration equations.

4.8 Dynamics — SYREN-QPT is dynamic. It yields balances of production, labor resources, and transport services for the last year of the periods of 10, 15, and 20 years.

4.9 Functional Forms — SYREN-QPT is linear and separable.

4.10 Solution Techniques — The model can be solved by linear and separable programming. Also, use is made of multiobjective optimization.

5 Estimation and Validation

5.1 Estimation — Parameters are obtained by various methods: one-point estimates, forecasts of input-output coefficients, expert information.

5.2 Validation — *Ex ante* forecasts have been carried out and confronted with actual outcomes. According to the model builder, the structural changes forecast by the model are confirmed by actual developments.

6 Model Use

6.1 Model Users — Various institutes of economic studies in the U.S.S.R. and GOSPLAN.

6.2 Main Applications — Generation of alternatives for the development of the national and regional economies (pre-planning studies and calculations for plans).

6.3 Documentation — Structure and limitations: available.
User manual, testing data: available to a certain extent.
How to replicate model : available to a certain extent.

7 Distinguishing Feature — Possibility of including detailed industrial and regional submodels.

CANADA

1   General Information

1.1 Model Name

FRET: Forecasting Regional Economies and Transportation, consisting of two interdependent submodels: the multiregional economic model TOMM (Transport Oriented Multiregional Model) and the transport model FRETNET (NETwork model of FRET).

1.2 Model Builder — C. Lardinois.

1.3 Responsible Organization — Centre de Recherche sur les Transports, Université de Montréal, Montréal, Canada.

1.4 Publication — Los, M. (1980), A Transportation-Oriented Multiregional Economic Model for Canada, *Centre de Recherche sur les Transports, Université de Montréal Publication 178.*

1.5 Development Stage — FRET will soon be operational.

1.6 Period — The main data are input-output data for 1974. FRET is meant for the medium term (5-10 years).

2   Model Purpose

2.1 General Purpose — 1. Planning studies (*ex ante*). 2. Forecasting studies. 3. Analytical studies.

2.2 Specific Purpose — FRET aims at an integrated analysis of the economy and the freight transportation system. It enables one to study: 1. the effects of regional economic development on the utilization of the freight transportation system; and 2. the effects of changes in the freight transportation system on the regional economies.

3   Model Elements

3.1 Model Size

Regions : TOMM: $R = 8$; FRETNET: 85, including 9 for the U.S.A. and 9 for the rest of the world.

Sectors : TOMM: $I = 62$ (90 commodities); FRETNET: 64 tradeable commodities.

Exogenous variables : TOMM: N.A.

Endogenous variables : TOMM: 4096.

Equations (and inequalities): TOMM: N.A.

3.2 Exogenous Variables

National: total volume of tradeable commodities, price indices for tradeable commodities.

Regional: price indices for nontradeable commodities, wage index, final demands per commodity, labor supply, capacity constraints per commodity, international exports and transit traffic (per commodity), network information (costs, etc.).

3.3 Endogenous Variables

National: —

Regional: interregional trade flows, production, employment, network utilization (including modal choice), aggregate interregional transport costs, international imports.

	Model Structure	
4	Model Structure	
4.1	Production Technology	Input-output; labor and capital are related to production levels by means of fixed technical coefficients.
4.2	Interregional and International Trade	In TOMM the volumes of international, interregional, and intraregional trade of various commodities are modeled by a programming model determining an optimum spatial allocation of economic activities. In FRETNET route and mode choice (approximately 7 transport modes have been distinguished) are determined at a less aggregated spatial and commodity level.
4.3	Other Interregional Links	None.
4.4	National-Regional Links	In TOMM the total volume of tradeable commodities is determined exogenously at the national level. This indicates that TOMM has a top-down structure.
4.5	Supply and Demand Considerations	In TOMM regional production levels are determined given exogenously specified final demand variables and labor and capacity constraints.
4.6	Equilibrium Assumptions	On the goods market, supply and demand are equal by definition. On the labor market excess supply may arise.
4.7	Treatment of Prices	Prices are exogenous in the model (except for aggregate interregional transport costs). They play an important role in determining the spatial allocation of activities and mode choice.
4.8	Dynamics	The model is static.
4.9	Functional Forms	TOMM is a programming model with linear constraints and an objective function that includes an information term, so that it is nonlinear. FRET consists of linear relationships.
4.10	Solution Techniques	The models have to be solved by convex and linear programming techniques.
5	Estimation and Validation	
5.1	Estimation	Model coefficients are determined by elementary operations (e.g., division) applied to observations from one year.
5.2	Validation	The model has not been validated.
6	Model Use	N.A.
7	Distinguishing Feature	Detailed modeling of the freight transportation sectors of the economy.

CANADA

1   General Information
1.1   Model Name   SCIOM: Statistics Canada Interprovincial Input-Output Model.
1.2   Model Builders   R. Hoffman, C. Gaston, and others.
1.3   Responsible Organization   Structural Analysis Division, Statistics Canada, Ottawa, Canada.
1.4   Publication   Hoffman, R., and J. Kent (1976), Design for Commodity by Industry Interregional Input-
                                            Output Models, in K.R. Polenske and J.V. Skolka (eds.), *Advances in Input-Output Analy-
                                            sis* (Ballinger, Cambridge, MA), pp. 251-262.
1.5   Development Stage   The model has been operational since about 1976.
1.6   Period   The database was compiled for 1966 and 1974. It will be compiled again for 1979.
1.7   Related Models   A two-region input-output model is being completed by the same model builders. The
                                            "regions" are Canada and the U.S.A. The number of industries is: 480 (U.S.A.) and
                                            200 (Canada). The number of commodities is: 480 (U.S.A.) and 650 (Canada).

2   Model Purpose
2.1   General Purpose   *Ex aequo:* analytical studies, planning studies.
2.2   Specific Purpose   The model is a multipurpose tool for interregional studies.

3   Model Elements
3.1   Model Size   Regions   : 11.
                                            Sectors   : 200 (650 commodities).
                                            Exogenous variables   : N.A.
                                            Endogenous variables: 2200.
                                            Equations   : 2200.
3.2   Exogenous Variables   National: —
                                            Regional: final demand.
3.3   Endogenous Variables   National: —
                                            Regional: sectoral outputs, interregional trade flows.

4   Model Structure
4.1   Production Technology   Input-output (commodity-by-industry methodology).
4.2   Interregional and   Included in the model.
        International Trade
4.3   Other Interregional Links   None.
4.4   National-Regional Links   In most cases a top-down approach is appropriate for final demand. A bottom-up
                                            approach is applied to sectoral outputs.
4.5   Supply and Demand   The model is demand driven.
        Considerations
4.6   Equilibrium Assumptions   Supply and demand are equal, by assumption.

4.7	Treatment of Prices	Prices are not included.
4.8	Dynamics	SCIIOM is static.
4.9	Functional Forms	SCIIOM is linear.
4.10	Solution Techniques	Standard methods for systems of linear equations.
5	Estimation and Validation	
5.1	Estimation	Coefficients: one-point estimates.
5.2	Validation	N.A.
6	Model Use	
6.1	Model Users	The model has been used by national and regional governmental agencies, private organizations, and universities.
6.2	Main Applications	N.A.
6.3	Documentation	Structure and limitations: available.
		User manual, testing data: N.A.
		How to replicate model : N.A. (data are in part confidential under the Statistics Act).
7	Distinguishing Feature	Commodity-by-industry method.

U.S.A.

1	General Information	
1.1	Model Name	MRIO: Multiregional Input-Output Model.
1.2	Model Builder	K.R. Polenske.
1.3	Responsible Organizations	MRIO has been developed by the Harvard Economic Research Project. It is now installed at the Massachusetts Institute of Technology, Cambridge, MA, U.S.A.
1.4	Publication	Polenske, K.R. (1981), *The U.S. Multiregional Input-Output Accounts and Model* (Lexington Books, Lexington, MA).
1.5	Development Stage	MRIO has been operational since about 1970.
1.6	Period	MRIO is based on an input-output table from 1963. The model is meant for the short and medium terms.
1.7	Related Models	The Poverty Institute (University of Wisconsin) has developed a model based on MRIO with endogenous consumption and employment.
2	Model Purpose	
2.1	General Purpose	1. Analytical studies. 2. Planning studies (*ex post*). 3. Forecasting studies.
2.2	Specific Purpose	MRIO is a comprehensive multipurpose tool for accounting, policy analysis, and forecasting.
3	Model Elements	
3.1	Model Size	Regions : 51. Sectors : 79. Exogenous variables : N.A. Endogenous variables: 4029. Equations : .4029.
3.2	Exogenous Variables	National: — Regional: final demand variables per sector (government expenditures, personal consumption, gross investments, foreign exports).
3.3	Endogenous Variables	National: — Regional: industrial outputs and interregional trade (by sector).
4	Model Structure	
4.1	Production Technology	Input-output.
4.2	Interregional and International Trade	A uniform import pattern for all industries in a certain region for a given commodity is assumed.
4.3	Other Interregional Links	None.
4.4	National-Regional Links	The determination of regional final demand variables falls outside the scope of MRIO. In most applications a top-down approach to these variables will be used. MRIO implies a bottom-up approach to sectoral outputs.

4.5	Supply and Demand Considerations	MRIO is driven by demand variables.
4.6	Equilibrium Assumptions	Supply and demand are equal in markets for goods, by assumption.
4.7	Treatment of Prices	Prices are not included in the standard version. In the dual version MRIO can be used to study the formation of regional prices.
4.8	Dynamics	MRIO is static.
4.9	Functional Forms	MRIO is linear.
4.10	Solution Techniques	MRIO is solved by standard methods for systems of linear equations.
5	Estimation and Validation	
5.1	Estimation	Different methods have been applied for each sector.
5.2	Validation	MRIO has been simulated for the base-year data (1963). Back-projections of the model to 1947 and 1958 state outputs.
6	Model Use	
6.1	Model Users	MRIO has been used by national and regional governmental agencies, universities, private organizations, and students.
6.2	Main Applications	Regional employment and income analyses, disparities in regional allocations, regional energy analyses, interregional transportation analyses and forecasts, analyses of the railroad industry.
6.3	Documentation	Structure and limitations: available. User manual, testing data: available. How to replicate model : available.
7	Distinguishing Features	Consistency of database. Extensive use by different analysts for alternative purposes.

U.S.A.

1	**General Information**	
1.1	Model Name	MULTIREGION.
1.2	Model Builders	D.J. Bjornstad, R. J. Olsen, P. Vogt.
1.3	Responsible Organizations	Oak Ridge National Laboratory, Oak Ridge, TN; Applied Business Research, Inc., Wellesley, MA; Charles River Associates, Inc., Boston, MA, U.S.A.
1.4	Publications	Olsen, R.J. et al. (1977), MULTIREGION: A Simulation-Forecasting Model of BEA Area Population and Employment, *Oak Ridge National Laboratory Report* ORNL/RUS 25. Bjornstad, D.J. (1980), Recent Modification to the Oak Ridge National Laboratory MULTIREGION Model, *Paper presented at the Conference on an Assessment of the State of the Art in Regional Modeling, MIT-Harvard Joint Center for Urban Studies, April.*
1.5	Development Stage	MULTIREGION has been operational since about 1977 and has been developed at O.R.N.L. At present two versions of the model exist: one is used at O.R.N.L., the other at C.R.A.
1.6	Period	Data are based on 1950-1970, some on 1975. The model is meant for the medium and long terms.
2	**Model Purpose**	
2.1	General Purpose	1. Forecasting studies. 2. Analytical studies. 3. Planning studies (*ex ante*).
2.2	Specific Purpose	To forecast regional population and employment.
3	**Model Elements**	
3.1	Model Size	Regions : 173.
		Sectors : 36.
		Exogenous variables : N.A.
		Endogenous variables: approx. 15 000.
		Equations : approx. 15 000.
3.2	Exogenous Variables	National: employment by sector, population by age-sex cohort.
		Regional: employment for certain sectors.
3.3	Endogenous Variables	National: —
		Regional: employment by sector, population by age-sex cohort.
4	**Model Structure**	
4.1	Production Technology	Production is not dealt with in an explicit way. MULTIREGION consists of two components, dealing with population and employment, respectively.
4.2	Interregional and International Trade	For certain sectors interregional backward or forward links are included by market accessibility measures of the gravity type based on truck transport times.
4.3	Other Interregional Links	Gross migration is explained by, among other things, employment pressure, climatic conditions, and population potential.

4.4	National-Regional Links	The model has a top-down structure.
4.5	Supply and Demand Considerations	Regional employment levels are determined by both supply and demand variables.
4.6	Equilibrium Assumptions	Various adjustment processes give rise to an approximation of regional labor market equilibrium.
4.7	Treatment of Prices	Prices are not included.
4.8	Dynamics	MULTIREGION is dynamic.
4.9	Functional Forms	MULTIREGION is linear.
4.10	Solution Techniques	MULTIREGION is solved by a multistage iterative computation process where last-period values of some explanatory variables are used to produce first-stage estimates of endogenous variables.
5	Estimation and Validation	
5.1	Estimation	Relations have been estimated by means of OLS and weighted least squares applied to pooled cross section time series.
5.2	Validation	MULTIREGION has been used in dynamic simulations. Given the results, the adjustment processes to disequilibrium on the regional labor markets have been revised.
6	Model Use	
6.1	Model Users	The model has been used by national and regional governmental agencies, private organizations, and at a university.
6.2	Main Applications	Long-term projections of regional population and employment. Basis for regional energy projections. Projections of demand for land for industrial purposes.
6.3	Documentation	Sturcture and limitations: available. User manual, testing data: available to a certain extent. How to replicate model : available to a certain extent.
7	Distinguishing Features	Large number of regions. Supply and demand interactions on the labor market.

U.S.A.

1	General Information	
1.1	Model Name	MAG: Multiregional Econometric Model of the U.S.A.
1.2	Model Builders	N.J. Glickman, F.G. Adams, W.J. Milne.
1.3	Responsible Organization	University of Pennsylvania, Philadelphia, PA, U.S.A.
1.4	Publication	Milne, W.J., N.J. Glickman, and F.G. Adams(1980), A Framework for Analyzing Regional Growth and Decline: A Multiregional Econometric Model of the United States, *Journal of Regional Science*, 20, 173-189.
1.5	Development Stage	The model has been operational since about 1979.
1.6	Period	Data are based on 1954-1976. The model is meant for the short term.

2	Model Purpose	
2.1	General Purpose	1. Forecasting studies. 2. Planning studies (*ex ante*). 3. Planning studies (*ex post*).
2.2	Specific Purpose	To study the effects of national economic growth on differential regional economic development and to forecast regional energy demand.

3	Model Elements	
3.1	Model Size	Regions : 9 (census regions).
		Sectors : 6.
		Exogenous variables : approx. 800.
		Endogenous variables: approx. 1600.
		Equations : approx. 1600.
3.2	Exogenous Variables	National: outputs in certain industries, wages, population size.
		Regional: energy prices.
3.3	Endogenous Variables	National: —
		Regional: sectoral output, sectoral employment, sectoral wages, nonwage income, energy consumption, population, interregional migration.

4	Model Structure	
4.1	Production Technology	Labor demand is based on a CES production function.
4.2	Interregional and International Trade	Not included.
4.3	Other Interregional Links	Regional wage rates depend, among other things, on the wage rates in surrounding regions. Interregional migration depends, among other things, on wage differentials between regions and relative unemployment rates.
4.4	National-Regional Links	The model is driven by national variables, forecast by the Wharton Annual Model.
4.5	Supply and Demand Considerations	In the manufacturing industries the regional shares depend on variables from the supply side: labor and energy costs. Regional output in the other industries depends on regional demand.

4.6	Equilibrium Assumptions	The market of manufacturing industries is in equilibrium at the national level. The markets of the other industries are in equilibrium at the regional level. On the labor market the possibility of excess supply is taken into account.
4.7	Treatment of Prices	Interregional differentials in wages and energy prices are determinants of the inter-regional allocation of production. The volume and consumption of regional energy demands are influenced by regional energy prices.
4.8	Dynamics	MAG is dynamic.
4.9	Functional Forms	MAG is. linear.
4.10	Solution Techniques	Usual methods to solve systems of linear equations.
5	Estimation and Validation	
5.1	Estimation	The model has been estimated by means of OLS.
5.2	Validation	*Ex post* simulations outside the sample period have been carried out.
6	Model Use	
6.1	Model Users	The model has been used by a national governmental agency and a private organization.
6.2	Main Applications	Energy demand forecasting.
6.3	Documentation	Structure and limitations: available to a certain extent. User manual, testing data: available to a certain extent. How to replicate model : available to a certain extent.

U.S.A.

1	General Information	
1.1	Model Name	IDIOM: Income Determination Input-Output Model.
1.2	Model Builders	S.P. Dresch, R.D. Goldberg, D.A. Updegrove.
1.3	Responsible Organization	Institute for Demographic and Economic Studies, New Haven, CN, U.S.A.
1.4	Publication	Dresch, S.P., and D.A. Updegrove (1980). IDIOM: A Disaggregated Policy-Impact Model of the U.S. Economy, in R. Haveman and K. Hollenbeck (eds.), *Microeconomic Simulation Models for Public Policy Analysis*, vol. 2. (Academic Press, New York, NY) pp. 213-249.
1.5	Development Stage	IDIOM has been operational since 1972.
1.6	Period	The main data are based on about 1973.

2	Model Purpose	
2.1	General Purpose	1. Planning studies (*ex ante*). 2. Analytical studies. 3. Educational purposes.
2.2	Specific Purpose	To assess the economic effects of changes in fiscal structure (taxes, transfers, expenditures) and other exogenous economic developments at a relatively high degree of disaggregation (by region, industry, and occupation).

3	Model Elements		
3.1	Model Size	Regions	: 51.
		Sectors	: 86 (60 national and 26 regional).
		Exogenous variables	: N.A.
		Endogenous variables	: approx. 3000.
		Equations	: approx. 3000.
3.2	Exogenous Variables	National:	components of final demand by sector (other than personal consumption).
		Regional:	components of final demand (other than personal consumption) in regional sectors.
3.3	Endogenous Variables	National:	labor and nonlabor income, personal consumption, output by sector, tax revenues, primary materials requirements, capital requirements by sector, employment by sector.
		Regional:	output by sector, employment.

4	Model Structure	
4.1	Production Technology	Input-output. Fixed technical coefficients are applied to labor and capital.
4.2	Interregional and International Trade	IDIOM assumes the existence of interregional trade, but it does not contain an explicit representation of such a trade pattern.
4.3	Other Interregional Links	None.
4.4	National-Regional Links	IDIOM is a top-down model. First, outputs of national sectors are determined on the national level. Then these outputs are distributed across regions according to the distribution of activity in a base period.

4.5	Supply and Demand Considerations	IDIOM is demand driven.
4.6	Equilibrium Assumptions	For national sectors, supply and demand are equal at the national level (transportation costs are assumed to be zero). For regional sectors, supply and demand are equal at the regional level (transport costs are assumed to be infinite). On the labor market unemployment may exist.
4.7	Treatment of Prices	Prices are not included.
4.8	Dynamics	IDIOM is static.
4.9	Functional Forms	IDIOM is linear.
4.10	Solution Techniques	Standard methods of solving system of linear equations.
5	Estimation and Validation	
5.1	Estimation	Coefficients have been obtained as one-point estimates.
5.2	Validation	Validation studies have not (yet) been carried out.
6	Model Use	
6.1	Model Users	IDIOM has been used by national and regional governmental agencies, private organizations (including consultants), and universities.
6.2	Main Applications	Impact analysis of: military expenditures, cut-back in arms exports, local public works, and a major earthquake.
6.3	Documentation	Structure and limitations: available. User manual, testing data: available. How to replicate model : available to a certain extent.
7	Distinguishing Feature	The use of the distinction between national and regional sectors to avoid the problem that interregional trade patterns have to be dealt with explicitly.

U.S.A.

1	**General Information**	
1.1	Model Name	NRIES: National-Regional Impact Evaluation System.
1.2	Model Builders	K. Ballard, J. Kort, R. Wendling, R. Gustely.
1.3	Responsible Organization	Bureau of Economic Analysis, U.S. Department of Commerce, Washington, DC, U.S.A.
1.4	Publication	Ballard, K.P., R.D. Gustely, and R.M. Wendling (1980), NRIES, Structure, Performance and Applications of a Bottom-up Interregional Econometric Model, *Bureau of Economic Analysis, U.S. Department of Commerce Report*.
1.5	Development Stage	NRIES has been operational since about 1979.
1.6	Period	NRIES is based on data from 1955 to 1976. It is meant for use in the short and medium terms.
2	**Model Purpose**	
2.1	General Purpose	*Ex aequo*: forecasting studies, planning studies (*ex ante*); planning studies (*ex post*).
2.2	Specific Purpose	Analysis of spatial distribution of impacts resulting from policy alternatives. Generation of medium-term forecasts of regional economic activity.
3	**Model Elements**	
3.1	Model Size	Regions : 51.
		Sectors : 12.
		Exogenous variables : N.A.
		Endogenous variables: 14000.
		Equations : 14000 (of which 3500 are behavioral equations).
3.2	Exogenous Variables	National: production indices in agriculture and mining, social security information, federal expenditures, balance of payments, minimum wage rate.
		Regional:
3.3	Endogenous Variables	National: output, population, employment, unemployment, wage rates, consumer prices, interest rate, etc.
		Regional: output, population, employment, unemployment, wage rates, income, taxes.
4	**Model Structure**	
4.1	Production Technology	A linear labor demand relation is assumed. This relation takes into account technological change.
4.2	Interregional and International Trade	In several sectors, regional production depends on distance deflated production or income in the other regions.
4.3	Other Interregional Links	None.
4.4	National-Regional Links	A bottom-up approach is applied to all main endogenous variables.
4.5	Supply and Demand Considerations	In NRIES regional production is mainly determined by variables from the demand side.

4.6	Equilibrium Assumptions	On the markets of goods and services, supply and demand are assumed to be equal. On the labor market, unemployment is taken into account.
4.7	Treatment of Prices	Wages play a role in, among other things, the determination of income and the inter-regional allocation of production.
4.8	Dynamics	NRIES is dynamic.
4.9	Functional Forms	NRIES is linear.
4.10	Solution Techniques	NRIES is solved by a Gauss-Seidel iterative solution technique.
5	Estimation and Validation	
5.1	Estimation	The model has been estimated by means of OLS (in some cases with Cochrane-Orcutt adjustments).
5.2	Validation	Dynamic simulations have been carried out with NRIES (within the sample period). For several regions MAPE statistics based on NRIES have been compared with MAPE statistics resulting from single-region models. In general, the statistics are of the same order of magnitude.
6	Model Use	
6.1	Model Users	NRIES has been used by national and regional governmental agencies.
6.2	Main Applications	Impact analysis of energy scenarios (solar, coal, oil, gas). Impact analysis of the federal government Grants-in-Aid Program. Impact analysis of local public works programs.
6.3	Documentation	Structure and limitations: available. User manual, testing data: available. How to replicate model : available.
7	Distinguishing Features	NRIES is a large-scale bottom-up model with an interesting treatment of interregional linkage features.

U.S.A.

1	**General Information**	
1.1	Model Name	MREED: Multiregional Model of the Economy, Environment and Energy Demand.
1.2	Model Builder	T.R. Lakshmanan.
1.3	Responsible Organization	Department of Geography, Boston University, Boston, MA, U.S.A.
1.4	Publication	Lakshmanan, T.R. (1979), A Multiregional Policy Model of the Economy, Environment and Energy, *Boston University, National Science Foundation Project Working Paper* NSF 79-1.
1.5	Development Stage	MREEED became operational in 1981.
1.6	Period	The main data are based on about 1966-1976. The model is meant for the short, medium, and long terms.

2	**Model Purpose**	
2.1	General Purpose	1. Analytical studies. 2. Planning studies (*ex ante*). 3. Planning studies (*ex post*).
2.2	Specific Purpose	MREED is a policy analysis model capable of determining the key economic-environmental-energy consequences associated with alternative national and regional public policies.

3	**Model Elements**	
3.1	Model Size	Regions : 50.
		Sectors : 53.
		Exogenous variables : N.A.
		Endogenous variables: approx. 880 per region.
		Equations : approx. 880 per region.
3.2	Exogenous Variables	National: taxes, depreciation, investment tax credit, interest rate, replacement capital rate.
		Regional: fuel prices, interregional transport costs by sector, heating days.
3.3	Endogenous Variables	National: some types of investment, employment.
		Regional: output by sector, capital, labor and energy demands, income, public expenditures, taxes, transportation energy demand, residential energy demand, aggregate energy price, environmental emissions, investment supply, unemployment, labor force, wage rates, consumption.

4	**Model Structure**	
4.1	Production Technology	Factor demand functions are based on a production function with production factors of capital, labor, and energy.
4.2	Interregional and International Trade	Interregional forward links are taken into account by means of a demand potential variable. This variable is defined as the weighted sum of demands in other regions, deflated by the costs of interregional communication. Further, regional investment supply depends on accessibility of input and output markets.

4.3	Other Interregional Links	None.
4.4	National-Regional Links	A top-down approach is applied to most variables, among which is investment supply in manufacturing industries. A bottom-up approach is used for investments in sectors whose output is determined in regional markets and some other variables.
4.5	Supply and Demand Considerations	Regional output is determined by variables from the demand side (demand potential) and variables from the supply side (prices of production factors).
4.6	Equilibrium Assumptions	Disequilibria are taken into account on the regional labor market.
4.7	Treatment of Prices	Prices are an important driving force behind substitution processes in production and interregional location.
4.8	Dynamics	MREEED is dynamic.
4.9	Functional Forms	A large variety of forms are used: e.g., translog production functions, log-linear energy demand, logit models, linear forms.
4.10	Solution Techniques	N.A.
5	Estimation and Validation	
5.1	Estimation	Various econometric methods are used: ordinary and two-stage least squares, instrumental variables, iterative Zellner, maximum likelihood, multinomial logit.
5.2	Validation	A validation plan has been written for MREEED, but it has not yet been carried out.
6	Model Use	N.A.
7	Distinguishing Features	Detailed treatment of energy sector. Use of flexible production and consumption functions. Use of the median voter model in public expenditure equations. Use of spatial market potential (based on truck transport time and distance) in output equations.

U.S.A.

1	**General Information**	
1.1	Model Name	MRMI: Multiregional, Multi-Industry Forecasting Model.
1.2	Model Builders	C.C. Harris, Jr., M. Nadji.
1.3	Responsible Organization	Bureau of Business and Economic Research, University of Maryland, MD, U.S.A.
1.4	Publication	Harris, C.C., Jr. (1980), New Developments and Extensions of the Multiregional, Multi-Industry Forecasting Model, *Journal of Regional Science*, vol. 20.
1.5	Development Stage	Operational since 1973.
1.6	Period	National data: 1958-1980. Regional data: 1970-1976. The model is meant for the medium and long terms.
2	**Model Purpose**	
2.1	General Purpose	1. Planning studies (*ex ante*). 2. Forecasting studies. 3. Planning studies (*ex post*).
2.2	Specific Purpose	Making baseline forecasts and doing long-run regional economic impact analyses.
3	**Model Elements**	
3.1	Model Size	Regions : 3103 counties, or 435 SMSAs and rest of economic areas, or 183 economic areas, or 51 states.
		Sectors : 108.
		Exogenous variables : N.A.
		Endogenous variables: 1129 per region.
		Equations 1129 per region plus auxiliary equations.
3.2	Exogenous Variables	National: all national variables from the Interindustry Forecasting Model (INFORUM) developed by C.B. Almon et al. at the University of Maryland.
		Regional: —
3.3	Endogenous Variables	National: —
		Regional: per sector: output, employment, total demand, investments, government expenditures, personal consumer expenditures, foreign imports and exports, transport costs; population, births, deaths, labor force, unemployment, personal income, value of land.
4	**Model Structure**	
4.1	Production Technology	Input-output analysis is used to estimate intermediate demand.
4.2	Interregional and International Trade	Interregional trade is dealt with by means of a linear programming transportation model. The shadow prices of this model indicate the marginal transportation costs of shipping goods out of each region and of obtaining inputs to each region. These shadow prices play an important role in the location of output among regions.
4.3	Other Interregional Links	None.
4.4	National-Regional Links	MRMI is a pure top-down model.

4.5	Supply and Demand Considerations	Regional outputs are determined by supply variables (production costs) and demand variables.
4.6	Equilibrium Assumptions	At the national level supply and demand for goods are equal. At the regional level supply and demand for labor and goods are not necessarily equal.
4.7	Treatment of Prices	Costs of transportation, labor, and land are important explanatory variables determining the interregional location of output.
4.8	Dynamics	MRMI is dynamic.
4.9	Functional Forms	MRMI is linear.
4.10	Solution Techniques	MRMI contains a linear programming transportation problem. The solution of the remaining part of the model is straightforward since it is recursive.
5	Estimation and Validation	
5.1	Estimation	Relations are estimated by OLS.
5.2	Validation	Forecasts for historical years have been compared with actual dates.
6	Model Use	
6.1	Model Users	The model has been used extensively by national and regional agencies, private organizations, and universities.
6.2	Main Applications	Regional economic effects of national highway systems, regional effects of locating the communications sector, on-shore impacts of off-shore oil wells, impacts of opening new coal mines, etc.
6.3	Documentation	Structure and limitations: available. User manual, testing data: N.A. How to replicate model : available to a certain extent.
7	Distinguishing Features	The model is greatly disaggregated. The use of a programming transportation model to deal with transportation costs. No predetermined regional values are needed.

U.S.A.

1	**General Information**	
1.1	Model Name	MEPA-III: Massachusetts Economic Policy Analysis Model (III refers to substate regional version).
1.2	Model Builders	G.I. Treyz et al.
1.3	Responsible Organization	MEPA Project, Economics Department, University of Massachusetts, Amherst, MA, U.S.A.
1.4	Publication	Treyz, G.I., A.F. Friedlaender, and B.H. Stevens (1980), The Employment Sector of a Regional Policy Simulation Model, *Review of Economics and Statistics*, 62, 63-73.
1.5	Development Stage	MEPA has been operational since 1977 as a single-region model. It has been proposed as a point of departure for a multiregional model for the U.S.A. Further, it has been planned to extend MEPA as a multiregional model for several subregions of Massachusetts. The following description is mainly based on the single-region version, but in some cases properties of the proposed multiregional version are reported.
1.6	Period	MEPA is a quarterly model, based on data from about 1954-1975. It is meant for the short, medium, and long terms.
2	**Model Purpose**	
2.1	General Purpose	1. Planning studies (*ex ante*). 2. Forecasting studies. 3. Planning studies (*ex post*).
2.2	Specific Purpose	To determine the effects of state policy initiatives and external events on the Massachusetts economy and to make economic and tax revenue forecasts.
3	**Model Elements**	
3.1	Model Size	Regions : 5 (subregions of Massachusetts).
		Sectors : 50.
		Exogenous variables : 355.
		Endogenous variables: 565.
		Equations : 565.
3.2	Exogenous Variables	National: employment and investments in various sectors, components of disposable income, wages, prices.
		Regional: direct consumer taxes, personal tax parameters, business taxes, government spending, fuel costs.
3.3	Endogenous Variables	National: —
		Regional: employment and investments in various sectors, unemployment, wages, prices, disposable income.
4	**Model Structure**	
4.1	Production Technology	A Cobb-Douglas production function is assumed; the production factors are labor, capital, and material inputs from each sector separately. This means that--unlike the traditional input-output analysis--the model permits factor substitution in response to

4.2 Interregional and International Trade	changes in relative input prices. Regional exports depend on the average cost of regional production relative to the average national production costs. In the proposed structure for the multiregional version, interregional trade is determined by interregional differences in production costs, taking into account interregional transportation costs.
4.3 Other Interregional Links	None.
4.4 National-Regional Links	The single-regional version of MEPA is obviously a top-down model. In the multiregional version a top-down approach is applied to employment, among other things, while a bottom-up approach is used for labor supply, among other things.
4.5 Supply and Demand Considerations	On the labor market, employment is determined by both supply (wage) and demand variables. Regional wages are determined by, among other things, the discrepancy between supply and demand of labor.
4.6 Equilibrium Assumptions	The model is based on a general equilibrium approach taking into account various processes of adjustment to changes in exogenous variables.
4.7 Treatment of Prices	Regional wages and prices are endogenous. They play a role in income formation, factor substitution, and interregional investment decisions.
4.8 Dynamics	MEPA is dynamic.
4.9 Functional Forms	MEPA consists of linear and log-linear forms.
4.10 Solution Techniques	N.A.
5 Estimation and Validation	
5.1 Estimation	Equations have been estimated by means of OLS and certain numerical methods.
5.2 Validation	An *ex ante* forecasting record for MEPA has been published for 1977–1979. Final revised actual data for these years are not yet available, however.
6 Model Use	
6.1 Model Users	MEPA has been used by the Massachusetts State Government.
6.2 Main Applications	Forecasts of main regional economic indicators. Regional effects of government tax and expenditures measures. Effects of expanding port facilities.
6.3 Documentation	Structure and limitations: available to a certain extent. User manual, testing data: available to a certain extent. How to replicate model : available to a certain extent.
7 Distinguishing Features	Treatment of input-output relations by means of Cobb-Douglas production functions. Inclusion of a submodel dealing with inequalities in the income distribution.

U.S.A.

1	General Information	
1.1	Model Name	ECESIS.
1.2	Model Builders	A. Isserman, P. Beaumont, D. Plane, P. Rogerson, D. McMillen.
1.3	Responsible Organization	U.S. Bureau of the Census, American Statistical Association, National Science Foundation, U.S.A.
1.4	Publication	(1982) ECESIS: An Interregional Economic-Demographic Forecasting Model of the States, *University of Iowa, Institute for Urban and Regional Research Working Paper.*
1.5	Development Stage	ECESIS has been built and is being validated. It will be operational in 1982.
1.6	Period	ECESIS is based on data from 1958-1978. It is meant for use in the short and medium terms.
2	Model Purpose	
2.1	General Purpose	1. Forecasting studies. 2. Planning studies (*ex ante*). 3. Planning studies (*ex post*).
2.2	Specific Purpose	To forecast state populations 20 years ahead and to study the importance of modeling population and economic conditions simultaneously.
3	Model Elements	
3.1	Model Size	Region : 51. Sectors : 3. Exogenous variables : 973. Endogenous variables: 7179. Equations : 7179.
3.2	Exogenous Variables	National: prices, interest rates, foreign immigration, birth and death rates by age, social insurance contribution rate. Regional: agricultural employment and income, labor force participation rates for the elderly and teenagers, death rates, productivity trend variable.
3.3	Endogenous Variables	National: all are sums or ratios of regional endogenous variables. Regional: employment, wages, income, population by age, output, investment, capital stock, unemployment, labor force, migration flows, births.
4	Model Structure	
4.1	Production Technology	A Cobb-Douglas production function is assumed for manufacturing with capital and labor as factors and constant but neutral technological change. The model is neoclassical but includes institutional factors, for instance, in wage determination.
4.2	Interregional and International Trade	Regional production depends on demand in other regions. This demand is weighted by historical trade flows for manufacturing and by distance for nonmanufacturing.

4.3	Other Interregional Links	Regional wages rates depend in part on wage rates in other regions according to distance and industrial structure. Interregional migration depends on employment opportunity and labor force supplies in each region.
4.4	National-Regional Links	All endogenous national variables are calculated from the regional levels; no regional variables are formed by disaggregating national variables.
4.5	Supply and Demand Considerations	Production is demand driven, but the model does include important supply constraints (capacity).
4.6	Equilibrium Assumptions	Equilibrium is assumed for manufacturing output (no inventory adjustment), but not for labor markets (unemployment).
4.7	Treatment of Prices	The consumer price index in each region is a constant portion of the national index.
4.8	Dynamics	ECESIS is dynamic.
4.9	Functional Forms	ECESIS consists primarily of linear and log-linear equations.
4.10	Solution Techniques	ECESIS is solved by a Gauss-Newton iterative solution technique.
5	Estimation and Validation	
5.1	Estimation	The model has been estimated by means of OLS with Cochrane-Orcutt adjustments where appropriate.
5.2	Validation	Dynamic simulations have been carried out within the sample period. Further validation is in progress.
6	Model Use	
6.1	Model Users	ECESIS is intended for use by the national government, but also may be used by state governments and research groups.
6.2	Main Applications	Allocating federal funds to the states for capital expenditures.
6.3	Documentation	Structure and limitations: available to an extent. User manual, testing data: N.A. How to replicate model : N.A. (yet).
7	Distinguishing Features	Linking of very complex demographic accounts (for economic forecasting models) with rather aggregated but elaborate structural econometric models. Modeling of economic-demographic feedbacks for a closed interregional system.

JAPAN

1	General Information
1.1	Model Name	RDM-II: Regional Dispersion Model (second version).
1.2	Model Builders	N. Suzuki, F. Kimura, Y. Yoshida.
1.3	Responsible Organization	Mitsubishi Research Institute, Inc., Tokyo, Japan.
1.4	Publication	Mitsubishi Research Institute, Inc. (1978), Regional Dispersion Policies and their Effects on Industries—Calculation based on Interregional Input-Output Model (Version II).

| 1.5 | Development Stage | Operational since about 1973. |
| 1.6 | Period | Input-output coefficients are based on 1970, coefficients of final demand equations are based on 1960-1972; the coefficients are being updated; the model is meant for the medium and long terms. |

2	Model Purpose
2.1	General Purpose	1. Planning studies (*ex ante*). 2. Forecasting studies. 3. Analytical studies.
2.2	Specific Purpose	Forecasting the effects of various policy measures on the regional distribution of economic activities (transportation network improvements, private and public investments, environmental standards, taxes).

3	Model Elements
3.1	Model Size	Regions : 9.
		Sectors : 11.
		Exogenous variables : approx. 750 (except environmental submodel).
		Endogenous variables: approx. 1250 (except environmental submodel).
		Equations : approx. 500.
3.2	Exogenous Variables	National: government consumptive expenditures and investments, exports, inventory formation.
		Regional: exports, inventory formation.
3.3	Endogenous Variables	National: production, value added.
		Regional: production, value added, investment, labor demand.

4	Model Structure
4.1	Production Technology	Input-output. A Cobb-Douglas production function is assumed with capital and labor as production factors.
4.2	Interregional and International Trade	All sectors of destination within a region are supposed to have the same pattern of imports. Trade coefficients are explained by time distances between regions and the share of the capital stock in the region of origin relative to the national capital stock.
4.3	Other Interregional Links	None.

4.4	National-Regional Links	A bottom-up approach is used for variables such as production and value added. A top-down approach is employed for government expenditures, exports, and inventory formation. Regional production is mainly determined by final demand. Supply constraints only play a role in the specification of interregional trade coefficients (via the capital variable).
4.5	Supply and Demand Considerations	
4.6	Equilibrium Assumptions	Commodity and labor markets are assumed to be in equilibrium. Prices and the interest rate are exogenous. They act as explanatory variables for regional investments.
4.7	Treatment of Prices	
4.8	Dynamics	RDM is mainly static; some parts are dynamic (capital formation). RDM is mainly linear. Trade coefficient equations are log-linear. The model is solved by standard methods for systems of equations.
4.9	Functional Forms	
4.10	Solution Techniques	
5	Estimation and Validation	
5.1	Estimation	Behavioral equations have been estimated by means of OLS. In some equations parameters have been modified given the results of calibrations.
5.2	Validation	Model simulations have been carried out and compared with actual data. The gaps between the two are reasonably small, according to the model builders.
6	Model Use	
6.1	Model Users	The model was designed for (and has been used by) the Economic Planning Agency of the national government. It has also been used by regional planning agencies.
6.2	Main Applications	Impact analysis of: trunkline transportation network improvement, large regional development investments, environmental controls, dispersion tax systems, regional distribution of government investments.
6.3	Documentation	Structure and limitations: available. User manual, testing data: available to a certain extent. How to replicate model : available to a certain extent.
7	Distinguishing Features	The model includes an environmental submodel dealing with the emission of water and air pollutants, and investments for waste disposal.

JAPAN

1   General Information

1.1   Model Name   BALAMO: Multiregional Balanced Input-Output Model.

1.2   Model Builders   T. Kawashima et al.

1.3   Responsible Organization   BALAMO has been developed by the model builders at the request of the Ministry of Construction of the Japanese Government.

1.4   Publication   Kawashima, T. (1978), Regional Impact Simulation Model BALAMO, in A. Straszak and B. Wagle (eds.), *Models for Regional Planning and Policy Making, Proceedings of the Joint IBM/IIASA Conference, Vienna.*

1.5   Development Stage   BALAMO has been operational since 1976.

1.6   Period   BALAMO is based on data from 1960 to 1970.   It is meant for the short and medium terms.

2   Model Purpose

2.1   General Purpose   1. Forecasting studies. 2. Planning studies (*ex ante*). 3. Analytical studies.

2.2   Specific Purpose   To measure impacts of public investments at the national level on regional economic activity. The model is meant as a tool for government decision makers dealing with public investments.

3   Model Elements

3.1   Model Size   Regions   :   8 (covering North Japan).
                                                     Sectors   :   8.
                                                     Exogenous variables :   approx. 60.
                                                     Endogenous variables :   192.
                                                     Equations   :   192 (apart from the input-output-related equations).

3.2   Exogenous Variables   National: public investment, final demand in certain sectors.
                                                     Regional: final demand in certain sectors.

3.3   Endogenous Variables   National: production pressure, output, employment (by sector).
                                                     Regional: *idem.*

4   Model Structure

4.1   Production Technology   Input-output. Production factors are labor and public capital (road stock). The production functions are linear or log-linear.

4.2   Interregional and   For certain sectors, interregional trade is taken into consideration. Trade coeffi-
       International Trade   cients are constant.

4.3   Other Interregional Links   None.

4.4   National-Regional Links   BALAMO is a top-down model.

4.5   Supply and Demand   BALAMO is characterized by supply and demand interactions; production levels are deter-
       Considerations   mined by both final demand and the availability of production factors.

4.6   Equilibrium Assumptions   On the market for goods, excess demand (or excess supply) may arise.

4.7	Treatment of Prices	Prices are not included in BALAMO.
4.8	Dynamics	BALAMO is dynamic.
4.9	Functional Forms	Linear and log-linear.
4.10	Solution Techniques	BALAMO is a recursive model so that the solution is straightforward.
5	Estimation and Validation	
5.1	Estimation	Coefficients have been estimated by means of ordinary and two-stage least squares.
5.2	Validation	In a strict sense, no validation has been carried out.
6	Model Use	
6.1	Model Users	BALAMO has been used by the Ministry of Construction of the Japanese Government.
6.2	Main Applications	To measure the impact of public investment for highway construction on regional economic activities and environmental degradation.
6.3	Documentation	Structure and limitations: available. User manual, testing data: available to a certain extent. How to replicate model : available to a certain extent.
7	Distinguishing Features	Detailed treatment of both regional and commodity hierarchies. The model is strongly application oriented.

JAPAN

1   General Information
1.1 Model Name   NRPEM: Nine Region Politico-Economic Model.
1.2 Model Builders   T. Fukuchi et al.
1.3 Responsible Organization   University of Tsukuba, Japan.
1.4 Publication   Fukuchi, T. (1978), Analyse Economico-Politique d'un Développement Régional Harmonisé, *Les Collections de l'INSEE*, C.61, 227-253.
1.5 Development Stage   A first version of the model has been operational since about 1976.
1.6 Period   The data are mainly based on 1966-1971. The model is meant for the medium term.
1.7 Related Models   This model is related to multiregional models built by Dr Fukuchi at the end of the 1960s. These models have been used (and partly still are used) for metropolitan and regional development planning. Special attention is paid in these models to public investments.

2   Model Purpose
2.1 General Purpose   1. Planning studies (*ex ante*). 2. Forecasting studies. 3. Analytical studies.
2.2 Specific Purpose   To identify the relation between political voting behavior and economic resource distribution.

3   Model Elements
3.1 Model Size
                                   Regions   :   9.
                                   Sectors   :   3.
                                   Exogenous variables : 38.
                                   Endogenous variables: 243.
                                   Equations   : 243.
3.2 Exogenous Variables   National: interest rate.
                                   Regional: cultivated land, sectoral exports.
3.3 Endogenous Variables   National: standard of living, voting shares of political parties.
                                   Regional: income, consumption, production, consumer's price, wage rate, employment, capital stock, population, social overhead capital (various categories).

4   Model Structure
4.1 Production Technology   Cobb-Douglas production functions have been used for the various sectors. Production factors are labor, private capital, and social overhead capital.
4.2 Interregional and   No explicit attention is paid to interregional trade.
     International Trade
4.3 Other Interregional Links   Interregional migration is dealt with in an implicit way.
4.4 National-Regional Links   The model has a bottom-up structure.

4.5	Supply and Demand Considerations	Regional production volumes are predominantly determined by variables from the supply side (availability of production factors).
4.6	Equilibrium Assumptions	Supply and demand are equal on the various markets. Equilibrium is attained by price adjustments, migration, and resource reallocation.
4.7	Treatment of Prices	Consumer prices and wages are endogenous.
4.8	Dynamics	NRPEM is dynamic.
4.9	Functional Forms	Most of the relations are log-linear.
4.10	Solution Techniques	The model is recursive; consequently, it can be solved in a straightforward way.
5	Estimation and Validation	
5.1	Estimation	Coefficients have been estimated by means of direct and iterative least squares.
5.2	Validation	The model has been simulated for the year 1980. According to the model builder the validity is reasonable.
6	Model Use	
6.1	Model Users	The model has been used by the model builders.
6.2	Main Applications	The model has, among other things, been used to study the sensitivity of the socio-economic structure and the voting behavior of the people for the interest rate.
6.3	Documentation	Structure and limitations: available to a certain extent. User manual, testing data: available to a certain extent. How to replicate model : available to a certain extent.
7	Distinguishing Feature	Integration of socioeconomic and political systems.

JAPAN

1	General Information	
1.1	Model Name	EPAM: Economic Planning Agency Model for Comprehensive Regional Development Plan.
1.2	Model Builders	T. Fukuchi et al.
1.3	Responsible Organization	Economic Planning Agency, Tokyo, Japan.
1.4	Publication	Fukuchi, T. et al. (1967), Study of Regional Development Planning Model, *Economic Planning Agency Series* 18, 1–569 (in Japanese).
1.5	Development Stage	Operational since 1967.
1.6	Time Period	Pooling data (1955–1962, nine regions).
1.7	Related Models	Succeeding National Land Agency model and models by T. Fukuchi.

2	Model Purpose	
2.1	General Purpose	1. Planning studies (*ex ante*). 2. Forecasting studies. 3. Analytical studies.
2.2	Specific Purpose	Calculate optimum pattern of public investment by 9 regions and by 4 categories in relation to growth, equity, and welfare targets.

3	Model Elements	
3.1	Model Size	Regions : 9.
		Sectors : 3.
		Exogenous variables : 138.
		Endogenous variables : 689.
		Equations (with regional dummies): 57.
3.2	Exogenous Variables	National: —
		Regional: investment fund supplies by sectors, export by sector, cultivated land, transfer from central government, economic distances for travelers and commodities.
3.3	Endogenous Variables	National: —
		Regional: income, consumption, production, capital stock (private: fixed and housing; public: four categories of social overhead capital), tax revenue, welfare indices, intraregional trade (agricultural and nonagricultural).

4	Model Structure	
4.1	Production Technology	Cobb-Douglas production function with private and public capital, labor, land, which includes scale of demand as a proxy for utilization rate.
4.2	Interregional and International Trade	Three interregional trades (travelers, agricultural, and nonagricultural goods) as functions of improved gravity type are included; regional export is included as an exogenous demand variable.
4.3	Other Interregional Links	Interregional migration is included.
4.4	National-Regional Links	The model has a bottom-up structure.

4.5	Supply and Demand Considerations	Demand influences indirectly through production factors, and directly through production (utilization) to the supply side.
4.6	Equilibrium Assumptions	Supply and demand are equal on the various markets. Equilibrium is attained by price adjustments, migration, and resource allocation.
4.7	Treatment of Prices	Treated as exogenous.
4.8	Dynamics	EPAM is dynamic.
4.9	Functional Forms	Log-linear and linear.
4.10	Solution Techniques	The model is recursive; consequently, it can be solved in a straightforward way.
5	**Estimation and Validation**	
5.1	Estimation	Coefficients have been estimated by means of direct and iterative least squares.
5.2	Validation	The model has been simulated for the year 1985. According to the model builder the validity is reasonable.
6	**Model Use**	
6.1	Model Users	The model has been used by the Economic Planning Agency of Japan.
6.2	Main Applications	The model is being used to construct the New Comprehensive Regional Development Plan of the Japanese Government.
6.3	Documentation	Structure and simulation results: available to a certain extent.
7	Distinguishing Feature	Inclusion of public capital by 9 regions and 4 categories and various interregional flows.

AUSTRALIA

1	General Information	
1.1	Model Name	INTEREG.
1.2	Model Builder	D.F. Batten.
1.3	Responsible Organization	Commonwealth Scientific and Industrial Research Organization, Highett, Victoria, Australia.
1.4	Publication	Batten, D.F. (1982), The Interregional Linkages between National and Regional Input-Output Models, *International Regional Science Review* (in press).
1.5	Development Stage	The model has been operational since 1980.
1.6	Period	The model is meant for the short and medium terms.

2	Model Purpose	
2.1	General Purpose	1. Analytical studies. 2. Education purposes. 3. Planning studies (*ex ante*).
2.2	Specific Purpose	To estimate the complete pattern of interregional commodity flows and input-output tables for a nominated set of interacting regions.

3	Model Elements	
3.1	Model Size	Regions : variable.
		Sectors : variable.
		Exogenous variables : variable.
		Endogenous variables : variable.
		Equations (inequalities): variable.
3.2	Exogenous Variables	National: outputs, intermediate and final demand by sector; input-output coefficients.
		Regional: outputs by sector; some information on final demand.
3.3	Endogenous Variables	National: —
		Regional: interregional and intersectoral flows, interregional and intraregional input-output coefficients.

4	Model Structure	
4.1	Production Technology	Input-output.
4.2	Interregional and International Trade	Interregional trade flows are estimated on the basis of some accounting constraints, capacity constraints in the transport network, and the principle of entropy maximization.
4.3	Other Interregional Links	None.
4.4	National-Regional Links	INTEREG is a top-down model.
4.5	Supply and Demand Considerations	INTEREG is mainly demand driven. Supply constraints are present in the form of capacity constraints in the transportation network. Regional and sectoral supply constraints can be taken into account.

4.6	Equilibrium Assumptions	At the national level, supply and demand are in equilibrium. At the regional level disequilibrium may occur.
4.7	Treatment of Prices	Prices are not included.
4.8	Dynamics	INTEREG is static; a version has been developed that can in principle be used in the context of dynamic input-output models.
4.9	Functional Forms	The maximand in INTEREG is an entropy function. The constraints are linear.
4.10	Solution Techniques	INTEREG is formulated as a mathematical programming problem. This problem is transformed into a system of nonlinear equations that is solved by means of Newton's method.

5   Estimation and Validation

| 5.1 | Estimation | The formulation of INTEREG is flexible so that given coefficients (e.g., cost or capacity coefficients from a transport system) may be incorporated. If they are not available, the solution of the model is less convincing, but still possible. |
| 5.2 | Validation | Survey-based interregional tables do not exist in Australia and Sweden. Hence, it is not possible to confront model outcomes with actual developments. |

6   Model Use

6.1	Model Users	INTEREG has been used by the CSIRO and at the University of Umeå, Sweden.
6.2	Main Applications	Estimation of interregional input-output tables. Examination of regional multiplier effects.
6.3	Documentation	Structure and limitations: available to a certain extent. User manual, testing data: available to a certain extent. How to replicate model : available.

| 7 | Distinguishing Feature | INTEREG is formulated in such a general way that it is suitable for applications involving any set of regions or nations. |

AUSTRALIA

1	Model Name	DREAM: Dynamic Regional Economic Allocation Model.
1.2	Model Builders	R. Sharpe†, A. Karlqvist‡, D. Batten†, J.F. Brotchie†.
1.3	Responsible Organization	†CSIRO, Division of Building Research, Highett, Victoria, Australia; ‡University of Linköping, Sweden.
1.4	Publication	Karlqvist, A., R. Sharpe, D.F. Batten, and J.F. Brotchie (1978), A Regional Planning Model and its Applications to South Eastern Australia, *Regional Science and Urban Economics*, 8, 57-86.
1.5	Development Stage	The model is still in a development and educational phase, but has been applied to 3 case studies.
1.6	Period	The model is predominantly based on data that are 5-10 years old. The model is meant for the short to medium terms.
2	Model Purpose	
2.1	General Purpose	1. Planning studies (*ex ante*). 2. Analytical studies. 3. Forecasting studies.
2.2	Specific Purpose	The model is formulated to analyze the feasibility, consistency, and trade-offs between different national and regional objectives in terms of populations, economic activities, and the transportation system.

3 Model Elements

3.1	Model Size	Regions : $R \leq 10$.
		Sectors : $I \leq 30$.
		Exogenous variables : variable, 1000 max.
		Endogenous variables : variable, 1000 max.
		Equations (and inequalities): variable, 1000 max.
3.2	Exogenous Variables	National: target production levels of national sectors, population, objectives, transport system.
		Regional: population.
3.3	Endogenous Variables	National: production, employment and investment, imports, exports.
		Regional: production, employment, investment, interregional commodity flows.
4	Model Structure	
4.1	Production Technology	The model contains input-output relations. Regional production levels are constrained by the regional labor force and capital stock, and structural employment changes.
4.2	Interregional and International Trade	For certain sectors, interregional and international trade are taken into account. The trade flows are modeled by means of an entropy maximizing method.
4.3	Other Interregional Links	At present the model does not contain other interregional links. An extension toward interregional population flows has been planned.

4.4	National-Regional Links	A top-down approach is applied to production levels in national sectors. A bottom-up approach is used for other variables.
4.5	Supply and Demand Considerations	The values of regional production are determined, given constraints on the supply of labor and minimum consumption. Consequently, DREAM has a mixed supply and demand orientation.
4.6	Equilibrium Assumptions	In DREAM, disequilibrium may occur in the markets for labor and capital at both regional and national levels.
4.7	Treatment of Prices	Transport costs play a role in determining the pattern of interregional trade flows.
4.8	Dynamics	DREAM is dynamic.
4.9	Functional Forms	DREAM contains linear constraints and an objective that may be in either linear or entropy form.
4.10	Solution Techniques	DREAM is solved by iterative linear or entropy programming techniques (choice is made by user).
5	Estimation and Validation	
5.1	Estimation	The coefficients of the model have been derived directly from the available data, e.g., an input-output table, supplemented with expert judgments.
5.2	Validation	The overall performance of the model has not been confronted with actual developments, because its main purpose is prescription rather than prediction.
6	Model Use	
6.1	Model Users	The model was originally designed for the National Department of Urban and Regional Development and State government authorities, and also for internal research purposes.
6.2	Main Applications	Evaluation of a growth center between two metropolises (Melbourne and Sydney). Evaluation of large mineral developments in Western Australia. Equity versus efficiency evaluations of regional development in Tasmania. Evaluation of a metropolis and its state (Melbourne, Victoria).
6.3	Documentation	Structure and limitations: available to a certain extent. User manual, testing data: available to a certain extent. How to replicate model : available to a certain extent.

REPUBLIC OF KOREA

1	General Information	
1.1	Model Name	OTSIS: Optimum Transportation Sector Investment Study.
1.2	Model Builder	T.J. Kim.
1.3	Responsible Organization	Korea Institute of Science and Technology, Seoul, Republic of Korea.
1.4	Publication	(1982) Coal/Clement Distribution and Optimum Transportation Sector Investment Study, *Korea Institute of Science and Technology Technical Report*.
1.5	Development Stage	The model has been operational since about 1980.
1.6	Period	The main database for OTSIS consists of a freight origin-destination survey, carried out once, and two input-output tables related to two years (with a time difference of 10 years). OTSIS is meant for the short term.

2	Model Purpose	
2.1	General Purpose	1. Planning studies (*ex ante*). 2. Forecasting studies. 3. Planning studies (*ex post*).
2.2	Specific Purpose	To generate transportation sector improvement programs that need to be implemented during the 5th Five-Year Development Program of 1981-1986 in Korea.

3	Model Elements	
3.1	Model Size	Regions : 31.
		Sectors : 5.
		Exogenous variables : 1411.
		Endogenous variables : 7322.
		Equations (and inequalities): 1364.
3.2	Exogenous Variables	National: imports and exports per sector.
		Regional: interregional passenger travel demand by mode.
3.3	Endogenous Variables	National: total welfare.
		Regional: production per sector, recommended number of lanes to be constructed for interregional transport for each transport system.

4	Model Structure	
4.1	Production Technology	Input-output.
4.2	Interregional and International Trade	Interregional transport is studied by system and by mode.
4.3	Other Interregional Links	None.
4.4	National-Regional Links	A top-down approach is used for imports and exports per sector. A bottom-up approach is used for transportation investments.
4.5	Supply and Demand Considerations	The model is demand driven. If it appears that the existing capacity of transportation systems is insufficient to meet the demands, the model generates the required expansions of ports and lanes.

4.6	Equilibrium Assumptions	Supply and demand are equal, by assumption.
4.7	Treatment of Prices	Prices do not play an explicit role in the model, apart from transport costs.
4.8	Dynamics	OTSIS is static.
4.9	Functional Forms	OTSIS is linear.
4.10	Solution Techniques	OTSIS is solved by linear programming.
5	Estimation and Validation	
5.1	Estimation	Coefficients have been obtained as one-point estimates.
5.2	Validation	The validity of the model will be tested by means of the *ex ante* forecasts for 1981-1986.
6	Model Use	
6.1	Model Users	The model has been used by the Ministry of Transportation of Korea.
6.2	Main Applications	Generation of recommendations for the transportation development programs for the 5th Five-Year Development Program in Korea.
6.3	Documentation	Structure and limitations: available. User manual, testing data: available. How to replicate model : available.
7	Distinguishing Feature	Detailed treatment of transportation sector and infrastructure.

KENYA

1	General Information	
1.1	Model Name	IIOSMK: Interregional Input-Output Simulation Model for Kenya.
1.2	Model Builder	A. Bigsten.
1.3	Responsible Organization	Gothenburg University, Sweden.
1.4	Publication	Bigsten, A., (1980), *Regional Inequality and Development, A Case Study of Kenya* (Gower, Farnborough, U.K.).
1.5	Development Stage	The model has been operational since about 1979.
1.6	Period	The model is based on data from 1967 to 1976. It is meant for the medium term.
2	Model Purpose	
2.1	General Purpose	1. Analytical studies. 2. Planning studies (*ex ante*).
2.2	Specific Purpose	To simulate the development of regional inequality in Kenya and to test the effects of various policy changes.
3	Model Elements	
3.1	Model Size	Regions : 8. Sectors : 9. Exogenous variables : N.A. Endogenous variables: N.A. Equations : N.A.
3.2	Exogenous Variables	National: final demand variables in base year. Regional: *idem*.
3.3	Endogenous Variables	National: final demand variables after base year. Regional: final demand variables after base year, income, employment.
4	Model Structure	
4.1	Production Technology	Input-output. A production function with fixed technical coefficients has been assumed for labor.
4.2	Interregional and International Trade	All sectors of destination within a region are assumed to have the same pattern of imports.
4.3	Other Interregional Links	Interregional income transfers are taken into account.
4.4	National-Regional Links	A top-down approach is applied to some of the final demand components. A bottom-up approach is used for income and employment.
4.5	Supply and Demand Consideration	IIOSMK is a demand driven model on both the commodity and the labor markets.
4.6	Equilibrium Assumptions	On the commodity markets, supply and demand are equal, by assumption. On the labor market, no attention is paid to unemployment for conceptual and statistical reasons.
4.7	Treatment of Prices	Prices do not play an explicit role.

4.8	Dynamics	IIOSMK is dynamic.
4.9	Functional Forms	IIOSMK is linear.
4.10	Solution Techniques	Standard.
5	Estimation and Validation	
5.1	Estimation	Interregional trade coefficients have been estimated by means of entropy maximizing methods. For other coefficients, use has been made of OLS.
5.2	Validation	*Ex post* simulations have been carried out.
6	Model Use	
6.1	Model Users	The model has been used by the model builder.
6.2	Main Applications	The effects on interregional income inequalities have been analyzed for policies concerning, among other things, the regional distribution of private investments and infrastructure.
6.3	Documentation	Structure and limitations: available. User manual, testing data: available to a certain extent. How to replicate model : available.

CONTRIBUTING AUTHORS

ISSAEV, Professor Boris, International Institute for Applied Systems Analysis, A-2361
    Laxenburg, Austria
NIJKAMP, Professor Peter, Department of Economics, Free University of Amsterdam, De
    Boelelaan 1105, Post Box 7161, 1007 MC Amsterdam, The Netherlands
RIETVELD, Dr. Piet, Department of Economics, Free University of Amsterdam, De Boele-
    laan 1105, Post Box 7161, 1007 MC Amsterdam, The Netherlands
SNICKARS, Dr. Folke, Stockholm Research and Statistical Office, Box 2242, S-10316
    Stockholm, Sweden

ANDERSSON, Professor Åke, Department of Economics, Umeå University, Box 718, S-90187
    Umeå, Sweden
BARANOV, Professor Edward, Deputy Director, Central Economic Mathematical Institute
    (CEMI), Department of Economics, Krasikova 32, Moscow 117418, USSR
BOLTON, Dr. Roger, Department of Economics, Fernald House, Williams College, Williams-
    town, Massachusetts 01267, USA
COURBIS, Professor Raymond, Applied Macroeconomic Analysis Group (G.A.M.A.), Univer-
    sity of Paris X-Nanterre, 2 Rue de Rouen, F-92000 Nanterre, France
GRANBERG, Professor Alexander, Deputy Director, Institute of Economics and Industrial
    Engineering, Siberian Branch of the Academy of Sciences of the USSR, Novosibirsk
    90, Prospekt Nauki 17, USSR
LAKSHMANAN, Professor T.R., Chairman of the Department of Geography and Director of
    the Center for Energy and Environment Studies, Boston University, 48 Cummington
    Street, Boston, Massachusetts 02215, USA
MATLIN, Dr. Ilya, Central Economic Mathematical Institute (CEMI), Department of
    Economics, Krasikova 32, Moscow 117418, USSR
MIZERA, Dr. Stephan, Scientific Institute of Regional Planning, Drienova 34, 82980
    Bratislava, Czechoslovakia
SAKASHITA, Professor Noboru, Institute of Socio-Economic Planning, University of
    Tsukuba, Sakura, Niihari, Ibaraki 305, Japan
SCHUBERT, Dr. Uwe, Interdisciplinary Institute for Regional Planning, University of
    Vienna, Hasenauerstrasse 42/8, 1190 Vienna, Austria